G00164147

SPIRITUAL WOUNDS

SPIRITUAL WOUNDS

TRAUMA, TESTIMONY AND THE IRISH CIVIL WAR

SÍOBHRA AIKEN

IRISH ACADEMIC PRESS

First published in 2022 by
Irish Academic Press
10 George's Street
Newbridge
Co. Kildare
Ireland
www.iap.ie

© Síobhra Aiken, 2022

978 1 78855 166 3 (Cloth)
978 1 78855 167 0 (Ebook)
978 1 78855 168 7 (PDF)

A CIP catalogue record for this book is available from the British Library.

Typeset in Minion Pro 11/15 pt

Cover design by Fiachra McCarthy

Front cover image: Catalina Bulfin MacBride, courtesy of Kilmainham Gaol Museum (KMGLM 20PC-1B52-11) and the White family.

Back cover image: Materials from 'The Book of Cells', Mountjoy Jail journal, 1922 (Ms 20,849), Rosamond Jacob diaries and papers (Ms 32,582/95; Ms 33,113/2/2), and Niall C. Harrington papers (Ms 40,685/2). Reproduced courtesy of the National Library of Ireland.

Irish Academic Press is a member of Publishing Ireland.

MIX
Paper from
responsible sources
FSC® C021394
www.fsc.org

i ndilchuimhne ar na mná misniúla a chuaigh romham,

a chuir síolta na réabhlóide –

ach nár thug leo an fómhar

Nano Aiken (1896–1972)

Nellie Stuart (1898–1985)

Maudie Davin (1898–1978)

Annie Cardwell (1904–1922)

CONTENTS

Introduction

The Unspeakable Irish Civil War?

'The Unspeakable War' was the title chosen by journalist Eoin Neeson for his series of articles on the Irish Civil War (1922–3), a 'story that nobody dared to tell' in 1958.[1] This emphasis on silence still lingers in public discourse and the academic study of one of the most contentious periods in modern Irish history. Historians refer to the civil war as the 'great silence upon which Irish national identity was constructed', arguing that 'silence was the preferred option of many' and that 'a veil of silence was drawn over much of the violence'.[2] Literary scholars, too, hold that the events of the war were 'all failures too bitter for speech', that most writers 'preferred to remain silent on the Civil War'.[3] The official state decade of centenaries programme even flirted with this silence: the original schedule of events (2012–22) omitted the latter half of the civil war, before the programme was extended to 2023.[4]

This book is concerned with how the overemphasis on the reticence surrounding the Irish Civil War has occluded the many voices that broke the silence. I started off by compiling a list of writings by civil war veterans produced in the decades immediately after the conflict. Over time, the list expanded into a catalogue of accounts and books, many of which were published before there was any talk of setting up the Bureau of Military History in 1947. This book reintroduces some of these testimonies into public debate and, in doing so, opens up an alternative archive of veteran testimony from the Irish Civil War. The testimonies discussed in the pages that follow were written by pro- and anti-treaty men and women, in both English and Irish. They appear in many guises but share one major characteristic: nearly all have been overlooked in historical enquiry to date. The wealth of this body of testimony suggests that the silence of the Irish Civil War was not necessarily a result of revolutionaries' reluctance to speak, but rather due to the unwillingness of the architects of official memory – journalists, historians, politicians – to listen to the testimony of civil war veterans.

The code of silence around the Irish Civil War is indicative of the widespread belief that particularly devastating events are followed by an extended period of silence and repression of memory. These perceived silences, as Guy Beiner explains, reflect the 'popular appeal of quasi-psychoanalytical models in which a traumatic event is considered, by definition, to be unspeakable until it resurfaces at a much later date'.[5] This type of traumatic silence takes on far greater political significance in post-civil war society, in which the forgetting of past contentious events is believed to be essential for reconciliation. As Anne Dolan asks in her influential study *Commemorating the Irish Civil War: History and Memory, 1923–2000* (2003), 'does civil war by its very nature demand silence?'[6] Indeed, even as the civil war divide set the fault line in Irish politics, public figures and politicians repressed personal stories and burned their civil war papers. Both leading political parties in the newly established Irish Free State, Fianna Fáil and Cumann na nGaedheal, ran election campaigns promising to 'heal the wounds of war' and to 'get rid of the *damnosa hereditas*' [cursed inheritance] of 'forgotten' civil war days.[7] For decades, school textbooks, memoirs and history books mysteriously ended with the truce in July 1921. Children of revolutionary veterans in particular shared the sense that 'the whole country seemed to have taken a vow of silence'.[8] Politicians made pleas from the floor of the Dáil to 'forget past differences and past history' for the 'common benefit of all the people we represent'.[9]

However, studies of civil wars internationally suggest that these calls to forget often paradoxically produce a commitment to remember. Indeed, civil wars, more so perhaps than other conflicts, often produce an abundance of narrative as '[a]midst enforced collective amnesia, public censorship and the maddening proliferation of competing versions, the task of fashioning historical narratives becomes all the [more] urgent as it is contentious'.[10] This was certainly the case in early twentieth-century Ireland. The civil war ushered in a 'highly competitive' commemorative print culture, as numerous revolutionaries traded in their weapons for pens, preferring to let 'them have it with ink'.[11]

Moreover, the idea of a 'traumatic silence' contains something of a paradox. As trauma theorist Roger Luckhurst reminds us, even if a traumatic event produces an initial shock that resists linguistic representation, this experience is often followed by the 'manic production of retrospective narratives that seek to explicate the trauma'.[12] Psychologist Dori Laub similarly stresses that people who live through traumatic events often carry an 'imperative to tell and to be heard'.[13] The strength of this often unexplainable desire to tell is borne out in almost every page of this book.

Testimonies of contentious events seldom appear in conventional form, however. The act of introducing private, often painful, experience into the public realm, especially when it challenged official memory-making (and especially forgetting), demanded the cautious deployment of self-protective narrative strategies. As a result, civil war testimony is often found in places where historians do not traditionally look: in accounts and stories that blur narrative genres, in seemingly artless fictionalised life writing, in autobiographically based fiction and drama, buried under the artifice of poetry, or hidden in Gothic and romance modes. The supposed dearth of published first-hand testimonies relating to the civil war is especially complicated by the proliferation of popular autobiographical novels, particularly in the 1920s and 1930s.

The Irish Civil War – When Did It Become 'Traumatic'?

For all the emphasis on silence, veterans were not shy about expressing their view that the civil war was particularly distressing: Síghle Humphreys lamented that there was nothing 'chomh holc le Cogadh na gCarad' [as bad as civil war]; for Mary Harpur, it was the 'tragedy of all tragedies'; Frank O'Connor wrote that 'the period from the end of 1922 to the spring of 1923 was one that I found almost unbearably painful'.[14]

In the strictest of historical terms, Ireland's civil war erupted over the acceptance of the Anglo-Irish Treaty in December 1921 and was fought from 28 June 1922 to 30 April 1923 between the Provisional Government's pro-treaty forces and the anti-treaty Irish Republican Army (IRA), who objected to the oath of allegiance to the British monarch and to partition. The brevity of the conflict was very much at odds with the lingering after-effects felt by many veterans. Families, friends, former comrades and even spouses found themselves split over the terms of the treaty. Others attempted to prevent the conflict or participated reluctantly. Leading revolutionaries on both sides lost their lives. The rate of executions and imprisonment superseded that of the earlier struggle for independence. Communal violence was a feature of daily life, roads and railway lines were disrupted, atrocities were committed by both sides. The war precipitated a period of economic instability. Thousands of people, north and south of the new border between the Irish Free State and Northern Ireland, became refugees. Former revolutionaries struggled to secure employment – particularly defeated anti-treaty supporters – and thousands emigrated in the years that followed. The language of psychological wounding rings through the writings of many veterans grappling with this difficult legacy: Desmond Ryan lamented that 'the deepest wounds of the Civil War were spiritual wounds'; P. S. O'Hegarty wrote that civil war 'tears and lacerates and tortures for generations'; Todd Andrews asserted that the split left 'a psychological wound which was largely unhealed until the Second World War'.[15]

Despite the currency of the terms 'post-war bitterness', 'collective silence' and 'traumatic civil war' in both popular and academic discourse,[16] relatively little scholarly attention has been devoted to the civil war or to its legacy.[17] For decades, historical studies of the Irish revolution ended in 1921. F. S. L. Lyons announced in 1971 that it was 'not yet possible for the historian to approach [the civil war] with [...] detailed knowledge or [...] objectivity', while David Fitzpatrick, in his influential *Politics and Irish Life* (1977), famously opted to leave the 'unsavory history' of the civil war to 'some other student of Chaos'.[18] Michael Hopkinson's *Green Against Green: The Irish Civil War* (1988) was the first major scholarly study of the conflict, following Eoin Neeson's and Calton Younger's popular histories published in 1966 and 1968 respectively.[19]

The relative neglect of the traumatic legacy popularly associated with the civil war can be attributed to the scepticism towards popular 'mythology' long associated with the 'scientific' approach in modern Irish historiography.[20] The lack of scholarly attention to popular ideas of civil war trauma may also reflect the 'history wars' between nationalist and revisionist approaches to Irish history. As Joseph Valente outlines, the 'deployment of trauma theory in Irish studies' has been associated with an 'embattled nationalist position [in the fight] against revisionism'.[21] Furthermore, there is a tendency in much historiography to downplay the trauma associated with the civil war by stressing the restrained violence, limited death toll and 'trivial' demographic displacement in contrast to contemporaneous

European conflicts, such as the Finnish Civil War (1918) and the Silesian Uprisings (1919–21).[22] While such comparative studies offer valuable insight, they can easily be employed to support Liam Kennedy's 'MOPE' motif, influenced by debates of false memory syndrome, according to which the Irish naively view themselves as the 'most oppressed people ever'.[23] For example, Dolan suggests that the comparatively low levels of violence and homicide rates during the civil war are worth considering 'when tempted [...] to give into our *Angela's Ashes* instincts; that worse than the ordinary miserable civil war is the miserable Irish Civil War'.[24]

This emphasis on levels of violence fails, however, to consider an event and the traumatic meaning it accrues as separate. Leading trauma theorist Cathy Caruth has famously argued that 'trauma is not locatable in the simple violent or original event in an individual's past'; trauma is rather a process of remembering, as the unassimilated event 'returns to haunt the survivor later on'.[25] While Caruth's concern is individual psychic trauma, sociologists have developed theories of 'collective trauma' and 'cultural trauma' to grapple with the ways in which people harness the language of trauma to describe events that affect them collectively as much as individually. Kai Erikson suggests that a 'collective trauma' involves 'a blow to the basic tissues of social life that damages the bonds attaching people together and impairs the prevailing sense of community'.[26] In his theorisation of 'cultural trauma', Jeffrey C. Alexander emphasises that a horrendous event only becomes a 'collective trauma' when it is socially interpreted and represented as such: '[E]vents do not in and of themselves create collective trauma. Events are not inherently traumatic. Trauma is a socially mediated attribution. The attribution may be made in real time, as an event unfolds; it may also be made before the event occurs, as an adumbration, or after the event has concluded'.[27]

In the context of the Irish Civil War, diaries, letters and newspaper reports written at the time all suggest that the conflict was instantaneously coded as particularly traumatic, including by those with little or no direct interaction with its violence.[28] However, the civil war was also narrativised as 'unspeakable' *before it happened*. Newspaper editorials in spring 1922 forewarned the destruction, cautioning of the 'unspeakable horror of civil war', warning that 'coga carad caoi namhad' [the war of friends is the opportunity of the enemy], and that civil war 'means the material ruin of the nation and the moral degradation of its people'.[29] Fr Robert O'Loughran lamented the dangers of disunity and recalled that 'civil war among rival chiefs' in the twelfth century had led to the invasion of Ireland and to 'seven centuries of deathless protest, of sacrifices numberless and untold, of suffering horrible and unspeakable'.[30] But Fr O'Loughran wasn't speaking in 1922 or 1923 – he was speaking about the Cavan by-election in June 1918. These discourses all illustrate the 'affective prememory' of civil war, since historical events, as Beiner reminds us, are 'invariably understood and remembered in their time through reference to memories of previous events'.[31] David Armitage, author of *Civil Wars: A History in Ideas*, posits that such a dynamic is key to understanding civil war; it is 'both a historical and cumulative concept: that is, that whenever the spectre of civil war arose, it did so in forms that recalled previous conflicts'.[32]

If the civil war was imagined as uniquely devastating before it even occurred, the traumatic memory of the Irish Civil War cannot be confined to the official chronology spanning from 28 June 1922 to the ceasefire order of 30 April 1923. Dublin volunteer Pádraig O'Horan highlights in his remarkable fictionalised testimony, *The Flame of Youth* (see Chapter Four), that the shock of the civil war was not viewed as a single, isolated traumatic episode. Rather the bombardment of the anti-treaty headquarters at Dublin's Four Courts in June 1922 was recalled through the lens of the violence and devastation that had preceded it: 'France–France–France, and Easter Week in Dublin. *And now this*' (my emphasis).[33]

While O'Horan viewed the civil war as the culmination of a series of traumatic events which included the First World War, 1916 Rising and independence struggle, the carefully curated and glorified memory of the Rising and the war of independence also led to the overshadowing of various episodes that did not adhere to the heroic template. Indeed, the 'unspeakable' civil war was immediately characterised by its contrast to the Rising and the 'four glorious years' of 1918–21.[34] For example, in his preface to Dan Breen's 1924 memoir, *My Fight for Irish Freedom*, Joseph McGarrity juxtaposed the 'physical suffering' of Breen during the 'Tan War' with the '*mental* torture' he '*must have* endured [...] on seeing his former comrades turn their arms against each other after the signing of the treaty in 1921' (my emphasis).[35] McGarrity's conceptualisation of the civil war as exclusively traumatic (arguably to the extent that traumas associated with other events were downplayed) reflects the strong binary that developed from the late eighteenth century between the 'misery and disaster' of civil war and the 'revelation and self-realization' offered by revolution.[36] The Capuchin friar

Fr Aloysius Travers was one of many to sum up this dichotomy: speaking in 1942, he defended his decision not to reflect on the 'sad days of civil war', calling instead on his audience to 'try to forget what is painful – let us remember what is heartening and inspiring'.[37]

However, in Ireland's case, the 'heartening' revolution and the 'painful' civil war did not obey a clear-cut chronology. Even the terminology of 'civil war' was contentious. Those of the pro-treaty side took exception to the designation of 'civil war' since it 'gave their opponents a degree of legitimacy their cause did not entitle them to'.[38] Anti-treatyites, too, called on their followers not to 'call it a civil war',[39] tending instead to portray the fighting as a continuation of war against the British. The term 'civil war' was also widely employed in contemporary reporting to account for sectarian hostilities in the north of Ireland in the early 1920s, although this does not generally feature in the historiography of the Irish Civil War. Peter Hart has identified a second 'unacknowledged civil war' in the targeting of spies and informers by the IRA.[40] There were, of course, many further examples of 'unacknowledged civil war' throughout the revolutionary period. Irish men served in the British military, in the Royal Irish Constabulary (RIC) and in the Dublin Metropolitan Police (DMP). Irish-on-Irish violence played out not only in assassinations, but also in arson attacks, intimidation, agrarian violence, the burning of 'Big Houses' (and small houses too) and the hair cropping by the IRA of women believed to be associated with British forces. There were many 'brother against brother' (and sister against sister) splits from well before the civil war; Máire Comerford recalls that 'brothers and sisters [were] prominently on different sides', as many female revolutionaries, like herself, had siblings in the British army.[41] These unacknowledged civil wars did not end with the 'dump arms' order in May 1923. The traumatic legacy associated with the civil war must be considered, therefore, as something of a euphemism for the many painful events, intimate conflicts and thwarted hopes during and following the strained years of the revolutionary period.

Trauma: An Ordinary Disease?

If the civil war, in its broadest sense, was mediated as a collectively experienced trauma, how do these ideas of collective trauma interact with evolving ideas regarding individual psychological trauma? Writing in his memoir *Vive Moi! An Autobiography* (1964), Seán O'Faoláin addressed the fact that the Irish experience of violence 'bore no comparison to the experiences endured so long and so tenaciously by later revolutionaries elsewhere.'[42] Such a comparison did little, however, to dampen the lingering effects of his experience of the 'war of nerves'. As he confessed, 'My "battle" began after the first stage of the Troubles was over, and we broke into civil war amongst ourselves [...] This battle of mine was to oppress me traumatically for many years.'[43]

However, despite O'Faoláin's allusion to 'trauma' in his 1964 memoir, the application of the framework of trauma to the earlier events of the Irish revolution, though widespread, is not without its hazards. Alan Gibbs cautions that it is 'dangerous and presumptuous, to homogenize history in this way, to suggest that humans have always suffered in the same way from trauma.'[44] As I write this book in the context of the COVID-19 pandemic, scholars postulate that we 'live in an age of trauma', while new quasi-psychological concepts like 'lockdown trauma', 'post-COVID-19 trauma' and 'pandemic burnout' gain ground.[45] However, the idea of trauma as an exceptional, if prevalent, experience is a phenomenon which has only developed in the course of the last century. As one psychologist has observed, '[t]he reason that trauma disorder has only recently been discussed as a problem [...] is not because it is more common now, but rather because it has only recently become uncommon enough to be considered beyond the norm.'[46]

The term 'trauma' derives from the ancient Greek τραῦμα, meaning wound, and was originally conceived to describe bodily harm. The shift in meaning to express psychological injury is generally associated with the rise of modernity. From the end of the nineteenth century, state institutions were forced to grapple with compensation claims for conditions like 'railway spine', which showed no visible bodily injuries and was generally associated with train accidents, but also with factory mishaps, shipwrecks and mining disasters.[47] The need to address the condition of thousands of soldiers during the First World War precipitated a boom in psychological literature on various war neuroses, such as 'shell shock', 'hysteria' and 'exhaustion'. It was not until the aftermath of the Vietnam War, however, that the current vocabulary of post-traumatic stress disorder (PTSD) entered mainstream discourse. According to its 1980 definition, PTSD is caused by personal experience of a traumatic event that is 'outside the range of normal experience' and that involves 'actual or threatened death or serious injury, or a physical threat to the physical integrity of the self'.[48]

The field of literary trauma theory developed from the 1990s in response to developments in psychology. These studies largely emerged from scholars interested in Holocaust studies, including Cathy Caruth, Shoshana Felman and Geoffrey Hartman. Drawing on deconstructionist and Freudian-inflected theories, their writings present trauma as an event that both shatters a survivor's identity and defies representation. These foundational theories dominate much cultural criticism, but they pose a number of issues, not least for historical enquiry.[49] More pluralistic approaches to trauma have thus emerged in more recent years; rather than focus on the pathological outcome of trauma, scholars like Michelle Baleav, Stef Craps and Roger Luckhurst emphasise the range of possible emotional responses to traumatic experience and underscore that these responses are always 'mediated by cultural values and narrative forms rooted in a place that allow or disallow certain emotions to be expressed'.[50]

The 'traditional event-based model of trauma' that associates PTSD with a sudden, catastrophic event 'outside the range of normal experience' has also come under much scrutiny. As feminist and postcolonial scholars highlight, this model fails to acknowledge that trauma can stem from a constellation of events as much as from singular occurrences, and can accrue from 'insidious' daily traumas connected to structural, social or patriarchal oppression.[51] Furthermore, if trauma, though possibly disruptive and dissociative, is not always pathological, the pluralistic approach also opens up the possibility of positive adaptations to traumatic experience, such as the relatively undertheorised idea of the human capacity for 'resilience'.[52] Nevertheless, the testimonies explored in this book caution against any overly optimistic expectation of recovery.

When mindful of the dangers of homogenising traumatic experience across time, the study of trauma in the context of the Irish revolution is nevertheless fruitful given that the conflict coincided with the opening up of ideas about the psychological legacies of war across Europe. The writings explored in this book illustrate that revolutionaries engaged with Freudian ideas of the subconscious – through the circulation of translations such as Barbara Low's *Psycho-Analysis: A Brief Account of the Freudian Theory* (1920) – but they also made sense of psychological injury through various, and often competing, religious, supernatural and medical discourses.

Of course, Irish hospitals, and Irish doctors and nurses, treated First World War soldiers suffering from 'nerve diseases'.[53] Yet whereas the figure of the shell-shocked soldier took on strong cultural significance in post-war Britain, the dominant commemorative narrative of the Irish revolution was largely structured around the image of the heroic male guerrilla fighter whose suffering and discomfort were rendered invisible. The Irish Military Service Pensions Board was slower to recognise psychic injury than compensation boards in Britain, such as the London-based Irish Grants Committee, which included 'shock' in its definition of 'physical injuries'.[54] In response perhaps to emasculating colonial stereotyping of the Irish, revolutionaries presented the English as effeminate and nervous in contrast to the more resilient Irish.[55] Applications for 'wound' or 'disability' pensions to the Pensions Board indicate that there was little consistency in medical diagnosis or treatment. Revolutionaries were diagnosed with a wide array of conditions including 'neurasthenia', 'nerves', 'neurosis', 'nervous breakdown', 'shock' and 'hysteria' during the early decades of the Free State. Many struggled to gain recognition or compensation for such 'diseases'.

The various treatments employed to 'manage' psychological injuries illustrate how understandings of 'nervous conditions' were highly gendered. The word 'hysteria' has its etymological roots in the Greek word for uterus, and 'insanity' was very much perceived to be a 'female malady'.[56] The Pensions Board even had a policy of sending female applicants claiming for wound/disability allowances for gynaecological testing; conditions such as endometriosis could even be read as evidence of a nervous condition.[57] There is also evidence to suggest that male and female revolutionaries were treated differently for their 'exhausted nerves'. While veterans were prescribed various electric shock, analeptic drug and nutritional treatments, men's treatment was more likely to be motivated towards swift recovery, continued military engagement or re-entry into the workforce. Women's treatment, on the other hand, often emphasised lengthy 'rest cures' at a remove from the stressful environment (see Chapter Two).[58] The gendered subtext of trauma also meant that female revolutionaries were perhaps more likely to admit to 'nervous breakdowns' given that the vocabulary was more readily at their disposal. Mental injuries among men, however, could be deemed as a failure in masculinity.

The taboo surrounding questions of masculinity and mental health is apparent in the weaponisation of the language of lunacy that took on particular resonance during the civil war. As Gavin Foster outlines in his insightful study *The Irish Civil War and Society* (2015), Free State news sources, like *The Freeman's Journal*, presented republicans – or 'Irregulars' as they were dubbed – as 'childish and irrational', and diagnosed them with pathological conditions such as 'neuroses', 'megalomania', 'hysteria' and 'madness'.[59] Equally, anti-treatyites mocked their pro-treaty opponents for being 'hysteric' and 'grossly insane' 'Freak Staters'.[60] Such deriding pseudomedical language was particularly targeted at female revolutionaries, who were branded by journalists, church leaders and politicians alike as 'harpies', 'half-crazed, hysterical women' and 'neurotic girls'.[61]

There is evidence that such political rhetoric led to the downplaying of actual psychic trauma. Síghle Humphreys recounts, in an unpublished account of her civil war internment, how a fellow prisoner, Sadie Dowling, was bedridden for days and groaning with pain despite having no visible injuries. When Dowling made a sudden recovery after a sentry shot through her cell window, Humphreys lamented that 'people like that give us all the name of being hysterical and neurotic'.[62] However, she retrospectively acknowledged the prevalence of such conditions of which she had previously been sceptical: 'And still I believe it is an ordinary disease, and a person can suffer as much with it, as with anything else, so I suppose I should not blame them, but I used to.'[63]

An Alternative Archive of Testimony

Humphreys' account illustrates the taboo around nervous conditions and indicates that the realities of individual, psychic trauma were more contentious than generalisations regarding the 'unspeakable horror', 'tragedy' and 'bitterness' of civil war. Nevertheless, a significant number of testimonial narratives were published, particularly in the 1920s and 1930s (but also as late as the 1990s), that set out both to counter the silence promoted in official discourse and also to highlight, exorcise and even narratively perform the psychological impact of war.[64] This urge to tell is connected to the need to assign *meaning* to traumatic experience, which is often considered to be a necessary step towards some form of healing.[65] This *meaning*, as Meg Jensen outlines, is achieved firstly through the construction of a 'coherent, listenable narrative of a traumatic experience' and, secondly, 'by sharing that narrative through a testimonial act'.[66]

Studies of the commemoration of the Irish revolution have not yet sufficiently addressed the phenomenon of popular testimonial narratives.

David Fitzpatrick sums up the early Free State's public commemorative policy as a 'chronicle of embarrassment'.[67] Dolan, too, observes that the official approach to the civil war was 'to suppress, to remember selectively, to try to forget'; this is indeed evident in the state's reluctance to commemorate the Free State army dead and its failure to maintain the cenotaph in remembrance of Michael Collins and Arthur Griffith on Leinster Lawn.[68] But even though Cumann na nGaedheal and Fianna Fáil shied away from public commemoration, there was little effort by successive governments to suppress published civil war testimonies, unlike other twentieth-century post-civil war states. As Frances Flanagan outlines, despite 'the Free State's notoriously ruthless treatment of "Irregulars", the new government was far from totalitarian in policing dissenting discourse about the revolution once the civil war had ended [...] It made no effort to actively suppress Republican accounts.'[69] It was not until 1942 that Fianna Fáil Minister for the Co-ordination of Defensive Measures Frank Aiken supported the repression of accounts of the revolution for fear that 'the animosities and bitterness of the Civil War would be disastrous to public morale and national security'.[70]

There is a strong belief that published memoirists had 'very little to say' about the civil war, based perhaps on the influential memoirs of IRA veterans Dan Breen, Michael Brennan and Tom Barry.[71] Indeed, despite the proliferation of autobiographies and memoirs, very few straight-up civil war narratives made their way into the revolutionary canon. Many of the best-known civil war memoirs were published posthumously; these include Ernie O'Malley's The Singing Flame (1978), Liam Deasy's Brother Against Brother (1982), Niall C. Harrington's Kerry Landing August 1922: An Episode of the Civil War (1992), and John A. Pinkman's In the Legion of the Vanguard (1998).[72] However, the belief that memoirists totally avoided the events of 1922–3 fails to consider how all revolutionary narratives were filtered through the memory of the civil war; it also overlooks popular published narratives, many of which adopted literary forms.

While historians refer to the 'collective silence' around the civil war, literary critic Peter Costello postulated as far back as 1977 that 'to think of the Civil War as a failure of imagination would be wrong. It was quite the otherwise.'[73] Indeed, a commentator in The Irish Book Lover observed in 1931 that 'the Civil War seems to inspire more literature than its forerunner and we wonder why'.[74] Less conventional literary narratives arguably enabled veterans to satisfy the conflict between the 'will to deny horrible events' and 'the will to proclaim them aloud' which Judith Herman has identified as the 'central dialectic of psychological trauma'.[75] The resort to fictionalised narratives is also indicative of wider European literary trends from the *fin de siècle*, as autobiography 'gets displaced towards fiction'.[76] Many testimonies by First World War soldiers – such as the writings of Erich Maria Remarque, Henri Barbusse or Ralph Hale Mottram – adopted fictionalised forms. Indeed, Leonard V. Smith contends in his study of French soldiers' writings that the novel 'came to dominate testimony, and altered testimony itself along the way'.[77] This type of hybrid autobiographical fiction also had a strong footing in Ireland; as Ronan Crowley has recently outlined, 'novels whose characters were based on real people' experienced a 'true burgeoning' in Ireland between 1916 and 1921, the most famous being James Joyce's *A Portrait of the Artist as a Young Man* (1916).[78] Though these 'confessional or tell-all literary forms' remain 'largely unexplored and underexamined',[79] these fictionalised self-portraits were highly popular among revolutionary veterans in the 1920s and 1930s. By 1934 it was observed that 'the latest generation of Irish writers appears to have turned from plays to novels as a vehicle for interpreting the events in which it has been engaged', while the editor of Talbot Press observed that same year that there had 'been many books published dealing with the historical aspect of the period 1916–1924, and, of course, more novels'.[80]

The critical neglect of these autobiographically based fictional writings has resulted in a lack of consistent terminology to describe them; they might be considered as autobiographical fiction, semifictional autobiography, autofiction (a 'text that purports to be both fictional and autobiographical'),[81] autobiografiction ('fiction which draws on biography and/or autobiography'),[82] testimonial fiction ('a fictional narrative with a large testimonial component')[83] or *romans à clef* (real-life behind a façade of fiction). By their very nature, however, these tantalising blends of fact and fiction defy easy categorisation. This book does not offer any satisfactory solution to this dilemma.

This book is concerned, rather, with how disparate literary and non-fictional narratives by veterans of the Irish revolution can be read as testimony. Testimony is understood here as an account (in any form) that 'bears witness' to events that were experienced first-hand, but that is also driven by a moral or ethical concern to make a statement, contest a silence or precipitate change.[84] Civil war veterans harnessed the testimonial possibilities of various non-fictional and fictional genres of life writing, including diaries, novels, memoirs, biographies, short stories, history textbooks, plays and poetry. However, personal stories only become testimonies when they are presented as such to the public. For this reason, this book is also the story of the readers who bought, shared and often carefully scrutinised the testimony of revolutionary veterans. These interactions shed light on the public validation of private stories on which 'testimonial resolution' relies.[85] Moreover, given that historical remembrance is generated through social interaction – in what Maurice Halbwachs famously described as the 'social frameworks of memory'[86] – the reading, sharing and discussion of these testimonies is essential to understanding how they facilitated a counter-memory which contested the 'amnesia' promoted in official discourse.

While literary narratives are often employed as flourishes in historical studies, historians of the Irish revolution – with the notable exception of Flanagan's sophisticated study *Remembering the Revolution: Dissent, Culture, and Nationalism in the Irish Free State* (2015) – overwhelmingly privilege published autobiographies, 'newly-released' archival material, witness statements and personal accounts from newspapers and journals, many of which were published or gathered in the 1950s or later. However, as Hayden White argued in 1978, all historical narratives should be understood as 'verbal fictions, the contents of which are as much invented as found and the forms of which have more in common with their counterparts in literature than they have with those in the sciences'.[87] Closer interrogations of apparently unmediated historical memoirs reveal that they are laden with vulnerabilities: revolutionary memoirists regularly narrate incidents at which they were not present;[88] they often draw on earlier fiction, such as the documented evocation of Frank O'Connor's short story 'Guests of the Nation' in Ernie O'Malley's memoir (see Chapter Five); and their accounts were no less susceptible to the controlling influences of editors, bureau investigators, publishers and translators than were literary testimonies. The interactions between fictionalised testimony and standard autobiographical narratives thus suggest that the fiction of the Irish revolution also 'altered testimony along the way'.

Furthermore, the literary nature of civil war narratives is symptomatic of the intertextuality often associated with civil war representation.

Armitage outlines that the Romans, who invented the term civil war (*bellum civile*) in the first century BCE, were the first to try to understand civil war through narrative, and that this idea of civil war was disseminated in the works of poets, orators and historians such as Appian, Augustine, Caesar, Florus, Lucan, Plutarch and Tacitus.[89] Nicholas McDowell thus argues that 'writing about the experience of civil war, whether in London in 1649, or in Dublin in 1923, or in Belfast in 1972, involves working within characteristic tropes and images of the genre, and these finally derive from the Roman tradition, whether or not the protagonists were fully aware of that tradition'.[90] This literary inheritance is clear in early commentary of the Irish Civil War, as journalists lamented that 'Roman was to Roman more hateful than the foe', referring to the conflict as a 'brother against brother' war, like that of Romulus and Remus.[91] These intertextual motifs arguably provided a means by which to indirectly address the taboo of civil war. As Janet Pérez contends, narratives of the Spanish Civil War are often 'allegorical or symbolical, mythical, or otherwise not strictly historical'; readers understood the 'war of the sexes' plot, the Cain–Abel motif and 'the symbolic marital conflict' to denote civil war.[92] Clair Wills has similarly observed the use of the 'trope of brothers divided' and the 'love triangle' by Irish writers to imply civil war.[93] Motifs from Irish mythology were also mobilised: the evocation of the battle between Cúchulainn and Ferdia was yet another way to hint at civil war.[94] These motifs worked against the 'merely local or straightforwardly historical' and were thus often effective in appealing to both sides of the conflict.[95]

Civil war narratives were also smuggled into texts which, on the surface at least, were located in other eras of history. Pro-treaty politician Piaras Béaslaí's 1928 play *An Danar* [The Dane] was set in tenth-century Dublin, although theatre viewers could easily see that its 'cogadh bráthar' [war of brothers] referred to more recent events.[96] Incidents from the civil war were also frequently concealed in narratives that apparently addressed the less contentious struggle for independence, while, by the 1930s, the Spanish Civil War became a site through which veterans articulated their thoughts on earlier events.[97] This obscuring of chronological time may have been a self-protective strategy, but it may also have been dictated by market demands. For example, Liam O'Flaherty's novel *The Informer* (1925) is set in the aftermath of the civil war, but the 1935 film version, directed by John Ford, was transposed to the earlier and less troublesome 'Black and Tan war'.[98]

These moving timeframes are a further reminder that a certain degree of periodic fluidity is required when tackling the memory of the civil war. Moreover, while the testimonies in this study all evoke 'civil war' in its various forms, the writers' commitment to breaking silence often leads them, both consciously and unconsciously, to address other 'zones of oblivion' overshadowed by the 'heartening and inspiring' narrative of revolution. The following five chapters focus on different dimensions of these silence-breaking projects. The chapters are thematic and also roughly chronological.

Chapter One interrogates contemporary psychoanalytical ideas regarding the therapeutic benefits of reading and writing testimony. The chapter takes as a point of departure revolutionary veteran Desmond Ryan's singling out in 1936 of three published testimonies by male revolutionaries that captured the 'spiritual wounds' of civil war. These testimonies were written by two anti-treaty republicans and a Free State army soldier – and all three experimented with fictional narrative forms. The chapter draws on Ryan's selection of writings in order to investigate how veterans mobilised the narrative templates available to them in order to tell and process their experience. It further explores how the subterfuge of fiction allowed veterans to offer alternative insights into the psychological effects of war on combatants, the devastation of civil war for local communities and the merits of narrative for both personal catharsis and post-civil war reconciliation.

Spiritual wounds, by default, were coded as male. Chapter Two addresses the particular challenges faced by female revolutionaries in writing, producing and sharing testimony in a commemorative culture that privileged men's stories. It explores how female revolutionaries covertly inserted testimony of their own experience into non-conventional writings and how these concealed testimonies contested the exclusion of women, and indeed the objectification of women's pain, in mainstream revolutionary remembrance. By the end of the 1930s, fictionalised renderings of the Irish Civil War by female revolutionary veterans in fact outweighed the number of published straight-up autobiographical accounts.

Despite the prevailing emphasis on the culture of sexual prudery in the socially conservative Irish Free State, Chapter Three points to inquisitive attitudes to sexual relations, including homosexuality, in fictionalised veteran testimonies. However, borders continually collapse between consensual and non-consensual intimacy. Indeed, fictionalised veteran accounts of the revolutionary period are littered with both implied and explicit representations of sexualised violence, including hair shearing, sexual humiliations, gender-specific torture, rape and domestic violence. These representations complicate the belief that revolutionary sexual violence was a 'hidden' crime. These writings pose ethical challenges for readers: while such representations break a silence, they also risk further coding sexuality or even eroticising sexual violence. Though fictionalised representations of sexual violence cannot be equated with real-life incidences, they are nevertheless integral to any study of sexual violence during the revolutionary period; these representations formed part of an economy of social, cultural, political and legal discourses that regulated the reporting and remembering of actual sexual assault.

Chapter Four addresses the sense of exile that motivated veterans' writings. The chapter underscores that the civil war not only provoked geographic displacement through high levels of emigration and internal migration, it also generated a sense of 'spiritual' or 'inner' exile among veterans who struggled to identify with the new political order. This is particularly pertinent in the context of partition and the establishment of Northern Ireland, as individuals found themselves 'exiled' depending on the side of the border on which they found themselves. While male veterans could readily tap into existing tropes of exile as a means to address this experience, these generally masculine exile tropes are less prominent in the women's writing included in this chapter. Indeed, for many women, emigration offered an escape and an alternative to inner exile. Some of these writings also work towards return migration, and possible reconciliation, as expressed in the fictional writings of one female former civil war prisoner through romantic reunifications between displaced Catholics and Protestants.

Finally, Chapter Five complicates the idea that veterans were silent regarding their role in committing violence during the revolution and particularly during the civil war. The perpetrator testimonies identified tend to revolve around two contrasting narrative templates: testimonies that evoke the empathy-between-foes motif epitomised in Frank O'Connor's influential short story 'Guests of the Nation' (1931) and testimonies that are characterised by an excess and even exaggeration of violence. This 'cult of violence' was a male domain; female revolutionaries did not have the available narrative models through which to process and recount their experience of enacting violence. This chapter also suggests that the urge to tell may have intensified among some veterans in later life, particularly as the Troubles broke out from the late 1960s. Indeed, two of the most significant civil war perpetrator testimonies were produced in the diaspora in the context of the Troubles – and both found shelter in non-conventional and fictionalised narrative forms.

This book does not dispute the many children and grandchildren of revolutionaries who can testify to the reticence of the revolutionary generation. As much as this book is concerned with those who set out to challenge the silence of the civil war, it also maps these silences, looking at the official and socially sanctioned construction of myths of silence, the active silencing of revolutionaries through canon formation, censorship and excommunication, as well as the self-censorship of revolutionaries themselves. For some, revisiting the civil war proved incredibly difficult. Joe Good's son, Maurice, recounts that his father could not include the civil war in his memoirs: 'whenever he came to thoughts of the Civil War there was a hiatus in his writing. He would just come to a stop'.[99] Breandán Ó hEithir equally observes that Séamus Ó Maoileoin could not complete a sequel to his war of independence memoir, *B'fhiú an Braon Fola* [The Drop of Blood was Worth It] (1958): 'Dúirt sé go raibh sé ag iarraidh tabhairt faoi ach go mba phionós aimsire, leis é. Tháinig na deora ina shúile nuair a labhair sé ar an bpeannaid a bhain le cur síos a dhéanamh ar eachtraí a bhain le seanchomrádaithe a chuaigh ar thaobh an tSaorstáit' [He said he wanted to do it, but that it was a punishing task. His eyes filled with tears when he spoke of the pain he felt when describing events relating to old comrades who took the Free State side].[100]

But for some, committing words to print was easier than speech. George Lennon rendered his IRA experience in hybridised drama/diary/memoir form, while simultaneously refusing to broach the 'unmentionable civil war' with his family.[101] Equally, the loquacity with which many revolutionaries professed their reticence to speak about the civil war is telling in itself. Indeed, declarations as to the impossibility of communication were frequently no more than a rhetorical device. In his 1966 autobiography *Cuimhne an tSeanpháiste* [Memory of the Old Child], author and revolutionary Micheál Breathnach professes his wish to forget the civil war: 'B'fhearr liom brat mór dubh a ligean anuas ar an tréimhse sin agus é a chur as mo chuimhne ar fad *dá bhféadfainn é* [I would rather draw a big black curtain down on that period and put it out of my memory altogether *if I could*] (my emphasis).[102] Even though Breathnach suggests that he welcomes the silence surrounding the civil war, closer inspection reveals that his disclaimer, in fact, serves as a prefatory remark to heighten emotional impact. In the next chapter, Breathnach proceeds to detail his efforts to maintain friendships despite tensions over the treaty, as former colleagues tried to convert him to both the pro- and anti-treaty positions.

Breathnach's account thus suggests that even silence could be decidedly effable. Like the veterans whose writings will be explored in the chapters that follow, his hope to banish the civil war from his memory, *if he could*, was in conflict with his 'imperative to tell and to be heard'.

This book does not assume that the veterans discussed would have been diagnosed with any sort of medical or psychiatric condition due to their wartime experience. It is concerned, rather, with the self-protective strategies they exploited in their writings to address traumatic experience and balance the simultaneous desire to forget and the inability to stop remembering. Whether neutral, pro- or anti-treaty, men or women, their highly politicised urge to testify was a direct affront to the widespread calls to 'forget what is painful'.

Chapter One

'Ridding Ourselves of the Past': Therapeutic Testimony

Desmond Ryan (1893–1964) lamented that the revolution had left 'a bloody gulf of Civil War memories that hardly a generation will wipe out'.[1] He responded by putting pen to paper. His 1934 memoir, *Remembering Sion: A Chronicle of Storm and Quiet*, documented his revolutionary experience from his political awakening as a child to his sudden departure from Ireland during the civil war. Critics were undecided. As one reviewer grumbled, 'Looking back is a sad business. Mr. Desmond Ryan is really too young to indulge in it, and the events on which he looks back are too near and too vivid for him or for any of this generation to write of them with impartiality.'[2] However, Ryan defended his personal project of remembrance. Having 'waited some ten years', he insisted that exorcising the 'grimmest' of these memories enabled him to 'recover' 'good tempers'.[3] This writing, he claimed, was a most rewarding endeavour:

> It is not harping or brooding on the past but ridding ourselves of the past, blowing off the worst and retaining the best, and getting the picture and the experience of the past in proportion. What's wrong with Ireland just at present is that Ireland won't blow off steam once and for all but keeps all the Civil War and other war memories festering in her subconsciousness.[4]

Ryan was one of many revolutionaries whose writing was driven by what Frances Flanagan refers to as a 'therapeutic goal'.[5] Rosamond Jacob's history

The Rise of the United Irishmen 1791–94 (1937) was purportedly written as 'an attempt to heal the wounds of the Civil War and the resulting splits in contemporary Irish life';[6] Frank O'Connor's 1937 biography of Michael Collins, *The Big Fellow* – against whom he fought – is described in the foreword as 'an act of reparation';[7] Seán O'Faoláin found that writing helped him to put his revolutionary memories 'in their place'.[8]

Ryan's interest lay not only in the personal catharsis writing could provide its author through the expression of the subconscious, but also in the narrativisation of these 'spiritual wounds' by others and how the sharing of testimony might cultivate mutual understanding across treaty lines. In his biography of Éamon de Valera, *Unique Dictator* (1936), he identified three veterans, who, like himself, had resorted to narrative as a means to grapple with the 'fester[ing]' 'wounds of the Irish Civil War':

> In the pages of Peadar O'Donnell's *The Gates Flew Open* [1932], in Francis Carty's *Legion of the Rearguard* [1934], in Patrick Mulloy's *Jackets Green* [1936], three Irish writers from different viewpoints have written from first-hand experience of the physical and spiritual ordeal through which a riven army and a sundered movement then passed, and few readers of their poignant pages, even if Ireland is to them only a name on a map, can escape the feeling that the deepest wounds of the Civil War were spiritual wounds ...[9]

The first two testimonies selected by Ryan – who was a supporter of the treaty – are written by anti-treaty republicans, the third by a Free State army veteran. Although Peadar O'Donnell's (1893–1986) prison memoir has a place in the revolutionary canon, the remarkable testimonies of Francis Carty (1899–1972) and Patrick Mulloy (1903–1978) have almost totally eluded scholarly attention. Indeed, all three testimonies defy the standard conventions of autobiography: O'Donnell's highly literary memoir builds on his depictions of civil war imprisonment in his earlier novel *The Knife* (1930), while Carty's and Mulloy's testimonies of their civil war experience take the form of novels.

This chapter interrogates the self-acknowledged therapeutic aims behind many civil war testimonies. Despite the critical neglect of such non-conventional writings, these projects of literary witnessing are of particular historical value given their foregrounding of experience effaced from official remembrance. The blend of fiction, autobiography and memoir endorsed by O'Donnell, Carty and Mulloy – and indeed by many other veterans – is also indicative of the competing imperatives of disclosure and secrecy strongly associated with trauma-telling. These disguised divulgences were perhaps further required given that the taboo of psychological distress threatened the idealised image of heroic masculinity central to commemoration of the Rising and the 'fight for Irish freedom'.

Spiritual Wounds?: Historicising 'Trauma'

Ryan's contention that 'the deepest wounds of the Civil War were spiritual wounds' points to the vocabulary available to articulate psychological trauma in early twentieth-century Ireland. While the metaphor of the 'wound' was popularly understood to hint at emotional upset, the term 'spiritual wounds' might reflect Ryan's exposure to spiritual philosophy (anthroposophy) as advanced by the Austrian philosopher Rudolf Steiner (1861–1925).[10] Steiner aimed to apply scientific thinking to human soul-life but was apprehensive of the ability of psychoanalysis – as advanced by Josef Breuer and Sigmund Freud – to capture the 'spiritual reality'.[11] This clash between psychoanalysis and spiritualism is very much indicative of the diversity of ideas regarding the architecture of the psyche during the late nineteenth and early twentieth centuries.[12] Revolutionaries approached psychological wounding from various – often competing – secular, spiritual, religious or even paranormal perspectives.

Ryan's convictions regarding the possibility of 'healing' spiritual wounds through narrative was also shaped by his own experience as a psychiatric casualty of war. Ryan was interned in Stafford Jail, Wormwood Scrubs and Frongoch following his role in the Easter Rising alongside other staff and pupils from Patrick Pearse's school, St Enda's. His diaries reveal that he was held in 'complete isolation' and suffered 'nerves'.[13] After his release, he worked at *The Freeman's Journal*, where he was tasked with reporting for the newspaper's 'blood column' on the many 'murders, reprisals, burnings [and] shootings' of the 'not so glorious' years of the independence struggle.[14] Although Ryan supported the treaty, he was so 'disillusioned' by the growing schism between the two sides that he left *The Freeman's* and fled to London. In his memoir, he frankly acknowledges the psychological implications of this 'crisis' and recounts that he had a 'minor nervous breakdown' as he was swept 'over the seas from Sion'.[15]

When recovering from his first bout of 'nerves' in 1917, Ryan had made a resolution in his diary to commit himself to 'one definite and absorbing aim in life': writing.[16] He rewrote his prison diary and circulated it confidentially among his family.[17] This decision to share his harrowing experience in written form was the beginning of a long career in chronicling the revolution. His first two books were biographies of Patrick Pearse (1919) and James Connolly (1924), whilst his next effort, *The Invisible Army* (1932), documented the life of Michael Collins in fictionalised form.[18] These biographies were part of an outpouring of accounts written by revolutionaries detailing the lives of their deceased comrades – these writings might be referred to as 'relational testimonies' given that the subject's biography is nearly always entwined with the writer's own autobiographical experience.[19] In *The Invisible Army*, journalist David Harding is clearly an author surrogate: the book concludes as Harding, like Ryan, takes the mailboat to England. Harding is distraught after witnessing landmines exploding and following the deaths of intimate friends, including Collins, the subject of the 'biography': 'He wanted one thing only: to forget. All feeling was numbed. The beliefs of a lifetime swayed and crashed and reeled to death. Friendship had gone as the volleys of firing parties crashed and spades clanked to open gaping graves. NOTHING ON EARTH WAS WORTH IT'.[20]

Yet Harding's desire to forget is offset by the author's need to tell. If this type of fictionalised biography opened up the possibility of self-reflection and allowed Ryan to 'banish' the 'grimmest' of his memories,[21] his confidence in addressing his own experience was further realised in his 1934 memoir *Remembering Sion*, in which, as he would later state, he 'coughed up a good deal, or, to use a more accurate and elegant expression, I released most of the pent-up feelings of twenty-five years'.[22] Despite anticipated criticism from 'professional critics', Ryan remained convinced that such evocations of the past were not 'whining' or 'sickly sentimentality' but rather 'one of the most useful tasks to which any Irish writer can apply himself, and, if it helps no one else, it at least helps the writer to rid his bosom of much perilous stuff'.[23]

As philosopher Richard Kearney has outlined, this idea of exorcising trauma through narrative can be traced back as far as Aristotle's theory of mythos-mimesis.[24] These ideas took on greater significance in early psychotherapies based on abreaction theory (such as Freud's and Breuer's 'talking cure' advanced in 1897), which proposed that healing could be facilitated by expurgating suppressed memories through techniques such as free association, automatic writing, suggestion or hypnosis. This idea of narrative therapy remains central to psychological practice and theory. As Leigh Gilmore sums up, words provide a 'therapeutic balm' as the 'unconscious language of repetition through which trauma initially speaks (flashbacks, nightmares, emotional flooding) is replaced by a conscious language that can be repeated in structured settings'.[25]

But while abreaction is often connected to the transference from patient to analyst in a clinical setting, Suzette A. Henke contends, in her influential study *Shattered Subjects*, that abreaction is essentially an experience of 'rememory' and thus not contingent on an analyst. Following this line of enquiry, Henke coined the term 'scriptotherapy' to describe 'the process of writing out and writing through traumatic experience in the mode of therapeutic reenactment'.[26] Indeed, it may be that 'writing therapy' preceded 'talk therapy' in early twentieth-century psychoanalysis.[27] Automatic writing – perhaps most associated in an Irish context with W. B. Yeats – was practised widely in revolutionary circles.[28] While automatic writing primarily served as a means to access the unconscious and was often exercised in social settings, it seems that writing was employed as a coping mechanism by a number of revolutionaries in lieu of any type of 'talk therapy'.

Even though there was an explosion in psychological literature following the First World War, there was a general distrust of psychoanalysis in Ireland due to the disapproval of the Catholic Church.[29] Writer Samuel Beckett travelled to London for treatment in the early 1930s as he claimed that 'psychoanalysis was not allowed in Dublin at that time'.[30] Rosamond Jacob (1888–1960), who was interned during the civil war, also travelled to London for psychoanalysis to address her interpersonal relations; her therapy in fact began in epistolary form.[31] In light of limited medical services and public reluctance to address the psychological consequences of the revolution, veterans were often compelled to self-medicate. Both Seosamh Mac Grianna (1900–1990) and Charles Dalton (1903–1974) seem to have had recourse to writing as a sort of coping strategy. Mac Grianna had been interned as an anti-treaty prisoner in the Curragh, and his wife, Margaret Green, contended that he had 'become ill since the Civil War'.[32] He was treated in Grangegorman Mental Asylum in 1935–6 and drafted up a self-help plan at this time which consisted of 'five years' complete isolation, temperance and chastity', and included a provision to 'write' weekly letters and to promote 'development of mind and body'.[33] His highly metafictional novel, *Dá mBíodh Ruball ar an Éan* [If the Bird Had a Tail] (1940), reflects on the cathartic benefits of writing. In the opening chapter, the first-person narrator contends that he is writing 'go dóchasach' [hopefully], as writing a book is 'deas don chroí ag an duine' [good for a person's heart].[34] Mac Grianna's condition improved little, however, and the novel went unfinished.[35] He spent much of his later life in St Conal's Hospital in Letterkenny.

Dalton, who was a member of Michael Collins' squad and later an officer in the Free State army, was also treated in Grangegorman. His fellow squad member Frank Saurin described Dalton's condition in a letter to the Pension Board in 1941:

> He became obsessed with the idea that his house was surrounded by men out to 'get him'. He bolted and locked all his doors and went as far as to climb the stairs on his hands and knees, thereby avoiding throwing his shadow on a drawn blind so that he would not present a target to his imaginary potential executioners.[36]

By this stage, Dalton had been diagnosed by various consultants with 'mixed psychosis', 'mental aberration' and '100% delusional insanity'; the Pension Board was willing to compensate Dalton for an injury sustained to his hand, but would 'not touch the question of the disease aspect of his disability'.[37] According to his daughter, Carol Mullan, Dalton's memoir, *With the Dublin Brigade* (1929), was 'a form of therapy, really' for her father.[38] Even though the memoir only covers the period until the truce and omits Dalton's more contentious civil war activities – namely his implication in the killings of three unarmed teenagers in October 1922 – it nevertheless includes remarkably frank acknowledgements of his emotional strain during IRA activities. However, Dalton's allusions to his knees 'shaking' and his sense of 'suffocating' due to the 'beating of my heart' provoked commentary and perhaps even a certain unease. A reviewer in *Kilkenny People* essentially neutralised Dalton's forthright descriptions of his psychological suffering by casting them in heroic terms, claiming that these comments give 'actuality to the narrative and carry conviction to the reader'.[39] While Mac Grianna's and Dalton's writing may have been motivated by a therapeutic objective, their severe cases underline the dangers of touting writing as a cure.

Brooding on the Past or Ridding Ourselves of It?

Indeed, for Ryan, the healing potential of narrative was dependent on a certain means of articulation: it was possible, not through 'harping or brooding on the past' (as practised by party politicians and their followers), but through 'ridding ourselves of the past, blowing off the worst and retaining the best'.[40] This distinction echoes the influential concepts of 'acting-out' and 'working through' expressed by Freud in his 1914 essay, 'Remembering, Repeating and Working-Through'.[41] As intellectual historian Dominick LaCapra explains, 'acting out' describes the condition of being 'haunted or possessed by the past and performatively caught up in the compulsive repetition of traumatic scenes'.[42] Meanwhile 'working through' indicates 'the effort to articulate or rearticulate affect and representation in a manner that may never transcend, but may to some viable extent counteract, a re-enactment, or acting out, of that disabling dissociation'.[43] Echoing LaCapra, Ryan did not envision this process of 'ridding ourselves of the past' as a straightforward, cause-effect relationship between traumatic experience and narrative healing. Although he felt 'whole and sane' after exorcising his memories in *Remembering Sion*, he admitted the incompleteness of his project, that 'all the best bits' were left out. Writing may have temporarily satisfied the 'imperative to tell', but he felt bound to 'always be *Still Remembering Sion*' (my emphasis).[44]

Nevertheless, Ryan felt that writers were particularly privileged in their ability to 'blow off steam' and thus had a duty to challenge the misuse of civil war memory at official level. The destabilisation of literary genres was a tool rather than a hindrance for this project; Ryan felt that the blend of fiction and biography he employed in *The Invisible Army* was effective both in attracting readers with little interest in 'straightforward historical works' and also in reviving 'the atmosphere of that very abnormal time, and yet not distort[ing] the truth'.[45] While it was remarked that the text was 'difficult to classify',[46] his blending of (auto)biography, fiction and history was generally accepted; a reviewer in *The Irish Book Lover* contended that '[t]he fictional style of the narrative breathes vital colour into it, and so transcends biography'.[47] His subsequent memoir, *Remembering Sion*, was also highly literary and self-consciously experimented with Joycean fragmented narration by throwing 'all commas, semi-colons, colons, dashes and dots and grammar and sense and all desiccated word-polishing and mincing phraseology and restraint itself to the very devil when it suited'.[48]

Curragh internee Francis Stuart (1902–2000) also experimented with fictional and autobiographical structures. He claimed the civil war days 'were the worst of my life, the most vicious. Nothing is worse'.[49] Like Ryan, he addressed the revolution in two early novels, *Pigeon Irish* (1932) and *The Coloured Dome* (1932); the former is set in a dystopian future civil war in which the executions of 1922 are used to justify further violence, while the latter follows the exploits of a female republican leader during 'hopeless civil war'.[50] In his memoir, *Things to Live For: Notes for an Autobiography* (1934), Stuart claimed that fiction had provided him a more comfortable medium of self-expression: 'I've written novels because until now that form has seemed the one best suited in which to express myself. Only in the drama of living can my ideas take shape. Only by depicting the battle can I show what I have dreamed of as the triumph of defeat'.[51] While Stuart directly recorded his civil war internment in *Things to Live For*, he, too, found much 'left unfinished'. He returned to his civil war internment – albeit through the author surrogate character of H – in his eccentric fictionalised memoir, *Black List, Section H* (1971).[52]

Between the Modernist Trauma Aesthetic and Revolutionary Realism

Much attention has been afforded to the deployment of modernist or avant-garde narrative forms in order to emphasise the possibly disruptive and temporally disjointed nature of traumatic experience.[53] Writing of testimonies of male combatants from the First World War, Margaret Higonnet remarks that:

> PTSD has offered literary critics a vocabulary to describe the symptoms of soldiers' mental disturbances that may figure in memoirs and other autobiographical accounts: nonsequential memory,

flashbacks, nightmares, and mutism or fragmented language. Those symptoms bear a suggestive resemblance to certain features of modernist experiment: decentering of the subject, montage, ellipses or gaps in narrative, and startlingly vivid images. This similarity – or, some would argue, connection – between a set of medical symptoms among veterans and a set of stylistic features in narrative has fostered a masculine canon of modernism.[54]

While such modernist techniques are evident in a number of narratives that address the complexities of the revolutionary period – such as writings by Dorothy Macardle, Frank Gallagher, Ernie O'Malley, Elizabeth Bowen and the aforementioned Francis Stuart – the privileging of the modernist aesthetic in trauma studies has more recently come under scrutiny. Roger Luckhurst calls for equal consideration of high, middle and low forms of traumatic representation – including safely non-experimental texts – given that, 'if trauma is a crisis in representation, then this generates narrative *possibility* just as much as *impossibility*'.[55] Postcolonial scholars, too, have voiced their concerns about equating 'authentic' trauma literature with disjointed language; this overlooks the cultural contexts in which such narratives are produced, underestimates the political nature of testimony that seeks 'to get the message across' and also goes against the very idea of narrative repair if the healing potential of trauma-telling is connected to its 'shareability'.[56]

Some veterans certainly experimented with modernist techniques, but much of the testimonial literature of the Irish revolution in the 1930s relied on realism, under the influence, perhaps, of popular English, French and German war novels. Newspaper advertisements likened Ryan's *Invisible Army* to Erich Maria Remarque's starkly realist novel *All Quiet on the Western Front*.[57] Even though realism is often dismissed in literary studies, with critics lamenting that 'so disillusioned, post-revolutionary literary Ireland seems to have thrown out the Modernist baby with the Romantic bathwater',[58] Michael Rothberg contends that realism was far from a conservative mode; rather, realist depiction in the 1930s could represent 'a revolutionary force that was a natural correlative of proletarian struggle'.[59]

Whether influenced by realist or modernist literary forms, or indeed both, fictionalised testimonies offered veterans a protected means through

which to tackle the project of 'ridding ourselves of the past' given the
political taboo, practical risks and libel fears provoked by writing about
the civil war.[60] James J. Comerford outlines in his self-published tome, *My
Kilkenny I.R.A. Days 1916–1922* (1980), that his colleagues were fearful
of writing memoirs because of the delicate nature of pre- and post-truce
service:

> I was told how in many cases jealousies arose over the books – because
> the names of some men who legitimately had pre-Truce IRA service
> and should be in the story were omitted inadvertently, and, likewise,
> because the names of some men were included, inadvertently, even
> though they had no pre-Truce records. As a result of such errors,
> writers of these books, together with their friends, were harshly
> criticised and in fact sometimes actually harassed.[61]

Memoirists frequently faced libel cases and official censure. Dalton's *With
the Dublin Brigade* was brought up in the House of Lords; his account of
the killings of Bloody Sunday led to debate as to 'whether it is advisable
that a book of this sort should be circulated'.[62] Ernie O'Malley famously lost
a libel case taken by Joseph O'Doherty, who protested against O'Malley's
claim that he had backed down from a raid due to the fact that he was
married.[63] Cases like these may explain why O'Malley's civil war memoir
(1978) was published after his death (with many names omitted in the first
edition). These cases also resulted in ambiguous disclaimers being placed
at the beginning of memoirs and fictionalised testimonies alike: 'All the
names mentioned in this story are names of purely fictitious persons.'[64]
One exception was the disclaimer in Mountjoy 'graduate' Francis Plunkett's
banned 1935 novel, *As the Fool*, in which he claimed that he had no
intention to 'fictionalise real people'.[65] This move backfired as Plunkett – a
pseudonym for the fascinating London-based anarchist (and former civil
war prisoner) Myles Mordaunt – landed himself in court for defamation
against Brigadier General F. P. Crozier, Auxiliary Division of the Royal Irish
Constabulary and author of a number of books, including *The Men I Killed*
(1937).[66]

Yet even testimonial endeavours under the camouflage of fiction did
not guarantee authorial freedom or possible unburdening. Accounts of
the revolutionary period came under deep scrutiny and had to convince

a knowledgeable readership who had lived through the period. Critics and publishing houses emphasised authenticity even in fictionalised writings and the reading public wrote corrections into the margins of novels and memoirs alike, eager to point out any historical inaccuracies.[67] Regardless of disclaimers that insisted that all persons were fictitious, readers actively sought to identify characters in the many autobiographically based novels published during this period. A reviewer of Eimar O'Duffy's novel *Miss Rudd and Some Lovers* (1924) was confident that 'his Irish, or at any rate his Dublin, readers will have no difficulty in recognising the distinguishing marks of some more or less public characters'.[68] Some writers even invited their readers to look past these fictional disguises. Robert Brennan, who was later director of publicity for the anti-treaty side, published a pseudonymised detective novel, *The False Finger Tip*, in 1921, which he had written during his war of independence imprisonment. The novel was dedicated to 'the man I have called SAMUEL LANIGAN' – one of the 'fictional' characters in the book – 'as a reprisal for having to endure his many conversations during many weary months [...]'.[69]

Fiction that failed to meet the criteria of empirical verifiability was not readily entertained, and reviewers and readers were less drawn to accounts of the revolution by 'outsiders'. English-born and US-based novelist Kathleen Pawle was harshly criticised for her 1936 novel *We in Captivity*, set during the Rising; one reviewer contended she had 'no business to set up to interpret Ireland'.[70] Dublin author J. S. Collis found that his autobiographically inflected novel *The Sounding Cataract* (1936) also met with censure. As a reviewer in the *Irish Independent* wrote, Collis 'may know the details of the Civil War, but he is quite unable to capture its atmosphere. It might be a civil war in China or Peru for all the relation it bears to the Ireland of 1922'.[71] Liverpool-born John Brophy's banned novel *The Rocky Road* (1932) was also dismissed outright, both for its 'too-incredible' and 'unnecessary' seduction scene, and because the author did 'not know his Dublin of this particular period'.[72]

Despite all these risks, many veterans were compelled to share their testimonies and search for a confirming audience: Ryan confessed that he resisted the temptation to leave his writings stashed away in 'the bottom drawer' and instead threw 'the manuscript at the public'.[73] These target readers included fellow veterans. Shirley Quill recounts in her memoir of her husband, anti-treaty veteran and trade union leader Mike Quill (and long-time New York resident), that she could not hamper her husband's desire to textually revisit his revolutionary days:

> 'Darling, for you the Civil War is still an open wound. If you don't stop reading this stuff, it will never heal.'
> 'You're right,' he replied quietly, 'but I can't help it. I can't stop reading.'[74]

Testimonies to traumatic experience often evoke 'vicarious' reactions, but these reactions can prove 'especially powerful' when the listener has 'first-hand traumas that are similar to those being portrayed'.[75] The compulsion of some veterans to write was thus matched by a compulsion by others to revisit the period as readers.

These confirming target audiences also influenced the narrative templates employed by veterans. Sidonie Smith and Julia Watson stress in their influential study of autobiography that individuals invariably tell their life stories 'by borrowing from and inventing upon models of life narratives that are culturally available to them'.[76] In the case of the civil war divide, the narrative templates were also shaped, to varying extents, by the distinct commemorative cultures of the pro- and anti-treaty sides. This is clear from the three testimonies identified by Ryan to which we will now turn. Peadar O'Donnell's layering of fiction and history in *The Gates Flew Open* tapped into a well-established republican narrative of redemptive, traumatic defeat that transcends time and place, and presents wartime trauma as collective as much as individual. Francis Carty's novel, *Legion of the Rearguard*, drew on the affirmative, rural realism of Daniel Corkery, whose short-story collection, *Hounds of Banba* (1920), established prose fiction as a key medium for addressing the events of the revolution. Yet, unlike Corkery's nationalistic collection, produced as the conflict was still ongoing, Carty's writings offer a solemn alternative to more glorified accounts of revolutionary activity and underscore the psychological devastation to family life in civil war. Free State army veteran Patrick Mulloy found little solace in the memory of the revolutionary dead, but rather resorted to grisly realism in *Jackets Green: A Novel* to convey the brutality of wartime violence to both his Irish and international readers. This mode was less amenable, perhaps, to the Irish reading establishment; as will be discussed, his testimony proved too unvarnished to please literary reviewers or the Censorship Board.

Peadar O'Donnell's *The Gates Flew Open*: The Triumphant Trauma of Defeat?

In light of the fact that politicians 'show no sign of ever really blowing off steam', Desmond Ryan called on writers to set 'down everything honestly and truthfully, even shocking themselves and all Ireland and all the world in the process'.[77] This 'shock' he identified first with James Joyce's *Ulysses* (1922), which 'left the most eloquent prologue to the Irish revolution ever written', and second with Peadar O'Donnell's *The Gates Flew Open* (1932). According to Ryan, '[w]hen Peadar O'Donnell wrote *The Gates Flew Open*, even if his gates hurled themselves against just and unjust, he told us what the jails had been thinking and left a picture of the Civil War which probably did something to deflate the blood feuds and passions of that time'.[78] Published in early 1932, O'Donnell's retrospective prison memoir was one of the first full-length published accounts detailing the conditions endured by some 12,000 anti-treaty prisoners.[79] O'Donnell had been highly active in the IRA in his native Donegal during the struggle for independence. He opposed the Anglo-Irish Treaty and joined the Four Courts garrison, but ultimately spent most of the civil war in prison. *The Gates Flew Open* documents his internment from summer 1922 until spring 1924; during this time he was held in Mountjoy, Kilmainham and the Curragh camp and also spent three months in solitary confinement in Finner camp, County Donegal, under threat of execution.

Ryan's belief that O'Donnell's eclectic memoir aided in easing tensions was not shared by contemporary reviewers; it was deemed a 'vulgar book [...] distinguished by its unreasoning bitterness',[80] that was 'disappointing' and 'too full of personal animosities'.[81] By this time, O'Donnell had published four novels to significant praise: *Storm: A Story of the Irish War* (1925), *Islanders* (1928), *Adrigoole* (1929) and *The Knife* (1930).[82] The stark depictions of rural poverty in these novels reflected O'Donnell's political aims, specifically his campaign against the payment of land annuities to the British state from 1926.[83] However, the political undertones of *The Gates Flew Open* were far less concealed than in his fiction, and the memoir was widely considered inimical to his literary reputation. A reviewer in *The Irish Book Lover* took issue with the 'gossipy and slovenly' style and declared that 'Peadar, who now has five books in his name, should be growing up'.[84]

In response to his critics, O'Donnell did not deny that the memoir was 'bitter and vulgar', but rather contended that 'therein lies its faithfulness to the inflamed spirits of the jails' and that there was 'nothing wrong with an artist truthfully reflecting his experiences'.[85] *The Gates Flew Open* was thus driven by a truth-telling motive that O'Donnell did not consider to be at odds with his artistic practice. Indeed, the memoir is highly literary and continuously draws attention to the slippages between fact and fiction, challenging thus conventional ideas of what constitutes testimonial evidence.

O'Donnell's testimony was also shaped by the political context of the early 1930s. By the time he was writing *The Gates Flew Open*, O'Donnell was essentially on the run due to his role as founder of Saor Éire, the far-left political wing of the IRA. His depiction in the memoir of the bishops' refusal to offer the sacraments to civil war prisoners was thus a direct affront to the Catholic Church, who had denounced Saor Éire as 'frankly communist' and the IRA as 'sinful and irreligious'.[86] *The Gates Flew Open* equally posed a challenge to the Cumann na nGaedheal government in the lead up to the 1932 election, in which Fianna Fáil successfully ran on a campaign to 'open the gaol gates' and release republican prisoners.

As much *The Gates Flew Open* is a personal testimony, it is also a political document with a collective aim. O'Donnell sets himself up as a 'moral witness' in the memoir in the sense that he writes from direct experience but is motivated to set the record straight and speak up on behalf of his fellow prisoners – 'the minds that were bruised in the prisons of 1922'.[87] This is all the more pertinent given that many tell 'stories so brilliantly', yet 'so few write'.[88] In particular, *The Gates Flew Open* pays tribute to O'Donnell's fellow republican prisoners – Liam Mellows, Joe McKelvey, Dick Barrett and Rory O'Connor – who were executed in December 1922 as a reprisal for the assassination of Free State TD Seán Hales.

In its testimonial aim to speak for a silenced, sometimes illiterate, community and in its honouring of the 'true witnesses' of the republican dead, O'Donnell's memoir taps into a long legacy of republican jail writing which highlighted the mistreatment of Irish prisoners in the British prison system and often cast this suffering through a redemptive lens; these include John Mitchel's *Jail Journal* (1854), Jeremiah O'Donovan Rossa's *My Years in English Jails* (1874), Michael Davitt's *Leaves from a Prison Diary* (1885) and Thomas Clarke's *Glimpses of an Irish Felon's Prison Life* (1922). These prison testimonies are essentially extensions of the daily resistance performed by republican prisoners as they flouted prison rules, wrecked cells, branded walls with graffiti, attempted escapes and engaged in hunger strikes for better conditions, privileges or release.

Intertextual Testimony: *The Gates Flew Open* and *The Knife*

Although *The Gates Flew Open* is established in the canon of republican writing, O'Donnell's 'imperative to tell' about his civil war internment first found a home in his fiction. The final section of his 1930 novel *The Knife* catalogues civil war prison conditions and pre-empts many scenes evoked two years later in *The Gates Flew Open* – including the contentious fallout between the prisoners and the clergy. *The Gates Flew Open* thus exists in intertextual dialogue with *The Knife,* and O'Donnell even draws the reader of the memoir towards its literary precedent: 'I went amid jail scenes with a soft light in *The Knife* and they were very angry.'[89] Both texts resist generic categorisation: literary critic Johann A. Norstedt is ambivalent about the merits of the final section of *The Knife,* as 'it is almost as though one is reading somebody's jail journal (O'Donnell's?), not the novel which began with Catholics and Protestants fighting over land in rural Donegal.'[90] Meanwhile, Alexander González considers *The Gates Flew Open* to be 'too rough and unpolished [...] to qualify it as autobiography in the formal tradition of Yeats, Moore, and O'Casey.'[91]

If O'Donnell's rural novels aimed to shock through their stark depictions of economic precarity, the descriptions of prison life in *The Knife* were equally provocative. The jail section of the novel opens as the eponymous protagonist, an anti-treaty prisoner, is subjected to what O'Donnell later described as a 'mock crucifixion':

> [A] flashlight stabbed into the cell to light up the figure of a man, hung by the wrists from a hook in the roof. The Knife had now been hung up for hours, his toes just touching the ground, his weight swinging on his wrists. Consciousness hovered like sleep mocks an exhausted car driver, a thing of jerks and flashes.[92]

Rather than focus on such brutality, however, O'Donnell's prison writings are more concerned with the daily routine and resistance of the prisoners, as they attend 'engineering' classes on how to blow up bridges, dig tunnels, thwart prison counts, organise sing-songs, light bonfires and play rounders. The prison guards, too, are generally sympathetic towards the prisoners; they provide newspapers, pass messages and even supply breakfast. Richard English attributes the 'japery, jollity, naive optimism, and boyish good humour' of O'Donnell's civil war internees to the influence of the British public-school novels of P. G. Wodehouse.[93]

Nevertheless, O'Donnell exploits the novel to openly lash out at the 'holy' bishops and leaders of the Free State side; the eponymous protagonist the Knife denounces the 'mean little mind' of Mulcahy and hopes to get 'one fist into the yellow blotched face of Glennon before I go'.[94] These are not fictional characters: Richard Mulcahy was commander-in-chief of the Free State army and Commandant Tom Glennon was in charge of Finner camp. Just as O'Donnell was repatriated to Donegal under threat of execution, the fictional republican prisoners are imprisoned in Dublin and subsequently are sent back 'to our own county' before being condemned to death on a false charge of possession of arms.[95] As they await their execution, the Knife insists, 'I do not want to die,' echoing the sentiments expressed in O'Donnell's later memoir, in which he recalls battling 'the fever to live'.[96] Nevertheless, *The Knife* is motivated by a reconciliatory aim, if crudely rendered. Reflecting O'Donnell's genuine hope of rebuilding the broken 'pattern of neighbourliness' after the civil war, the novel emphasises how small Catholic landowners had more in common with their Protestant neighbours than the burgeoning middle-class supporters of the new state; the Knife is saved from the Free State firing squad by his neighbour, an Orangeman.[97]

One of the more striking features of both the novel and the memoir is the use of black humour in the face of trauma. In *The Gates Flew Open*, machine-gun fire from the prison guards is met 'with derisive cheers'.[98] The tragedy of the death of Peadar Breslin, who was shot in an attempted escape from Mountjoy, is dissipated by the arrival of Andy Cooney wearing 'a pair of trousers that reached a little below his knees and were as tight-fitting as a stocking'.[99] With the threat of execution looming over him, O'Donnell recalls entertaining himself by putting the 'heart crossways' in the prison guards by warning that 'if I'm killed here I'll come back and tell you which one of us is right'.[100] Meanwhile, after his hunger strike, O'Donnell jocularly quips that the physical and psychological strain was worth it for his post-hunger strike feast: 'You have missed one of life's great moments if you haven't tasted a brandy egg-flip after a forty one days' fast.'[101]

This humour is not only an extension of the resistance of prisoners, it also might have offered a defence mechanism in extreme situations. George A. Bonanno, who postulates that 'resilience in the face of loss or potential trauma is more common than is often believed', sees laughter as an adaptive response that can '[increase] the psychological distance from distress and [enhance] social relations'.[102] This black humour is drawn out in the memoir through imaginary, fictional sketches; for example, in describing the executions, O'Donnell comically imagines that Dick Barrett had time 'to remember the cigarette famine when a twenty box of Players was put before him'.[103]

This blurring of boundaries between fact and fiction is further extended through the many intertextual literary references littered throughout *The Gates Flew Open*. Just as O'Donnell's jovial prison atmosphere is inflected by his reading of Wodehouse, the prisoners make sense of their experience through the lens of the prison literature they have read. In *The Knife*, prisoner Sam Rowan comes up with a plan to tear down the bars on the windows based on tactics explained in the popular serial novel *Convict 99: A True Story of Penal Servitude* (1898).[104] In *The Gates Flew Open*, O'Donnell recalls the execution of his four comrades in December 1922 through reference to Ethel Voynich's novel *The Gadfly* (1897), in which the execution turns into a butchery as each member of the firing squad aims aside, hoping not to fire the death-shot.[105]

But it is not only previously read works of fiction that shape O'Donnell's memories. He also recalls his experience through reference to the dramatic autobiographical play *Journey's End: A Play in Three Acts* (1928) by R. C. Sherriff, based on the experience of a British army infantry in 1918, and Arnold Zweig's autobiographical war novel *Der Streit um den Sergeanten Grischa* [The Case of Sergeant Grischa] (1927), which dramatically recounts the execution of a Russian escapee from a German prison camp. Both these accounts were published *after* O'Donnell's imprisonment; these literary references thus illustrate how revolutionaries relived their experience through reading the testimony of others and how personal memory is always 'multidirectional', to use Rothberg's term, in that it is always 'subject to ongoing negotiation, cross-referencing, and borrowing; as productive and not private'.[106] Through these literary allusions, O'Donnell couples the suffering of republican prisoners with that of other oppressed groups, including soldiers in the British and Russian armies. This not only reflects O'Donnell's international socialist agenda, it also speaks to Kalí Tal's contention, in her consideration of Vietnam soldiers' testimonies, that those who have experienced trauma often seek to identify with a wider community of 'survivors' in an effort to contextualise their suffering and 'to connect it across history to other atrocities, committed at other times'.[107]

The End of a Chapter – Not the End of a Book

The Gates Flew Open ends on a victorious note as O'Donnell escapes from the Curragh. He dramatically recounts how he was directed out of the camp by the light of the North Star as the prison gates mysteriously 'flew open' before him. This open-ended conclusion – reinforced even in the memoir's title – reflects the cyclical-linear framework of republican remembrance, as traumatic defeat is framed within a 'recurring pattern of struggle and defeat' working 'towards future triumph'.[108] This model of redemptive republican trauma is an example of what LaCapra refers to as a 'founding trauma': a trauma which paradoxically becomes 'the valorized or intensely cathected basis of identity for an individual or a group'.[109] Although such 'founding trauma' templates can allow an oppressed group 'to reclaim a history and to transform it into a more or less enabling basis of life in the present', LaCapra also argues that such sacralising myths may undermine the need to come to terms with the past.[110] In particular, 'individuals may resist working through because of what might almost be termed a fidelity to trauma, a feeling that one must somehow keep faith with it'. LaCapra further suggests that this 'fidelity' to a traumatic past is often associated with one's 'bond with the dead, especially with dead intimates', as reliving such trauma is seen as 'a painful but necessary commemoration or memorial'.[111] This bond with the republican dead is, of course, at the heart of *The Gates Flew Open*. The 'fidelity' to a traumatic past, rather than Ryan's idea of 'ridding' ourselves of it, may explain the vocal reticence of many civil war veterans whose silence served to further highlight the 'unspoken' event.

The open-endedness of *The Gates Flew Open* – it was 'not the end of a book', in O'Donnell's terms, 'but the end of a chapter'[112] – also allowed O'Donnell to conclude on an affirmative note that would appeal to his republican readership. The dialogic nature of testimony is particularly clear from O'Donnell's dedications in his two accounts: *The Knife* was written 'For the IRA, of the IRA,' while the first edition of *The Gates Flew Open* included the inscription, 'To the Unbreakables; the men and women who milled the Stampede of 1922.'[113] However, O'Donnell's upbeat escape narrative demanded a certain (further) fictionalisation of his experience. O'Donnell's co-prisoners later admitted that they were 'very sore' that O'Donnell had escaped in place of Jack Keogh, who they had planned to break out to evade court martial.[114] Keogh was later considered to have become 'insane' 'as result of ill-treatment'.[115] This point of contention complicates the idea of solidarity between prisoners, let alone among a wider 'unbreakable' republican community. The imaginative rewriting of the escape plot points to the strength of individual survival instinct and suggests that O'Donnell's heroic ending may have clouded actualities of fear, discordance and even mental illness that did not find space in his redemptive trauma testimony.

War and Mental Illness in O'Donnell's Rural Novels

Yet if *The Gates Flew Open* is charactered by hope in a redemptive traumatic defeat, this optimism is less apparent in O'Donnell's earlier novels, a number of which were developed and written during his internment. *Storm* was advertised as having been written 'in Mountjoy and Kilmainham'.[116] O'Donnell included a clause in his will that this first novel never be reissued, and historians and critics have largely supported his judgement, referring to the novel's 'crude propagandist glorification' and 'unadorned simplicity'.[117] But *Storm* is a loosely fictionalised testimony of the author's revolutionary experience: Eamon Gallagher is a 'Godless' IRA schoolteacher on Arranmore island (where O'Donnell himself worked as a teacher), and many of the incidents, such as raids on RIC barracks in Milford and Derry, reflect O'Donnell's involvement in similar events.[118] If *The Gates Flew Open* illustrates O'Donnell's use of black humour to supersede trauma, *Storm* suggests this is a mere strategy: Gallagher smiles and jokes in the face of his death, but his love interest, Máire, acknowledges that 'only a few will guess that inside in him there is a set of thoughts only God sees'.[119] The eulogising of republican martyrs evident in *The Gates Flew Open* is also complicated by O'Donnell's attention to the realities of poverty, as the young volunteer Conal O'Boyle laments he could never 'play Robert Emmet in a rig like this'.[120]

The economic struggle of rural communities is central to O'Donnell's second novel, *Islanders*, in which the revolution has no more than a tangential impact, as the island community is faced with more pressing concerns. However, O'Donnell directly addresses the psychological devastation of civil war in his third novel, *Adrigoole* (1929), which was inspired by news of the death by starvation of a family in Castletownbere, County Cork, in 1927 due to lack of economic opportunities after the evacuation of the British fleet. He transposes the situation to his native Donegal, where married couple Brigid and Hughie Dálach – who appear briefly in *Storm* as Hughdie and Máire Bheag – harbour 'tired republican soldiers' but worry that 'their supply of potatoes would be used up with all the traffic'.[121] These difficulties are augmented with the slide to civil war. The republicans still arrive but now the Dálachs are met with suspicion from their neighbours. The children are even tricked by the local schoolteacher into divulging the presence of the men on the run. Hughie Dálach and Brigid's uncle, Neddie Brian, are mistaken for republicans and, while rounding up lambs in the fields, are accidentally shot by Free State soldiers. The bonds of the community are further shaken when young Grania Dálach dies from a fever and the locals keep their distance. Hughie is arrested for poteen distilling, sentenced to twelve months in prison and discovers on release that Brigid and the children have starved to death in his absence. In the concluding lines of the novel, Hughie is goaded into a motor car 'that would take him to the asylum'.[122]

This connection between war and mental illness is at odds with the more hopeful narrative of redemptive republican trauma foregrounded in *The Gates Flew Open*. Yet even O'Donnell was uneasy with the ending of *Adrigoole*: he later expressed regret about Hughie's tragic demise and remarked that he wished he'd had Hughie emigrate instead of being institutionalised.[123]

'I Couldn't Think of Anything Else to Write about': O'Donnell's Civil War Archive

O'Donnell's revisiting of his civil war imprisonment in both memoir and fiction points to his urge to document and perhaps process his experience:

he claimed that *The Gates Flew Open* was a 'potboiler' written because 'I couldn't think of anything else to write about'.[124] Yet despite producing two civil war prison testimonies in the early 1930s, O'Donnell's urge to tell was matched with desire to conceal: like a number of IRA leaders, he destroyed his military papers for fear they could start 'the Civil War all over again'.[125] *The Knife* and *The Gates Flew Open* were thus part of an effort by O'Donnell to create and curate a written archive of *his* civil war by tapping into the established republican model of trauma testimony available to him. His intertextual fictional and non-fictional testimonies hint at the difficulties of categorising his experience and at the complexities of telling, especially when endeavouring to speak on behalf of others. It is often in his fiction, freer from the pressures of conventional first-person autobiography, that his strongest political and emotional concerns are addressed.

Fiction did not always provide a foolproof cover, however. Not long after the publication of *The Gates Flew Open*, O'Donnell was made to account publicly for the anti-clerical comments in both *The Gates Flew Open* and *The Knife* during a libel case he brought against the Dominican magazine, *The Irish Rosary*, on account of an article that alleged that O'Donnell had travelled to Moscow to study 'the technique of revolution' and hoped, as a founder of the organisation Saor Éire, to establish an 'anti-God state' in Ireland. The judge ruled that an allegation of 'Sovietism' was not defamatory and the case was a financial disaster for O'Donnell. The cross-examination in court also illustrated that the fictional character of the Knife was read as an author surrogate, with the defence asking O'Donnell, 'who is The Knife? [...] He is speaking your own thoughts?' O'Donnell neither confirmed nor denied any autobiographical connection and responded that the Knife 'was created in order to interpret a very difficult phase in Irish history'.[126]

O'Donnell's unsuccessful case, as well as the litigation cases in which IRA memoirists Dan Breen and Ernie O'Malley were embroiled in 1932 and 1937 respectively, illustrates, in critic Nicholas Allen's view, 'the difficulty of looking to literature for any confirmation of a cherished past'.[127] For all the difficulty, however, these cases did not mark the end of the publication of civil war testimony. They may indeed have further pushed authors to explore alternative narrative forms – as in Carty's and Mulloy's works, which grapple more directly with the psychological impact of war.

Francis Carty's *Legion of the Rearguard*: 'I must work it off my system'

While O'Donnell's *The Gates Flew Open* was decried for its rancour, Francis Carty's *Legion of the Rearguard* was praised for being 'devoid of bitter partisanship'.[128] The novel opens at the truce of July 1921 and traces the events of the civil war in Wexford through the fictional character of Paul Davin. Carty's writings had a clear therapeutic aim; one of his protagonists writes, as his 'urge for mental activity found an outlet in writing'.[129] Carty further elucidated the cathartic nature of his writing process in a 1930s interview with poet and architect Niall Montgomery. Though Carty 'couldn't say he liked it [writing]', he confessed that his novels were a project of 'emotion remembered in tranquillity' and that he had a strong urge to document his experience: 'I feel that I have to record the Civil War because it made such a deep impression on me and I must work it off my system.'[130] Carty found in the novel a genre that was perhaps uniquely capable of tackling Ryan's idea of 'ridding ourselves of the past' rather than 'brooding' over it. Unlike the 'open-ended temporality' of non-fictional testimony – typified in the 'open' gates of O'Donnell's memoir – Leonard V. Smith contends, in his study of First World War soldier testimonies, that the novel 'is a genre that testifies to a search for closure, which would give experience an end that would make it historically specific'.[131]

Carty was something of an 'improbable revolutionary'.[132] He joined the publicity committee of Sinn Féin in his native Wexford after the Rising, served as registrar of the republican arbitration court and subsequently joined the Irish Volunteers. He supported the anti-treaty side and spent most of the civil war in internment. The family found themselves 'exile[d] from the old county' and relocated to Dublin, where their new home in Rathmines became something of an IRA headquarters.[133] During the 1930s, Carty was the manager of a hairdressing salon – although he did not want to be known as the 'hairdresser author'.[134] He went on to enjoy a long career in journalism and editing: he was manager for The Parkside Press and C. J. Fallon publishers, editor of Éamon de Valera's *The Irish Press* from 1957, editor of *The Sunday Press* from 1962 and editorial director of *The Irish Digest* and *The English Digest*.[135]

The majority of first-hand, non-fictional testimonies of IRA activity – such as those of Dan Breen (1924), Ernie O'Malley (1936) and Tom

Barry (1956) – were from the pens of leading figures who had significant insight into the politics of the national organisation. Carty's activities, by contrast, were restricted and localised. He was even disparagingly referred to as 'head bottle-washer' before a Military Pension advisory committee.[136] Given that Carty was arguably not considered 'qualified' to provide a straight-up autobiographical account of his experience, the blend of fiction and history enabled him to tell his story, while also highlighting the impact of war on combatants and ordinary citizens. *Legion of the Rearguard* (1934) was published following Carty's Tailteann prize-winning novel *The Irish Volunteer* (1932), which ended with the announcement of the truce in 1921. Although the novels are not strictly sequential – Art Russell is the protagonist of *The Irish Volunteer*, while Paul Davin is the leading character of *Legion of the Rearguard* – both protagonists share Carty's upbringing in a petty bourgeois Wexford family with initial sympathies for the Home Rule Party. Carty's detailed thirty-five-page witness statement to the Bureau of Military History in 1954 parallels the novels in terms of narrative sequence, factual descriptions and even use of vocabulary.[137] Indeed, it is hard to imagine that his fictional writings of the early thirties did not crystallise his later recollections.

'The Work of an Eye-witness'

Like O'Donnell's testimonies, *Legion of the Rearguard* defied generic categorisation. Advertised as 'the work of an eye-witness',[138] reviewers agreed that *Legion of the Rearguard* was 'not a novel in a sense, but rather a history of this internecine quarrel'.[139] The first section of the novel offers prolonged faux-journalistic descriptions of the treaty debates and provides pen portraits of the leading politicians of the period. While reviewers commented on the author's 'earnest desire to deal fairly with both sides',[140] Carty was a strong supporter of Fianna Fáil. In the lead-up to the 1932 election, he was vocal in his opposition to Cumann na nGaedheal's economic policy, arguing that the payment of land annuities to the British government was a betrayal of the principles of the deceased pro-treaty leader Arthur Griffith.[141] Indeed, his Fianna Fáil allegiances were abundantly clear from the portrait of party leader Éamon de Valera on the cover of the novel – not to mention the fact that the title echoes de Valera's famous call on the 'Soldiers of the Republic – Legion of the Rearguard' accompanying the IRA dump arms order in May

1923. Given Fianna Fáil's entrance into government in February 1932, the hopes for reconciliation expressed in *Legion of the Rearguard* were coming from a position of newly acquired political authority and Carty's genuine belief that this new government could offer a clean slate to both republicans and 'republican' treaty supporters, following the lineage of Griffith.

The activities of Paul Davin in *Legion of the Rearguard* strongly reflect Carty's civil war experience. As officer commanding the 4th Battalion, South Wexford Brigade, Carty initially registered in the Free State army and was even fitted with a uniform. However, as the anti-treaty forces under Rory O'Connor occupied the Four Courts, the brigade transferred their allegiance. Carty, though uncertain, followed suit. He was subsequently appointed divisional training officer and ran a training camp outside New Ross. After hostilities erupted in June 1922, he was active in the republican takeover of Enniscorthy Castle by siege on 7 July 1922. No less than a week later, he was rounded up in Ferns by the better-equipped Free State army and interned until early 1924.

Battles and Cups of Tea

The strength of *Legion of the Rearguard* lies not in its bare reproduction of fact, but rather in its detailed, even photographic, depictions of family and communal life. As one reviewer described it, '[b]attles alternate [...] with cups of tea'.[142] Throughout the novel, war invades domestic spaces: in the opening pages, Sarah Davin laments that, because the carpets had been removed due to Black and Tan raids, 'your feet made a hollow sound, as if there was nobody living in the place'.[143] The characters continue their daily social routines regardless; Nancy O'Shea is more concerned about whether her haircut is too short than with her mounting debt, while Bridget, the Davin's maid, makes the most of the family rosary to simultaneously pray and dry her hair.[144] Carty also gives an insight into the intimate relations of men on the run absent from many straight historical accounts: volunteers sleep together on a mattress, are secretly consoled by the 'Sacred Heart badges' (or wind-up badges) made for them by the nuns and sheepishly rub sulphur ointment into each other's backs to reduce scabies.[145] Nevertheless, the anxiety of war shines through: Paul's father, Jamesy, has no appetite and surreptitiously feeds his meals to the dog; Paul's comrade Ned Coyne can no longer maintain the sobriety required among the volunteers due to his 'strained nerves'; Dempsey, another volunteer, finds himself overcome by hunger and sleeplessness, and dreads that the 'first rifle-crack might [...] send him cowering for cover'.[146]

English novelist Graham Greene (1904–1991), who reported from Dublin in the direct aftermath of the civil war,[147] recognised that Carty's novel presented 'what history cannot do, the curious mental contrasts of a local, a provincial war, the shy romantic prudish affections of gunmen on the run'.[148] The affirmative realism of Carty's novel reflects the influence of Daniel Corkery, rather than the more disillusioned realist aesthetic of Frank O'Connor or Seán O'Faoláin. Unlike writers as diverse as Aodh de Blácam, P. S. O'Hegarty and the aforementioned O'Connor and O'Faoláin, Carty, in a public lecture in 1934, supported Corkery's contentious claim that Irish writers should be motivated by three key facets of Irish life: the religious consciousness of the people, Irish nationalism and the land.[149] Yet while Corkery's collection of revolutionary stories, *The Hounds of Banba* (1920), appeared in the midst of the war of independence and embraced 'bald expressions of revolutionary exaltation',[150] Carty's revolution is characterised, in his own words, by 'anti-climax'.[151] His volunteers, though earnest, are impoverished to the extent they feel 'the stones through the soles of their boots' and find that more often than not their operations are thwarted by inexperience, poor planning or self-doubt.[152] And while Carty felt that Catholicism was a key aspect of Irish life (he later produced two books on Irish saints),[153] *Legion of the Rearguard* reflects his sense that he was a 'bad Catholic' who, as he confessed, was indifferent to the '*ipso facto* excommunication' applied to republicans during the civil war.[154]

Carty's emphasis on the war's invasion into domestic life is particularly clear in his decision to creatively locate a devastating attack, redolent of Carty's actual surrender in Ferns, into the Davin family home. In his witness statement, Carty documents how the republicans retreated to Ferns post office due to mechanical trouble with their lorry after having blown up a bridge north of the village. The men were resting on the footpath outside the post office when a Free State armoured car 'came chasing around the corner, opening fire'.[155] In the novel, the men retreat due to engine failure after a similar operation to halt Free State army advances – although they put down roadblocks rather than the more contentious reality of blowing up bridges. They are sitting on the footpath with their backs to the Davin family home when the Free State army car dashes into sight:

The armoured car came level with the yard gate. Bullets crashed through the stable door in front of him. He [Paul] flung himself sideways through the kitchen door [...] sprawling across the table, scattering cups and saucers about the floor. His mother stood stiff with terror between the table and the fire-place. She held a big teapot in her hand. With a sudden cry she dropped the teapot, which smashed on the tiles, filling the kitchen with steam.[156]

The crashing teapot becomes integrated into the soundscape of war, indicating the perceived intimacy, or even unnaturalness, of civil conflict. The raiding party, although mostly made up of Dublin Guards, also includes Paul's childhood friends and former comrades in arms Milo Burke and Ned Coyne. Far from presenting a simplified victim-perpetrator binary, the fictional omniscient narrator highlights the impact that carrying out this attack had on the Free State army soldiers: 'It was a dirty job having to turn a machine-gun on the house which had so often opened its doors to them [...] they had only done their duty as soldiers. They felt ashamed, all the same.'[157]

This attack on the Davin home results in the deaths of two of Paul's comrades, reflecting Carty's first-hand testimony of witnessing two deaths during the siege of Enniscorthy. In his witness statement, Carty recounts that '[a]s we reached the corner of the lane they opened fire on us. Volunteer Maurice Spillane was killed outright and Paddy O'Brien was wounded. [...] Paddy Fleming, O'Sullivan and myself carried Paddy O'Brien along the lane and he was removed to the hospital where I visited him the next day and found him dying'.[158] Ernie O'Malley documents the same incident at Enniscorthy in the posthumous *The Singing Flame* (written in the 1930s but not published until 1978). Rather than rely on unembellished description as Carty does, O'Malley's description of the sudden death of Spillane and shooting of O'Brien moves from the unsettling to the comic, concluding with a Rabelaisian image of a stout, unsoldierly soldier:

The noise of bursting cases, then silence. *A sudden rifle crack and a boy beside me fell*. A few more sharp cracks from some distance, then Paddy O'Brien in front staggered, sprawled forward. His collar and neck were stained with quickly flowing blood. I banged slowly with my revolver in the direction of rifle fire; I reloaded and emptied again. When I looked behind me I saw the men carrying Paddy disappear round the end of the lane. The other man lay flat on his back. He moaned; his face was a whitish grey. His eyes were staring. I pulled him in close to the wall. I took cover beside him against a shallow gate entrance and heard him begin an Act of Contrition, say 'O my God ... my God I am heartily sorry ...' slowly, haltingly, seemingly unconscious [...] *There was a little shuddering gurgle and he was dead.* At the gate above me was a Wexford officer. He was pressed against the gate but he was too fat to be under cover; his posterior protruded and shook with nervousness. *I laughed. He turned his head in surprise. Then when I had pointed out the cause of my mirth, he laughed too.* [my emphasis][159]

While Carty's description of these deaths are rather matter-of-fact in his witness statement, he also resorts to ironic humour in *Legion of the Rearguard* to reflect on the senselessness of the deaths of Paul's two comrades. Like Spillane (the boy in O'Malley's account), Pax Murphy's death is more or less immediate.[160] Neale Rowan's pain is more visible, however, as he wriggles in a pool of dark blood, muttering 'I'm not going to die.'[161] The seriousness of his condition evades the parish priest, Father Meyler, who mistakes Rowan's delirious singing for jeering, asking, 'What about the poor people all over the country, robbed and oppressed by you and the likes of you?'[162] Only on realising that he is indeed in the presence of death does the priest administer the last rites. This 'irony-assisted recall' has been identified by historian Paul Fussell as a quintessential motif of First World War literature, as former tropes of tragic, heroic death were replaced by ironic disillusion.[163]

The fictional narrator's gaze also draws attention to the various reactions that witnessing death evokes among the characters – particularly the women. Paul's mother, Sarah, helplessly cradles Pax Murphy, watching as the 'poor boy's life was ebbing away before her eyes'.[164] Bridget's 'frail body shook so violently with sobbing that she spilt most of the water'.[165] Paul is particularly affected by the corporeal manifestations of Bridget's pain and her 'pathetic expression *almost* made him cry' (my emphasis).[166] In this sense, the women's responses, as much as the actual scenes of violence, are presented as emotional triggers. That the women's distress is more visceral is indicative of how trauma, through the language of 'nerve troubles' or 'hysteria', was considered a natural response for women within the social and cultural conventions of the time. In both fictional and non-fictional veteran narratives, the female body often constitutes an analogy for men's (repressed) suffering. For example, in Mossie Hartnett's posthumous revolutionary memoir *Victory and Woe: The West Limerick Brigade in the War of Independence* (2002), the recurring allusions to Hartnett's aunt's 'nervous breakdowns' can be read as a vehicle through which he draws attention to the psychological impact of the conflict more generally. At one point, he explicitly draws a comparison between his aunt's embodiment of trauma and his own 'suffering in silence': '[W]e rushed into the kitchen to see my aunt in a state of collapse [...] It was a truly frightening experience for anyone to undergo, much less a woman [...] I usually had to suffer in silence the recriminations that came my way as a result of this and other episodes at that time.'[167]

Fiction and What If?

In an interview with historian Calton Younger, Carty recounted how he unsuccessfully attempted to escape from a local schoolhouse after his arrest at the post office in Ferns.[168] In *Legion of the Rearguard*, Paul is successful in his escape attempt, thus allowing Carty to imaginatively tease out what could have been. Yet escape, the novel suggests, would have only prolonged the despair, and Paul grows to doubt 'the wisdom of pushing principles to their logical conclusion'.[169] The republicans ultimately stand little chance and Paul, as commanding officer, is forced to give the rather inglorious orders to disband. Shortly afterwards, he is shot, arrested and interned. He escapes court martial due to his injuries, but his comrade, Dempsey, is executed. Fiction enables Carty to work in a subtle critique of the class-motivated selection of men for execution: 'Why the staters, as a rule, shot members of the rank and file rather than influential officers, was not clear; they may have hoped thus to create a more salutary and demoralising effect.'[170]

Carty's descriptions of jail life, like those of O'Donnell, continue the performance of resistance typical of republican prison narratives. But the novel nevertheless hints at the emotional worries of the prisoners as Paul dreads that hunger striking would 'permanently injure his brain'.[171] In a clear reference to O'Donnell's *The Gates Flew Open*, the end of the mass strike of October 1923 is heralded by the 'arrival of the egg-flip'. In the novel, however, this note of victory is quickly replaced by 'consciousness of defeat', the 'full realization of their mistake' and, in particular, an understanding of 'the cruel mockery it was to make one's parents the victims of propaganda'.[172] On his release, Paul's parents embody the destruction of the war: Jamesy's hair had gone white, while Sarah's dazzlingly white apron 'was no longer a symbol of her bustling vitality, but seemed merely to emphasize the defeat of the spirit whose body it shielded'.[173] For Paul, the 'continuous agony of mind which had afflicted his parents' was 'more intense than physical trouble' endured by active combatants.[174]

The Civil War Love Triangle

Carty weaves a strong romance plot through the novel that counterbalances such utterances of dismay and carries the narrative towards a sense of closure. Readers of such war documentary novels were not, it seems, turned off by such romantic elements.[175] M. J. MacManus of *The Irish Press* contended that the 'slight thread of fiction' upon which Carty's narrative was hung did not 'matter very much' given the 'power in this story, and sincerity, and honest, vigorous writing'.[176] Yet while easily dismissible, the metaphor of the love triangle was a key narrative strategy for evoking the pain of civil conflict. Paul and Milo Burke both find themselves drawn to the feisty Rosaleen O'Shea, who smokes cigarettes behind the nuns' backs and flouts gender boundaries by arriving at the male-only IRA training camp on the same day as de Valera's much anticipated visit. Early in the novel, 'Rosaleen stood in the middle, one hand on Paul's shoulder, the other on Milo's. Dragging the boys closer together, she stepped back a bit. They felt her affectionate face between their shoulders.'[177] This triangle foreshadows the split between the two friends, as Milo Burke joins the Free State army and Paul sides with the republicans.

These love triangle plots are employed in numerous renderings of the civil war. A particularly powerful example is found in the remarkable autobiographically informed novel *Camps on the Hearthstone* (1956) by trade unionist activist and later Labour politician Patrick Hogan (1885–1969); the novel deals with the period from the 1913 lockout through to the civil war and clearly draws on the author's own experience.[178] The protagonist, Jack, finds himself between two suitors – Norah Cremins, a working-class Dubliner (evoking Henrik Ibsen's Nora), and Kathleen

Keatinge, a middle-class Gaelic Leaguer (representing Kathleen Ní Houlihan). Jack's decision to reject Norah and pursue Kathleen as a suitor thus functions as an allegory for the protagonist's choice to put the utopian nationalistic dreams of the nation before more socially progressive aims.[179]

As narratologist Patrick Colm Hogan outlines in his study of Hogan's novel, the love triangle motif evident in many civil war narratives is a particular feature of postcolonial writing: 'Perhaps the most common structure for national allegory is a sort of love triangle. The nation is represented as a man or woman and different possibilities for national development, different political directions, are represented as rival suitors for the love of that man or woman.'[180] Hogan's novel is unusual in its adoption of a female/male/female triangle. More typical in civil war novels is the male/female/male homosocial triangle, in which males compete for an often passively rendered female. This particular trope locates the female figure at the root of the romantic (and military) conflict and thus mirrors the widespread vilification of republican women for initiating the slide to civil war. O'Donnell's aforementioned novel *The Knife* also draws on the romance triangle to point to political possibilities, as the unusually strongminded female protagonist, Nuala Godfrey Dhu, rejects the advances of James Burns (who subsequently joins the Free State army), in favour of Orangeman Sam Rowan.

In *Legion of the Rearguard,* the break-up of the love triangle comes quickly. Milo Burke proposes to Paul's sister, Grace, leaving Rosaleen and Paul free to make a match. Like the allegorical female characters in Hogan's novel, Rosaleen is a personification of Ireland as 'Dark Rosaleen'. Paul is faced with the dilemma, therefore, of reconciling his 'love for Rosaleen with his duty to the national cause', knowing that he can only marry Rosaleen in the Catholic Church if he renounces his loyalties to the Republic.[181] He chooses the latter and paradoxically withdraws from Rosaleen in order to continue waging war to defend her allegorical namesake. As his dismay with the republican campaign increases, Paul's abandonment of Rosaleen becomes a source of regret; 'after his rotten behaviour towards Rosaleen, he could not very well criticize others'.[182]

Aside from evoking intense emotions and teasing out political allegiances, the romance plot also enabled Carty to sensitively portray the inner turmoil of Paul's childhood friend and Free State officer:

From Milo Burke's standpoint, things looked almost as bad. On his appointment to the command of Tassagh, Milo had confidently hoped for a speedy and complete triumph. He had pictured himself happily married to Grace, an officer of high rank in the National Army, helping to build up the new state and put the country on its feet. [...] Then, instead of petering out, as he anticipated, the stupid struggle kept dragging on.[183]

This empathy for the enemy is characteristic of many veterans' testimonies (see Chapter Five). But Carty's concerted effort to present a reconciliatory picture of the civil war arguably involved a certain sanitisation of his own experience. Most notably, Carty chose not to fictionally recreate his organisation of the Killurin train ambush on 24 July 1922, which, Carty believed, led to the deaths of eight Free State soldiers.[184] Following the ambush, the republican prisoners were 'lined up against the wall' and shot at by a number of Free State soldiers, including commanding officer of the National Army at Enniscorthy and Wexford 1916 veteran Seán Gallagher. As Carty explains in his witness statement:

I do not think that we were fired on direct. I remember seeing some of the officers flashing their revolvers towards the pavement and sending out ricochet bullets. One of the prisoners was, however, injured and died subsequently, and on the following morning I found a flattened revolver bullet in the heel of the boot of one of the men who had been beside me.[185]

Seán Gallagher, his 'nemesis', figured vividly in Carty's family stories. As Francis Xavier Carty recounts: 'Mother and Father were walking down Grafton Street in Dublin when Father suddenly froze and a look of horror came into his face. Mother could not understand. "Seán Gallagher," he said, "has just passed by. He is the man who twice tried to shoot me."'[186] The fictional character of Milo Burke is suggestive of Gallagher; the description of Burke's reluctant surrender at Tassagh, 'due to water shortages', echoes Gallagher's refusal to surrender after the siege of Enniscorthy until his garrison were compelled to 'through lack of food and water'.[187] By voicing Burke's interior thoughts in the novel, Carty places himself in the shoes of his opponents, and one reviewer even commented that Carty could have 'written a novel, with Milo Burke, the National Army Officer, as the hero'.[188] Moreover, Burke's marriage to Paul's sister, Grace, unites the two opponents through blood and points to the need for rekindling relationships in the aftermath of the conflict.

The novel's closing sentence further affirms Paul's decision to make amends after his release from internment: 'He got out his bicycle after tea and rode down to visit Rosaleen ...'[189] This sentence, followed by an ellipsis, signals not only the end of the conflict, but also Paul's break from the allure of ideological nationalist allegories and the beginning of the prisoner's reintegration into civilian and family life. This search for a 'mythical healing female' is an identified feature of soldiers' testimonies.[190] But, as Kalí Tal cautions in her consideration of Vietnam veterans' writings, for many, '[s]uch a homecoming as they might wish for is always unreachable, because it is based on returning not only to a place, but to a time when they were innocent of war – the pre-trauma state'.[191] Whether returning to civilian life was as straightforward or not for the author, *Legion of the Rearguard* attests to a desire for narrative closure through its clear demarcation between past and present – unlike the established republican memoirs that end with a continued commitment to the struggle.

Carty's Lifelong Memory-searching

Carty's novel was part of a lifelong project of remembering the revolution. In addition to the novels, he addressed the period in short stories and, on his death, was still working on a fictionalised account of the revolution in Wexford entitled 'Blood in the Main Street'.[192] His son Francis Xavier further attests to this reoccurring urge to 'tell': '[H]e used [to] tell us on Sunday mornings about his part in the War of Independence. We were sometimes bored by the repetition'.[193]

If this need to tell is accompanied by the need to find a confirming readership, the question of audience for veterans' testimonial writings was complicated by their publication by British printing presses. Journalist Aodh de Blácam lamented the popularity of formulaic war novels in Britain that were, in his view, characterised by 'the queerest oaths and drink and hysteria', yet purported to 'Tell the Truth about the Irish revolution for the First Time.'[194] Indeed, Carty's publishers, the reputable J. M. Dent & Sons, had recently published Rearden Conner's seemingly autobiographically based novel, *Shake Hands with the Devil* (1933), which was censored in Ireland and criticised for pandering to 'a certain market in England [...] for unpleasant books about Ireland' (see Chapter Three).[195] In a public lecture, Carty distanced himself from such authors who 'worked with one eye on England and the other on America' and 'traded largely on lust [...] and scenes of violence'.[196] There are a number of examples of dramatic irony in Carty's novel that suggest he was writing with an intimate audience in mind, perhaps his former colleagues, many of whom were 'away in Wales' by the time of writing.[197] For example, the fictional narrator denounces gunrunning against the orders of GHQ; his fellow volunteers would have known that Carty himself organised such an operation in defiance of orders and sent two men to Salisbury Plains in England where they retrieved thirty rifles.[198] Furthermore, while Paul disciplines his men for the 'blackguardism' of raiding banks,[199] Carty admits to raiding a number of banks himself, albeit in IRA-sanctioned operations.[200]

While Carty's fiction won awards, sold well and was serialised in *The Irish Press*,[201] he was not considered among the writers identified by O'Faoláin in 1935 as the representatives of 'the brutal literature of despair' whose works would subsequently form the canon (these writers included Seán O'Casey, Peadar O'Donnell, Liam O'Flaherty and Frank O'Connor).[202] Carty's endorsement of a more affirmative, rural community realism and support of Corkery's views on Irish literature was arguably at odds with O'Faoláin, who opposed the 'nativist' views of Corkery, his former mentor. This difference in viewpoint was evident as far back as September 1924, when O'Faoláin objected to a number of articles by Frank Gallagher on the so-called 'Volunteer Spirit' in the pages of the daily newspaper *Sinn Féin*. O'Faoláin complained that the 'reiteration of Propaganda is offensive' and suggested 'that it was time for Irish republicanism to formulate an integrated policy and expend its energies on issues of pressing concern, such as poverty, schooling, and the language revival'.[203] Refuting O'Faoláin, Carty contended in a letter published in *Sinn Féin* that '[o]ur people in 1922 and often before followed men like the pro-treaty leaders who preached lies and withheld facts, they have so often believed falsehoods about nationalists and acted according to such beliefs with such disastrous consequences, that we cannot repeat too often the fundamental principles of our national faith'.[204]

Nevertheless, Carty's literary project was far from the 'isolationist, Sinn Féinish approach' associated with early twentieth-century Irish republicanism.[205] His writings are better understood as part of the canon of European interwar literature: for British author and communist activist Helen Gosse, Carty's *The Irish Volunteer* was akin to Ralph Hale Mottram's *The Spanish Farm Trilogy* (1924), which offered intimate portraits of the First World War from a civilian perspective based on the author's experience in France and Flanders.[206] While Carty is absent from literary and historical study, his reputation at the time is clear from the fact that he was included in a 1930s unpublished essay series by Niall Montgomery alongside writers and artists such as Seán O'Faoláin, Mary Manning, Frank O'Connor, Samuel Beckett, Maurice McGonigal and Francis Stuart. Carty indeed had a strong bond with the eccentric Stuart; they had known each other since their civil war imprisonment days and both of them turned to fiction to tease out this experience. However, reflecting the diversity of responses to the civil war, Montgomery quipped that 'they have neither of them read the other's book'.[207]

Shouting Instead of Whispering: Patrick Mulloy's *Jackets Green*

Patrick Mulloy's *Jackets Green: A Novel* (1936) is less mellow and forgiving than Carty's writings. Rather than advance reconciliation, the restorative potential of Mulloy's fictionalised testimony is connected to his commitment to truth-telling and his employment of a naturalist-realist aesthetic to confront the full gamut of wartime disillusion. *Jackets Green* is a warning to future generations: Mulloy dedicated his book to 'THE RANK AND FILE OF EVERY NATIONAL MOVEMENT AND SECRET SOCIETY IN EVERY COUNTRY, TO REMIND THEM THAT MANY A PATH OF GLORY LEADS TO A GRAVEYARD OF SOULS'.[208] The novel tells the stories of three friends – Tim, Mike and Dan – who develop strong ties of comradeship while imprisoned in an unnamed camp in the north of the country during the war of independence, only to find their paths diverge during the civil war. In this sense, Mulloy's civil war is remembered as the result of a gradual process of brutalisation, as the strain of years of conflict takes its toll and hopes for unity are frustrated again and again. In his stated aim to caution future generations, both in Ireland and internationally, Mulloy does not hold back from graphic portrayals of violence nor from 'soldiers' talk'. He does not shy away either from taboos such as the mental strain of the conflict, the men's recourse to alcohol and prostitution, and even hints at homosexuality in the prisons.

Mulloy's 'graveyard of souls' was at odds with O'Faoláin's idea of the 'brutal literature of despair' which 'found a mid-way position between reality and romance'.[209] In a review of *Jackets Green* in *The Spectator*, O'Faoláin remarked that: 'In the divisions caused by the Civil War, Mr. Mulloy finds the material for his comment on the cruelty of all idealism. The trouble is that he shouts it instead of whispering it.'[210] In fact, O'Faoláin shared his scepticism of Mulloy's aesthetic in no less than three separate reviews, considering it to be 'the Troubles *sans phrase*' and 'over-brutally done'.[211] It was not the sense of disillusion portrayed that caused him concern, nor Mulloy's ability as a writer, but rather his lack of restraint. As O'Faoláin highlighted in a review of Jake Wynne's similarly brutal – and similarly overlooked – autobiographically based novel, *Ugly Brew* (1936), from the perspective of a Free State soldier (see Chapter Three), there was little doubt about their authenticity: 'If we are so fond of realism, here it is. It all sounds true enough to me, and we do not, I trust, wish to fool ourselves into thinking that such things as war can ever be pretty, or that ideals can be defended by fine speeches and elegant behaviour.'[212]

O'Faoláin nevertheless acknowledged that *Jackets Green* was one of the first novels to 'look at the Civil War period from the point of view of the young Free State army officer'.[213] As Anne Dolan has illustrated, commemorating the pro-treaty victory in the civil war was more 'troubled' than anti-treaty commemoration, as even the Cumann na nGaedheal government was hesitant to commemorate the Free State dead.[214] Mulloy thus had fewer narrative templates at his disposal than his anti-treaty opponents through which to relay his experience. In his original (unpublished) preface to the novel, Mulloy attempted to distance himself from the more hagiographical accounts of revolutionary martyrs and leaders endorsed by both pro- and anti-treatyites, specifying that his was not 'a story of a Movement; nor of martyrs – nor of heroes'. He aimed rather to present 'a tale of plain people caught in the mad whirl of revolution' given that 'history records [the leaders]'.[215]

Mulloy was probably never invited to submit a statement to the Bureau of Military History, which tended to collect material from more senior and connected revolutionaries. But available records affirm the strong similarities between the author and Tim, the novel's survivor-protagonist. A native of Dún Laoghaire, County Dublin, Mulloy joined the Volunteers as a teenager and spent much of the war of independence period imprisoned in Ballykinlar camp, County Down – just like his fictional characters.[216] Many of these prisoners were rounded up in the aftermath of Bloody Sunday in November 1920 and interned until December 1921, after the signing of the Anglo-Irish Treaty. In February 1922, Mulloy joined the Free State army at Beggar's Bush and by November had been appointed to the rank of captain at the age of just twenty.[217] Stationed at Baldonnel aerodrome, he supported the army mutineers who delivered an ultimatum to the government in March 1924 in response to army demobilisation, demanding the resignation of the Army Council and that steps be taken towards Michael Collins' ideal of an all-Ireland Republic. He was one of over 300 'absconders' to walk out with their arms.[218] After tensions abated, Mulloy became a clerk in the Department of Agriculture. However, the civil war split had caused social and communal rifts. Before long, Mulloy relocated to London, where he was employed at the Irish Free State High Commissioner's Office and Irish Embassy for thirty-six years.[219] 'Lonely' when he first emigrated, he set up the Irish Club in Eaton Square, which he managed with 'fatherly care' for the rest of his life.[220] Through the club, he became a 'well-known member of the Irish community', regularly contributed to the London-Irish weekly paper, the *Irish Leader*, and earned a reputation as a prize-winning playwright and children's author.[221]

The factual basis of the novel is further hinted at by Mulloy's intention to include a paratextual contract of truthfulness at the opening of *Jackets Green*, contending that '[a]ll the incidents related are true, the entire story being based on a series of true incidents, which have come within the author's personal experience'.[222] This preface was never published – and, quite paradoxically, this original version of the novel was intended to be published under the pseudonym Fionn O'Malley, illustrating thus 'the twin imperatives of truthtelling and secrecy' associated with stories of trauma.[223]

Whatever the reason for the retraction of this original preface, Mulloy's desire to set the historical record straight and give a warning to future generations suggests the influence of popular First World War autobiographical novels. For example, Remarque's *All Quiet on the Western Front* opens with the aim 'simply to tell of a generation who, even though they may have escaped its shells, were destroyed by the war'.[224] In many of these First World War accounts, the bare reproduction of fact was seen as essential both for conveying the horrors of war to the reader and for upholding the writer's claim of truth-telling.[225] However, Mulloy's documentary descriptions of violent scenes also tested the boundaries of realism. Tim witnesses '[s]omething dripped from overhead' only to discover that 'the telegraph wires were festooned with human intestine' after a mine explosion. He sees '[b]its of a tender were strewn like matchwood, while little rivulets of blood streamed across the road and trickled into a sewer'.[226] O'Faoláin took particular offence at this description, while for reviewer and author Francis Mac Manus, *Jackets Green* was 'realist but quite unreal'.[227] In this sense, Mulloy's aesthetic evokes the narrative conventions of what Michael Rothberg refers to as 'traumatic realism': 'a realism in which the claims of reference live on, but so does the traumatic extremity that disables realist representation as usual'.[228]

Mulloy's grisly realism also exists in a grey zone, as does much war literature, between the 'didacticism of educating readers about the horrors of the battlefields and the enticement that stems from drawing on extreme emotions'.[229] This ethical discomfort is reflected in the persistent concerns of nationalist commentators regarding the perceived appeal of 'unpleasant' books about Ireland among English readers. Like Carty's novel, *Jackets Green* was published in London, this time by Grayson and Grayson, who had previously published Liam O'Flaherty's autobiography *Shame the Devil* (1934) and O'Faoláin's short story, *There's a Birdie in the Cage* (1935). Nevertheless, Mulloy's graphic, take-no-prisoners approach was perhaps more successful in appealing to both sides of the treaty divide than the testimonies of O'Donnell and Carty. As Norah Hoult argued in her review of the novel, 'this is a vigorous very much alive book, in which the author has no axe to grind, and is refreshingly detached'.[230] Writing in *The Irish Press* on Mulloy's death, A. O'R, who worked with Mulloy in the civil service from 1924, also recalled that the author was 'highly popular with all his colleagues, despite the prejudices arising out of the Civil War'.[231]

Subverting the Gender Norms of Prison Life

Jackets Green opens with the arrest of Tim at his family home sometime during the war of independence; this is the beginning of a path of brutalisation destined towards civil war. The trauma of the First World War and of the revolution collide as Tim's mother clings to a shrapnel helmet which belonged to her son who was killed in France. Far from embodying patriotic motherhood, she exclaims that 'no mother is proud when she's told that her son has been killed'.[232] Tim, alongside his comrades Dan and Mick, is later transferred by tender to an unnamed camp in the north of the country. As they dismount, they are surrounded by a 'howling, leering mob' who shower them with sectarian abuse.[233] Ironically, officers from 'His Majesty's Forces' protect the prisoners from the rowdy crowds who 'booed and waved Union Jacks', shouting 'Hell roast the Pope!'[234]

The descriptions of such rioting – referred to in contemporary accounts as 'Belfast confetti' – indicate that the fictional camp is based on Ballykinlar camp, County Down.[235] Much of the prison section revolves around attempts to conceal Dan's identity, as he is ordered back to Dublin 'for trial for high treason' on the orders of British officer Igo – who is most likely based on the notorious RIC Constable Eugene Igoe.[236] Mick pretends to be Dan and is sent back to Dublin – only to be sent back to the camp again after his identity is revealed. The various methods of concealing prisoners – such as adding them to the 'sick parade' – echo veterans' accounts of Ballykinlar, Camp II.[237] Numerous escape plans are also concocted. After a frustrated attempt to escape via a tunnel, the prisoners crawl out under the barbed wire during a football match. This attempt fails when the escapees are spotted in the grass by an orderly; the camp is lit 'up by the brilliant glare of the searchlight' and 'the camp sirens' shriek.[238] This elaborate escape plan is almost identical to that documented by Ballykinlar prisoner Francis O'Duffy in his witness statement.[239]

The novel also includes details of prison life that add to contemporary accounts: the prisoners drink out of condensed milk tins called 'Charlie Bakers', sing songs such as 'Tim Muggin's Ass', use the handles of bread knives to make rings out of coins, and tie twine together to make bags.[240] Joanna Bruck has argued that these 'domestic' prison crafts, as well as the popularity of theatre and cross-dressing, illustrate the subversion of traditional gender norms in Irish internment camps.[241] Mulloy's novel elucidates a more taboo aspect of this ambivalent masculinity: the possibility of homosexual relationships between prisoners. Tim confides to Dan that 'a fellow in a hut near us tries to treat me like one [a woman]'. His fellow prisoner 'starts pawing me and putting his arms around me, and calling me "dear" and "darling" and all sorts of silly names like that'. He also tries to bring Tim back to his hut:

'He didn't want yeh ta sleep with him, be any chance?' asked Dan.
'I think that's what he wanted me to shift into his hut for.'[242]

Mulloy's reference to homosexuality may not only reflect the lived experience of IRA internees, it also unsettles the emphasis on masculine values promoted in the canon of 'fighting stories', perhaps advanced to counter negative, effeminate colonial stereotypes of the Irish.[243]

While much of the prison section of the novel is light-hearted, Mulloy also bears witness to distress caused by the claustrophobia of camp life and the shooting of prisoners by sentries:

> 'We've had enough of this camp.'
> 'Let's burn it.'
> 'Yes, burn the bloody kipp to the ground.'
> 'We'll be mowed down.'
> 'Let them mow us down – we'll be shot one by one, anyhow.'
> 'Three have been shot already.'
> 'Seven have died because they couldn't stick it.'
> 'One went mad.'[244]

A number of prisoners in Ballykinlar were indeed diagnosed for neurasthenia, including one man who was kept in a guardroom for weeks before being released to Richmond psychiatric hospital.[245] The shooting of three prisoners refers to the deaths of Joseph Tormey and Patrick Sloane (17 January 1921) and Tadhg Barry (15 November 1921) who were shot by prison sentries. Accounts from Ballykinlar prisoners, including Louis J. Walsh's memoirs *On My Keeping and Theirs* (1921), testify to the disruption these shootings provoked.[246] In his novel, Mulloy focuses less on the contentious circumstances of the prisoners' deaths, but rather on the psychological impact of the shootings on the surviving prisoners:

> When they reached the gate, they found a crowd of roughly five hundred prisoners kneeling and mumbling the responses of the rosary around a prisoner lying dead on the ground: shot through the heart by a sentry. Transfixed eyes were staring at the contorted features of a dead comrade, and the last remnants of restraint seemed to have disappeared from the faces around [...] The shooting of a

comrade playing heavily on the minds of the prisoners. Their nerves, taut by weary months of imprisonment and deferred hopes, were ready to snap.[247]

In his capacity as a novelist, Mulloy could thus establish himself as a 'moral witness' to his fellow prisoners' suffering.

The Civil War: 'A Graveyard of Souls'

The taut nerves of the prisoners set the context for the tragedy to come. As in Carty's account, the devastating split between friends is foreshadowed by a love triangle. Throughout his imprisonment, Tim remained in contact with his sweetheart Sheila but, on his release in December 1921, she begins to question her affection for him: 'Sheila, linked between Dan and Tim, was glancing from one to the other: she loved Tim, she told herself, but Dan attracted her. Tim was a handsome boy, kind, affectionate, and over-anxious to be attentive, while Dan, rugged and weather-beaten, did not appear to take the slightest notice of her presence.'[248]

The women are presented in stereotypical terms as vociferous in their denouncement of the treaty. Tim's sister Maureen claims she is 'ashamed of him' for joining the Free State, while Sheila leaves him for Dan – the only one of the three friends to take the republican side. There is a sense that the romantic patriotism of the women is ill-informed and nourished by binary perceptions of the Black and Tans as bloodthirsty savages in contrast to the heroic, saintly Volunteers. Mick disputes such a view: 'An' what do yeh think our fellows did? [...] Just wait in the ditches wid prayer-books, then sprinkle the tenders wid holy water, an' blow them up in the name a the Father, Son and Holy Ghost, an' expect a plenary indulgence?'[249]

Unlike the many revolutionary memoirs which emphasis the respectability of the officers and legitimise the use of violence, Mulloy's disillusion with the civil war is reflected through the total lack of professionalism of combatants on both sides. Republican recruits run home at the first sight of danger, including the supposedly bellicose republican commander 'The Gunner'.[250] Meanwhile, in the Free State camp, civil war is accompanied by heavy drinking and sex, as summed up by an ex-British army officer who boasts 'of the battles he had won, of the wine he had drunk, and of the women with whom he had slept'.[251] There are casual references to combatants seeking out domestic servants after raids, others are mocked for putting 'some jane in the family way' and the contraction of venereal diseases from prostitutes is also indicated.[252]

Women who transgress the gender norms of warfare are equally sexually degraded (as further explored in Chapter Three). On her arrest for carrying arms and dispatches for the republicans, Sheila is shamed as a 'bloody whore *de combat*, the dirty little spitfire.'[253] The female prisoner's body becomes a site of further conquest where the Free State soldiers can prove themselves. One soldier enters Sheila's cell in an attempt to woo her: he emerges dishevelled and we later learn that Sheila's clothing is torn.[254] Dan, who dresses in a Free State uniform in order to break Sheila out, mocks the soldiers for not knowing 'how to handle a judy.'[255] He escapes with Sheila by making a bet with the soldiers that he is enough of a 'ladykiller' to not only 'get away wid it', but also to manage to take her for a 'walk.'[256] As Dan and Sheila flee, the sentry calls out that '[i]f yeh want any square-pushin', do it upstairs. A bed's more comfortable anyhow.'[257]

Nevertheless, the soldiers are presented as having little control over the circumstances that have tragically pitted them against each other. Enlistment in the Free State army, for many, is an alternative to unemployment.[258] Throughout the novel, Mulloy paints humane sketches of friendships between 'enemies': Dan assists an injured Black and Tan in an ambush, Tim plays cards with the British officers imprisoning him, and the returned prisoners drink bottles of 'nigger's blood' – a slang for an alcoholic beverage – with a corporal in the British army.[259] Relations are amiable between the three friends, even when Mick and Tim remain on the Free State side and are imprisoned by their anti-treaty comrades, including Dan, in a military camp in the Wicklow Mountains.

For Tim, joining the Free State army means sacrificing his sweetheart, but getting a 'jackets green' army uniform 'was the proudest moment of his life.'[260] As the war progresses, however, the soldiers see that the tasks being assigned to them are in stark contrast to the 'flags', 'parades' and 'colour' they had associated with the 'gold paved streets' of the memory of the Easter Rising.[261] When ordered to reclaim a barracks from a brigade of republicans, one Free State soldier confesses, 'I feel as though I'm taking something that doesn't belong to me: a robbing the dead sort of feeling.'[262] Tim watches, dismayed, as some of his fellow soldiers revel in their newly acquired power: 'They had come from prisons and camps; some even from the condemned cell; from mountain haunts, from hay-lofts and ditches, from cellars and caves, to be placed in power: they were hysterical with reaction.'[263] This power translates into senseless killing taken out first on the natural world and later on the civilian population. As Tim laments: 'Nobody quite knew what they were firing at, and when a frightened pheasant rose out of the heather a soldier had a shot at it – just for fun; blood lust was aroused, and it was something to kill.'[264] Both Mike Delaney – an old concertina player who knows little about the 'row on in Dublin' – and his daughter, Kitty, are collateral damage: they unwittingly find themselves in the middle of a gun battle between republicans and Free State soldiers in their own farmhouse.[265]

The powerlessness of the individual against this collective brutalisation is reflected in Tim's feeble response to the tortures carried out by his fellow officer, Jobson:

> Smiling the demonical smile of a sadist, the officer walked towards the prisoner, his Sam Browne belt hanging loosely in his hands. The prisoner recoiled. [...] Before the prisoner could say any more he received the full force of the Sam Browne belt across the face. With a scream he tried to protect himself with his hands, while the officer started to tear off his waistcoat and shirt.[266]

Despite his best efforts, Tim finds himself caught up in this spiral of brutality. Raiding homes becomes routine; he no longer paid 'attention to the women's abuse; nor to the little crowd outside; nor to the grubby kids around the door; nor to the pair of hawk-like eyes in the window opposite; nor did he notice the signals when his car moved off'.[267]

Drinking becomes a coping mechanism. Tim previously only drank 'dry ginger'.[268] However, after hearing 'the swish of the Sam Browne and a [prisoner's] scream', he discovers that he 'liked the effect of it [porter]. It gave him courage.'[269] By the times of Michael Collins' assassination, Tim had been 'tight nearly every night' for three weeks.[270] Having witnessed the deaths of civilians, republicans and Free State soldiers alike, Tim throws wine over his tunic to conceal the blood stains on his 'jacket green'.[271]

The mental strain endured by the soldiers is further expressed by their frequenting of 'digs' or 'kipps' after a night's drinking. Despite Tim's initial shock that girls could drink or be so forward, he is suddenly overcome by a wild desire 'to see the girl undressed'.[272] However, when the prostitutes sneeringly nickname the soldiers 'Green and Tans', one man whips out his revolver and shoots a jug that smashes 'into smithereens over the woman's head'.[273] The other soldiers, including Tim, trash the brothel when they are refused alcohol: 'Each officer then drew his revolver and started to blaze at everything he could see: cups, saucers, jugs, bottles, lamps, flower vases. Demented and half-naked women rushed into the street screaming at the tops of their voices; men ran out of the houses and finished their dressing as they ran up the street [...]'.[274] Mike, too, allows himself to be led away by a prostitute on Grafton Street when he is tasked with bringing his friend, Dan, in front of a firing squad. Over the brothel bed hangs the Madonna and child; in perhaps the only recent literary appraisal of Mulloy's novel, Allen contends that this portrait signals the civil war's 'poison of the relations held between sign and salvation'.[275]

The most probable outcome of the 'orgy of sadism' of civil war is death.[276] Sheila is shot in an ambush and, following the civil war accidental shooting motif (most famously associated with Liam O'Flaherty's 1922 short story 'The Sniper'),[277] anti-treatyite Dan inadvertently shoots his Free State friend, Mick. Mulloy perhaps takes this accidental shooting plot a step further: when Tim discovers his two friends' dead bodies, circumstances suggest that Dan committed suicide after unintentionally killing his friend.[278] Suicide, or implied suicide, emerges in a number of revolutionary veterans' writings, and indeed in civil war writing internationally, to convey the inner destruction and self-division caused by internecine conflict.[279]

The novel's conclusion thus refers back to the aim outlined in the dedication to remind readers that 'many a path of glory leads to a graveyard of souls'. Tim emerges as the sole survivor of his direct associates and is the only living witness to tell the tale. He struggles to 'blot out the memory' of the 'ghastly sights' he has witnessed. After Sheila's death in hospital, his 'reaction was hysteria [...] And before anybody could stop him, Tim was chasing through the corridors of the hospital like a frenzied maniac'.[280] Whereas Carty's novel concludes with an optimistic sense of closure marking the re-establishment of social and romantic relationships, Mulloy's ending underscores the distance between the survivor of war and the civilian. Tim's reminiscences of happier days with Dan and Mick are disrupted by the sound of a patriotic tune coming from an upstairs window.

There is no sense of 'mythical female healing' as in Carty's novel. Brutalised and disenchanted by patriotism, Tim, in his final line of the novel, screams at the woman above to turn off her gramophone: 'Jesus Christ! Stop it, or I'll kill you!'[281]

Mulloy's Unlistened-to Story

In the first month after its release in March 1936, the sales of *Jackets Green* exceeded Mulloy's expectations. The novel sold nearly 600 copies in Ireland, made the Dublin bestseller list and two film companies expressed an interest in the story.[282] However, the novel's success was shortlived. Not only was Mulloy's novel sidelined from the canon of revolutionary fiction in reviews by O'Faoláin, it did not stay long in Irish bookstores. By June, the Irish Censorship Board had banned *Jackets Green*.[283] This was the beginning of a long and financially disastrous battle for Mulloy, which lasted until his death, as he strove to defend his novel's merit, revoke its censorship and republish it. The dismissal of his novel, and particularly the doubting of its authenticity, cut deep. That his story was told, but not heard, speaks to Holocaust survivor Primo Levi's observation of the problem of the 'unlistened-to story': that is to say, a story that is told without being truly listened to and that continues to haunt the teller in their dreams.[284]

Although Mulloy speculated that there may have been political reasons for the banning of his novel, he acknowledged that it was regarded as 'obscene' because of the brothel scenes.[285] Intriguingly, the censors were not concerned with the brutal descriptions of violence, as, in Mulloy's view, 'the cult of violence had been accepted in Ireland' (see Chapter Five).[286] Nevertheless, a significant body of fiction relating to the revolutionary period was banned by the Irish Censorship Board, often because of sexual 'impropriety' rather than politics (see Chapter Four). These include Seán O'Faoláin's *Midsummer Night Madness: And Other Stories* (1932), John Brophy's *The Rocky Road: A Novel* (1932), Liam O'Flaherty's *The Martyr* (1933), Rearden Conner's *Shake Hands with the Devil: A Novel* (1933), Francis Plunkett's *As the Fool* (1935) and Jim Phelan's *Lifer* (1938) (also containing references to homosexual relationships among prisoners).[287]

Some authors may have welcomed the *succès de scandale* offered by censorship and may indeed have been drawn to the controversy of civil war for that very reason. Liam O'Flaherty wrote his satirical civil war novel, *The Martyr*, with the intention to 'stir them up'.[288] Séamus MacCall – who participated in the First World War and subsequently fought on the anti-treaty side – wrote a seemingly autobiographically based novel *Gods in Motley* (1935) in which the imprisoned republican protagonist awaiting execution hoped that 'writing would stir the sluggish backwaters of his crowded mind'.[289] On receiving the manuscript, the editor of Talbot Press asked, 'are you not afraid that it will be censored by the Free State?'[290]

Even though Mulloy could not appeal the decision of the Irish Censorship Board, he defended his novel through a highly publicised case against the Irish edition of the *Daily Express* for defamation. He took libel action against the newspaper for an article that suggested the novel was 'indecent' and reprinted a quote by Mr William Magennis, a professor at the National University of Ireland and a member of the Censorship Board, who claimed that there was not 'a single redeeming feature about the book'. A contentious aspect of the trial was whether 'certain references to sex' – namely 'a reference to homosexuality and a graphic account of scenes in a brothel' – should be considered 'indecent'.[291] The jury found that the article was defamatory of Mulloy's book, that the statement attributed to Professor Magennis was accurate, that the article was fair criticism of Mulloy's book and that the words complained of – that the book had not a 'single redeeming feature' – were untrue.[292] However, the newspaper pleaded 'fair comment' and the judge dismissed the damages of £500 awarded to Mulloy.[293] Mulloy was thus obliged to pay the defendants' costs of £571 – a ruling he unsuccessfully appealed – and was left almost bankrupt.[294] This decision also led to the false opinion that Mulloy had sued the newspaper for £500, as suggested in an article in *The Irish Times* in 1945.[295]

The objections to Mulloy's novel – in literary criticism, censorship and in court – underscore the difficulties for combat veterans in negotiating their wartime experience with the social expectations of civilian life. Even the 'coarseness' of language was deemed offensive for the public, to which Mulloy responded that such 'soldiers' talk' was 'most expressive'. When cross-examined, Mulloy, echoing O'Donnell, maintained that the novel could not be considered 'indecent' as it was true to his experience. He held that the book was 'photogenic', held up 'the mirror to nature', and that only 'smug' people would doubt the occurrence of such events.

When it was suggested to him that 'it was unpleasant' to read extracts of the book 'to a jury on which there were two women', Mulloy responded that '[i]t was just as unpleasant for me to write'.[296]

Mulloy's continued attempts to find a 'listening community' in Ireland are clear from the fact that he donated the original manuscript of the novel to the National Library in 1947 after carefully guarding it throughout the London Blitz.[297] Although Mulloy could not convince publishers to reprint his novel after the ban was finally lifted in 1968, he revisited the civil war in other writings.[298] His play, *Harvest of the Wind*, produced by the Little Theatre Club in Garrick Yard in 1968, again addressed the author's civil war experience.[299] Like *Jackets Green*, the play centres on three released IRA prisoners who take opposing positions on the treaty; once again, this split is represented through a love triangle, as the female love interest rejects her pro-treaty fiancé, Simon, in favour of his more stridently republican friend, Gerry. Simon is killed in an anti-treaty ambush when travelling to Dublin on a 'mission of mercy' to save Gerry from execution. The play ends as the sole survivor of the three, Con, is left in the Free State Military Camp in the Wicklow Mountains in the company of a female prostitute, who 'sidles coquettishly toward the couch as the curtain falls slowly'.[300]

Harvest of the Wind was expressly written to contest the silence surrounding the conflict, as Mulloy argued that the civil war had so far been 'eschewed by dramatists', even though 'the conflicts and clashes of character of the time are the very essence of drama, ready made'.[301] In 1975, Mulloy also issued a pamphlet entitled *Mutiny Without Malice*, which detailed his role in the Army Mutiny of 1924. The pamphlet was again motivated by a sense of moral duty as a surviving witness; Mulloy was 'one of the few remaining survivors of the 300 former Free State army officers involved'.[302] While a reviewer in *An Cosantóir*, the official magazine of the Irish Defence Force, was unconvinced by Mulloy's 'kindly and benevolent' account, Mulloy was nevertheless credited with challenging officialdom, 'whose technique has been simply to throw a blanket of silence over the whole business and consign it to oblivion'.[303] While Mulloy's writings for adults highlighted the violent underbelly of war, his children's writings – described by Brendan Behan as 'excellent'[304] – advocated against violence. His popular illustrated novel *Andy Tinpockets* (1950) follows the adventures of three young children in Ireland and their outrage against the abuse of farm animals.[305]

Conclusion

By the end of the 1930s, a plethora of fictionalised records of the civil war had made it to press, flying in the face of calls on the floor of the Dáil to 'let us forget past differences and past history'.[306] The writings of Peadar O'Donnell, Francis Carty and Patrick Mulloy illustrate the influence of international cultural debates regarding the psychological legacies of war in the aftermath of the First World War. Their writings also underscore the generative impulse at the heart of traumatic experience and highlight the collaborative nature of testimony as veterans hoped that their accounts would be received by confirming audiences. One narrative revisit was often not enough to satisfy the urge to tell, however. O'Donnell, Carty and Mulloy penned a number of civil war accounts at various points in their lives, told from different vantage points, in different genres, real and imagined.

Although Carty's novel works towards closure with Paul visit's to Rosaleen heralding the republican prisoner's return to civilian life, the conclusion of Mulloy's novel offers no such consolation, pointing instead to the rift between the Free State soldier and civil society. Meanwhile, O'Donnell's prison diary participates in a longstanding model of republican remembrance in which trauma stories are chapters within a continual cycle of suffering building towards a better future. The tragic experience of witnessing the death of comrades is also addressed from three very different perspectives: O'Donnell resorts to black humour in his descriptions of his executed comrades; Carty sees death through ironic eyes; while for Mulloy death causes taut nerves and, eventually, an urge to commit further violence. The question of perpetrating violence is one to which we will return in Chapter Five.

But before that, it is necessary to look beyond the distinctly masculine perspective of civil war evident in O'Donnell's, Carty's and Mulloy's testimonies. For even as these veterans drew attention to the mental strain of wartime experience and thus troubled more heroic narratives of revolution, their writings nevertheless present war as a male domain. The fact that *Jackets Green* was deemed 'unpleasant' for, and even harmful to, the female jurists during Mulloy's libel case underscores the exclusion of women from wartime remembrance, expressed here through the language of safeguarding. Even though Desmond Ryan was supportive of gender equality, his own writings include stereotypical one-dimensional representations of female revolutionaries: in *The Invisible Army*, civil war is signalled by the presence of 'rogues, looters, wasters and *hysterical women wrapping petty crimes and private griefs in the tricolour*, too soon dyed red in the blood of the brothers of yesterday' (my emphasis).[307] The following chapter will thus consider a number of female-authored texts that could equally have been selected for their evocation of the 'spiritual wounds' of civil war.

Chapter Two

From Rest to Writing Cures: Testifying to Women's Pain

Before its banning in Ireland, Patrick Mulloy's *Jackets Green* appeared in *The Irish Times* bestseller list alongside yet another autobiographical novel of the revolutionary period, Kenneth Sarr's *Somewhere to the Sea* (1936).[1] Sarr had been a lawyer in the underground Sinn Féin courts prior to the treaty, and reviewers praised his 'first-hand' picture of the 'troubles'.[2] Among the readership was playwright and critic Mary Manning (1906–1999), who had recently relocated to Boston. For Manning, Sarr's novel was the first such account that 'realized the existence of a great solid mass of quiet people who went on living and eating and laughing and sleeping or trying to sleep, during those years'.[3] She opened her review of *Somewhere to the Sea* with an autobiographical sketch of the rather mundane nuisance caused by the Battle of the Dublin to the bathers of Blackrock:

> I remember as a child bathing at Seapoint, where all the nice little suburban children bathed, swimming out beyond the rocks, turning suddenly to look towards Dublin, and seeing the city more or less in flames. I felt very little surprise, only the mildest stirring of excitement, for it was the year Nineteen Twenty-two. The Irish Civil War was in full progress and for the second time in six years O'Connell Street was on fire. I could never feel much surprise again, having been brought up in troubled times and since my seventh year having been conscious of little else but wars and rumors of wars. And then I

heard our nurse screaming at us from the shore to come in outer that or no jam for tea. Her remarks were punctuated by distant gunfire, but her concern I learnt on reaching the shore was not inspired by sounds of warfare but rather that we might stay in too long and get cramps! And sure enough all the other nannies and governesses and mammas did not seem to be unduly alarmed but went on knitting and gossiping and keeping their eyes on their charges.[4]

Manning's criticism of the many accounts of the revolution that only dealt with 'those taking an active part' highlights the gendered silences in the dominant commemorative narrative of 'heroic and unblemished freedom fighters'.[5] Unlike the testimonies discussed in Chapter One in which the female protagonists are often reduced to symbolic importance,[6] the female characters in *Somewhere to the Sea* – Miriam Joyce and artist Estella Marlay – are complex, relatable characters, capable of their own successes and mistakes. Sarr, too, highlights how armed action is not divorced from seemingly private gendered traumas. In one instance, the shock of a raid on her home causes Muriel MacDermott to go into labour prematurely; this, although dramatic, resonates with contemporary accounts.[7]

Manning's review highlights how readers assimilated the testimonies of others through the lens of their own (gendered) experience. It also underscores the precarious position in which female readers of accounts of the Irish revolution found themselves, especially given that reviewers often saw their task as one of verifying, or challenging, the 'authenticity' of such writings. However, rather than yield to the 'masculinisation of the female reader',[8] Manning purposely exploited her review of Sarr's novel to bear witness on behalf of the ordinary citizens of Dublin suburbia. She extended her criticism of the overshadowing of women's actual experience two years later in her comic novel *Mount Venus* (1938), which was published in Boston, but never printed in Ireland or Britain due to libel fears.[9] The matriarch, Caroline d'Acosta (referred to as 'the Doña') is purportedly based on Maud Gonne MacBride and is imprisoned over eight times for sedition. Concealed behind the satire, Manning draws attention to taboos often omitted from the grand narrative: the Doña had been 'living in really dreadful sin' before getting married; she is cast off by her brother, an officer in the British army, for her politics; and the death caused by the influenza epidemic is placed on a par with loss of life during the revolution.[10]

This chapter examines a number of civil war testimonies by female revolutionaries, many of which swerve from the conventions of standard autobiography. The majority of the women included here opposed the treaty, including Garrett O'Driscoll, the pen name of Peggie Kelly (1902–1969), Annie M. P. Smithson (1873–1948), Dorothy Macardle (1889–1958) and Máirín Cregan (1891–1975). The writings of Máiréad Ní Ghráda (1896–1971) bring a pro-treaty perspective. The discussion of women's experiences following a chapter on men's testimonies is not intended to reify a gender hierarchy by contrasting women's testimonies to an assumed male standard. Male and female revolutionary veterans experienced many of the same challenges in attempting to satisfy the competing compulsions to both divulge and conceal at the heart of the trauma testimonial project. Nevertheless, women's testimonies are further complicated by the inherently gendered understandings of trauma. Whereas it was assumed that men yielded to effeminate, hysteria-like symptoms due to the physical shock of accidents or warfare, women's bodies were deemed to be symptomatic by nature.[11] The idea that so many of women's ordinary experiences were traumatic – from arranged marriage, to pregnancy, to childbirth – paradoxically rendered their lives not traumatic at all.

As is typical of post-conflict commemoration internationally, women's suffering was exploited in revolutionary remembrance for symbolic significance – women's wounded bodies often served as a conduit for expressing men's trauma, while woman and nation were conflated in the pervasive tropes of 'Mother Ireland', 'Dark Rosaleen' or 'Kathleen Ni Houlihan'.[12] Meanwhile, the lived experience of female revolutionaries was sidelined from official narratives, their actual suffering trivialised and branded as indicative of the innate madness of 'furies', 'die-hards' and 'neurotic girls'.[13] Even the gender-exclusive motifs employed internationally to denote internecine conflict – such as brother against brother; father against son; *guerre fratricide*; *Bruderkrieg*; *cogadh na mbráthar* – visibly erase women from the civil war narrative.

Female revolutionaries, in giving testimony, were thus tasked with renegotiating the simultaneous dismissal, objectification and even commercialisation of women's pain in much revolutionary remembrance. The two main processes of trauma-telling also pose particular challenges for female testifying-subjects. Firstly, the private construction of a 'coherent, listenable narrative of a traumatic experience'[14] is complicated by the restraints placed on female self-expression. As Elaine Showalter argues, this problem is not tied to language itself, but rather that 'women have been denied the full resources of language and have been forced into silence, euphemism and circumlocution'.[15] More challenging than the question of representation, however, is the second task of sharing one's story through a public testimonial act. The difficulties of finding an attuned witnessing audience for women's testimony is clear from the extra challenges they experienced in publicising, publishing and transmitting their testimonies in a commemorative environment that privileged men's accounts of revolution. As a result, perhaps, the liminal space between fiction and non-fiction became one of the most significant sites for the exploration of women's 'spiritual wounds' of civil war. Not only did the subterfuge of fiction offer a means to testify to personal experience, female revolutionaries also exploited the freedom offered by fiction to reframe mainstream revolutionary remembrance by linking daily social and structural traumas to wartime trauma, and by presenting domestic spaces as battlefronts no less immune to war and revolution than conventional frontlines.

The 'Female Malady' and Women Revolutionaries

Much of the rhetoric employed by journalists, church leaders and politicians to condemn female revolutionaries was couched in the pseudomedical language of madness and lunacy. While male republicans were 'diagnosed' with pathological conditions such as 'neuroses', 'megalomania' and 'hysteria' by their opponents, such invective was specifically targeted at female anti-treatyites.[16] Even though women were divided on the question of the Anglo-Irish Treaty, they were popularly held responsible for the slide to civil war due, perhaps, to the vocal rejection of the settlement by all six female TDs and the anti-treaty stance of Cumann na mBan.[17] The idea that the treaty divide reflected a 'difference of opinion along sex lines' was promulgated by Hanna Sheehy-Skeffington, among others, who claimed that 'wives, daughters and sisters are in one camp (Republican) and their menfolk in the other (Free State)'.[18] During the conflict itself, anti-treaty women took on riskier tasks than during the previous war of independence and were often responsible for storing and carrying guns and ammunition, particularly as men in possession of arms could be summarily executed following the Public Safety Bill of October 1922. Over 600 women were interned in the Irish Free State for political activities and associations (not to mention the internment of female activists in the north of Ireland); these levels of incarceration far exceeded that of the period 1916–21.[19] Despite this, women's diverse roles were 'completely absent', 'reduced to footnotes' and 'utterly [neglected]' in key studies of the Irish Civil War (an oversight that is being redressed in more recent scholarship).[20] The internment and mistreatment of republican women was again justified through their reduction to 'harpies, ill-suited for rational political discourse'.[21]

Gendered conceptions of trauma also played out in the medical treatment prescribed to female revolutionaries for 'exhausted nerves'.[22] In her memoir, *The Hope and the Sadness: Personal Recollections of Troubled Times in Ireland* (1980), female activist Siobhán Lankford recounts that she travelled from Cork to Dublin in the aftermath of the civil war to seek treatment from well-known republican sympathiser Dr Robert Farnan. She found his consulting rooms in Merrion Square were crowded with 'women who had been straining every nerve to assist in the fight for freedom'.[23] Dr Farnan was in fact a gynaecologist; that he treated patients for nervous conditions underscores that 'weak nerves' were inherently connected to the female reproductive system. Lankford was prescribed 'six weeks complete rest in the Mater Hospital' followed by a period 'living in Malahide and Sutton, and Dr. Farnan's care for a whole year'.[24] This type of treatment reflects the highly disciplined and gender-specific 'rest cure' first developed by Philadelphian neurologist Silas Weir Mitchell in the late nineteenth century. Mitchell's rest cure was devised primarily for well-to-do ladies and was based on the removal of the patient from her usual surroundings, which sometimes, as in Lankford's case, involved a retreat to the countryside or to the seaside. In its most regimented form, the patient was expected to lie in bed for six weeks to two months and was not allowed to read, write or have visitors.

However, Dr Farnan seems to have adopted a different approach for male combatants; IRA leader Michael Collins sent his men to Dr Farnan and he was known to 'cure by merely speaking to the men'.[25] Whereas it is suggested that men's treatment for 'nerves' endorsed a form of 'talk therapy' to facilitate their swift re-entry into combat, women's treatment excluded them from public life.

From Rest to Writing Cures?

The curtailment of women's self-expression in the medical domain is reflected in the suppression of the voices of female revolutionaries during the revolution and its aftermath. Resistance to the circulation of women's writings was a feature of the revolutionary period; documents were often confiscated during house raids given the significant roles of female couriers and propagandists. Fiction, too, had political significance. Kathleen Goodfellow, a member of Cumann na mBan, published a collection of short stories (under the pseudonym Michael Scot), *Three Tales of the Times*, in 1921. Her graphic depictions of the Black and Tans and her reflections on the impact that witnessing violence had on children was a direct challenge to the British military.[26] In autumn 1921, Emily Ussher's novel *The Trail of the Black & Tans* (published under the pseudonym 'The Hurler on the Ditch') was purportedly removed from bookshop windows by the Cork RIC due to its depictions of atrocities carried out by British forces.[27]

However, when Ussher wrote a follow-up novel, it was deemed 'too sad and depressing' to publish in the context of the 'agreement between Free Stater and Republican'.[28] While many women chronicled their revolutionary experiences with a sense that it was 'worth remembering',[29] securing a publisher in the post-independence period became increasingly difficult. Sheehy-Skeffington found her 'Dublin Memories' rejected by Talbot Press in 1934, as, although 'chatty and enjoyable', its 'literary value' was 'slender'.[30] Margaret Buckley's *The Jangle of the Keys* (1938) is the only full-length published civil war jail memoir by a female prisoner.[31] Many other memoirs were simply never published, such as those of Eithne Coyle and Síghle Humphreys,[32] while Máire Comerford's overlooked memoir was serialised in its Irish translation in *Agus* magazine from 1981 to 1990.

Even the etymology of the term 'testimony' – believed to be connected to the Latin 'testes' – points to the longstanding gendering of the 'witness' as male. Leigh Gilmore has argued that women are routinely conceived of as 'untrustworthy witnesses' in the public sphere in such a way that 'women's witness is discredited'.[33] This tendency to mistrust women's testimonies is indeed clear from the scholarly emphasis on the 'the lies' found in Maud Gonne's writings, such as her 1938 autobiography *Servant of the Queen*.[34] Women's voices, too, were marginalised in major commemorative projects, such as the appropriately titled 1940s series, *Fighting Story 1916–21: Told by the Men Who Made It*.[35] Women made up less than 10 per cent of those interviewed by the Bureau of Military History (1947–57), while Ernie O'Malley only included a handful of women among the over 450 veterans he interviewed between the late 1930s and early 1950s; some of these have been published in the series *The Men Will Talk to Me*.[36] As recently released witness statements and pension files increasingly demonstrate, women's names and activities are often conspicuously absent, or even consciously expunged, from male veterans' accounts.[37]

These hurdles in terms of production, publication and being believed may explain the reluctance of many female revolutionaries to place themselves at the centre of their own narratives. Despite the wealth of testimonies by female revolutionaries – in the form of diaries, witness statements, interviews and a handful of published memoirs – Lucy McDiarmid suggests that women's accounts of the 1916 Rising are characterised by 'exteriority' as they construct themselves 'as part of a collective'.[38] For female revolutionaries, writing about the self, in Karen Steele's view, could prove 'liberating but also alienating'.[39] Síghle Humphreys, in an unpublished account of her imprisonment, humorously apologises for her use of first-person narration: 'I'm afraid it will be more an account about myself than the women prisoners, all I hope is that I wont [*sic*] be as bad as Benjamin Franklin'.[40] The ambiguities surrounding women's agency as writers are also played out in co-authored narratives, such as those of the Power and Cooney sisters.[41] Both Eithne Coyle and Dorothy Macardle wrote about Maud Gonne MacBride as a means to reveal information about their own lives.[42] Women also often mediated the transmission of men's accounts: Moya Llewelyn Davies most probably had a hand in Charles Dalton's and Batt O'Connor's memoirs published by her nephew, Peter Davis, in 1929; she also prepared notes for Michael Collins' *The Path to Freedom* (1922), which then 'passed through' Kathleen McKenna.[43] However, this work was largely unaccredited, and even unremunerated, as in the case of Kitty O'Doherty, who apparently was the ghostwriter of Dan Breen's *My Fight For Irish Freedom* (1924).[44] Other women, such as Lily MacManus, inserted quotes from leading male figures into their writings as a vehicle for expressing their own opinions.[45]

In light of the fact that political women could only write about the self 'in the most restricted or disguised of terms',[46] the espousal of generic hybridity, or the blending of fiction and personal experience, is of particular pertinence for female revolutionaries. Cumann na mBan founder Alice Cashel's young adult novel, *The Lights of Leaca Bán*, highlights Cashel's own feminism: when the young female protagonist wonders whether only men could contribute to the 'noble' national cause, she is reassured that 'it's you and all the other girls like you who will really save Ireland'.[47] Equally, Lily O'Brennan employed covert narrative strategies to highlight women's roles in the conflict: her unpublished children's novel, *Leading a Dog's Life in Ireland*, chronicles the period 1916–21 through the eyes of a dog, stressing that '[r]epublican women went reluctantly to bed at night, and could hardly sleep listening for the clamourous [*sic*] knock that meant the arrest of those they sheltered'.[48] Her earlier novel, *The Call to Arms: A Tale of the Land League Days*, published in 1929 under the pen name Esther Graham to little critical acclaim, shares the explicit aim of highlighting the 'priceless services of the heroes and the heroines of the Land War, for the women were in it, too'.[49]

This flight to the past was yet another enabling strategy for addressing the experience of female revolutionaries. Rosamond Jacob recalled that a document of hers concerning 'British cruelty and aggression' was seized by military in a house raid during the war of independence. However, she defended herself by claiming, truthfully, that the account was not propaganda, but a historical document relating to the failed rebellion of 1798.[50] That female revolutionaries were concerned about the omission of women activists from standard histories even as the revolution was still unfolding suggests that they shared anxieties not only about how they might be remembered – but also about how they might be forgotten.

Garrett O'Driscoll: Talking to your Childhood 'With Pen Dipped, not on Ink, but in Tears'

Steele laments that 'life stories' by female revolutionaries 'rarely produced personal or political transformations'.[51] But what were the cathartic aims behind female-authored fictional projects of remembrance? Garrett O'Driscoll's poem 'The Plain People' was printed just days before Éamon de Valera's call to the 'Legion of the Rearguard' to dump arms in 24 May 1923 and end the civil war. The speaker forcefully decries 'the plain people' who have repudiated the principles that they so cherished 'yesterday':

The Plain People

We have builded on the day,
    Of the clay,
We have striven and achieved
We have listened and believed
And ye left us without warning
    On the way,
With the Golden City sighted,
With the wrongs of years unrighted,
At the breaking of the morning
    of the Day.

We have buried in the clay
    Of the clay,
Youth and gladness, love and laughter,
Sent to face the great Hereafter
At your bidding, all we cherished
    Yesterday –
For a dream, was it? – a blunder?
(Oh, the severings asunder
When they smiled and prayed and perished,
    Who shall say?)

We have mingled with the clay,
    Of the clay,
Tears of women, blood of men;
We have given – given again
Home and kindred, father, brother
    For (you say)
A poor fairy thing? – a gleam? –
A now half-forgotten dream?
(Ah, ye called it other, other
    Yesterday).[52]

Evoking the collective voice, the speaker conjures up a sense of betrayal felt by the republican side as 'ye left us without warning / On the way'. Yet while the collective voice is tied to the political, the recollections of those who 'smiled and prayed and perished' suggest an intimate relationship between the speaker and the civil war dead – and equally an anxiety surrounding the forgetting of their legacy: 'a now half-forgotten dream'.

The poem 'The Plain People' could easily be forgotten among the many poems that appeared in newspapers and propaganda sheets throughout the civil war. But O'Driscoll carved out a literary reputation the following year for the Tailteann prize-winning novel *Noreen*. The assertive poetic voice hiding behind a male penname in fact belonged to Cumann na mBan revolutionary Margaret 'Peggie' Kelly.[53] Peggie and her sister Winifred spent much of their youth in St Mary's Dominican convent in Dún Laoghaire after the death of their mother Marion Kelly (née Sheils) in October 1909.[54] From 1919, however, they became lodgers at 15 Marino Crescent, Clontarf, the Boland family home and 'a favourite resort of gunman and repository of guns'.[55] By day, the sisters typed documents, transported arms and ran dispatches, while at night they worked as couriers.[56] In early 1921, the Kelly sisters were discovered burning documents in an open fire and fled to Glasgow, fearing arrest.[57] After their father died at sea in March 1922, they returned to Ireland and once again took up residency in Marino Crescent. They remained in Clontarf during the civil war; a number of their acquaintances lost their lives in the conflict, including Harry Boland, who was shot on 2 August 1922 by a former companion who had joined the Free State army.

Peggie Kelly was decidedly reticent about her revolutionary exploits and left no written record, it seems, of her activities. Her life and works were only recently recuperated in an article by Jody Allen-Randolph, who stumbled across Kelly when writing a biography of Kelly's acclaimed niece, poet Eavan Boland.[58] Although Kelly passed on little more than 'mere fragments' of her experience,[59] Garrett O'Driscoll documented the revolution in a number of short stories published between 1922 and 1925, and most notably in her 1924 novel *Noreen*, published by London publisher George Roberts in 1929.[60] O'Driscoll's interest in the psychological legacies of war is clear from her later concerns for the many 'able-bodied' but 'not quite able-minded' ex-IRA men who found themselves desolate as they could not qualify for a wound pension.[61] Her writings, too, underscore the medicalisation of women's emotional health and connect women's subjugation to their linguistic behaviour, as reflected in her recourse to a male pseudonym.

A Project of Scriptotherapy?

Noreen can be read as an exercise in scriptotherapy or therapeutic writing. The idea of narrative catharsis is inscribed into the novel itself. Noreen's brother, Con, hides his 'old copy-book of effusions' in the bottom of a press in which he 'laid bare' 'so much of his inner heart'.[62] Writing provides a means of coping; at night, words come to him 'easily' and bring 'a gleam [...] in his dark eyes'.[63] It is not hard to imagine that Con's practice may be reflective of the author's own writing given the circumstances in which *Noreen* was produced. As Allen-Randolph elucidates:

> Peggie Kelly started writing this novel during the War of Independence when she and others worked 'tirelessly for the lads', taking the reins of revolution from an older generation [...] She saw many of them die for a new Ireland shaped by their own youthful hopes. She worked on the novel while on the run in Glasgow, with the deaths of the Civil War, including Harry Boland and Liam Mellows, before her. She finished her novel after the Civil War drew to a close in April 1923 while her future husband was interned by Free State forces. Shadowing her life in words, her fiction mines both personal and national grief, and the poignant rooms where one blurred into the other.[64]

The novel, which might be described as a female anti-*Bildungsroman*, traces the development of the eponymous protagonist, Noreen, from her birth to the drama of the Easter Rising. Thwarting the upward mobility narrative associated with the *Bildungsroman*, the novel's conclusion is marked by tragedy. In lines that echo the poem 'The Plain People', Noreen finds 'Death around her, and about her, and before her and behind her. What is Death? White stones above white bones in the silent clay? Or a great door wherethrough there passes, once, for always, the soul that is not clay?'[65] Even though the novel relates to the period leading up to the Rising, it was written through the independence struggle and civil war, and thus offers testimony in real time to the contentious atmosphere of the period. The novel shows, too, how the shadow of the memory of 1916 lingered over succeeding events – yet, unlike more celebratory evocations of the Rising, the outcome of O'Driscoll's novel speaks to the same sense of disillusion outlined in her 1923 poem.

Like Carty's novel, which was decorated with an image of Éamon de Valera, O'Driscoll established her republican allegiances in *Noreen* by dedicating the first section of the book to 'The Chief'. This first section follows the Donegan family, living in rural Ballygrath, from the birth of the youngest and only daughter – Nora Kathleen – to the tragic death of the eldest of the four siblings, Con, from consumption. It was this treatment of rural Irish family life that particularly impressed critics, including Edward Compton Mackenzie, who heralded *Noreen* as 'one of the most tender pictures of childhood I have ever seen'.[66] However, O'Driscoll's dedication of this first section to de Valera intertwines the routines of childhood with the wider political struggle.

Indeed, unlike the many testimonies that present idyllic, innocent pictures of childhood as a contrast to the later turmoil, O'Driscoll's sketches of childhood are beset by impending sadness and offer little nostalgic respite from the present. Evoking the poetry of Alice Meynell, childhood is recalled 'with pen dipped, not in ink, but in tears'.[67] The friendship that develops between Michael Donegan and the Scottish schoolmaster Mac is disturbed by the voice of the omniscient narrator, who cries back through the prism of foresight to warn them of the split between green and brown uniforms that would later divide them: 'And oh, Michael, Michael *agradh*! Isn't it many a thought you'll give Mulligan's field in the turbulent years to come?'[68]

The themes of violence and death are a feature of early childhood, expressed through the mistreatment of Noreen's cat, Lickylips. Despite Noreen's protests, her father decrees that Lickylips' litter of kittens be 'drownded', causing the cat to wail 'forlornly around the house'.[69] This emphasis on the welfare of animals reflects O'Driscoll's interest in antivivisection campaigns; the question of violence against animals could also provide a means of commenting on social or political violence, and was often married to campaigns for women's rights during this period.[70] The cat's death unearths incredibly strong emotions in the young protagonist: 'She did not want to be alive. She wanted to *die*.'[71]

Lickylips' death anticipates the death of Noreen's older brother, Con. Con is described as an 'idealist' and a 'dreamer' and his mother worries that he is not eating, doesn't sleep, and she wonders 'is he very fond of himself?'[72] Con rebels constantly and is beaten by his father, as his mother looks on 'powerless'.[73] His rebelliousness is further illustrated through his repudiation of the Catholic Church, upsetting both his family and the local priest. His rejection of God is connected to his sense of the injustices of the world, as he finds it impossible to reconcile himself with *the sadness of things* [...] It's like a cold river always flowing over me, things and people struggling with evil, and going down – getting swamped, getting damned.'[74] Con's illness is thus psychological as much as physical; his preference for writing over eating takes a toll on his body.[75] After a brief period studying medicine in Dublin, he writes to his mother that he has contracted consumption and is 'coming home for good'.[76] He dies five months after his return to Ballygrath, 'swamped by the sadness of things'.[77] However, in line with the emphasis on collective experience in the writings of female revolutionaries, the trauma depicted in *Noreen* is always collective, insidious and contagious, rather than based around a single, sudden event. As the narrator reflects, 'And that is life. I suffer. You suffer. I suffer because you suffer, and you because I suffer. So we bear a burden other than the burden of the day.'[78]

The Gendered Subtext of Trauma and Politics

The second section of *Noreen* is set in Dublin after an elapse of twelve years with the First World War and the approaching Rising as a backdrop. Noreen follows Con's legacy in rebelling against her social environment. As is often the case in narratives of civil war, the military conflict becomes 'a metaphor for inner conflicts', which, as Margaret Higonnet argues, is frequently accompanied by an inversion of gender roles and 'reversals in emotional and sexual relationships'.[79] While the Donegan brothers, Michael and Derry, join the Gaelic League, host debates on the national question and join the Irish Volunteers, Noreen's revolution is tied to her status as a woman. She finds her match in Lila Panther, a childhood friend with whom she becomes reacquainted. The 'exquisite' and exotic Lila symbolises the social progress being made in early twentieth-century Ireland. Described as a 'tomboy', she smokes her brother's cigarettes, enjoys frequent trips to the theatre and shares a sympathy for the 'downtrodden' not quite appreciated by her English fiancé, Bernie.[80]

The plainer Noreen – described in characteristically oxymoronic terms as being 'not ugly, neither was she pretty'[81] – resists social norms more forcibly than Lila, although this is less discernible from outside appearances. Unlike Lila's dramatic fashion, Noreen dresses sensibly, as her 'father frowned on bare throats and transparent stockings'.[82] Her father symbolises the patriarchy: she laments that he 'thinks because I'm a girl I've no right to be in the world', declares that she is 'not his property', nor 'a piece of his furniture', and insists that she does not 'want to be *ladylike*'.[83] After a quarrel with her father, in which he criticises her deceased brother, Con, Noreen runs away from home, threatens to escape to America and takes flight to Glasgow, to where Lila is staying.

This conflict in gender roles is connected to the political struggle through the prevalence of military metaphors: Noreen walks 'like a warrior', gives the poker 'a warlike twirl' and challenges her father 'to a wordy battle'.[84] Indeed, O'Driscoll repeatedly subverts gender roles in her writings. Noreen insists her cat, Lickylips, is a boy, although 'he' bears a litter of kittens; Lila refers to rescued orphan girl Estelle Amy as a 'small boy'; Michael has a light touch 'like a woman's'; and Lila – who holds herself 'boyishly' – exclaims that her fiancé, Bernie, is 'the lady' in the relationship and treats her in a 'motherly' way.[85] This undercutting of conventional notions of gender and sexuality is further evident in O'Driscoll's short stories, such as the ambiguous story 'Mettle' in which the teacher, Guifoyle, admits that he had been 'crossed in love' but never 'loved a woman'.[86] Like Mulloy's allusions to homosexual relations, O'Driscoll's subtle questioning of the conventions of heterosexual love is at odds with the rigid gender dichotomies often associated with the post-independence national project.

O'Driscoll's writings, too, hint at the tendency to prescribe rest-based therapies to 'nervous' women who transgressed social boundaries. Lila's fiancé finds her to be 'irritable and unstrung' and arranges for her to take a month's recuperation in Glasgow.[87] O'Driscoll's first published short story, 'A Flippant Young Man'[88] – published during the civil war in November 1922 and believed to contain 'strong autobiographical elements'[89] – also points to the prescription of 'rest'. The eccentric 21-year-old narrator, Mabel Puck, had led an 'unregenerate' life in Dublin where she knew 'a lot of boys', but on becoming 'very queer, and very, very tired' after her aunt's death, she retreats to an isolated country cottage bought with her inheritance money.[90] On doctor's orders, she must eat eggs and is catered for by the local women. She is contented that 'there is no war here – among the fairies'.[91] Yet Mabel's removal from public life fails; she falls in love with an injured IRA man whom she discovers in her garden.

If relief from trauma is achieved through abreaction, women's access to self-expression is also constantly problematised in O'Driscoll's writings: Derry admonishes Noreen 'paternally' that '[l]ittle girls should be seen and not heard', while Father Seagrave reminds her that '[l]ittle girls must never put out their tongues' and 'should not wink'.[92] When Noreen uses language unbecoming of a little girl (she exclaims that the kettle is 'as hot as blazes'), she is sternly chastised.[93] Even in adult life, Noreen is censured for using 'unladylike language'.[94]

Trauma and Romance

Like the employment of the love triangle in Carty's and Mulloy's novels, romantic conflict is essential to the exploration of trauma in *Noreen*. When Lila's engagement to Bernie is broken off, she proposes to her true love, Derry Donegan. Yet romance is bittersweet. The narrator warns that 'who would have the rose must have the thorn, and who taketh the Lily taketh the Shadow too'.[95] Love is also tainted by sorrow for Noreen. She finally admits to herself that she has fallen in love with Kenneth, Lila's brother, who is on leave due to injury from the British army. Despite her affection for Kenneth – unlike her apathy towards the third vertex in the love triangle, doctor and IRA activist, Fergus O'Hara – Noreen does not pursue the relationship with Kenneth and sacrifices her happiness in order to appease her nationalistic brothers.[96] This decision marks the end of her girlhood, as conveyed through an uncanny moment of self-division as she takes one final glimpse at her youthful self in the mirror:

> She stood awhile at the mirror before changing her clothes [...] Through half-shut eyes she saw herself as she had been when she had been, for the first and only time in her whole life, pretty: took a last, long look at the slim silk-clad ankles, the black-brown, waved, dishevelled hair, the bare arms. No one would ever think her pretty again – not even Kenn, so changed in this one night she was. She was no longer now a girl, but a woman, with her whole life under shadow ...[97]

For Jean-Michel Ganteau and Susana Onega, the 'formal affinity with the romance as a mode' is often evoked 'whenever realism fails to evoke extreme situations'.[98] This may explain the prevalent thematic coupling of romance and civil war. Indeed, one of the earliest civil war novels was IRA veteran Martin T. Henry's *Ambushed Lovers: A Tale of The Troubled Times in Ireland* (1929), which addressed the intra-nationalist struggle through the characters of two sisters whose respective male partners take opposing stances on the treaty.[99] The deflection from civil war to romance can also be observed in a number of autobiographically inflected novels, such as Peadar Ó Dubhda's *Brian* and Éamonn Mac Giolla Iasachta's novel *Toil Dé*.[100] First-hand testimonies, such as the memoirs of Sheila Hartnett (1906–1975), similarly highlight how romance fell victim to the civil war and that 'love letters' were confiscated as dangerous literature by the newly established state.[101] The intense feelings of love and heartache were evidently a powerful vehicle for conveying personal trauma in a society in which emotions were often repressed.

In O'Driscoll's novel, Noreen's termination of her relationship with the British soldier brings the story to its traumatic climax. Noreen's dissociative view of herself in the mirror as a 'pretty' girl who would never again possess such innocence is indicative of the trope of 'splitting' identified in women's writings of trauma; it points to the idea that '[e]xtreme trauma creates a second self [...] It's a form of doubling in the traumatized person.'[102] This heartbreak is followed shortly after by the tragedy of the Rising. Despite her pleas to mobilise with her brothers and her cry 'I wish I was a man!', Noreen stays at home with her brother's reassurance that 'the harder part is yours [...] the greater and better part'.[103] The two brothers are both killed and the novel ends with the image of three women and an old man waiting by the fire 'for the dawn'.[104] The trauma evoked in *Noreen* is associated not only with the death of her brothers in the Rising, but also with her realisation of her subjugated position and the understanding that romantic desire is secondary to that of the nation. The women's figurative resemblance to Ireland is even hinted at in their names: Noreen is affectionately referred to as Dark Nosaleen (a pun on Dark Rosaleen), while Lila's name evokes the symbol of the lily, which was to become a feature of Cumann na mBan campaigns in the coming years. That the surviving characters are left 'waiting for the dawn' again points to the cyclical-linear nature of redemptive republican trauma narratives which defy closure.

O'Driscoll's authorial intent is difficult to ascertain. Was she celebrating her protagonist's sacrifice to the nationalist cause in dedicating the first section of the book to Éamon de Valera? Her writings, like that of many female revolutionaries, point to the problematic relationship between the national cause and that of women. She was a supporter of Fianna Fáil, and her 1935 short story 'The Bean-a-Tighe Looks Back' celebrates the domesticity of rural women and claims that country people were better off than ever before.[105] Yet other writings highlight the difficulties for rural communities in the post-independence period (see Chapter Four) and indeed, O'Driscoll was one of a number of female writers to sign a petition opposing the 1937 Constitution which defined women's place as in the home.[106]

The personal circumstances that inspired the events described in *Noreen* equally remain open to speculation. Does Noreen's escape to Glasgow mirror the author's own getaway to that same city to avoid arrest? How does the tragic death of Con relate to the death of Kelly's older sister, Catherine, who also died at the age of eighteen from bovine tuberculosis? And how did the author relate to the orphaned street girl, Estelle Amy, described in Yeatsian terms as one of the 'children of Reverie'? Estelle's father had died two years previously 'leaving behind him a broken little body that shuddered at his memory'.[107] Does this speak to Kelly's own loss of her father, a sea-captain who was sent to a 'sanatorium usually reserved for perilously ill inmates' on his return from the Great War, only to drown in a shipwreck in March 1922?[108] How does Noreen's mourning for her brothers at the conclusion of *Noreen* relate to the deaths of Kelly's IRA comrades during the civil war?

Perhaps the most direct confrontation with the death of comrades comes in O'Driscoll's later short story 'The Lacklander', published in *Green and Gold* magazine in 1925 and advertised on the cover as a 'great and unique story of the Black and Tan terror'.[109] The story is set in a safe house furnished with rifles, medicine chests, books and a bomb-distillery (reminiscent, perhaps, of 15 Marino Crescent). The protagonist, Maggie, works 'day in, day out [...] for the lads', rolling bandages 'round fractured limbs' and converting dressings into pull-throughs for rifles.[110] As the struggle intensifies, Maggie's comrades are killed one after another. She claims, 'I wish I was dead' and finds that the 'only familiar things' left were 'The Lacklander' and the 'little kettle'.[111] The Lacklander – the nickname for Paul Ormond, who was much-loathed for remaining 'neutral and unmoved' in the midst of the struggle – too, meets his death; it emerges at the story's conclusion that he only refrained from military activity as he had been 'crocked' when carrying dispatches for De Valera. Evoking the same sense of loneliness evident in both the poem 'The Plain People' and in *Noreen*, Maggie emerges as the sole survivor: 'You're the last of them – the old crowd – gone on me – in such a little time. It will be winter now, for me, forever.'[112]

Allen-Randolph asks how did 'a woman writer who inscribed female characters into revolutionary events in her fiction – something the new literature often overlooked – become erased from the national canon?'[113] However, O'Driscoll was just one of a number of female revolutionaries to find expression in fiction and one of a number of revolutionaries to contribute autobiographically informed writings to the short-lived literary journal, *Green and Gold*. Waterford Cumann na mBan activist Teresa Deevy (1894–1963), later a prolific playwright, left little recollections of her revolutionary exploits. Yet her 1924 short story 'Just Yesterday' directly addresses the civil war, as did her first play, *The Reapers*, the script of which has since been lost.[114]

Annie M. P. Smithson: Writing and Revolting

Another contributor to *Green and Gold* was Waterford-based Cumann na mBan activist, Red Cross nurse and novelist Annie M. P. Smithson. Smithson built a writing career on chronicling the revolution, although her works have received little scholarly attention.[115] Though one of the best-selling novelists of the twentieth century, her romance novels have been dismissed, perhaps due to their repetitive plots and predictable religious conversion stories. Moreover, her works are deemed less amenable to feminist readings; recent criticism suggests that Smithson's 'political beliefs did not impinge […] on her writing, nor did her predominantly romantic fiction empathize with female emancipation'.[116] Such dismissals dogged Smithson throughout her career. A review in *An Lóchrann* scoffed at her first novel, *Her Irish Heritage* (1917), lamenting 'is ró-léir gur bean a scríobh' [it is too clear that it was written by a woman].[117] In characteristically pseudomedical language, author Eimar O'Duffy claimed that the characters in Smithson's later novel, *The Walk of a Queen* (1922), lived in a 'state of chronic patriotic hysteria'.[118] Yet the screen of pious romance enabled Smithson to address transgressive topics, such as marital breakdown, the impact of stillbirth (and denial of burial rites by the Catholic Church) and the psychological legacies of revolutionary violence. In fact, discussions of Smithson's novels were known to provoke 'not in front of the child' signals.[119] And while O'Duffy criticised the inflated patriotism of *The Walk of a Queen*, contemporary reviewers remarked on Smithson's representation of women's active roles in the revolution and her insights into 'the life of the girls in digs of lodgings'.[120]

Smithson's body of writings also indicates that women's fiction proved more lucrative than memoir. While Smithson's revolutionary novel *The Walk of a Queen* was a bestseller, she also edited the memoirs of nurse Linda Kearns published that same year under the title *In Times of Peril*. However, the memoir proved a 'hopeless failure' and did not elicit 'a single repeat order'.[121] Her fictional writings were also written with a testimonial aim, particularly the novel *The Marriage of Nurse Harding* (1935), in which she boldly inscribed her experience as a nurse during the Battle of the Four Courts and her subsequent imprisonment.

Indeed, much of Smithson's fiction includes 'portraits of her own life' and is considered by Oonagh Walsh to be a type of 'working-through'.[122] Many of her romance novels include lonely female characters whose isolation is resolved through religious conversion. These themes speak to Smithson's biography: her father, Raynor Smithson, a Protestant barrister, died when she was three years old, leaving her mother almost destitute.[123] After squandering her inheritance, Smithson was required to leave school and fled Dublin to her aunt in London. Estranged from her mother, she abandoned her ambition to be a journalist and was encouraged to pursue a career in nursing, as she was not 'blessed with much in the way of brains'.[124] After training as a nurse, Smithson took up a position in Gilford, County Down, where she fell in love with a married doctor. The breakdown of this relationship had a deep impact on her; a number of her later novels document ill-fated romances between doctors and nurses. Feeling 'not well either in body or in soul', she found solace in Catholicism and converted in 1907.[125] She also developed a strong interest in nationalist politics, which was further motivated by her discovery that her father had supported the Fenians in 1867. By 1916, she was warned by her employers to keep her republican sympathies hidden. Possibly due to her politics, she resigned from her position as a nurse in Dundrum and relocated to Waterford, where she provided nursing training to the local branch of Cumann na mBan.[126]

As a nurse, Smithson had a keen interest in the manifestations of psychic wounds on the body. Her writings reflect strongly on the medical treatments prescribed to the wounded and illustrate evolving conceptions of the psychological wounds of warfare. In an early short story, 'Hills o' Home', an Irish shell-shocked soldier in a London hospital begs a nurse to 'let me talk to you and unburden my mind', despite talking being prohibited among the patients.[127] Smithson was remarkably frank regarding her own bouts of depression; her 1944 autobiography even addressed her contemplation of suicide.[128] She was treated with a number of 'rest cures' – including once in July 1921, when she was advised by Dr Kennedy to leave her nursing position in Waterford 'and return if possible to my native air'.[129] Letters from Mr H. Doak, the editor of Talbot Press, to Smithson in the 1940s also refer to the fact that Smithson had been prescribed 'a rest' by Dr Young. Doak reflects on the docility such treatments demanded, teasing Smithson that she had better not be a 'very rebellious patient'.[130] Smithson also seems to have found solace in a sort of bibliotherapy; for her, reading W. W. Jacob's comic stories helped her to keep her 'reason' 'at a very wretched period'.[131]

If reading was a source of comfort, so, too, was writing. Smithson's first novel, *Her Irish Heritage*, was dedicated to the memory of the rebels of Easter 1916 and was followed by the more autobiographical *By Strange Paths* (1919). Her next novel, *The Walk of a Queen*, was received by her publishers in Talbot Press as the civil war erupted in May 1922.[132] In advance of publication, the press decided to award the novel a 100-guinea prize, which Smithson later spent on provisions for wounded and injured IRA men.[133]

'Lovesick Boys' in *The Walk of a Queen*

Although *The Walk of a Queen* is strongly patriotic, it nevertheless captures a particular historical moment from the perspective of a female revolutionary. That said, as Danae O'Regan outlines, Smithson's novel is less provocative than Rosamond Jacob's (1888–1960) novel *The Troubled House* (1938), which, although written in 1922 or 1923, was not published until much later.[134] Jacob was also a member of Waterford Cumann na mBan and was another contributor to *Green and Gold*. Her novel is set against the backdrop of Bloody Sunday in November 1920 and ends with the accidental killing of a father by his own son. This itself can be read as an evocation of 'father against son' civil war but may also have been informed by Jacob's reading of Freud's *Totem and Taboo* which reflects on patricide.[135] While Jacob's character Kate Ryan is charged with organisational responsibilities for the IRA, Smithson's protagonist, Geraldine Moore, is a health worker (like Smithson) who works as a messenger for the republican movement. Smithson gives the men the prime revolutionary roles, as represented through the characters of twin brothers Desmond and Anthony Ryan, who were interned in Frongoch during the Rising. Jacob is also more willing to reflect on the ethics of violence and highlights the psychological implications of enacting violence through the character of Liam, who is treated with a sort of man-to-man talk therapy after his involvement in the killings of Bloody Sunday.[136] Typical of republican propaganda, Smithson emphasises the lurid violence of the Black and Tans; this is underscored by their willingness to shoot at women and through coded reference to sexual attacks on vulnerable women in rural communities.[137]

While Smithson's novels have been associated with a 'simple, unquestioning belief in the absolute virtues of republicanism and Catholicism',[138] her more conservative outlook may reflect the views of many of her time. Nevertheless, she provides unusual commentary on the nature of women's work and female relationships. Geraldine dismisses 'masculine acts of mere courtesy' and contends it is 'women who are doing the world's work today'.[139] Not unlike the writing of O'Driscoll, the thwarting of gender roles which often accompanies civil conflict leads to the questioning of heterosexual love. In *The Walk of a Queen*, the 'new woman' Jill Devereux – who is introduced from behind a cloud of cigarette smoke, has short, bobbed hair and takes little interest in her appearance – finds herself infatuated by the mysterious French woman (and spy) Yvonne Delauney. She confesses that she feels like 'a lovesick boy' and further contemplates that, 'men, as a sex, seldom appealed, although as intellectual comrades she enjoyed their company'.[140] By the novel's conclusion, however, Jill's 'extremely unconventional' social convictions, agnostic religious views (and, perhaps, sexuality) are resolved: she converts to Catholicism after the apparition of the ghost of Desmond and marries his brother, Anthony.[141] Despite such resolution and conformism, Smithson's conversion narratives provide a means for the novelist to sketch, mostly sympathetically, unconventional, non-conforming characters. Furthermore, as observed elsewhere, conversion narratives may have been a useful narrative template through which traumatic experience becomes 'reconstituting rather than destructive'.[142]

The Walk of a Queen is revealing in terms of the currency of ideas regarding shell shock, psychoanalysis and suggestion/hypnosis during the civil war itself. The husband of Desmond's and Anthony's sister Sheila returns from the war in France with 'shell shock'; he has not been 'really normal since' and resorts to drinking.[143] This sense of heightened stress is not just a concern for male combatants: Geraldine Moore is described as being on 'the verge of a physical and nervous breakdown' due to the anxieties of the conflict and her financial insecurity.[144] IRA activist Dr O'Connor is equipped with the knowledge to ease her condition. Doubting the benefits of taking 'rest' abroad, he treats Geraldine's insomnia with hypnosis: 'Hypnotism – or suggestion – is very removed from nonsense [...] [W]hen used properly it is now recognised by the faculty as of great value in the treatment of many diseases. It is likely in the near future that suggestion and psychoanalysis will largely take the place of drugs.'[145]

These new secular ideas of psychoanalysis were not cut off from spiritual or metaphysical explanations. Smithson shared an interest in the extrasensory, as did many female revolutionaries, including Maud Gonne MacBride and Rosamond Jacob. Smithson's interest in the supernatural did not compromise her religious beliefs, however. The ghost of Desmond appears to Jill and precipitates her conversion to Catholicism. Religion itself prevents madness: it is his 'Catholic faith alone' that keeps Desmond sane before his execution, preventing him 'from putting a revolver to his head'.[146]

While *The Walk of a Queen* is set during the war of independence, it nevertheless speaks to the uncertainties of the split loyalties that had erupted as Smithson completed her manuscript. The novel ends with the marriages of the two female protagonists. However, this sense of happily-ever-after is problematised by fears of impending civil war outlined in the final passage: 'Peace was in Ireland, too, at last, but – for how long? Was the fight over – the battle won? Or must our people again go through the Crucible of suffering and temptation, to come forth from that fiery trial either as worthless dross – or pure gold? The answer – like the future – lies in God's Hands.'[147]

The Walk of a Queen is thus a historical document expressing the looming sense of civil war in real time. As the publishers considered Smithson's manuscript for an award, she was embroiled in the Battle of Dublin. On orders from Cumann na mBan, she was stationed at Moran's Hotel, where she cared for injured men in the midst of some of the more violent fighting witnessed in the city. She was among the last to vacate the hotel, leaving only after a mine had been set off to 'make matters more difficult for the enemy'.[148] Shortly afterwards, she was sent on a Red Cross mission to Mullingar, but on arrival, she was held up at gunpoint and bundled into a van by Free State soldiers. As the van drove victoriously into town, it was fired on by a patrol; the sergeant, James McNamee, was shot dead before Smithson's eyes.[149] It later emerged that the shooters had attacked in a case of friendly fire. Smithson was interned for over a week before being released after threatening hunger strike.

'An Authentic Picture of the Irish Civil War': The Marriage of Nurse Harding

Smithson depicted these events through a very thin veil of fiction in her 1935 novel The Marriage of Nurse Harding. She originally entitled the novel 'To What End?', betraying, perhaps, a sense of disillusion with regard to the outcome of the revolution. However, Doak, her editor, was unconvinced that this was a 'selling title' and coined a more sanitised option, which evoked Mary Augusta Ward's bestselling novel The Marriage of William Ashe (1905).[150] The publishers also played up the novel's tantalising blend of fact and fiction and promoted the book as 'an authentic picture of the tragic events of the Irish Civil War of 1922'.[151] In her later memoir Myself – and Others: An Autobiography (1944), Smithson intertextually directs the reader back to her novel for an account of this period, noting that she had 'described a good deal of that week in my book – The Marriage of Nurse Harding'.[152] As in Peadar O'Donnell's two connected intertextual testimonies of civil war imprisonment – The Knife and The Gates Flew Open – Smithson's retelling speaks both to the lifelong 'imperative to tell' and also expressly challenges conventional understandings of what constitutes testimonial evidence.

For contemporary reviewers of The Marriage of Nurse Harding, the lightly fictionalised sections that detailed the civil war were 'the most interesting part[s] of the book' and 'the strongest, showing first-hand knowledge and observations'.[153] Like Smithson, Nurse Nora Harding finds herself posted as a Red Cross nurse in Doran's Hotel; this was clearly identifiable as Moran's Hotel, which was occupied by the anti-treaty IRA during the Battle for Dublin. Smithson's IRA comrades are given equally flimsy disguises: Dr Bobby Givor is patently Captain Bobby Ievers, then a medical student, and Tom Miley – described 'as belonging to one of the most ultra-Unionist families in Dublin' – is the brother of R. M. Smyllie, later editor of *The Irish Times*.[154] Meanwhile Mullingar becomes the 'fair sized town in the midlands' of 'Margallin'.

On the surface, the tragic tone of the autobiographical account is stronger than in the novel. The civil war is described as the 'terrible time' when 'brother fought against brother' and when 'for the second time within a few years, our city was the scene of war and desolation'.[155] Nevertheless, the autobiography exhibits many of the ambiguities characteristic of women's autobiography. As reflected in the title itself, *Myself – and Others*, Smithson routinely deflects attention from herself – or 'redirects the spotlight'.[156] The male officers on duty with Smithson are all identified in a way that musters them as authenticating witnesses to Smithson's testimony. Smithson also stresses the collective achievements of her female comrades by drawing attention to Tilly Simpson's bravery and suggesting that Kathleen O'Connell, de Valera's long-time secretary, should publish her memoirs.

The novel may offer a more feminist critique than the autobiography. One of the most dramatic incidents relayed by Smithson is the occasion on which all women and prisoners in the Gresham Hotel were ordered to 'leave the building at once' as the Battle of Dublin drew to a close in July 1922.[157] The consternation these orders provoked is recorded in a number of testimonies, including Carty's novel *Legion of the Rearguard*, in which he matter-of-factly recounts that '[p]hysical force was almost needed to make them leave the Gresham'.[158] In her autobiography, Smithson expresses her dismay at the order but ultimately submits to de Valera's authority: 'I felt this order bitterly. Surely as a nurse I should have been allowed to remain! But the order came from the Chief himself – thus in those days did we call de Valera – and was definite and not to be changed.'[159] The fictionalised rendering presents this incident as more humiliating and also emphasises the injustice of gender inequality:

> It came as a thunderclap – hardly could they believe their ears. Never, for one moment, had they anticipated this. They might be shot dead, the building might be set on fire, but that they should be ordered to leave it – to go away *just because they were women*, to be sent out of

the hotel, not be allowed to stay and see the finish – it was beyond belief. They even dared to protest, to detain the harassed adjutant who had come with the order. It was useless. They were to leave – and immediately [my emphasis].[160]

The novel also indirectly draws attention to the mistreatment of the female prisoners; Nora worries during her arrest about how she 'would be treated' and reminisces after their release that the prisoners 'had a nasty' experience and had 'gone through the most unpleasant time'.[161] Nonetheless, Smithson also points to women's roles in reinforcing patriarchal hierarchies: Nora chastises her fellow nurse, Rose O'Daly, for daring to go out with the men when they obtained, sometimes at gunpoint, essential supplies from shopkeepers.

In Smithson's testimonies, traumatic experience is not conveyed through absence or inexpressibility as often emphasised in studies of modernist literature, but rather through augmented narrative detail, supporting neurobiological studies which suggest that emotional stress can enhance and strengthen memory, rather than hindering it.[162] She claims in her autobiography that her civil war memories are 'rather a kaleidoscopic character, a series of moving pictures, passing back and forth before me'.[163] This sensory detail is also evoked in the fictionalised testimony:

> In after years, the events of that evening were more or less blurred in Nora's memory. She remembered sitting on the floor in one of the rooms in that public-house; she sat between two windows from both of which the men were replying to the fire of the enemy, as fast as they could; she was consumed with a terrific thirst and some one gave her a bottle of lemonade, and one of soda water.[164]

The attention to detail is particularly apparent in the descriptions of being held up at gunpoint on the bridge in Mullingar in *Myself – and Others*:

> 'Halt! Halt – or we fire!' Our driver stopped and the van was at once surrounded. 'Get out – put up your hands – well above your head!'
>   Lined up on the bridge, we stood there, hands up, facing a group of men, some in uniform, some not, revolvers in their hands [...] It was not comfortable on the bridge, my arms ached and it was

chilly and dark. I never hear the words, 'I stood on the bridge at midnight,' without seeing again the bridge outside Mullingar town, and the particular individual who was facing me, holding a revolver in a rather shaky hand. I did wish he were not so nervous and would hold the gun in a steadier grip.[165]

This incident is similarly rendered in the earlier fictionalised testimony, *The Marriage of Nurse Harding*:

'Hands up! Put them up! Line up on the bridge there, and be quick about it!'

Nora Harding, standing thus on the bridge hands stretched above her head, arms growing tired, gazed into the face of the man who stood in front of her, revolver in hand. He did not seem too sure as to how it should be held, the hand holding it being decidedly shaky. She wished he did not look so nervous.[166]

In the novel, however, Smithson further develops the emotional consequences of this incident. The fictional narrator returns to the site of trauma at the bridge at 'Margallin' three times, as Nora experiences recurring post-traumatic nightmares: she would 'visit again in her sleep the bridge outside Margallin, and the man with the shaky hand would stand in front of her brandishing his revolver'.[167] A believer that 'the mind affects the body in everyone', Smithson also mobilises the body to articulate trauma: Nora's arms cramp, she suffers 'cold of nervousness' or 'nervous tension' and feels 'decidedly shivery'.[168]

This discussion of the emotional toll of the civil war is less apparent in the autobiography, where Smithson emphasises that the men 'were splendid' and highlights their professionalism by ascertaining that 'there was no hysteria, no loss of self control amongst us'.[169] On the other hand, Nora's tasks include caring for shocked civilians, including a young boy who accidentally finds himself at the heart of the battle and who was 'losing his head entirely'. She speaks to the boy to 'allay his fear', gets him some hot milk and later sends him home 'with two cheery Boy scouts'.[170]

The main difference between the novel and the autobiography is that in *The Marriage of Nurse Harding* the attack on the van causes the deaths of a young republican, Hugh Hewdon, as well as the Free State sergeant.

In line with popular civil war motifs, this tragedy is exacerbated by the fact that Hewdon's father, Major Victor Hewdon, is in the Free State army and gave the order to shoot the approaching vehicle. Smithson's novel thus literally evokes the motif of 'brother against brother, father against son'. Yet overall, the fictionalised testimony deviates little from the straight-up autobiography. Even the language used to describe the death of the Free State sergeant is practically identical:

> He was stone dead, literally riddled by bullets.[171]
> He was stone dead, simply riddled with bullets.[172]

The mask of seemingly artless romance fiction enabled Smithson to testify to her civil war experience almost ten years before she produced her autobiography.

The Ghostly Remnants of Civil War: Dorothy Macardle's *Earth-bound*

While the genre of romance could provide a subterfuge for testimony, the Gothic – a mode of writing characterised by its foreboding environments, ghostly presences and uncanny revelations – became one of the more popular modes in women's writings in the early decades of the Irish Free State.[173] Even Smithson's romance fiction was littered with Gothic and supernatural inflections. The generic conventions of the Gothic were particularly powerful in articulating repressed traumatic experience and juxtaposing confused personal anxieties against 'dominant discourses of order and regulation'.[174] Moreover, the Gothic preoccupation with the memory of the dead was particularly pertinent in the post-First World War context. It was also a mode that resonated with the Irish republican imagination; as Siobhán Kilfeather argues, the formal repetition of Gothic plots was appropriated by Irish writers, dating back to the failed rebellion of 1798, to convey the linear-cyclical conception of republican memory as a history that is always 'repeating itself'.[175] For example, Smithson's short story 'The Guide', follows a demoralised volunteer, Brendan Meehan, fleeing arrest after the 1916 Rising. He goes astray in the Dublin mountains but is led to safety by a 'strange-looking' person with 'longish hair' – who, it emerges, is the ghost of Robert Emmet.[176]

Perhaps more than any woman revolutionary, Dorothy Macardle is known for her use of Gothic forms. The title story of Macardle's 1924 short-story collection, *Earth-bound*, directly mirrors Smithson's 'The Guide': two rebels get lost in the Wicklow mountains after escaping from Mountjoy Gaol but are saved from a search party – or possible death by frostbite – by the ghost of Art O'Neill. O'Neill had died of hypothermia in the same location in 1591 after escaping from Dublin Castle with Aodh Ruadh O'Donnell.

Earth-bound (1924) stands out from popular republican Gothic fables. Not only were the nine stories written *in extremis* during her civil war imprisonment, Macardle also artfully evoked the formal structures of the Gothic to reflect on the cathartic benefits of testimony. A self-described 'unashamed propagandist', Macardle was one of the most significant republican chroniclers of the civil war. She was reared in a prosperous Dundalk business family and joined Cumann na mBan in late 1918 or early 1919. As a professor of English in Alexandra College, she encouraged a number of her pupils, including Mary Manning, to take up writing. Macardle was dismissed from her position, however, after her arrest in November 1922. Following her release in summer 1923, she published a number of propagandist articles in *Éire*, a republican paper published in Glasgow to avoid suppression, and attempted to publish a collection of poetry.[177] *Earth-bound* was reluctantly rejected by Talbot Press, who felt that some of the stories were 'pure genius' and 'better than Daniel Corkery's, who is supposed to be the best short-story writer in Ireland', but feared that there was no market for them.[178] The collection was later published by the Harrigan Press in Worcester, Massachusetts, in 1924 and subsequently self-issued from Countess Markievicz's residence in Frankfort House, Dartry, and published by Emton Press, Dublin.

Macardle's influential account of some of the most contentious atrocities of the civil war, *The Tragedies of Kerry*, also appeared in 1924. In the foreword to that book, Macardle outlined that her aim was to provide an 'infinitesimal fragment of the truth' based on her 'intimate question [*sic*] of witnesses' and that the account consisted of 'clear, indisputable facts [...] without art or artifice, as they were told'.[179] But such denial of 'art or artifice' is complicated by the fact that even Macardle's historical writing relies on the Gothic: in the opening pages of her monumental history of the republican movement, *The Irish Republic* (1937), she renders the Republic as 'an invisible within a visible, an intangible within the tangible State'.[180] These Gothic inflections reflect the wide interest in parapsychology among the revolutionary generation. Macardle joined the Society for Psychical Research (SPR) in 1920 and attended séances, perhaps in an attempt to contact her younger brother, Kenneth, who died in the Somme in 1916.[181] Her later novels further illustrate her interest in the extrasensory and cast doubt on psychoanalysis by indicating that Freud himself had come around to the 'idea of telepathy'.[182]

The importance of collaborative witnessing in the telling of trauma is enacted in the very structure of *Earth-bound*. The nine stories are situated within an overarching frame story of a group of activists sheltering in the 'hospitable studio' of a republican newspaper, the *Tri-Colour*, in Philadelphia.[183] In each story, the latest arrival to the exiles' haven is asked to give testimony of their experience; these include IRA men seeking rehabilitation in America, a Norwegian folklorist, a survivor of hunger strike, a priest, an artist, a domestic servant and the wife of an IRA leader. The visitors sometimes give their testimony towards the end of their stay, emphasising the speaker's need to exteriorise that which has been previously unsaid. This 'imperative to tell' is also accompanied by the need 'to be heard'; Liam Daly confesses that 'there is a story I have to tell – sometime, somewhere', but is only willing to speak 'if you'll listen'.[184] The sympathetic reception of these exercises in truth-telling supports their narration: Nesta McAllister is known for her 'sensitive response to one's precise meaning […] which made the talk grow subtler when she was there'.[185] The translation of these traumatic stories from the repressed unconscious to a coherent sharable story that is received orally by a confirming audience is also linked to the public transmission of these oral stories *in print*. In the story 'The Prisoner', the ghost of the prisoner of 1798 begs his comrade to record and publish his story on his behalf, proclaiming that 'You must tell it [the truth] – it must be remembered; *it must be written down*' (my emphasis).[186] The editors of *Tri-Colour* facilitate the testimony by transcribing and, it can be assumed, publishing it in their paper.

The collection thus reflects on the cathartic potential of truth-telling, the significance of attuned listening and the translation of oral stories to public *written* testimonies in order to contest official memory-making. Yet given such an emphasis on the collective, interpersonal dynamics of testimony, how does *Earth-bound* testify to Macardle's own experience? Like many female revolutionaries, Macardle's published writings are ambiguous regarding her own experience. In her early journalistic writings, her prison experience is often depicted in collective terms,[187] she frequently deflects from her experience to focus on more celebrated female republican activists, her witness statement to the Bureau of Military History is only three pages long, and several of her later prison recollections are overcoloured by nostalgia, glossing over her experience of hunger striking.[188] Her poetry often perpetuates traditionally defined gender roles,[189] while her historical writing, too, claims that 'the history of the Republican army can never be told unless by *men* who fought in it' (my emphasis).[190] However, as Leeann Lane contends, fiction was a 'dissident vehicle of expression' for Macardle.[191]

'On the Verge of Madness': Layers of Testimony

On the surface, at least, the stories in *Earth-bound* reflect very little on Macardle's own prison experience; reviewers could celebrate that '[h]appily only in one of them, the last, is there any allusion to the civil war'.[192] However, Macardle's prison experience 'centrally informs' the collection.[193] That the stories are presented as oral testimonies suggests that they were perhaps first delivered verbally to Macardle's fellow prisoners.[194] The eliciting of testimony within the stories also reflects the place of composition; like in prison, the latest arrivals are invited to testify while their comrades lend a witnessing ear. Moreover, the stories 'The Prisoner' and 'A Story Without an End' contain concealed testimony of aspects of Macardle's own prison experience. This is achieved through a layering, palimpsest approach in which 'surface designs', as feminist literary scholars Sandra Gilbert and Susan Gubar famously argued, 'conceal or obscure deeper, less accessible (and less socially acceptable) levels of meaning'.[195]

'The Prisoner' is the only story that directly deals with incarceration. Considered a 'heroic male narrative of rebellion',[196] it details the anguish and hallucinations of a hunger striker, Liam Daly, in a condemned cell in Kilmainham, who finds solace in the company of a 'young lad with thin, starved features and deep eye-sockets like a skull's'.[197] Redolent of republican Gothic tales, the 'young lad' is in fact a ghost who was condemned to death for his support of the 1798 rebellion. This disruption in temporality evokes the sense of linear displacement associated with traumatic experience: prison is likened to 'a whirlpool' in which time goes 'back again to yesterday and round to today and back to yesterday again.'[198] The prisoner's plight is powerfully conveyed in first-person narration:

> I was in a punishment cell, a 'noisome dungeon' right enough, complete with rats and all, dark always, and dead quiet; none of the others were in that wing. It amounted to solitary confinement, of course, and on hunger-strike that's bad, the trouble is to keep hold of your mind. I think it was about the thirtieth day I began to be afraid – afraid of going queer. It's not a pretty story.[199]

Macardle's story about a male prisoner might suggest, as Gerardine Meaney contends, that she 'could not or would not write of female hunger-strikers'.[200] However, the use of a fictive male narrating subject, like O'Driscoll's use of a (male) pseudonym, could have been exploited as an 'authorizing strategy' in order to 'temper a women's usurpation of public authority'.[201]

Moreover, the gendering of the prisoner as male is complicated by the story's dedication to 'E. C.', most likely Macardle's fellow prisoner Eithne Coyle (1897–1985). Indeed, all of the stories in *Earth-bound* are dedicated to a fellow female revolutionary and their biographical experience often adds an extra layer of meaning to the story.[202] The dedication of 'The Prisoner' to Eithne Coyle was not coincidental. Coyle was known for responding to any injustices with a casual 'why don't we have a hunger strike?' and was purportedly on her seventh strike by November 1923.[203] She was one of the first women to be arrested in the civil war and went on hunger strike in Ballyshannon barracks in September 1922 in protest against being kept in an isolated cell, like 'The Prisoner'.[204] As Coyle recalls, 'I decided if I was kept there much longer that I would be a fit subject for the nearest lunatic asylum.'[205] Margaret Buckley euphemistically insinuates that Coyle's mistreatment may have included a sexual threat, as her 'cell was invaded at all hours of the night by members of a drunken guard, an undisciplined mob, until sheer force of terrible and unchristian conditions compelled her to go on hunger-strike for more human conditions'.[206] The emotional distress described in 'The Prisoner' can thus be read as an act of bearing witness to Coyle's experience of solitary confinement.

But Macardle adds another layer to her narrative to suggest the story could be a reflection on her own experience of hunger striking. 'The

Prisoner' is often assumed, as in the reviewer comments above, to be set during the war of independence. However, on its initial publication, in *Éire* in September 1924, the story carried the title 'The Prisoners: 1798–1923'.[207] This original tagline firmly locates Daly's plight in the context of the civil war. Its omission on the second publication is illustrative of the widespread blurring of historical dates to avoid the more contentious internecine strife. However, in *Earth-bound*, Macardle added the inscription 'Mountjoy/Kilmainham' at the end of the story. This suggests that 'The Prisoner' was composed between Macardle's time in Mountjoy and her time in Kilmainham, which included her week-long hunger strike.[208] As Irina Ruppo Malone observes, this revelation makes 'the readers realize that what they have taken to be a fictional account may in fact be a survival-account of the author's own imprisonment'.[209] Lane, based on her study of Macardle's intimate jail diary, agrees that Macardle 'may have rewritten the story in light of her own involvement in a hunger strike'.[210]

"Tis Better for Me to Tell': Collaborative Witnessing

The final story in *Earth-bound*, 'A Story Without an End', also employs a palimpsestic approach to address the traumatic experience of the female prisoners – and possibly Macardle's own experience. The reserved Nesta McAllister, who has recently fled to Philadelphia, struggles to share her anxieties with the group of attentive exiles. As her face 'had gone white and her eyes wide and dark', her audience suggests that maybe it would be 'better' not 'telling it'.[211] However, Nesta remains convinced of the cathartic benefits of narration: 'No, no – I'll get rid of it – 'tis better for me to tell'.[212] Nesta relates a dream in which she saw four men carrying a dying IRA man on a stretcher into her home. Her first dream is followed by a second, more disturbing, apparition in which her husband is executed in prison:

> There were high stone walls and a dark yard; everything was cold; it was dawn. The yard was full of stones; it was narrow and long; there was a dark hole dug in the earth. There was a man standing near it, against the wall; his hands were behind his back and his eyes were bandaged; there was a bright red mark over his heart. It was Roger; he was going to be killed. Soldiers formed up with rifles and stood covering him. There were nine; I counted them; it was all quite clear.

[…] I heard him shout 'Fire!' and heard the volley, and saw Roger fall, and saw that man go over to him with his revolver and shoot – Oh, it was horrible. I can't.[213]

Nesta hopes that her audience will reassure her that 'the dream could never come true'. However, such a promise is difficult to make, especially when Nesta recounts that her first nightmare came true. Not only that, but the injured man who is brought into her home in her first dream appears as the executioner in the second. The execution party were dressed in 'green uniforms', which, for Nesta, is 'so absurd' 'it couldn't come true'.[214] For the reader, however, the green uniforms clearly refer to the uniform of the Free State army. As Malone contends, it is the reality of the civil war, 'rather than the supernatural, that becomes the source of dread for the reader'.[215]

The palimpsestic effect of the dedication adds further intensity to the story. In this case, the story is dedicated to N. C. – most likely Nora Connolly. Famously, Connolly's father James was placed on a chair before his execution in Kilmainham for his role in the 1916 Rising.[216] Macardle observed in her prison diary that Nora was distressed at being imprisoned in the same location: 'She is struggling out of a nervous breakdown which has hung over her ever since her father was executed in this prison.'[217]

Aside from conjuring up an image of James Connolly's execution, the story is dated 'Mountjoy, December 1922'. This, of course, refers to the executions of Rory O'Connor, Liam Mellows, Joe McKelvey and Richard Barrett on 8 December 1922. The dedication to Nora Connolly reflects her strong ties with Mellows, whom she had helped escape from Reading Gaol in early 1916. She describes the shock of his death in her 1981 memoirs: 'I had just gone out of the house for something, and bought a newspaper and opened it, and saw that Liam had been executed. I nearly died.'[218]

Yet 'A Story Without an End' also draws on Macardle's own experience. Nora Connolly was not in fact imprisoned until after the December 1922 executions. Macardle, however, was interned at this time and captures the impact of the executions in her poem 'Mountjoy':

> How could we bear the death
>   Of noble men in the dawn
> The volley that broke our breath
>   Their lives with the echoes gone;

> But that we knew their blood
> Would cry from the altar-stone
> Till the hearts of the multitude
> Grew as brave as their own?[219]

While the poem evokes the collective ('the volley that broke *our* breath') and is hagiographical in its focus on the republican dead ('brave as their own'), the fictional story offers a more pronounced individual female view of the distress of witnessing execution: Nesta's fears for her husband's safety are at odds with the hope for redemptive male sacrifice in the poem. Moreover, Nesta's account of hearing the execution shots – '*There were nine*; I counted them; it was all quite clear' (my emphasis) – is disguised testimony of the author's own experience. Macardle and her fellow prisoners had been told the executions were to take place and listened to the shots from the women's section of Mountjoy that December morning in 1922. As Peadar O'Donnell recalled in *The Gates Flew Open*, 'Dorothy Macardle has told us of it. They heard the volley and then they heard the single shots which they counted. There were *nine single shots* [...]' (my emphasis).[220]

Dual-marginalisation: Máiréad Ní Ghráda's *An Bheirt Dearbhráthar agus Scéalta Eile*

The Gothic mode employed in *Earth-bound* is central to Macardle's later novels *Uneasy Freehold* (1941), *The Unforeseen* (1946) and *The Dark Enchantment* (1953). Indeed, the Gothic took on increased significance in women's writing in the post-revolutionary period. As Caoilfhionn Ní Bheacháin highlights, members of Cumann na mBan described themselves as 'Ghosts' from 1927, reflecting how 'they understood themselves as ghostly revenants in the public life of the new Free State'.[221]

Máiréad Ní Ghráda was also drawn to Gothic tropes to address the 'unspeakable' legacy of the revolutionary period – and specifically the civil war. Ní Ghráda is widely known for her later plays, including *An Triail* [The Trial] (1964) and *Breithiúnas* [Judgement] (1968); the former addresses the institutionalisation of unmarried mothers, while the latter centres on the posthumous trial by public opinion of the politician Marcas de Grás, who had built his career on spurious reports of his revolutionary exploits. Ní Ghráda's commitment to unveil the societal oppression of women and lay bare the falsified roots of revolutionary commemoration can be traced back to her 1939 short-story collection, *An Bheirt Dearbhráthar agus Scéalta Eile* [The Two Brothers and Other Stories]. To date, this collection of revolutionary stories has received scant critical attention, though not for lack of literary merit. Brian Ó Nualláin, better known as Flann O'Brien, reviewed the collection in *The Irish Times* and averred that Ní Ghráda's stories were 'more successful than many who have bigger names among her contemporaries' on account of the fact that she foregrounded character development over the bare facts of the 'troubled times'.[222] Critic Philip O'Leary, too, considers Ní Ghráda to be 'the most original Gaelic writer of fiction on the war'.[223]

While Ní Ghráda's stories address various episodes during the period 1916–23, her specific focus on the civil war is evident from the motif of brothers divided in the collection's title. The collection also includes a host of metaphors that denote civil war, such as the Cain–Abel motif in 'Cain' [Cain], a father-son killing in 'An Díthreabhach' [The Recluse] and the love triangle in 'An Bheirt Dearbhráthar' [The Two Brothers]. Even though a number of the stories are conformist in their depiction of men and women in traditional military and maternal roles, these more conventional narratives buffer the subversive critique of the construction of mainstream revolutionary remembrance running through the collection. Ní Ghráda's decision to write in Irish – a language that was facing sharp decline in rural Ireland, including in her native Kilmaley, County Clare – also powerfully extends the deployment of Gothic motifs to reflect on the marginalisation of women in the new state.

Ní Ghráda's fiction includes what might be considered testimony of aspects of her own experience. For example, the female protagonist in 'Sos Comhraic' [Truce] is, like the author, a County Clare native who is active in the Gaelic League while studying at university in Dublin. Indeed, Ní Ghráda earned an MA in Irish under the supervision of Douglas Hyde in University College Dublin (UCD). She was later employed as a *timire* [organiser] for Ernest Blythe, who was Minister for Trade and Commerce in the First Dáil from 1919. She served as secretary to Blythe, a supporter of the Anglo-Irish Treaty, throughout the civil war.[224] As Blythe affirmed in his witness statement to the Bureau of Military History, '[she] interviewed any person in town or through the country I could not arrange to meet myself owing to being on the run. She was very good at the job and could be relied on to handle any negotiation very well.'[225] Ní Ghráda's short stories are thus an important addition to the relatively small archive of writings by women who supported the pro-treaty side.[226]

The fictionalised testimony buried in *An Bheirt Dearbhráthar agus Scéalta Eile* is all the more significant given that, like most of the authors discussed, Ní Ghráda's personal papers haven't survived. One of the most insightful sources of information with regards to her revolutionary activism is a 1969 radio interview with Aedín Ní Chaoimh in which Ní Ghráda recalls her involvement in the UCD branch of Cumann na mBan and her imprisonment, along with at least three other women, in November 1919 for 'obstructing thoroughfares' when selling Gaelic League flags on Grafton Street.[227] Not unlike Macardle's nostalgic recollections of imprisonment, Ní Ghráda portrays her time in Mountjoy as a period of excitement: '[D]o thaitin sé liom go seoigh, bhíos óg ag an am agus ba bhreá liom é, an dtuigeann tú, bhuel mar phíosa spóirt a cheapas a bheith sa bpríosún' [Of course I thoroughly enjoyed it, I was young at the time and I loved it, you know, well I thought it was a bit of fun to be in prison].[228]

Ní Ghráda was known for her 'disarming modesty'[229] and contemporary newspaper reports imply that the flag sellers were more militant than Ní Ghráda's interview might suggest. The women were initially held due to their refusal to give their names or addresses in English, were imprisoned because they refused to pay a fine of 5s each and would not accept packages that were not addressed in Irish.[230] Three of the flag sellers (who are not named in the newspapers) caused havoc by smashing windows and mugs in Chancery Police Station. These three women also ate grapes, read books and laughed amongst themselves during court proceedings. As they left the dock, they shouted 'Up the Republic[!]' 'Up de Valera[!]'.[231]

Whatever excitement Ní Ghráda felt during her imprisonment, her short stories suggest that her hopes for the new state had dwindled by the end of the 1930s. Despite earning a reputation as the first female radio announcer in Ireland or Britain for 2RN radio service, Ní Ghráda was expected to retire from her position in May 1935 in accordance with Fianna Fáil's institutionalisation of the marriage bar in order to create positions for male civil servants who had been dismissed on political grounds. Ironically, it seems that Ní Ghráda's husband, Richard Kissane, was reinstated on the condition that his wife resigned.[232] Richard had been in the Free State civic guard and supported the pro-treaty government during the Curragh mutiny, but many of his family was on the republican side and his brother, Éamonn, became a Fianna Fáil TD and was later parliamentary secretary to de Valera.[233] The 'brother against brother' motif at the centre of *An Bheirt Dearbhráthar agus Scéalta Eile* was not far removed, then, from Ní Ghráda's personal circumstances. Her history book for school children, *A Primary History of Ireland* (1966), suggests that the events of 1922–3 had a strong impact on her. She describes the 'disastrous Civil War' as the 'saddest thing in the history of our country', lamenting that '[m]en, who for years had fought as comrades, now turned their guns against each other.'[234]

An Bheirt Dearbhráthar agus Scéalta Eile was not Ní Ghráda's only attempt to document the revolution in fiction. She also wrote a play *Stailc Ocrais* [Hunger Strike] based on Frank Gallagher's hunger strike journal *Days of Fear* (1928). However, it seems that the play was rejected by the Abbey Theatre in 1939. It wasn't produced until over twenty years later, in 1962.[235] Although *Stailc Ocrais* is an adaptation of a male combatant's diary, writing about the psychological turmoil of hunger striking, as in Macardle's 'The Prisoner', offered an alternative to heroic representations of IRA guerrilla fighters. Ní Ghráda also added a distinct female dimension in her adaptation of Gallagher's diary; she replaced the prisoner's father with the mother as a key character and included a choir of female voices in the play, reflecting the nightly vigils outside the gates of Mountjoy during such strikes.

This was indeed an environment that Ní Ghráda was familiar with from her brief imprisonment: Ní Ghráda thus selected and re-adapted a male-authored text – and indeed, listed 'Proinnsias Ó Gallchobhair' as a co-author – in order tease out an experience close to her own heart. While Ní Ghráda may have cited Gallagher as a co-author in order to credit his composition of the original text, the disguise of a male co-author may have also offered a convenient protective shield. Indeed, the Abbey Theatre had already returned another of her plays in 1936 – the English-language *Brothers* by 'Máiréad Kissane'.[236] Although the manuscript of *Brothers* is not extant, the title is reminiscent of her short-story collection. Furthermore, though Gallagher's authorship is credited in a number of sources, Tomás Mac Anna, who produced the play when it was finally staged in 1962, insisted in a later interview that Ní Ghráda was the true author of *Stailc Ocrais*.[237]

'[Ní] Raibh ina Chuid Cainte ach Gliogar' [His Talk was All Blather]: Dismantling Revolutionary Remembrance

Despite difficulties in producing her stage works, Ní Ghráda was successful in publishing her short stories in Irish. Some of these appeared in the Capuchin journal *Bonaventura* and were then published as a collection by government publisher Oifig an tSoláthair. Following the stock Gothic motif, a number of the stories relate to city visitors who venture out into the desolate and recalcitrant territories of rural Clare in the early 1930s. There they are faced with lingering material evidence of the revolution: there are bloodstains on the floor of an abandoned house, a local barfly bears a scar on his forehead, and a ghostly figure, likened to the supernatural figure of Erlkönig in German folklore, haunts the landscape. The ghost, it transpires, is actually a father who has refused to speak a word since he unintentionally shot his son, an anti-treaty activist, while serving in the Free State army. Like Macardle's *Earth-bound*, many of the stories contain frame stories, or stories within stories, as the city visitors elicit testimony from locals about the tragic events of the revolutionary period.

This emphasis on orality arguably tapped into an Irish-language market for folklore-based writings; Ní Ghráda's earlier short-story collection for children, *An Giolla Deacair agus Scéalta Eile* [The Troublesome Lad and Other Stories] (1936) carried the subtitle 'Máiréad Ní Ghráda do scríobh, ar lorg na sean-scéal' [written by Máiréad Ní Ghráda, based on old tales]. But these Gothic tropes also allowed Ní Ghráda to destabilise what is narratively understood as real and thus mount a powerful critique of the now-established revolutionary narrative. In the title story of *An Bheirt Dearbhráthar agus Scéalta Eile*, a visiting Dublin-based public works civil servant is unnerved by his surroundings and particularly by his discovery of a haunted house. He learns from his hostess that the house was the location of the killing of IRA activist Seán Mac Cárrthaigh by the Black and Tans. Seán's own brother, Roibeard, had informed on him after finding Seán in the company of Roibeard's young bride-to-be, Hélen. Ní Ghráda is particularly interested in the present-day consequences of this fallout: at the end of story, the civil servant asks his hostess what happened to the mythical 'Hélen' 'gur deineadh ár agus argain agus dortadh fola le grá di' [for love of whom slaughter, plunder and bloodshed was committed]. It emerges that 'Hélen an Chláir' [Helen of Clare] is in fact Neilí, the maid, who was serving him in the guest house.[238] This first story not only reflects the lingering psychological legacies of war, it also hints at the urban civil service's lack of understanding of the needs of rural Ireland, while also artfully dismantling the reduction of women to symbolic significance in much revolutionary remembrance.

Not all the stories contain such feminist commentary. Some of the characters comply with stereotypical representations of Irish mothers as they patriotically send their sons out to fight.[239] But Ní Ghráda suggests that compliance with these Mother Ireland tropes is performative. In 'Máthair an tSaighdiúra' [The Soldier's Mother], the eponymous mother is mute and motionless when she is informed by a troop of soldiers that her son has died in the service of the Free State army. This story was criticised in a review by C. Ó. N. (Ciarán Ó Nualláin) for its lack of emotional depth: 'ní mór na dinn-mhothuigheacha [sic] atá ar obair a nochtadh ar dhóigh éigin a bhogfhas croídhe an léightheora' [you must reveal the deep feelings in a way that will move the reader's heart].[240] However, in this case, the mother's composure is strategic. When the soldiers come to her door, she is hiding the young IRA man responsible for her own son's death; she breaks her silence only to protect the young man she is harbouring. The mother's performed public stoicism is undercut at the story's conclusion as her keening echoes through the glen. The mother's keening also furthers the Gothic emphasis on suppressed anxieties by underscoring the capacity of the oral Gaelic tradition to articulate intense concealed emotions and to challenge dominant social order.

The story 'An tOifigeach' [The Officer] more clearly addresses the dangers of the romanticisation of maternal sacrifice. A tellingly unnamed widow harbours her son and his flying column during the war of independence. Ní Ghráda documents the many tasks the mother dutifully fulfils, from soothing the men back to sleep when they are disturbed by nightmares, to waking them up as they make for an ambush in Kilmichael, to preparing them a breakfast of duck eggs, sliced bread and tea.[241] The mother masterfully conceals her distress throughout: 'Níor dhóigh le héinne a bheadh ag éisteacht léi go raibh aon ualach ar a haigne' [No one listening to her would have ever suspected that there was any burden on her mind].[242] After the civil war ends, she travels to the city to surprise her son, who is now a high-ranking officer in the Free State army. She also needs to seek financial support from him in order to evade eviction. On her arrival at the barracks, however, she is greeted curtly by a young soldier on guard. When she pushes open the door of her son's office, she finds him infatuated by a finely dressed young lady. The expensive jewellery of the female civil servants is juxtaposed with the mother's dishevelled attire, as she wears a 'hata de'n tsean-dhéanamh a bhí fíorsceochach' [an old-style hat full of brambles].[243] Sensing her son's shame, the mother turns on her heel and makes the long journey home again. There is little ambiguity here: the institutions of the newly conceived state, from which Ní Ghráda herself had recently been expelled, is a hostile place for those women who 'sacrificed' so much for 'the cause'. Such critique is all the more ironic given that An Bheirt Dearbhráthar agus Scéalta Eile was published by the government publication office.

Ní Ghráda's collection strategically foregrounds a number of 'heroic' male revolutionaries, such as the appropriately named Seán Ó Laochdha (whose surname evokes the word 'laoch' [hero]), who, along with his IRA comrades, selflessly places himself 'i mbeárnain an baoghail' [in the line of fire].[244] However, this conformity to the patriarchal nationalist narrative is matched by subversion. Ní Ghráda's main interest is in the men who suffered due to the many 'unacknowledged civil wars' of the revolutionary period. One story explores the distress of a man mistakenly identified as a spy by the nationalist movement, another addresses the tragedy of a man whose alcohol addiction led him to spy on the IRA and finally take his own life. The story 'An tSochraid' [The Funeral] offers an intimate psychological portrait of an RIC officer attending the funeral of one of his colleagues. He contemplates leaving the service but is worried about the shame he would bring on his impoverished Armagh Protestant family. The collection also implies violence against women: a returned emigrant businessman defends a young woman who is fleeing from a drunken British soldier, her unravelled clothing perhaps hinting at her sexual vulnerability.[245]

Ní Ghráda further exploits the ironic narrative strategies of the Gothic mode through her inclusion of fraudulent narrators. In 'Cain' [Cain], the narrator's poignant account of heroically shooting his brother to save him from a certain death at the hands of the Black and Tans is revealed to be no more than a figment of his whiskey-fuelled imagination.[246] The testimony in 'Airgead i bhFolach' [Hidden Money] is also undermined, as the narrator speculates 'ná raibh ina chuid cainte ach gliogar' [that his talk was all blather].[247] Ní Ghráda thus casts doubt on the reliability of narrative itself and, in doing so, troubles the heroic narrative of the 'fight for Irish freedom'. This vigorous critique of revolutionary commemoration was extended in her 1968 play *Breithiúnas*, in which the lead character, an assassinated politician, reflects on the fact that his entire political career was based on falsified reports of his exploits as an IRA activist. Ní Ghráda's fiction thus offered an alternative perspective to her historical educational writings advertised as providing insight into 'the *lives of men* who served high ideals' (my emphasis).[248]

Máirín Cregan's *Hunger-strike: A Play in Two Acts*: 'Torture of Mind' on the Domestic Battlefront

While Ní Ghráda's play *An Triail* (1964) is highly regarded, she was well known as a children's writer to the extent that *An Bheirt Dearbhráthar agus Scéalta Eile* has not only eluded scholarly attention, it has also been miscatalogued as a children's book.[249] The strong association of women writers with children's fiction is also a feature of Máirín Cregan's literary career. Cregan was once internationally regarded for her children's books, including *Old John* (1936) and *Rathina* (1942) but, as Susan Cahill writes, 'she is now an unknown figure; her children's literature is forgotten, and her significance has not yet been analysed'.[250] Cahill views Cregan's children's literature as an extension of Fianna Fáil 'agricultural politics' in that she promulgates 'strategic constructions of Ireland, which insist upon a rural, self-sufficient nation populated with "clear-eyed, happy-hearted children"'.[251] However, her works include two highly political plays for adults: *Curlew's Call* (1940), which deals with female emigration (discussed in Chapter Four), and *Hunger-strike: A Play in Two Acts* (1932).

Hunger-strike perhaps offers the most direct testimony of the psychological implications of civil war from the pen of a female revolutionary. The play outlines the emotional breakdown of a young woman, Nano Grady, whose husband Ned is one of some 7,000 republican prisoners to participate in the mass hunger strike of October 1923. The dedication of the play, 'To Jim, With my Love', indicates the play's autobiographical nature given that Cregan's husband, Wexford Fianna Fáil TD Dr James Ryan, participated in the strike and was reported on his thirtieth day to be 'in a precarious condition.'[252] Cregan, too, played an active role in the revolution. She transported 'a violin case full of automatics and ammunition' to Kerry in the lead-up to the Rising.[253] This resulted in her dismissal from her post as a teacher; she later joined Cumann na mBan.[254] She was separated from her eight-month-old baby in February 1921 when she was interned in Wexford Jail for refusing to display a poster which read 'God Save the King' in the window of her home. After her release, she went 'on the run' to Dublin where she worked in the Department of Foreign Affairs and delivered dispatches to London and Paris. Her statement to the Bureau of Military History concludes with the line: 'When the Four Courts was attacked I joined up with Irish republican forces and left Foreign Affairs.'[255] While she gives no further details to the Bureau, she 'acted continuously' in support of the republican side from June 1922 and even delivered messages to Geneva, Berlin, London, Paris and Rome.[256]

Cregan's play is somewhat at odds with her own experience. The fictional protagonist is not engaged in military activities but rather experiences the civil war from a distance as a housewife in a rural farmhouse. Nevertheless, the play demonstrates a confident authorial voice less evident in Cregan's non-fictional writings. Indeed, she wrote a third-person account of her journey to Tralee in the lead-up to 1916 in which she refers to herself as 'a young girl'.[257] She often mediated men's accounts of the revolution, as evident in a 'thrilling story' detailing her husband's 1916 experience, a radio talk on the life of Seán Mac Diarmada and a sketch of James Connolly.[258] Cregan's statement to the Bureau of Military History, which was collected by Sinéad Ní Chiosáin, Ní Ghráda's sister-in-law, gives a detailed factual description of her pre-civil war activities, but interestingly enough, Cregan added a number of appendices to her witness statement, including newspaper cut-outs, as though she needed to prove the veracity of her account. Cregan was one of just a handful of women interviewed by IRA intellectual Ernie O'Malley. While this interview provides important insight into her civil war diplomatic exploits, Cregan was interviewed alongside her husband and her interview is less formalised, therefore, than many of O'Malley's one-on-one interviews with male veterans.[259] For all the apparent conformism of *Hunger-strike*, the fictional surrogate of Nano offers a far more intimate portrayal of the implications of the author's revolutionary experience than conventional autobiography allowed.

'Placing in her Proper Setting and Due Prominence the Irish Woman, the Irish Wife and the Irish Mother'

If the 'imperative to tell' is accompanied by the need to find a 'confirming' readership, Cregan's play is a prime example of the difficulties experienced by women in sharing their testimonies. *Hunger-strike* was submitted to the Abbey Theatre in 1931 but was considered 'unsuitable' 'for various reasons'.[260] Dublin publishers M. H. Gill and Sons offered to publish the play at the author's expense for £26.5.0.[261] The initial response to its publication was less than positive. The publishers lamented that the play was 'too true to realities' and, as a result, 'it has fallen desperately flat so far, and the unfortunate hunger strike recently has put the tin hat on it properly'.[262] The *Standard* refused to print a review given the 'theologically debatable' theme.[263] Perhaps Cregan's play was too direct; she didn't hide behind a male pseudonym or adopt 'safe' narrative modes like the other female revolutionaries discussed in this chapter. As Francis Carty's brother, James, advised her, 'if it was translated from some Scandinavian language they [the Abbey] would find no fault with it'.[264]

Cregan's emphasis on Nano Grady's struggle to keep herself 'from going mad' as she supports her husband Ned's strike also prompted a variety of responses.[265] The renowned literary critic, Daniel Corkery, admitted that 'many parts of it [the play] are quite perfect'. Interestingly, however, he recommended to Cregan that she add a third act in which Ned appears on stage 'reconciled and prepared to carry on'.[266] Such advice indicates a certain resistance to Cregan's foregrounding of the female protagonist and her divergence from more heroic depictions of the conflict. Nevertheless, contemporary reviews focused on the conformist aspects of the play. One reviewer bizarrely noted in *Dublin Magazine* that Nano's husband's character 'is clearly defined', although, the reviewer adds, 'he does not appear on the stage'.[267] More telling still is a review in the *Catholic Bulletin* which praised the play for 'placing in her proper setting and due prominence the Irish woman, the Irish wife and the Irish mother in the particular phase of the struggle for Irish Freedom'.[268]

Public Stoicism vs Private Suffering

At the opening, Nano does indeed embody the values of stoicism and composure popularly associated with republican women. She supports her husband on his hunger strike, hoping 'he'll be let die in peace'.[269] As the play progresses, however, the conflict between her public stoicism and private suffering becomes apparent. Nano lets down her cover in the presence of her old Fenian neighbour, Davy Lucey, and struggles to articulate her personal doubts about the strike: 'I don't know if – if I want Ned to hold out – if –'.[270] She cannot sleep and is overwhelmed by the guilt she feels for encouraging others to 'lend a hand and fight':

> Last night I dreamt (*She looks fixedly at something before her*) – I dreamt I saw Ned lying on an old torn mattress on the floor of a stable and that I had my two hands on his throat, choking him. I could see his face getting purple and eyes bulging, and he kept crying to me, 'What are you killing me for? What are you killing me for?' and I kept laughing and saying, 'For fun.'[271]

Nano's nightmarish representation speaks to contemporary depictions of female republicans who, in pro-treatyite writer P. S. O'Hegarty's words, were 'practically unsexed, their mother's milk blackened to make gunpowder, their minds working on nothing save hate and blood'.[272] Nano's confused sense of guilt is compounded by the juxtaposition of her disturbing night terrors with the more benevolent dream of her young son who 'was dreaming daddy came home'.[273] The divisions between Nano's public stoicism, her private suffering and her nightmarish evil self further exemplify the use of the split personality trope, evident in *Noreen*, to indicate psychological injury and, in the context of women's writings, perhaps, to hint at the emotional repression demanded of women in a patriarchal society.[274] Nano's nightmares also highlight a psychological complexity obliterated by official constructions of maternal sacrifice and even point to how female revolutionaries may have internalised the widespread negative stereotyping of republican women in popular discourse.

The domestic implications of civil war splits are illustrated through the clashes between Nano and her fur-clothed aunt Julia, who exerts enormous pressure on her to convince her husband to come off the strike. Julia even suggests that her husband, in his derangement, may wonder if she had thoughts for another man. As Nano notes in an aside, 'Nobody in the world can ever be half as cruel to you as your own relations.'[275] Nano's distress has a physical impact and, like her husband on strike, she grows emaciated in her worry, becoming 'paler and thinner, her face expressionless'.[276] Like the ghostly presences in Macardle's and Ní Ghráda's fiction, Nano is reduced to a phantasm and walks up the stairs 'like a ghost'.[277]

Cregan makes subtle reference to women's activism throughout: Nano wishes to escape from her domestic base and her family disparage her Cumann na mBan activism.[278] Davy also calls attention to the oft-forgotten female strikers, commenting that some of them were 'only slips of girls'.[279] This is all the more pertinent given that Nell Ryan, Cregan's sister-in-law, survived a thirty-four-day strike in April 1923.[280] The domestic divisions in the play would also have resonated with readers in light of the fact that the Ryan family, which was at the centre of a Dublin 'network of radicals', famously split over the treaty.[281] Min Ryan was married to Free State Minister for Defence Richard Mulcahy, who oversaw the internment of a number of the Ryan siblings. Kit Ryan tried to convince her sister to leave her husband,[282] suggesting that the clashes in the play between Nano and Aunt Julia may be more sanitised than the realities.

The play concludes with the announcement that Ned has discontinued the strike. While on the one hand Nano laments 'we're beaten again', there is a sense that the certainty of death would bring as much relief as the unknowability of survival. Just before the curtain closes, Nano privately reads out a telegram from Ned: 'All men off strike. *Suspend – your – judgement – for the – present.* Writing to-night. – Ned' (my emphasis).[283] The fact that Ned assumes Nano would be disappointed by his failure to become a martyr hints at the gulf between them. While the published play opens with a dedication to Cregan's husband Jim, the dialogue concludes as Nano calls for her Fenian neighbour, who proves a more comforting figure than the absent hunger striker:

> (*She puts her hand to her head.*) I wish my head would stop buzzing. (*She takes a few steps in front of table and suddenly clutches it*). I think I must be getting weak. (*She sways and makes as if to lie on table. Raising her voice*): Davy! Da-a-a-avy. (*She swoons.*)
>
> (CURTAIN)[284]

There is no respite for Nano. Davy symbolically tells her that the struggle will continue, as, 'though the cow is dead itself, she has left after her the finest red heifer calf we had yet'.[285] This ambiguous ending suggests that Nano's individual suffering risks being consumed by the continued public struggle of anti-treaty republicans within the newly founded state. While Mary McWhorter recalls meeting Cregan in 1922 and claimed that she had 'the happy faculty of making fun out of tragedy',[286] messages smuggled out from the Battle of the Four Courts from her husband, Jim, resonate with the emotional turmoil that the fictional husband's telegrams evoke. In one note, written as the Four Courts were under siege, Jim reassured her, 'Don't mind the big guns, they are harmless to us.'[287]

'[It] Gave Me a Tremendous Thrill': A Confirming Audience

Hunger-strike's only national performance, it seems, was on Radio Athlone in May 1936.[288] Tomás Ó Maoláin, who himself participated in a forty-one-day fast in Mountjoy in 1923, was particularly affected by the play, highlighting how such testimonies resonated with those who had had similar experiences. Writing to the author, Ó Maoláin contended that 'the dramatic atmosphere which you were so successful in creating was true to life and gave me a tremendous thrill. My father, who listened in with me and who went through all the torture of mind so well portrayed by Nano, was very much affected by the realism of the production.'[289]

There were other attempts to stage the play. Mary Manning – who decried the erasure from the official historical narrative of the 'quiet people who went on living and eating and laughing and sleeping or trying to sleep' – expressed an interest in producing Cregan's play in 1933 with a group of players associated with the Irish Women Workers' Union.[290] However, there is no indication that it was ever produced. Just a year later, Manning emigrated to Boston, where she remained for the rest of her life. The large-scale emigration that characterised Ireland in the 1920s and 1930s – particularly the high levels of female emigration – thus further obscured the experience of female activists from revolutionary remembrance.

Conclusion

Margaret Buckley's prison memoir, *The Jangle of the Keys*, appeared in print in 1938, offering the first full-length, first-person account of women's civil war internment. However, by the time her memoir was published, women activists had already documented their civil war experience in testimonial fiction. Despite production and publication challenges, fiction not only attracted a wider readership, it also seems to have offered more narrative freedom than conventional first-person testimonies. While fiction could be a constraining genre for women, given the widespread stereotyping of female revolutionaries in men's fiction (see Chapter Three), it nevertheless allowed women to take ownership of wartime trauma and illustrate both how women engaged directly with military activity and how war invaded domestic life.

The fictionalised testimonies of female revolutionaries directly challenged efforts to forget the civil war and the sidelining of women's activism during this period. Their writings also challenge conventional understandings of wartime trauma as associated with sudden, catastrophic blows and illustrate the everyday social traumas omitted from heroic commemorations. Their testimonies reflect developing medical discourses regarding psychic trauma and hint at the medicalisation of women's 'nervous conditions' as a means by which to further suppress female expression. Their writings also underscore the psychological complexities of women's responses to war and thwart simplistic constructions of women as passive victims by drawing attention to women's regulation of other women's behaviour and by conjuring up images of female perpetration (see Chapter Five).

Access to language was a constant problem for these women. They felt a stronger need than their male comrades to hide behind protective narrative masks, as evident in the use of male pseudonyms, male-authorising masks, the retreat to gothic and romance modes, and the exploitation of the protection offered by the Irish language. However, subversion in their writings is almost always balanced by conformism. As much as these female revolutionaries pushed boundaries and claimed ownership of the civil war in fiction, their projects of remembrance are full of contradictions. Female revolutionaries could cast doubt on the developing masculine discourse of war in fiction while simultaneously consolidating and mediating that same hero narrative in school textbooks, history books and biographical sketches.

Publicly sharing private stories was understood as a means through which to exorcise difficult memories. Nevertheless, as in the previous chapter, these testimonies do not suggest a straightforward connection between recounting traumatic events and personal healing. Unlike the male revolutionaries discussed in Chapter One who revisited their revolutionary experience throughout their lives, female revolutionaries tended to move away (or, indeed, were pushed away) from political subjects during their writing careers. While there is a visible difference between Mulloy's grisly realist novel *Jackets Green* and the more redemptive narratives of stridently anti-treaty writers, there is less of a contrast between Ní Ghráda's fiction and that of her anti-treaty counterparts, suggesting that the question of gender, by the 1930s, could transcend civil war allegiances.

There are many more women whose autobiographically based fictional writing merits inclusion in studies of the Irish revolution. The subsequent chapters will address the testimonies of both men and women: the remarkable testimonial writings of female emigrants Eilish Dolan (also known as Eily O'Horan and Elizabeth Brennan) and Kathleen Hoagland will be addressed in Chapter Four, while women's perspectives on the implications of perpetrating revolutionary violence will be addressed in Chapter Five, with particular mention of the writings of Úna Bean Uí Dhiosca, Margaret Barrington, Rosamond Jacob and Elizabeth Connor (the pen name of Úna Troy).

Despite the creative deployment of self-protective narrative strategies by female authors to point to the psychological toll of civil war, there were, nevertheless, certain aspects of revolutionary experience that were more contentious. The following chapter will consider one such aspect, namely testimonies of gender-based and sexual violence.

Chapter Three

Hidden in Plain Sight: Witnesses to Sexual Violence

The testimonies in the previous chapters illustrate the strategies employed by veterans of the civil war to insert private, often painful, experience into the public realm in spite of reticence at official level. While these testimonies demonstrate the 'imperative to tell' shared by those who have experienced traumatic events, telling was always accompanied by the need to conceal. The taboos surrounding sexual trauma in 1920s Ireland, in particular, complicated any full disclosure. As Lindsey Earner-Byrne outlines in her microstudy of sexual violence in the civil war, the reporting of rape was hindered, firstly by 'the fear of not being believed' and secondly by 'the contemporary conviction that a woman was contaminated by rape'.[1] The foundation of the Irish Free State was accompanied by the reification of (hetero)normative gender norms and the promotion of repressive social conventions, according to which sexual relations outside marriage were regarded as immoral and even punishable. The stress on patriarchal gender and sexual norms in post-independence Ireland is arguably reflected in the reluctance to address psychological trauma among veterans of the revolution, as explored in previous chapters. 'Nervous' male veterans threatened the foregrounded image of the unblemished, heroic freedom fighter, while psychic injury among female revolutionaries could be concealed by branding them as 'unmanageable' 'Amazons', whose social transgression was indicative of some sort of psychosexual disorder.[2]

The issue of sexual trauma during the Irish revolution and civil war has generated vibrant scholarship in recent times.[3] The extent of rape and sexual violence remains a moot point, however. For Marie Coleman and Gemma Clark, (systematic) sexual violence was 'rare' and 'relative[ly] [scarce]' in comparison to other twentieth-century European conflicts, while Linda Connolly has been central in advocating for further understanding of this 'hidden' and 'forgotten' war crime.[4]

This chapter does not seek to grapple with the complexities of quantifying sexual violence as either 'rare', 'widespread' or 'relatively scarce'. Rather, it complicates the belief that such violence 'disappeared from public discourse for decades after the Civil War' and must, therefore, be recovered from 'emerging stories and evidence' in 'newly accessible' files.[5] Recent historiography of the Irish revolution has indeed been strongly informed by an emphasis on 'newly released archival material' and 'completely new sources' – largely thanks to material being published online from the Bureau of Military History and Military Service Pensions Collection.[6] While this rich archive of state and military documentation has transformed understanding of the revolutionary period, such strong focus on 'new' sources has occluded earlier underappreciated material. Moreover, the historical and popular emphasis on emerging source material is indicative of what Guy Beiner refers to as 'the popular appeal of quasi-psychoanalytical models in which a traumatic event is considered, by definition, to be unspeakable until it resurfaces at a much later date'.[7]

By focusing instead on representations of sexualised violence in testimonies by veterans, this chapter first outlines the challenges of testifying to sexual violence first-hand and, second, addresses representations of sexual transgression and violation in published fictionalised writings by veterans themselves. Despite the prevailing emphasis on the 'Catholic culture of self-abnegation' that accompanied the foundation of the new state,[8] popular autobiographically informed fiction did not shy away from questions of sexuality. Moreover, the distinction between consensual and non-consensual sexual intimacy is repeatedly blurred: fictionalised accounts of the revolutionary period are peppered with descriptions of gender-based and sexual violence, including implied and explicit representations of hair shearing, sexual humiliations (including stripping and naked public exposure), gender-specific torture, rape and domestic violence (for discussion of domestic violence see Chapters Four and Five). While many of these writings are male-authored and document violence against women, fictionalised testimonies also point to the sexualised humiliation of men and resultant psychological trauma. The supposedly hidden crime of sexual violence in fact proliferated in literary narratives in the decades immediately after the civil war.

The study of such popular narratives is as necessary as any archival study of pension applications, compensation claims or court proceedings – particularly in the context of sexual violence. As Shani D'Cruze outlines, the 'historical study of this topic (perhaps more than most others) is necessarily a discourse on and around the surviving evidences, not an unmediated description of "what happened".[9] While careful to distinguish representations of sexual violence from actual occurrences, the prevalence of sexual violence in popular literature nevertheless raises questions regarding the connection between representations of sexual violence and the social reality. As Sabine Sielke argues in her historical study of the rhetoric of rape, 'cultural literacy' determines 'the signifying power of real rape'.[10] Jody Freeman similarly claims that both legal and literary representations of rape 'draw on and produce images that are already prevalent; they are part of what might be called the existing representational economy'.[11] Popular narratives of sexual violence should thus be understood in the context of the wider economy of legal, political and cultural representations; these discourses acted as 'gatekeepers' that regulated the reporting of actual sexual assault.[12]

Unlike the two previous chapters which underscore the strength of veterans' urges to testify, few of the writings in this chapter detail sexual violence first-hand; rather, narratives of sexual trauma – whether female- or male-authored – tend to 'bear witness' to the 'pain of others'. As explored by scholars such as Sorcha Gunne, Zoe Brigley Thompson, Lynn A. Higgins, Brenda R. Silver and others, this ventriloquism raises a host of questions regarding the ethics of 'telling' and 'reading' sexual violence.[13] Problematic blurred boundaries emerge between the real and the imagined, between testifying and eroticising, between reading and engaging in voyeurism. Furthermore, this chapter considers the possibility that narrative, as much as it may open debate and aid the abreaction of traumatic experience, can also perpetuate a culture of sexual violence and, through graphic depiction, even enact a further (textual) violation.

Women's Testimonies of Sexual Violence

The lack of first-hand testimonies of sexual violence during the Irish revolution does not mean that such attacks did not occur. The contentiousness of sexual violence meant that allusions to such assaults were usually shrouded in euphemisms: women were 'roughly handled', 'taken away' or 'outraged'.[14] The damage that sexual relations outside marriage posed to a woman's reputation is inferred in the memoirs of Free State soldier and Liverpool native John Pinkman. Pinkman could quickly silence a young woman who was courting an IRA man by threatening to 'tell everyone downstairs that you've had a fellow in bed with you'.[15] Regardless of whether relations were consensual or not, women could be held responsible for men's sexual behaviour. Cumann na mBan activist Kathleen Behan (née Kearney), for example, refers in her memoirs to the 'man who'd tried to rape me'. When she told her mother-in-law of this assault, she was told that she 'must have encouraged him'.[16]

The tendency to view women as 'tainted witnesses' – as evident in Behan's account and as explored in Chapter Two – is not only apparent in contemporary responses. It is also a default position evident in more recent scholarship. In a 2000 article, Louise Ryan drew attention to a number of explicit first-hand testimonies of sexual assault that were published in the republican gazette, the *Irish Bulletin*, in 1921. These include Mary Kelly's testimony of being assaulted by Crown forces during a raid on her family home in Enniscorthy, County Wexford; Nellie O'Mahony's testimony of being sexually assaulted in her home at Knockduff, Dunmanway, County Cork; and Norah Healy's report of being raped, when heavily pregnant, in her home on 106 Griffin Street, Blackrock, Cork.[17] Rather than unpack these graphic testimonies and tease out the context of their production, historians have doubted their reliability and significance, suggesting that 'the veracity of these reports is difficult to judge given the propaganda nature of the *Irish Bulletin* and lack of any other evidence' and that Ryan's 'supposedly "convincing evidence" of widespread attacks and sexual violence [...] is actually based on only a handful of examples'.[18] However, both Healy's and O'Mahony's testimonies can be cross-referenced with other sources. Healy's original handwritten affidavit still exists.[19] Handwritten testimonies of O'Mahony also survive, while census records corroborate her given address, as well as the names of her mother, father and brothers, Peter and William, which were included in her published account.[20]

Healy's, O'Mahony's and Kelly's testimonies were published during the war of independence. However, sexual violence during the civil war may have further hindered reporting. As Earner-Byrne explains:

> The story of an Irish woman raped during the War of Independence by a British soldier, particularly one of the hated Black and Tans, lent itself more readily to the accepted national telling of that war – the bad British army against the good Irish people. In contrast, the stories of Irish women being raped by Irish men who had claimed Republican credentials were far more difficult to absorb into the already fraught cultural framing of the Civil War.[21]

Sexual violence is often perceived to be less likely during civil war, due perhaps to the fact that the rhetoric of rape has been historically characterised by the 'specter of the rapist "other"'.[22] Historians widely accepted until recently that the American Civil War was a 'low rape war'.[23] Sexual violence committed by Jewish men against Jewish women during the Holocaust remains contentious, while sexual violence committed during the Spanish Civil War continues to be marginalised.[24]

Aside from potential shaming, questions of credibility and the taboo of civil war sexual assault, female revolutionaries may also have chosen not to report sexual violence in an effort to privilege resistance over victimhood. In her study of the testimony of female republicans in the Spanish Civil War, Gina Herrmann outlines that female republicans seldom testify to first-hand experience of sexual violence or rape, yet refer to the sexualised violations of others. This ventriloquism is evident in Kathleen Clarke's memoir in which she recounts that a British soldier sat down beside an unnamed Cumann na mBan woman, 'flung his arms around her and attempted to kiss her'.[25] Clarke's interest, however, is not in the soldier's actions but in the girl's valiant response: 'She boxed him thoroughly, resumed her seat and continued reading [...] she was a girl anyone would be proud of.'[26]

Laura McAtackney's study of the autograph books of female republican prisoners in Kilmainham Jail also highlights the inmates' tendency to celebrate their resistance against night-time raids on their cells. For example, Brigid Reed's autograph book includes the note: 'Don't forget Bridie when the soldier raided our dormitorys [sic] at 3 in the morning when we were asleep, when they came the next night they got a let down, for we had our doors barracaded [*sic*] and when they tried to force them in but failed.'[27] This celebration of political resistance is reflected in the memoirs of Spanish republican women, which, as Hermann contends, 'ask the audience to be attuned to the power of the Republican ideal, not to the power of the regime that employed violence'. In telling their stories, Spanish women thus aimed to rescue 'their publicly celebrated militancy from the strain of rape and sexual torture', to the extent that their testimonies include denials of sexual humiliations.[28]

There are similar efforts to minimise physical contact in the testimonies of Irish female revolutionaries. Peg Broderick of Galway, in a rare statement to Bureau of Military History from a female activist who had her hair shaved, outlines that 'they took me out and closed the door, then grabbed my hair, saying "What wonderful curls you've got" and then proceeded to cut off all my hair to the scalp with very blunt scissors'. However, she includes the disclaimer that: 'I might say that *they did not handle me too roughly*, which is strange to say' (my emphasis).[29] It is hard to imagine how such an attack was not 'too rough', raising the possibility, therefore, that this disclaimer served as a safeguard for her 'publicly celebrated militancy'.

The Donegal Amazon: Eithne Coyle's Revised Testimony

Eithne Coyle (to whom, as discussed already, it seems Macardle dedicated the story 'The Prisoner') includes a similar disclaimer in her testimony of her arrest by British forces in December 1920: despite the verbal abuse she received, she reported that 'physically I was not in any way ill-treated'.[30] As in the case of many female revolutionaries, Coyle's militancy led to the questioning of her gender conformity; she was referred to in a number of accounts as having done 'a man's work'.[31] But her sexual conformity, too, was hinted at. Headlines in contemporary newspapers referred to Coyle as the 'Donegal Amazon' – a designation that is inherently sexual in its evocation of mythical Amazonian warriors who 'cut off their right breasts so that they could better use bows and arrows'.[32] The unease regarding Coyle's militancy (and sexuality) plays out in the subtle variations between her statement to the Bureau of Military History, gathered by Sinéad Ní Chiosáin in 1952, and a later unpublished memoir, signed 12 July 1972, which, based on numerous repeated turns of phrase, seems to be a redraft of the earlier statement.[33]

There are a number of discrepancies between the two accounts. Of interest is the fact that Coyle's militancy is less pronounced in the 1952 witness statement. In the second memoir, Coyle notes that she was presented with a working revolver by the IRA after the Free State army made an attempt on her life as she returned from Arranmore Island in summer 1922.[34] The handover of the revolver is absent from her account of the same ambush in the 1952 statement. Indeed, her earlier statement does not explicitly refer to her possession of a working revolver, but rather alludes to her having an 'old revolver with no trigger'.[35] Furthermore, in the earlier statement, Coyle mentions that 'at Clady I participated while armed *in an attack* on a Special's post'(my emphasis).[36] However, the second memoir stresses that she was active in more than one attack: 'along the border to Clady where most of the fighting took place. I took part *in most of the attacks* on the infamous B Specials around the area' (my emphasis).[37]

The second testimony also has stronger undertones of sexual misconduct. As mentioned in Chapter Two, Margaret Buckley felt that Coyle was subject to 'unchristian conditions' during her civil war imprisonment. Coyle describes this term of imprisonment in her 1952 statement as follows:

> The soldiers used to come into the guardroom beside my door and I had my heart in my mouth for fear they would break into my cell which was locked from the outside [...] I made a protest to the O/C. – McGowan – and he replied that I had been doing a man's work and that I should put up with any treatment that would be given to a man in my position. At last I went on hunger-strike and remained on hunger-strike until I was brought to Buncrana military barracks. There was a woman attendant there and I did not take food until I got a guarantee that I would get proper treatment.[38]

In the second testimony, from her 1972 memoir, the emphasis is placed not on 'proper treatment' but on 'protection': Coyle once again recalls her unsuccessful appeal to the OC and recounts that 'I was on hunger strike from that moment until I was released or transferred to some *civilized* place, where I would have the *protection* of a female attendant' (my emphasis).[39]

There are also subtle differences between Coyle's descriptions of her imprisonment in Athlone Military Barracks in early 1921. In the 1952 statement, Coyle outlines that there was a 'pretty big opening in the wall beside the door.'[40] She notes, 'I tried to keep it covered with papers, but every time I did that the sentry outside stuck his rifle through the opening, so that I was not able to undress.'[41] In the 1972 narrative, the 'big opening' becomes a 'glory hole', placing a stronger emphasis on voyeurism: 'I was unable to undress while I was there. I filled up the glory hole with newspaper and my faithful guardian outside pushed them into my cell with his rifle.'[42] Furthermore, Coyle delights in the fact that she was moved downstairs in the barracks after a few days and no longer had to 'contend with a peeping Tommie for the rest of the night'.[43] This language of the 'peeping Tommie' is absent from her earlier witness statement.

The subtle differences between Coyle's 1952 and 1972 testimonies suggests the possible influence of Bureau officials, that Coyle may have rewritten her narrative following further processing of her experience or that her narrative changed in light of second-wave feminism (at one point in her later memoir, she added the exclamation, 'Women's Lib, Take Notice!').[44] These divergences underscore the interconnected minimising of female militancy (Coyle's presentation with a working revolver by the IRA) and of the possibly sexualised nature of their treatment (the need for 'protection', the 'glory hole' and the 'peeping Tommie').

Men's Autobiography vs Men's Fiction

Men's autobiographies can be similarly unforthcoming in relation to matters of sex, never mind sexual violence. According to Diarmaid Ferriter 'any search for sex in the memoirs and biographies written by Irish republicans of this era will be in vain. The same is true of the Bureau of Military History. What the reader gets, instead, is a depiction of chivalrous masculinity, brotherhood and camaraderie.'[45] C. S. Andrews famously claimed, in a much-cited letter to Seán O'Faoláin in 1965, that 'the absence of sexual relations between the men and women of the republican movement was one of its most peculiar features. I suppose all revolutionaries are basically Puritanical, otherwise they wouldn't be revolutionaries.'[46]

However, despite the belief that 'Irish prudery kept a veil over issues of sex and sexuality until recent decades',[47] writings by revolutionaries that swerve from the conventions of autobiography complicate the supposed sexual innocence of the revolutionary generation. Indeed, Louise Ryan includes the 'fictional' writings of Frank O'Connor in her study of male republicans' writings, arguing his fiction shows that 'despite their claims to piety, Republican men did engage in romantic relationships with young women'.[48] Michael Cronin has also challenged the failure of historians to critically examine literary sources to gauge attitudes towards sex, suggesting that such omission can lead to a 'one-dimensional, linear historical reading', which privileges official attitudes towards sex and sexuality.[49]

Though Roy Foster addresses the romance and sexual concerns of revolutionaries in his study *Vivid Faces*, he nevertheless asserts that 'the world of sex' is 'more or less absent from the drama written and acted by the future revolutionaries'.[50] However, popular autobiographically based fiction pertaining to the revolution frequently addresses sexuality, including sexual violence, in ways that first-hand accounts do not. Indeed, if historians point to the lack of evidence regarding the sex lives of Irish revolutionaries, literary critic Nicholas Allen observes that 'sex and the revolution' became a popular, if contentious, topic from the 1930s as 'the War of Independence gained a lurid afterglow'.[51] In line with the popularity of (anti-)*Bildungsroman* narrative forms, many popular autobiographical novels tease out the protagonist's sexual awakening. Even in Carty's seemingly innocuous novel *The Irish Volunteer*, Art's transition into adulthood is illustrated through his growing awareness of his own sexuality as he is upset by the 'disturbing thoughts' evoked by the 'dark shapes lying against the ditch' in the lovers' place of Brisket's Lane.[52] References to sex education through pornographic literature also emerge. In Carty's *Legion of the Rearguard*, Rosaleen sends Paul a presumably pornographic cartoon postcard from Paris, while the British soldiers in Mulloy's *Jackets Green* also have 'female picture[s]' hanging on the walls.[53] As highlighted in the two previous chapters, fictionalised accounts also subvert hegemonic conceptions of sexuality and even hint at homosexual partnerships. These accounts challenge Andrews' oft-cited assertion that '[d]irty stories were rare and homosexuality unknown'.[54]

'There were no Brothels': Documenting and Denying Commercial Sex

One of the arguments supporting the 'relative scarcity of sexual abuse' during the revolution is that the IRA perceived the 'humane treatment of women' to be a facet of their 'soldierly behaviour'.[55] In opposition to colonial stereotypes of the Irish, revolutionaries were at pains to present themselves as rational, pious and dutiful in accordance with an 'Irish Catholic middle-class puritanism and code of respectability'.[56] The Free State army even hired an official photographer to communicate the professionalism associated with the army uniform.[57] On the other hand, anti-treaty republicans sought to present themselves as sober and disciplined, in contrast with recently recruited 'trucileers', whose behaviour, as Gavin Foster sums up, was characterised by 'loose morals, drunkenness, "vile language" and "shocking" behaviour towards women'.[58] For Clark, such discourses meant that 'Irish militants seldom took pleasure in attacks on the private sphere – and, by extension, female bodies'.[59]

This model of military behaviour is undermined by the engagement of revolutionaries in commercial sex – a question that has yet to be fully addressed. Mulloy's novel *Jackets Green*, discussed in Chapter One, was deemed 'obscene' because of a brothel scene. As the author sardonically responded, 'of course, in the island of saints and scholars, there were no brothels'.[60] These attempts to hush up the nature of prostitution reflected the new regulation of sexual behaviour in the new state, as Dublin's vibrant red light district was shut down due to opposition from lobby groups, such as the Legion of Mary.[61] While anti-prostitution lobby groups in Britain, Belfast and Dublin were often made up of middle-class unionists and suffragettes, John Borgonovo outlines that in Cork, the anti-prostitution vigilante was spearheaded by Sinn Féin activists.[62] Nevertheless, '[r]epublican records largely omit mention of these activities'.[63]

If republicans were reticent to document opposition to prostitution, their reliance on prostitutes to gather intelligence was even more contentious. Dan Breen mentioned in his 1959 witness statement that the 'lady prostitutes' at Phil Shanahan's public house on Foley Street 'used to pinch the guns and ammunition from the Auxiliaries or Tans at night' to pass on to the IRA.[64] Yet while Breen recounts his frequenting of Shanahan's pub in his (most likely ghostwritten) memoir, *My Fight for Irish Freedom*, he does not dwell on the assistance provided by prostitutes. However, the frequenting of brothels by male revolutionaries features strongly in popular novels. Rearden Conner's (1907–1991) first novel, *Shake Hands with the Devil: A Novel* (1933), documents the assistance granted to IRA men in Dublin by prostitutes in its opening pages. The protagonist, Gaelic Leaguer Kerry Sutton, stumbles across a Black and Tan ambush and is dragged to safety in a 'filthy hole' 'in the Dublin slums'.[65] He is cared for by two prostitutes who chant, '['t]is one of the boys, God help him'.[66] The novel later presents extramarital sex not as immoral but as a natural outcome of the strain of warfare as, '[w]hen numbers of men are herded together they lose self-control and self-respect, unless the will is very strong. Quite decent fellows do strange things under such circumstances'.[67] The protagonist's comrade agrees that 'war does bring out the animalism in man', but reassures him that '[t]here are such people as prostitutes in the world, Sutton!'[68]

Unsurprisingly, Conner's graphic thriller was banned in Ireland.[69] As the author reflected in his later autobiography, 'God help the Irish writer who […] dares to suggest that such a creature as a prostitute exists in Ireland!'[70] Nor was the novel accepted into the canon of revolutionary fiction, despite its commercial, and later cinematic, success. For Ernest Boyd, '[t]he inaccuracy of the local references and the impossibility of the dialect placed in the mouths of the characters are symbolic of the general distortion of the picture as a whole'.[71] This sort of critical hostility may also have been a response to Conner's ambivalence towards the nationalist movement – he was the son of an RIC policeman and had been educated by the Christian Brothers in Cork – and in *Shake Hands with the Devil*, he presents the degradation of the both the IRA and Black and Tans. There seems to be an autobiographical strain running through the novel; as one reviewer noted, Conner's hero 'is a man who might well be his own prototype – a young medical student in Dublin who is hurled into the midst of the struggle'.[72]

Louis Lynch d'Alton (1900–1951) also reflects on prostitution in his anti-*Bildungsroman*, *Death is So Fair* (1936). Active on the fringes of the IRA as a messenger,[73] d'Alton claimed he wrote *Death is So Fair* 'in order to cure myself of the writing mania which my mother deplored in us all'.[74] The novel presents the corruption of the protagonist's virtuousness as indicative of the disillusion which shadowed the events of the revolution: Manus Considine is forced to set aside his ambitions to become a priest due to his IRA activism and, echoing Conner's novel, has no option but to accept the assistance of Dublin prostitutes: 'Considine remembered how he had once shrunk from a woman such as this. He had touched the grim side of life too often since then.'[75] The corrosion of his piety is also manifested though his 'sordid' sexual relationship with Norah Cogan and the priest's refusal to grant Considine absolution for his being an 'accessory' to murder.[76] The novel ends as the protagonist gives himself up to the Auxiliaries, essentially committing suicide. Although *Death is So Fair* was not banned, Aodh de Blácam, writing in *The Irish Press*, strongly refuted that such 'immoral' behaviour would have been exhibited by the 'patriots': 'We might remark that the fighting men of Ireland were men of honour and cleanness, perhaps more truly so than any other army.'[77]

Despite such claims of exceptional Irish piety, these popular novels not only reflect the social upheaval of the revolution, they also reveal wider post-war concerns regarding the impact of war on sexual behaviour, particularly male sexual behaviour. While prior to the First World War, war was considered to redeem traditional conceptions of male heterosexuality, the end of the war generated fears that 'war had obliterated the sexual instinct in men, or at least had shifted men's sexual drives away from women and towards other men and the desire for further violence.'[78] As Jason Crouthamel contends in relation to sexual discourses in Weimar Germany, '[a]s men grew accustomed to killing, it was believed, they became addicted to it as a heightened experience that drained sexual drives and turned men impotent'.[79] According to such anxieties, the soldiers' association with female prostitutes, though perhaps uncomfortable, was excusable in the context of war.

The idea, as evident in *Jackets Green*, that visiting brothels constituted both a release of pent-up anxiety and a bonding experience for combatants also features in Jake Wynne's *Ugly Brew*. Published in 1936, *Ugly Brew* was described by reviewers as 'mostly autobiographical' and seemingly written 'from first-hand experience'.[80] It was certainly set up to be read as autobiographical: a tantalising disclaimer in the opening pages claims that 'the locality of all real incidents has been purposely misplaced'.[81] Though Jake Wynne was most likely a penname, the author affirmed in letters to his publisher that the events were portrayed 'sincerely as I myself had seen it'.[82] The novel traces the life of Dublin-born Martin O'Neill from his childhood, through his involvement in the Easter Rising and independence struggle, until his emigration after the civil war. Wynne strongly stresses the mental strain of warfare, drawing attention, as one reviewer observed, to the 'appalling state of nerves which their dreadful work created amongst the gunmen'.[83] According to writer Norah Hoult, *Ugly Brew* was '[p]robably the most detached account of the 1916 rebellion and afterwards that has been written from within'.[84] Seán O'Faoláin also reviewed the novel favourably – though apprehensive of its 'brutalism' – and contended that many of the incidents described are 'recognisable as operations of the Squad'.[85]

Ugly Brew is a remarkable testimony to the disillusionment of disenfranchised Free State soldiers in the context of the sexual politics of the period. The trauma of warfare is explicitly connected to the protagonist's 'sense of sex-guilt' from growing up in Catholic Ireland. Twelve-year-old Martin is terrified of forgetting his lessons for school, as 'failure to memorise it would mean another throbbing hand'.[86] In markedly feminist commentary, Martin's mother's life is characterised by 'the bearing of the children, the rearing of them, the slavery of the house, the nagging worry over meagre finances and the submission to an irascible husband'.[87] Despite her piety, Martin's mother 'made many attempts [...] to instruct him in sexual matters, but could never get beyond dark and veiled hints as to some dreadful evil thing'.[88] This need for sexual education is born out of fear, as the mother warns her son to 'keep away from "queer" companions, never to go near certain streets in Dublin, to avoid advances from strangers in the street'.[89] Wynne's hint at children's vulnerability to possible sexual assault went against efforts by the 'purity movement' to conceal the extent of child abuse.[90] This social commentary was not appreciated by all: a disapproving reader of my own second-hand copy of *Ugly Brew* wrote a scrawl in the margins: 'This book is written by a woman!'

As in Mulloy's *Jackets Green*, Wynne presents sexual brutalisation as a particular symptom of the brutalisation of civil war. After the signing of the Anglo-Irish Treaty, Martin gets wrapped up in the 'home-made' 'Terror' and enlists in the Free State army. He quickly and disturbingly becomes absorbed in his work: 'This time Martin was a hunter, and truth to tell, he enjoyed it.'[91] However, the thrill Martin gets from shooting, arresting and carrying out raids takes its toll. He resorts to alcohol, considers suicide and eventually flees from Ireland to try his chances in South Africa. Martin's moral and psychological decline is illustrated through his visit to the brothels of the Monto, along with a number of his fellow soldiers: 'By the time the crowds began swarming out of the music-hall, and the bar was about to close, the four were thoroughly drunk. The tables and lights seemed to Martin to be the flickering parts of a mirage. His speech was thick and his eyes glazed.'[92] While his colleagues are regulars at the brothel, Martin seems to be embarrassed in this new environment, feeling 'he ought to pull himself together, for the sake of good manners'.[93] He asks to excuse himself but is led into one of the upper bedrooms by a prostitute. The subsequent events are only referred to euphemistically: 'He was feeling very sick. The woman came and loosened the hooks on his high collar. That was the last he remembered.'[94]

Despite the restrained description of Martin's encounter with the prostitute, Wynne's novel was criticised for this sexual scene. A reviewer in *The Irish Book Lover* hoped the novel would be on the censor's list because 'patriotism is exploited for the enjoyment of its mockers, and the poor are exploited to provide sordid sex incidents'.[95] The novel evaded censorship, however. In fact, it was a bestseller in Dublin and was reissued in 1937.[96]

Mulloy's and Wynne's novels offer similar descriptions of soldiers visiting brothels under the influence of alcohol. However, consumption of alcohol is not intended to justify their actions. The narrator in *Ugly Brew* suggests that had Martin been aware of the situation, he still 'probably would not have minded'.[97] Meanwhile, Tim's search for sexual, romantic relief in *Jackets Green* is presented as the result of uncontrollable natural instinct. Alcohol is no more than a convenient mask: 'He had a sudden wild desire to see the girl undressed – and to undress her himself. He argued with himself that if there was any wrong in it, he would be excused on account of the wine he had taken, and then he put his arm round the girl and bent down to kiss her.'[98]

Fictionalised testimonial writings thus forcibly broke the silence around Irish revolutionaries' frequenting of brothels. Indeed, rates of venereal disease were a cause of concern after the civil war, as such behaviour could no longer be solely attributed to British forces. In 1926, Jesuit priest and social reformer Richard Devane blamed all parties for the epidemic:

> In the past few years we have had wave after wave of men passing over the country – Black and Tans, British soldiers, Auxiliaries, Irregulars, Free-State troops – *all of whom* have been living under war conditions, with all that means in a soldier's life, as far as vice is conceived, and to whom the prostitute made a ready appeal every opportunity 'leave' was granted. [my emphasis][99]

In *Ugly Brew*, Martin's inferred intimacy with the prostitute is revealed when he 'began to experience acute discomfort of a disgusting nature', to which the doctor laughs, 'you've been with a woman lately'.[100] Mulloy's *Jackets Green* also alludes to venereal disease, as Mick, a captain in the Free State army, orders his men to stay away from the local women: 'I warned yeh not to have anythin' to do wid Molly Dolan. Yeh know what happened to Skitter Doyle'.[101] Venereal disease (VD) is also referred to in interviews collected by Ernie O'Malley: Dubliner Larry Nelson confessed that IRA men were lectured on VD and given lime juice to 'keep them cool as they were getting too hot with the women'.[102] Meanwhile, Patrick McLogan commented that a number of 'neutral' IRA combatants refused to participate in a compulsory venereal disease inspection in the Curragh camp.[103] This refusal to take part in the inspection perhaps underscores the men's attempts to disassociate themselves from promiscuous sexual behaviour, but may also suggest an attempt to conceal sexual transgressions within the ranks.

As Devane's statement suggests, prostitutes were routinely viewed as responsible for the spread of disease, as they made 'a ready appeal' to men at 'every opportunity'.[104] If male sexual frustration was an unavoidable consequence of war, female prostitutes were thus the culpable party and were widely vilified. In *Ugly Brew*, not only does the prostitute seduce Martin and 'pass on' a venereal disease, the 'bitch' also steals several pound notes that he had left in his pocket.[105] In *Jackets Green*, the women are again debased and accused of 'encouraging' the soldiers, despite the parish priest's insistence that Molly is 'the best girl in the village, goes to Mass every morning, attends Sodality regularly, and is as pure as the snow'.[106] One of the prostitutes is even named Phyllis – in the original (unedited) manuscript, one of the characters makes this pun explicit by commenting that 'Syphilis would be more appropriate'.[107] When the soldiers are refused drinks, they trash the brothel and 'wreck every joint in the place'. In an adjoining house, the men physically assault a 'drunken woman lying sprawled on her face on a couch in the parlour': 'One of the party went over, lifted up her skirt, and gave her four hefty smacks'.[108] Sexual brutalisation, and even violence against prostitutes, is thus conveyed in both novels as an uncontrollable outcome of the strain of warfare. But if violence against prostitutes was easily ascribed to the heightened stress of war, did this tolerance of violence against prostitutes also apply to other forms of violence against civilians and female revolutionaries?

Regulating Sexuality and the Legitimisation of Sexual Violence

The punishment of and violence against prostitutes reflect the moral sexual policing that republicans often prided themselves on. While IRA activists frequented brothels and contracted venereal disease, they also actively punished women who were associated, or were believed to be associated, with the enemy and who were deemed to jeopardise the republican cause. Although Crown forces used similar tactics against women and civilians to undermine the republican guerrilla campaign, the IRA adopted hair shearing as a 'targeted and widespread' means of disciplining potential female spies.[109] Other forms of humiliations included tarring and feathering, the branding of anti-treaty women 'with green paint' and, on one occasion in Belfast in 1922, a woman was reported to have been covered in petrol and set alight.[110] All of these attacks involved public humiliation with the aim of symbolically undermining a woman's femininity. As Gabrielle Machnik-Kekesi contends, 'punishing women for the transgression of gender – informing, spying, and consorting with the enemy – was not simply an intrinsically militarized and politicized act, but also a way of performing masculinity and punishing transgressions of Irish femininity'.[111] Ironically, therefore, the ideals of honour and cleanliness allowed for sexualised violence, specifically against women, in the name of preserving such honour.

Though mostly known for his autobiographical writings, Ernie O'Malley was another revolutionary to try his hand at fiction – and it is in his fiction that he reflects on the IRA's regulation of sexuality. In the humorous unpublished short story 'High Seas Piracy', a group of exiled republicans in New York city recall holding up a Cunard liner off Cobh in order to try and force a young bank clerk to marry a girl, the sister of one of their dead comrades, who had gotten 'into trouble'. The men seek to redress the woman's affront to public morality by arranging her marriage, whether or not the 'boyo' was actually responsible: 'We heard that he wasn't the only one that had been playing around her and that maybe had been true enough for she wasn't up to much, but we were thinking of her brother.'[112]

Nevertheless, the 'unacknowledged civil war' of sexually controlling violence by Irish men against Irish women occupies an uncomfortable position in revolutionary remembrance. Writing in the early 1960s, Máirtín Ó Cadhain (1906–1970), writer and IRA volunteer, addressed the silence regarding the practice of hair cropping:

Fágfaidh mé faoi dhaoine a throid ar son na hÉireann cuntas a thabhairt faoin gcaoi a ndéanaidís plaiteacháin de mhná a bhíodh ag tabhairt comhluadair do Dhúchrónaigh agus do shíothmhaoir eascoiteannaithe Rí Shasana. Is rud é nach bhfaca mé aon trácht sna leabhair air, ach tá mé cinnte go bhfuil sé ar fad cnuasaithe isteach ar sheilfeanna na Staire Míleata. Tá súil agam go bhfuil fear maith acu le hortha na luch a chur san áras úd. Theagmhódh gurb é sin an ghné dár gcuid cogaíocht is mó a gcuirfidh ár sliocht suim ann.[113]

[I will leave it to those who fought for Ireland to document how they used to shave off the hair of women who kept company with Black and Tans and with ostracised police officers in the service of the Crown. It is not something I have seen mentioned in books but I am sure that it is all gathered on the shelves of the [Bureau of] Military History. I hope there is someone good enough in there to banish the mice from the building. I would chance that this is the aspect of our war that future generations will be most interested in.]

Literary testimonies are far from silent on the practice of hair cropping, however. Before considering such representations, it is important to highlight that the impact of these humiliations was not just related to the physical attack of the hair shearing. Rather, the humiliation was extended through the public shaming that followed and in which the wider community was complicit. Fictional representations of hair shearing and other sexualised assaults thus risk perpetuating this shaming effect.

Fiction is also a problematic term to use in relation to testimony of sexual violence given the many ways in which the reliability of survivor testimony is called into question. Nevertheless, Emma V. Miller argues that in 'a social environment so often averse to hearing about the realities of sexual violence, fiction has provided a unique testimonial opportunity without the personally directed censure connected to the narrating of first-hand experiences'.[114] In women's fiction, such as that of Smithson and Ní Ghráda discussed in the previous chapter, sexualised violence is implied through references to unravelling clothing or in coded allusions to attacks on vulnerable women in rural – and, significantly, faraway – communities. While these indirect representations draw attention to such occurrences and to the widespread fears of vulnerability to sexual violence, they nevertheless shy away from direct representation. Violence against women is not quite 'unspeakable' but is nevertheless 'unseeable'.

Fictionalising Hair Shearing

This type of indirect representation is most common in the case of hair shearing. In a number of male-authored texts, such 'disciplinary' attacks are casually presented as a natural aspect of the conflict. Michael Farrell's autobiographically based novel, *Thy Tears Might Cease*, published posthumously in 1964 but purportedly written by 1937,[115] includes a passing reference to hair cutting: 'There were Auxiliaries in the neighbourhood and already an old man had been killed, a woman's head cropped, and a twelve-year-old boy was in bandages.'[116] Farrell's reference does not clarify whether the attack was carried out by Crown forces or the IRA. In d'Alton's novel, *Death is So Fair*, the protagonist elicits various 'trifles of information' from another local, including the news that Katie Tumulty's hair was 'cropped close by the boys' for having been seen talking to Tans.[117] Connemara IRA volunteer, Colm Ó Gaora, also wrote an ambiguous short story, 'An Díoghaltas' [The Revenge], about a father who burns all his daughter's possessions for falling in love with a British officer and then sets off to London to avenge her elopement.[118]

While these accounts might seem to endorse the punishment of women who transgress purity norms, d'Alton hints at the double standards underpinning such attacks. IRA commandant Hanly recounts that '[s]ome o' the lads' who 'were for getting virtuous' were planning to crop Norah Cogan's hair.[119] Norah's crime was 'being in trouble'.[120] Ironically, the putative father was an IRA volunteer. However, the violence of such haircutting is downplayed. Hanly succeeds in distracting his fellow volunteers from carrying out the assault by suggesting, '[s]ure, that only puts women in the fashion nowadays instead o' making an example o' them'.[121] This reflects an observed tendency to trivialise haircutting by associating 'cropping' with women's fashion.[122] Elizabeth Bowen's novel *The Last September* (1929) similarly belittles the brutality of such attacks by evoking contemporary flapper-style fashions. The character of Lois, who had her eye on a British officer, claims she 'should be bobbed', suggesting that she would be happy to pay the consequences for her sexual transgression. She has to be reminded by Lady Naylor of the malicious nature of these attacks: 'But masked men [...] would be a very nasty experience for a girl your age.'[123]

Hidden in Plain Sight: Tomás Bairéad's 'An Dath a d'Athraigh' [The Colour that Changed]

A more complex representation of hair shearing emerges in Tomás Bairéad's (1893–1973) 'An Dath a d'Athraigh' [The Colour that Changed] (1938), a short story described by Philip O'Leary as 'an unidealised account in which the heads of suspected female collaborators are shaved'.[124] Active in the Moycullen group of volunteers from 1916, Bairéad was imprisoned in Galway Gaol during the struggle for independence and worked for the *Irish Independent* in Dublin during the civil war.[125] Bairéad's 'An Dath a d'Athraigh', echoes accounts of other IRA veterans in its calm allusion to the necessity of shearing the hair of promiscuous young women in order to prevent them from associating with police officer Pislín:

> Bhí triúr ná ceathrar de na cailíní splannctha ina dhiaidh, cé nach ndeacha cailín as a' bparráiste seo in éindigh le póilín ná le saighdiúr leis na bliadhanta roimhe sin. Na cailíní is mó a shanntuigh sé, má b'fhíor dó féin, iad seo a raibh dearbhráithaireacha ná gaolta acu in Arm na hÉireann le eólas a phiocadh astu. Agus mo náire iad – d'éirigh leis cúpla babhta. Cuireadh an scéal amach go raibh sé pósta agus go raibh a bhean ina comhnuidhe i gconndae éigin eile, ach ní raibh aon mhaith ann go ndearnadh diogháil ar ghruaig bheirt ná triúr acu.[126]

> [There were three or four girls who were after him, even though no girls from this parish had courted a guard or a soldier for years before that. The women he was most interested in, if he was to be believed, were those who had brothers or relatives in the IRA so he could gather information from them. And shame on them, he was successful on a number of occasions. A rumour was spread around that he was married and that his wife lived in another county, but it was no good until two or three of them had their hair docked.]

However, Pislín has a change of heart and becomes one of the most successful IRA combatants during the war of independence. As the war draws to an end, he makes plans to marry Máire Phádraic Bhig, one of the girls whose hair had been cropped.[127] By suggesting that Máire was genuinely and romantically in love with Pislín, Bairéad complicates the earlier indication

– 'mo náire iad' [shame on them] – that the women were driven by unmanageable desire. But Pislín's change of 'colours' also highlights that this violence against the women was arbitrary and contingent not on their own allegiances, but on the allegiances of men. Pislín and Máire Phádraic Bhig never marry. The groom-to-be is shot by Free State soldiers just before his wedding day, reflecting perhaps Bairéad's genuine dismay at the events of 1922–3.[128] The story was published in the 1938 collection *An Geall a Briseadh* [The Broken Pledge], which was the recipient of the Douglas Hyde Literary Fund and was praised for being written in the 'purest quality [Irish] as spoken in Connemara'.[129] Bairéad's collection, which included such an ambiguous account of violence against women, made the *Irish Times* bestseller list, was reprinted at least four times and was on school syllabuses for years.[130] The often perceived 'hidden' crimes against women were 'hidden' in plain sight.

'The Terrible Irish Punishment': Jim Phelan's *Green Volcano*

Unlike the many generalised, and sometimes ambiguous, accounts of such 'disciplinary' violence, Jim Phelan's (1895–1966) thriller *Green Volcano* (1938) includes a graphic depiction of an assault on schoolteacher Molly Coolin for 'belonging' 'to the enemy':

> On the previous evening *a crowd of men and girls* had seized Molly, torn her clothes from her, and driven her naked out of the village. Half insane with fear and shame, she had run from house to house, only to be coldly repulsed by all. Then she had wandered in the fields by the river, seven miles, *shunned or reviled by everyone who met her*.
>
> Ben knew already the terrible Irish punishment for a spy-woman. Ruthless with a male traitor, it was only seldom, and in the most aggravated cases, the revolution executed a woman spy. Usually the known female traitor was treated as Molly had been treated – a punishment quite as efficient as the death penalty. [my emphasis][131]

Phelan's novel, too, drew on his own revolutionary experience. A native of Dublin, he participated in the occupation of the Rotunda in January 1922 along with Liam O'Flaherty and subsequently travelled to Cork with

O'Flaherty and Seán McAteer to establish Irish Citizen Army branches.[132] From March 1922, he engaged in occasional gunrunning from Liverpool to Ireland. After being involved in a botched robbery of a post office, apparently ordered by the IRA, Phelan was sentenced to death by hanging – later commuted to life imprisonment – for the killing of a postal clerk. His 1938 novel touches on some of this experience; it follows Glasgow native Ben Robinson on a mission across Ireland to seek revenge on the spy who had betrayed his gunrunning father, documenting both the struggle for independence and the emergence of self-declared rural soviets in Munster during the civil war. Although Phelan was an incredibly prolific writer of both fiction and autobiography, his son, Séamus Phelan, contends that this novel is essential to understanding his father's revolutionary life:

> Jim's part in the Irish War of Independence [...] became a defining event of his early life. To understand this, you have to read *Green Volcano*, his 1938 novel of the Irish struggle which he called 'the most important book'. This will tell you all you need to know about Jim's views on the formation of the Irish state, and how and why he was involved.[133]

Phelan's frank treatment of sexual matters is characteristic of all his work. In his autobiography, *The Name's Phelan* (1948), he claims that he was disowned by his family for being seen entering a lodging house: 'If I had been infected with leprosy and tuberculosis, had my arms and legs amputated, and was then carried off to a prison for lifelong torture, that would have been trivial, in their eyes, compared with the story they had heard.'[134] He thus came to be a strong opposer of the 'highly moral' culture of Ireland that was responsible, to his mind, for a 'good many cases of repressed or frustrated people going over the line of mind-safety'.[135] His jail writing, including the novel *Lifer* (1938) and the memoirs *Jail Journey* (1940) and *Tramp at Anchor* (1954), address both consensual and forced homosexual behaviour in prison. Reviewing *Jail Journey*, George Orwell commended Phelan for this indictment of the 'genuinely horrible' psychosexual consequences of life in the penal system. Orwell asserted that Phelan's 'straightforward discussions' were 'not just pornography in disguise'. Rather, he regarded him as a reliable witness who aimed to record an aspect of prison life that could not 'be hinted at in any public discussion of the subject'.[136]

Not surprisingly, Phelan's writing frequently fell foul of the Censorship Board. However, despite its usual insights into the nature of gender-based violence during the revolution, *Green Volcano* evaded censorship. While hair shearing is often presented in vague but nevertheless justified terms in male veterans' accounts, Phelan underscores the entire community's involvement in such shaming. Not only was Molly seized by 'a crowd of men and girls' and stripped naked, she was also 'shunned or reviled by everyone who met her'. Not unlike the female character in Bairéad's short story, Molly was unaware of her own transgression. The charge against her was her relationship with Liam Donohue who, unbeknownst to Molly, was deemed a 'traitor'. Although the protagonist, Ben, understood that Molly was 'blameless', he doubted that any 'court would hold her so, much less an impromptu village meeting'.[137]

Phelan's fictionalised account not only highlights the injustice of such attacks, it also suggests that 'the terrible punishment for a spy-woman' included public shaming through being stripped naked. While there has been a tendency in some scholarship to distinguish between sexual violence and targeted humiliations such as hair shearing, Phelan's account underscores that 'the terrible Irish punishment' was, as Connolly argues, 'intrinsically *sexual*'.[138] Moreover, although contemporary newspapers tended to depict such attacks as being perpetrated by masked men at night,[139] Phelan's fictionalised depiction is a reminder that the targeted humiliation of suspected women spies was contingent upon the sanction and even collaboration of the wider community. For Molly, this sense of shame is worse than death. Sobbing, she exclaims, 'now my mind and body are branded for ever'.[140]

'Unsexed Amazon[s]': The Sexual Objectification of Female Revolutionaries

While the IRA disciplined young women deemed to be too friendly with the enemy, women who actively supported the revolutionary cause were also deemed a sexual abomination – as 'unsexed Amazon[s]'.[141] Women's militarism was widely perceived as a challenge to both traditional gender conventions and to men's military and sexual prowess. As Lucy Noakes observes, female militants in First World War Britain were sexualised 'as both "mannish" lesbians, taking advantage of the opportunities the war offered to dress and act as men [...] and as promiscuous heterosexuals, motivated to join the women's service because of the access it offered to the male combatant'.[142]

The latter image of the sexually promiscuous female revolutionary was particularly widespread in the Irish context – hinted at even in the popular civil war love triangle motif (see Chapter One). Seán O'Faoláin's 1932 short-story collection, *Midsummer Night Madness: And Other Stories* – another text to be targeted by the Censorship Board – was one of many to eroticise revolutionary activity. Even the delivery of messages by female activists is sexualised; a narrator recalls how a woman revolutionary turned 'modesty aside to undo the top buttons of her blouse, drew out the usual small envelope, and handed it to me, warm as usual from its nest'.[143] Séamus MacCall's *Gods in Motley* refers to an activist who had the 'eye of a woman thinking two [IRA men] were better than one'.[144] In *Shake Hands with the Devil*, Rearden Conner documents how female revolutionaries 'carried revolvers in their handbags or concealed them on their persons and passed them to their menfolk at the psychological moment' and that republican men and women sometimes 'shared the same quarter, though not officially'.[145] He expounded on this eroticisation of military women in his 1937 memoir, *A Plain Tale from the Bogs*, in which he argued that republican women in Cork 'wear revolvers at their waists. They stalk around with their men, and live with them in the abandoned military and police barracks.'[146]

Conner's comments were met with censure: a reviewer quipped that '[s]urely it is not correct to say of the last stand of the Irregulars at Cork'.[147] However, these representations of female revolutionaries happily endeavouring to sexually satisfy the male volunteers were pervasive. Even in Carty's relatively mild novel, *Legion of the Rearguard*, the male protagonist wonders 'wouldn't any girl feel excited in the presence of a young man whose daring exploits were the talk of the countryside?'[148] In *Green Volcano*, Bridget Whalen, the love interest, embodies such representations: '"Tis not sure whether we live or die," said Bridget, seriously. "It is sure that we hate the Tans and we love our boys. An', faith," she added, laughing again, "the boys have need of a little lovin' now an' then, with the life they have to lead on the hills."'[149] In Francis Stuart's *The Coloured Dome* (1932), it emerges that Tulloolagh, 'the finest leader that the Irish Republican Army had ever had', is in fact a young mother in cross dress.[150] When awaiting execution in a Mountjoy cell with a fellow IRA man, she decides she 'wanted to give herself to him'.[151] Her militarism and sexuality are explicitly tied together in an erotic passage describing her naked body which is marked with a 'scar of a bullet wound in her left thigh'.[152] Francis Plunkett's *As the Fool* (1936), too, refers to Irish women whose 'knickers' are 'full of revolvers and ammunition', while in Liam O'Flaherty's *The Assassin* (1928), Kitty Mellett personifies the 'mixture of sex and idealism which is so strange a characteristic of women revolutionaries'.[153]

A number of fictional accounts document the warnings given to the IRA to behave well, yet even such warnings hint at their inevitable transgression. In O'Flaherty's banned civil war novel *The Martyr* (1933), the Free State soldiers are told they can '[f]lirt with the girls, but don't put them in the family way, because one girl with a bastard in her shawl at the barrack gate is enough to ruin the reputation of a whole regiment'.[154] In *Jackets Green*, Mulloy also highlights how certain volunteers attempted to mellow their fellow 'soldiers' talk':

> 'How would yeh like ta share yer bed wid her?' said somebody.
> 'Anythin' wid a skirt on id do me', said another.
> 'I'd prefer the skirt off', said a third.
> 'Aw, here, you fellows, chuck that talk. You ought to be ashamed of yourselves, behaving like a lot of corner boys; *you're letting us down*' [my emphasis].[155]

The fine line between discipline and transgression is particularly apparent in Frank O'Connor's 1929 short story, 'September Dawn'. An IRA commander on the run, Hickey, chastises a junior soldier for his drinking and for taking an inappropriate interest in Sheela, the young girl harbouring them. However, despite Hickey's disciplining of his junior, he finds himself overwhelmed by 'the desire for some human contact' and, when he encounters the young girl early in the morning, he 'took her in his arms and kissed her'.[156] Sheela's promiscuousness is again hinted at through her non-conformity to traditional models of femininity. She is described as 'another terrible rebel', wears 'men's boots twice too big for her' and has never been 'prouder' than when aiding the rebels.[157]

Female revolutionaries did indeed harness their sexuality, or were even expected to, in order to gather information or to escape from difficult situations. IRA leader Michael Brennan recounts that the Punch sisters protected the IRA men they were harbouring by inviting British officers into their home and entertaining them under the same roof.[158] Síghle Humphreys, too, recalls that she and her comrade, Nora Brick, evaded arrest by Free State soldiers by using their 'considerable charm'.[159] Yet the realities of these expectations were demeaned by the widespread sexual degradation of female revolutionaries in cultural representations; this might explain why female activists attempted to distance themselves from the possibly sexualised nature of their activities in their testimonies. Peg Broderick, a key Cumann na mBan activist in Galway city, was tasked with luring British soldiers down to the city's docks. She finishes her witness statement by identifying this as the task she most regretted having to do: 'Before concluding, I would like to say the job I hated most was enticing British soldiers down the docks in order to have them relieved of their arms by the volunteers.'[160] Katty Shinners of Ennis, County Clare, also reassured the Pensions Board in 1941 that 'there were only ten girls in our Cumann na mBan who could be accused of going with British soldiers and they aren't claiming Pensions [sic]'.[161] Despite the intelligence work which may have required women to socialise with soldiers, it seems that these women were denied recognition.

The eroticisation and masculinisation of female activists in literary narratives was connected to their vulnerability to physical, and even sexual, discipline. In O'Flaherty's *The Martyr*, for example, a woman revolutionary holding 'the ammunition drum' is chastised by Free State officer Crackers Sheehan, who angrily exclaims, 'That's a nice powder puff for a respectable girl [...] If I were your father, I'd redden your bottom for you.'[162] Such a threat of violence underscores Sharon Crozier-De Rosa's contention that female militants 'by enacting violence publicly, [...] jeopardised the existence of codes of chivalry that were established to protect them'.[163] As Noakes further evinces, these discourses left female activists 'vulnerable to both rumours regarding their sexuality as, by having stepped outside of traditional discourses of femininity they are seen as woman "out of place" and are thus unprotected by ideas regarding "respectable" female sexuality, and to physical sexual assault by male soldiers'.[164]

This conflation of female militancy and sexual promiscuity may explain why Eithne Coyle's 1952 witness statement elides the fact that she was presented with a new revolver and minimises the possibly sexualised nature of her mistreatment. Moreover, if female revolutionaries were culturally represented as promiscuous, might this have deterred them from reporting actual attacks for fear of undermining their political agency?

Sexual Assault in Fiction by Male Revolutionaries: Seán Óg Ó Caomhánaigh's *Fánaí*

The supposed lack of evidence regarding sexual violence during the Irish revolution is at odds with the prevalence of sexual violence as a theme in literature from the 1920s. As Allen asserts, Liam O'Flaherty, Lennox Robinson and William Butler Yeats 'all used sexual violence as [a] motif of Irish culture post-independence'.[165] As much as a cultural motif, however, such representations must be considered in terms of their relationship with the social reality.

One of the first novels to be censored in the Free State for its depiction both of female sexuality and sexual assault was completed in the Curragh camp by anti-treaty internee Seán Óg Ó Caomhánaigh (1885–1947), better known as Seán a' Chóta. Published at the end of 1927, *Fánaí* [Wanderer] was a romanticised version of the author's life based on his experience in the docks and mills of New England, and on a ranch in Dakota. However, there were complaints from the clergy that certain extracts recalled 'French sex-psychology literature' and were not suitable for school children.[166] The publisher, An Gúm, recalled the novel from shops and eighteen separate extracts were removed before its reissue.

Nearly all of the offensive scenes were semi-erotic extracts which emphasised the female protagonist's sexuality:

> Dhruid sí níos giorra dó. D'ardaigh a ghlac is an chros chun a beola. Chaith sé a ghéaga ina timpeall. Ghéill sí dó agus neadaigh ina bhaclainn, a haghaidh iompaithe in airde chuige. Shír a bheola a beola agus dhlúthaíodar [...] B'shin é an chéad uair riamh d'fhreagair sí bréagadh fir. B'é an rud a b'iontaí ar domhan é agus bhí áthas uirthi gurbh é an chéad fhear é.[167]

> [She moved closer to him. She brought his hand and belt to her lips. He put his arms around her. She yielded to him and nestled into his arms, her face turned up towards his. His lips sought her lips and they came together [...] It was the first time she had responded to

a man's seduction. It was the most extraordinary thing in the world
and she was happy that he was her first man.]

Ó Caomhánaigh's response to the redaction of such extracts was that
'nothing was in my mind other than language heard very very often among
mixed company in the Gaeltacht'.[168] Indeed, Ó Caomhánaigh's civil war
prison diary – transcribed and edited by Micheál Ó Catháin, but omitted
to date from historical scholarship – complicates the scholarly emphasis on
the puritanical attitudes of IRA activists.

Ó Caomhánaigh asserts in his diary that he had no less than forty
intimate relationships: 'dachad bean gur bhfeas dom a n-uile rún – ach
b'fhéidir rún mo mheallta [forty women whose every secret I knew –
except perhaps the secret of luring me].[169] Indeed, the Dunquin native
corresponded with numerous women during his internment, including
two women named Eibhlín and Síghle, whose acquaintance he made
in Kilmallock, County Limerick, during the civil war, and the latter
of whom assisted in smuggling his diary out of the Curragh. He also
maintained contact with previous lovers, such as New York-based Máire
Husae, whom he purports was a 'gariníon' [adopted daughter] of Michael
Collins' sister, and newly elected TD, Margaret Collins-O'Driscoll.[170]
His diaries make regular references to the packages received, including
cigarettes, letter paper, money, rosary beads and even a fountain pen
from New York – these packages were adorned with messages of 'grádh,
póga, teannadh/cogarnach agus díoghrais croidhe' [love, kisses, cuddle/
whispering and fervent affection].[171] Ó Caomhánaigh's dramatic dilemma
was how to choose between his many suitors: '[N]íl duine aca ná fuil go
hionmhianta ach, mo lagar! Connus is féidir liom seisear seachtar, ochtar
aca do bheith agam?' [There is not one of them that I do not desire,
but alas! How can I have six, seven, eight of them?][172] This openness to
sexual matters surprised his fellow internee and poet Joseph Campbell,
who wrote in his diary that Ó Caomhánaigh 'told me stories of his early
puberty. The tall woman of Dunquin at turf-rick up in the bog. She 45,
he 15.'[173]

Ó Caomhánaigh's diary includes a number of semi-erotic passages
that are not unlike the redacted passages in his novel. Many of these
relate to his unrequited affection for Neans Ní Theácháin (often referred
to as 'Ceann Dubh' [Dark Head]), whose walks through Central Park

he reminisced about at night-time.[174] The line between fact and fiction in many of his romantic diary entries is hard to decipher, however. On 5 November 1923, he made a plan both to work on his novel and also to write a short account of all the women he had ever met.[175] One such incomplete sketch is an imaginative reworking of a romantic encounter with 'Ceann Dubh' told from the perspective of the young woman. Set in an 'extremist' basement club under surveillance during the First World War, a group of communist women tell tales of their romantic adventures, trips to the theatre and secret jaunts to roadhouses on the edge of the city. Reflecting the connections between politically active women and sexual promiscuity, Ceann Dubh sees 'an flaith' [the prince] entering the club and ponders, 'Ní fheadar an bhfuil sé ionphógtha?' [I wonder if he is kissable?].[176]

The contentious sexual assault in Ó Caomhánaigh's novel *Fánaí* is connected to the supposed sexual liberation of modern women. The perpetrator, Ó Seansánaigh, apparently did not understand the difference between Peig de Róiste and the women he had met in lounges and bars in Canada. As the extract shows, Ó Seansánaigh did not take well to being rejected by Peig:

'An mbeidh tú mar bhean agam, a Pheig', ar seisean.

'Ní bheidh mé', ar sise go daingean, 'agus tóg aghaidh do chaoraíocht díom. Níl aon cheart agat teacht faoi mo dhéin ar an tslí seo agus muna bhfágann tú mé glaofaidh mé ar mo dheartháir'.

Ach níor staon sé. Dhruid sé léi agus thug iarracht ar a ghéaga a chur ina timpeall. Chúlaigh sí uaidh céim eile gur bhuail I gcoinne an fhalla. Ní fhéadfadh sí teitheadh uaidh. An rud nach bhfaigheadh sé le bladar gheobhadh sé le neart é [...][177]

['Will you be my woman, Peig', he said.

'I won't', she strongly replied, 'and take your abuse elsewhere. You have no right to come after me like this and if you don't leave me be I'll call my brother.'

But he didn't stop. He drew close to her and tried to put his arms around her. She pulled a step back from him until she hit the wall. She couldn't escape from him. What he couldn't achieve with charm he would achieve with force.]

The novel arguably does not endorse his actions, however: Ó Seansánaigh is clearly the villain in *Fánaí* and is almost successful in his attempt to murder Peig's partner, Seán. Though the main concern of critics at the time seemed to be the 'sentimental love scenes', a reviewer in *The Irish Times* did not think the assault was plausible: 'We could wish that a book thus recommended were free from such incidents as a woman's struggle against male violence, recalling the brutality of the American film.'[178]

In contrast, a reviewer in *The Irishman* objected to the censorship given that, '[after] all, life has its brutalities and most certainly so have manual labour and war [...] Are these things to be hidden in the new literature of the Irish, to be glossed over and slurred over as if they did not exist[?]'.[179] Ó Caomhánaigh himself was long of the belief that the writer's duty was to be 'chomh fírinneach don bheatha agus a bhíonn an stairí do staid a thráchtais' [as true to life as the historian to the period of his thesis].[180]

The case of *Fánaí* suggests that the celebration of female sexuality was as problematic as sexual violence. Moreover, the idea that sexual violence was the province of American films or of French sexual psychology highlights the promotion of a myth that sexual violence was not committed by Irishmen. However, there are many further representations of sexual assault by Irish revolutionaries in veterans' fictional writings. Much autobiographically informed fiction that eroticises female revolutionaries also casually hints at women's limited bodily agency. Within this context, the line between consensual and non-consensual intimacy is repeatedly blurred. In Anthony O'Connor's 1975 testimonial novel, *He's Somewhere in There* (discussed in Chapter Five), the senior male characters casually grope the young women, as Mr Corrigan unproblematically 'gave Maureen a pat on the bottom as she went by'.[181] The Free State captain's description of his youthful sexual relationships in the bustling military town of Athlone includes a highly problematic description of a woman's lack of consent: 'I'd gone the whole way with a few charming, willing girls, and except for Nellie Hogan who had cried bitterly, they'd come out of it with eyes sparkling and looking even more beautiful.'[182] In Phelan's *Green Volcano*, IRA activist/spy Liam Donohue writes to Molly in what seems to be an apology letter for forcing himself on her: 'Dear Molly, Do not blame me. Shall explain everything later. I am proud – really proud – that your body knew it was I, even when your mind said no. You always refused my urging. Laugh with me, as we will in the future, at the consummation of our courtship ...'[183]

These problematic references all highlight what international scholarship on civil war sexual violence reveals (as, indeed, do more general studies): that despite an emphasis on wartime gang rape by external armies, 'rape and other forms of sexual violence perpetrated by those known to the victim – and especially by intimate partners – is far more common than rape by combatants'.[184]

The Dangers of the Love Triangle Motif: Peadar O'Donnell's *The Knife*

While Ó Caomhánaigh's novel was censored, sexual violence also appeared in writings that dodged censorship. Indeed, Peadar O'Donnell's 1930 novel *The Knife* (discussed in Chapter One) depicts the assault of female revolutionary, Nuala Godfrey Dhu. As in many popular novels, the female-centred romance triangle (or quadrangle, in this case), is employed to tease out civil war loyalties, as all three suitors betray their own cause to woo Nuala. The apolitical Protestant Dr Henry agrees to treat Nuala's injured brother, an IRA rebel, in order to impress her, while Orangeman Sam Rowan hides rebels on her behalf, despite the risk of falling out with his community. The third suitor, Catholic James Burns, is motivated to leave the republican fight and join the Free State army after Nuala rejects his advances. This scene, reminiscent of the assault in *Fánaí*, is marked by an ellipsis:

> 'Will you marry me, Nuala?' he whispered.
> 'I have no feeling for anybody that way,' she said.
> 'But I have feeling like that for you.'
> 'I have tried to feel that way,' she said: 'it was no good; it is no good.'
> 'But you must marry me.'
> [...]
> 'I want you now.'
> He put his arms under her knees, and lifted her across his legs.
> [...]
> She pushed his arms away and got to her feet. He locked his arms around her knees, and looked up into her face.
> [...]

'We all fight for something. I fight because I want you.'

He drew her in to him, and kissed her, tore her blouse and kissed her breast, her neck ... 'Now will you marry me?'

'James, can't you see, all this means nothing to me.'[185]

Burns' advances point to the dangers of the love triangle, as the male characters ardently compete for the attentions of the central female character. O'Donnell's portrayal of the Free State soldier's violence towards women may have been a politically motivated attempt to degrade the soldiers and liken them to cultural representations of the brutish Black and Tans. The consequences of Burns' assault on Nuala are not teased out. However, when Nuala tears her knee on barbed wire, the visible trail of her female blood alarms the characters: 'There was a day, if blood was seen on Nuala!'[186] This sense of horror seems to suggest that, unlike the previous conflict when the spilt blood of women would cause outcry, the disorder of the civil war has normalised violence against women.

The implied assault of Nuala was not appreciated by P. C. Trimble in *The Irish Book Lover*, who lamented that 'Poor Nuala' is 'made to play the loved in a mawkish love-scene which recalls Hollywood at its worst. We just don't believe that Nuala, as we conceive her, would have stood for that sort of stuff.'[187] Like the case of *Fánaí*, critics were more concerned with condemning 'immoral', 'sentimental' and 'mawkish' representations of sexuality associated with American media than contemplating the possibilities of actual violence against women. Nuala, too, is held responsible for standing 'for that sort of stuff'.

Seduction/Rape?: Liam O'Flaherty's *The Martyr*

Liam O'Flaherty's satirical novel *The Martyr* (1933) presents perhaps the most explicit account of sexual assault in the context of the civil war. O'Flaherty was one of the earliest chroniclers of the civil war. His short story 'The Sniper', published in *New Leader* in September 1922, epitomised the 'brother against brother' motif of civil war (a republican sniper shoots at a Free State soldier during the Battle of the Four Courts only to realise he has shot his own brother). O'Flaherty's later Dublin novels, *The Informer* (1925) and *The Assassin* (1928), also exploit civil war themes; the former relates to an 'informer' who is hunted by his former comrades in arms, while the latter has been read as a reflection on the assassination of pro-treaty government minister Kevin O'Higgins in 1927.

For critics, O'Flaherty's writings could easily be read through the lens of his experience: a native of the Aran islands, O'Flaherty was severely wounded during his service in the Irish Guards in the First World War. Returning to Ireland in late 1921, he opposed the Anglo-Irish Treaty and participated in the communist seizure of the Rotunda concert hall in Dublin in January 1922. Purportedly a member of the anti-treaty garrison during the battle of the Four Courts, O'Flaherty emigrated to London shortly after the outbreak of the civil war. However, O'Flaherty famously mocked critics who were too quick to view his novels as empirical fact. As he contended regarding *The Informer*:

> The literary critics, almost to a man, hailed it as a brilliant piece of work and talked pompously about having at last been given inside knowledge of the Irish revolution and the secret organizations that had brought it about. This amused me intensely, as whatever 'facts' were used in the book were taken from happenings in a Saxon town, during the sporadic Communist insurrection of about nineteen twenty-two or three.[188]

Nevertheless, the historical context, as Danine Farquharson highlights, is central to *The Martyr*.[189] O'Flaherty sets his novel in Kerry during the final days of the civil war, the location of some of the most contentious atrocities of the period. In its satirical undermining of the belief systems of both anti-treaty republicans and Free State officials, *The Martyr* is filled with '[b]loodshed, rape, cruelty, whisky-bibbling, bawdy laughter and political madness', which, as one critic observed, 'tear around between the covers of this book like laughing hyenas on a rabies rampage'.[190] In the midst of the political madness is an unsettling scene in which a Free State officer, 'Crackers' Sheehan, 'seduces' secret agent, Kitty Grealey:

> 'What do you want, Crackers?' she said.
> 'Whatever is going. Anything left for me?'
> 'There's nothing left for you or anybody. I'm done in.'
> 'You will be, if you give me any more of yer impudence.'

He pulled off his tunic and slung it along the floor. Then he came
over to the bed and said briskly:
'Let me pull off yer things for ye. I'm used to jobs like this.'
'Leave me alone,' she said, drawing back.[191]

Despite Kitty's protests, Sheehan perseveres. The sexual encounter is
conceived of as an extension of warfare, as Sheehan insists on reclaiming
Kitty, despite the fact that she is promised to another man. The fear of
impending death in the context of war, too, has altered usual sexual
norms:

'I'll give ye a clip in the jaw if ye say another word,' he said, pulling off
her second stocking. 'Lie back there now and close yer eyes. I won't
be a tick. What ails ye, Kit? Ye used to offer me [a] sugar stick for it
once. Don't ye love us any more?'
      She offered no further resistance, but she lay back and covered
her face with her hands.
      'You have no right to do this,' she said, 'because I'm promised to
Charley Murphy. He'll kill ye if he hears about this.'
      'What's the good of being promised to a dead man?' said Sheehan,
loosening her skirt. 'The poor bastard is dead by now.'
      'God forgive you! What's that yer sayin'?' she cried, sitting up.
      'That's right. Sit up, till I get this dress over yer head. Hup! There
it goes.'
      'What's that you said about Charley? No. Don't take off any more.'
      'Off it all comes. Let go. [...] You should be ashamed of yerself.
Not another word now.'[192]

Despite the violence of the scene, the tone shifts after this point as Kitty is
suddenly seduced and 'began to look at him appraisingly as he undressed'.[193]
The reader's understanding of the scene as a sexual violation is undercut, as
Kitty throws 'back the clothes to receive him, as he leaped into bed, wearing
his revolver and his string of holy medals'.[194] O'Flaherty's scene thus draws
on classical narratives of rape, most famously Ovid's epic *Metamorphoses*,
which blur the boundaries between seduction and rape. The use of
force is reconceived as a seductive technique given that, according to
established cultural stereotypes, 'women are supposed to be coy about

their sexual availability'.[195] In line with the widespread sexualisation of female revolutionaries, Kitty is likened to a prostitute; it is suggested earlier in the novel that her work as a secret agent had led to her 'giving herself promiscuously' and '[t]hough not actually a whore, her conduct had of late not been far removed from that profession'.[196]

O'Flaherty's novel raises a host of questions regarding the ethics of representing and reading rape. While the indirect or coded renderings of rape (as outlined earlier) perpetuate the experience of sexualised violence as 'unsayable', O'Flaherty's insistent exposure is equally troublesome and risks inviting voyeurism. Indeed, the rape scene demonstrates key features identified by Emy Koopman as ethically problematic in depictions of rape: '1. the perpetrator is a sympathetic protagonist throughout the rest of the novel, 2. the scene is described in a way that is blatantly erotic, inviting voyeuristic impulses of the reader, 3. the scene employs an ironic discourse, inviting laughter.'[197] O'Flaherty's scene shares all three characteristics: though brutish and violent towards women, Sheehan was written as a character that would elicit a certain amount of respect, the success of which is evident in his description in a contemporary review as 'a fine, brave, unintelligent fighting machine'.[198] The resistance of Kitty serves to increase arousal, while there is an ironic, and minimising, twist when Kitty is suddenly charmed by Sheehan. The 'assault' is thus reframed as consensual.

'I am Sheila Doon of Magheraliffe ...': Public Testimonies in Jim Phelan's *Green Volcano*

O'Flaherty's Citizen Army comrade, Jim Phelan, once again presents an alternative insight into revolutionary sexual violence. *Green Volcano* includes a number of hard-hitting references to sexualised violence, including in a description of the sacking of a rural town by the Black and Tans: 'Down in Magheraliffe there was crying [...] For early that morning two lorries had whirled into the village, spouting death. Death and destruction and fire were behind as the lorries drove away. For nearly three hours only it had taken to rape the village, for nearly all the men were away. Over the Clare side maybe.'[199]

The reference to the 'rape' of the 'village' points to the widespread use of rape as a convenient metaphor for colonialism in Irish nationalist propaganda.[200] The use of such metaphors often occludes the actual experience of rape. As Meg Samuelson argues, in war zones 'women's bodies are simultaneously saturated with and stripped of meaning; in the process, they are rendered invisible. The raped female body suffers a similar fate: figured as a rhetorical sign, its disfigurements slip from view.'[201]

However, Phelan, quite unusually, highlights the perspective of the violated women and the affective and emotional dimensions of their experience. Unlike in *The Martyr*, he does not aesthetically represent rape, but rather hints at the abuse suffered by the women during the raid. Jack Keelahan, an IRA volunteer in Magheraliffe, nonchalantly notes, as if 'reporting the score of a football match', that the Tans, '[d]one up the rest in the ornery way'.[202] Maura Keenan is described as 'alive, but she walked slowly and in pain, holding the remnants of her clothes about her'.[203] Their mistreatment leads the women of the village to engage in the 'revolution'. Having been 'disciplined', 'the women naturally swung to the other extreme' and even enact revenge on a number of Black and Tans by stoning them to death.[204]

Phelan's dramatised account of such pillaging perhaps owes something to the reports of atrocities committed across the continent during the First World War, though his autobiographical writings also suggest the sack of Balbriggan may have provided further inspiration.[205] Phelan's depiction of sexual violence was not appreciated by critic Francis MacManus, who felt that Phelan was trying to be 'Goya' as '[e]verything that could happen in a war is made to happen: savage killing, women battering men to death, mutilation, rape, not to speak of monotonous swearing'.[206] However, a number of other reviewers focused on the novel's historical import. Writer Forrest Reid admitted that '[t]he book reveals an aspect of the war new to me, much of it being concerned with the intrigues of the rival secret services'.[207] A reviewer in *The Irish Times* even noted that 'Phelan took an active part in the mobile struggle, and every line bears the stamp of truth'.[208]

What is remarkable about Phelan's novel is not the various references to violence, including sexualised violence, against women, but the fact that the women are afforded the opportunity to voice their distress. In fact, the women exorcise their traumatic experiences by giving first-hand testimony at the trial of five uniformed British soldiers in a republican court: 'I am Sheila Doon of Magheraliffe ... I am the wife of an Imperial soldier – God help me. When the lorries came I did not run away. I thought I would be safe. With my papers. One of the men from the lorries tore my clothes. He dragged me on a sofa, but I got away.'[209]

The schoolteacher Molly Coolin, who was seriously assaulted, also testifies, albeit through ellipses:

> Molly Coolin came next, her look of embarrassment and shame giving way to cold calm as she faced the prisoners.
>
> 'I am Molly Coolin, schoolmistress of Magheraliffe,' she commenced. 'Last Saturday some men attacked my mother. These are two of the men, he and he.' She pointed to Duncan and James. 'A man from the lorry –'
>
> 'Yes?' from Tim Rooney, unemotionally.
>
> 'A man –'
>
> 'Did one of the men from the lorry rape you in your house?' asked the prosecutor.
>
> 'Yes.'[210]

By affording his female characters the opportunity to testify to their traumatic personal experiences in their own names, Phelan's court scene is at odds with representations of the violated female body as a symbol of the nation, employed to 'exalt a masculinized war narrative of victory and defeat.'[211] The extent to which Phelan's court scenes reflect the legal system of the time is questionable. Nevertheless, the local republican courts, or Dáil courts, which operated from 1920 until 1924, certainly were progressive. A number of women served as judges and the offences dealt with included abuses against women.[212] However, the sentencing of the perpetrators in the novel is in contrast to the non-prosecution of sexual crime at national level, such as the cover-up of the assault of Florrie and Jessie MacCarthy by Free State soldiers in Kenmare, County Kerry, in June 1923.[213]

Phelan even addresses the psychological consequences of such violations, most notably in the case of the character of Molly. When recalling the raid, Molly euphemistically exclaims that '[w]e have been *civilised* – this morning. That is what happened'.[214] She trembles at the sight of the location of her attack: '"No, not in there," she said in a strained voice. Her face was very pale, and she trembled a little, as if the sight of the room had reminded her of something terrifying.'[215]

After testifying in court, she resorts to similar ellipsis, busting into tears and exclaiming: 'I've had a - terrible experience, and I hardly know what I'm saying.'[216] When Molly is later stripped naked by the community for her association with the supposed spy, Irishman Liam Donohue, Ben still feels that the 'terrible experience' of this humiliation paled in comparison with 'the even more terrible happening to which it was the sequel'.[217] Moreover, it later transpires Molly was not raped by one of the British soldiers as she believed, but by Irish spy Donohue, who later becomes her lover. Phelan thus pointedly dismantles the dominant notion that brutality was exclusive to the Black and Tans. Molly's pain following these two assaults is contagious: Ben could not sleep 'remembering her strange, horrible crying and the curious, dreamlike unreality of the scene'.[218]

Phelan's attempt to address women's psychological trauma goes against the widespread tendency, until the latter part of the twentieth century, to gloss over sexual trauma. Joanna Bourke's extensive study of nineteenth- and twentieth-century medical, psychiatric and legal literature on psychiatric trauma reveals scant instances of sexual violence being identified as the cause of conditions such as hysteria, panic attacks or seizures.[219] Those involved in accidents or soldiers suffering from 'shock' were 'passive victims of calamity', but female rape victims were often presented as somehow complicit in their own misfortune.[220] This is evident, too, in Ireland: even though the Military Service Pensions Board sent female revolutionaries claiming for nervous conditions for gynaecological examinations, there is little evidence to suggest that possible sexual traumas were investigated.

By contrast to Phelan's novel, most literary representations indirectly document violence against women and shrug off the emotional consequences of such sexual attacks. In fact, in O'Flaherty's *The Martyr* the female character is actively silenced: 'Crackers' Sheehan threatens Kitty: 'I'll give ye a clip in the jaw if ye say another word.'[221] Though these writings are fictitious, they nevertheless were part of the wider economy of representations of sexual violence that functioned as 'gatekeepers' in the sense that they closed out stories of sexual violence that did not fit the established models.[222] From the denial that sexual violence occurred in Ireland in the reception of Seán Ó Caomhánaigh's *Fánaí* and the relative insignificance, and perhaps normalisation, of sexual assault in Peadar O'Donnell's *The Knife*, to the reframing of sexual violence as consensual (and the victim as promiscuous) in Liam O'Flaherty's *The Martyr*, these writings all boldly reflect on a taboo aspect of the revolution. Yet as much as they break a silence, these accounts authored by male revolutionaries nevertheless partake in a discourse in which female victims could easily be presented as culpable, in which graphic representation risked furthering and normalising such violence, and in which the reporting of sexual violence continued to be a highly risky venture.

Sexualised Violence against Men

If sexualised violence against women was taboo, sexual violence against men was even more contentious. Phelan's novel is again unusual in pointing to sexual violence against men. In a scene that hints at castration, it is reported that when Dave was captured by the Tans, they 'amused themselves' and 'cut' him. In response, Dave's partner, Dora seeks revenge on the man responsible and posts his 'alive' back from London as proof that 'he [the Black and Tan responsible] will not be marrying any more than Dave Keeler'.[223] This tale is presented as gossip and not necessarily factual. That said, such an account may reflect stories that circulated at the time or since. There are reports in popular histories, however hard to determine, that a number of anti-treaty civil war prisoners were castrated.[224]

While the widespread depiction, and even acceptance, of women as victims has facilitated research on sexual violence carried out against women, the issue of sexual violence perpetrated against men remains understudied internationally. Yet the sexual humiliation of men is hinted at in various contemporary accounts. Lady Gregory's diary refers to men in Mayo in 1921 being 'stripped naked on a bridge, beaten with rifles, indecently treated and then thrown over the bridge into the river'.[225] Seán a' Chóta's Curragh diary documents the medical inspections required of anti-treaty prisoners and hints at the humiliation of the shaving of pubic hair and being stripped naked in front of others.[226] In Mulloy's *Jackets Green*, British soldiers pull IRA prisoners naked from their beds, saying 'Come along, show a leg, show a leg' [...] 'Come along there, Paddy [...] Up and kiss the sergeant.'[227] The sexualised abuse of prisoners is more strongly suggested in Mulloy's description of civil war torture methods: as mentioned in Chapter One, Captain Jobson of the Free State army forces republican prisoners to strip off their clothes as he watches on with the 'demoniacal smile of a sadist'.[228]

Public Humiliation in Dermot Barry's *Tom Creagan*

The psychological consequences of such sexualised humiliations are perhaps most strongly suggested in the novel *Tom Creagan* (1931) by Dermot Barry. This 'quintessential Irish Bildungsroman' has been described as indicative of the disillusioned self-expression of James Joyce's *Portrait of the Artist as a Young Man* (1916).[229] The novel traces the inner turmoil of the eponymous protagonist, Tom, who joins the Irish Volunteers and is interned in Wales for his role in the Rising. Gradually, however, he turns away from violent means. Although more or less absent from critical study, the novel was awarded a Tailteann prize for Literature in 1928 and was regarded as 'one of the best stories of the period dealt with'.[230]

Like many such novels, the young revolutionaries' sexual awareness is directly addressed, as they 'pick up' three young 'girls' – one of whom is referred to as a 'tart' – on the Circular Road. The excitement of war was more socially acceptable, however, than the protagonist's awakening sexuality: 'a moment's foul thought of those girls bathing on the beach was a sin, but he delighted in war'.[231] While Tom may have been thrilled by the war initially, he turns to pacifism following a number of pivotal events, including the death of a comrade during the 1916 Rising, having to sacrifice his romantic desires due to his activism, his friendship with an English 'conscientious objector' and his disapproval of IRA targeting of supposed 'spies'. Another catalyst is the humiliation of the protagonist when he is strip-searched on the streets of Dublin: 'For a half-hour, Tom stood half-clothed in the miserable night, while the slow, absurd, search went on [...] and how ridiculous he was making himself, with all the people looking at him, and some of them, the girls, tittering, as the officer pulled up his shirt'.[232]

Shortly afterwards, Tom dies from grief following the death of his brother in active service and his mother being sent 'in a cab to the asylum'.[233] Though *Tom Creagan* was successful in Ireland, the blend of fiction and autobiography was perhaps of less interest to those unaware of the events described; a perceptive Australian-based reviewer observed that 'the appeal of the book is to Irishmen rather than to students of literature, especially to those Irishmen who have vivid personal recollections of the Easter rebellion'.[234] Indeed, the novel was read as autobiographical: it includes the rather tantalising disclaimer that 'some of the incidents are possibilities rather than records of actual historical events'. As one critic argued in a review of *Tom Creagan* and the short-story collection of David Hogan (penname of anti-treatyite Frank Gallagher), *Dark Mountain*, 'they could not have the qualities they possess unless actual experience had guided the authors' pens'.[235]

The individual behind the pseudonym of Dermot Barry (or sometimes Denis Barry) was Tadhg Gahan (1895–1962). The protagonist's revolutionary experience mirrors that of the author. A native of Wood Quay, Dublin, Gahan studied commerce at UCD, was a member of the Irish Volunteers and was stationed at Jacob's factory. This resulted in his imprisonment in Frongoch in the aftermath of the Rising. On his release in August 1916, he rejoined 'C' Company, Battalion II, Dublin Brigade and claims that during this period, he attended weekly drills and 'all other parades as ordered'.[236]

However, and quite unusually, Gahan retired from active duty in May 1920. When being interviewed before an Advisory Committee for a military service pension on 8 June 1928, he attributed his resignation to the fact that he had moved to Rathfarnham.[237] This reason did not sit well with him, however. The following day he wrote to the pension board to clarify that his resignation was not 'due to my going to live in the country'.[238] While he did not offer an alternative reason, the ideological reservations expressed in *Tom Creagan* might hint at Gahan's true doubts about the use of physical force and his distress on account of what he later referred to as the 'desultorily cruel civil war'.[239] Though the novel ends before the truce, 'unacknowledged civil war' characterises the narrative throughout: Seán Delaney is killed in 1916 after he is informed on by an Irish middle-class family, while Tom finds the English Quaker to be 'nearer me than the Gael at my side'.[240] Gahan discovered a medium, in fiction, which allowed for the suggestion of personal humiliations, among other traumas.

Conclusion

While Gahan's remarkable novel indicates that fiction could provide a self-protective means of addressing sexualised trauma, most of the texts discussed point to the problems of writing sexual violence. The various strategies of evasion in women's testimonies pose more questions than they answer regarding the nature of sexual violence during the revolution. Nevertheless, the oft-assumed culture of silence surrounding sexual violence was clearly not as pervasive as often suggested. Fictionalised testimonies written by male revolutionaries complicate the emphasis on sexual innocence, cleanliness and honour advanced in official remembrance, foregrounded in much self-representation and further promoted in historical studies. These accounts, rather problematically, often normalise violence against women as a natural consequence of the excess of masculine anxiety during wartime. Moreover, violence against women, which could be sexualised in its nature, could paradoxically be justified as a means with which to regulate sexual promiscuity. The widespread sexualisation of female revolutionaries in popular discourse was also accompanied by the suggestion that militant women, having transgressed accepted social norms, were no longer protected by established norms of respectability; they were, therefore, particularly vulnerable to physical and sexual assault.

Popular representations of sexual violence against women highlight the fine line between consensual and non-consensual relations, and underscore that, despite an insistence on the sexual brutality of the Black and Tans, Irish-on-Irish sexual violence was its own 'unacknowledged civil war'. Jim Phelan's writings are something of an anomaly in his attention to the psychological consequences of such assaults. Debates around these representations associate sexual violence with the influence of French psychology or Hollywood movies. These discourses governed the reporting and remembering of actual sexual violence: testimonies of sexual assault were closed out by the culturally and socially consolidated myth that such violations did not occur in Ireland or by the idea that the victim – and particularly the 'promiscuous' female revolutionary – was responsible for their own suffering. Moreover, it would appear from censoring practices that depictions of men's 'immorality' were as offensive as representations of violence against women.

Testimony is always dialogic and relies on its reception to be complete. Audiences willing to hear about sexual violence first-hand were arguably limited. The next chapter considers another rich body of testimony that struggled to find a reception in post-revolutionary Ireland: the testimony of veterans who found themselves displaced in the aftermath of the civil war.

Chapter Four

'A Dispossessed People': Spiritual Exiles and Exiled Emigrants

For prolific novelist Elizabeth Brennan (1907–1981), the 'recipe' for her fictional plots was simple: 'plenty of love, but not much sex, and no violence'.[1] During the 1960s and 1970s, Brennan produced at least twelve romance novels that were recommended to housewives who liked 'to curl up with a book when the washing-up is done'.[2] Yet her earlier writing – published under the name Eily O'Horan – shied away from neither sex nor violence. These 1930s and 1940s short stories, some of which addressed the revolutionary period, were published in literary journals in England, Ireland and the United States. Her credentials as a writer were solidified by the fact that she had been imprisoned in Kilmainham in the same section as Mary MacSwiney, Maud Gonne MacBride and Grace Plunkett. Biographical sketches dated her internment to 1921, but this, once again, was a convenient blurring of historical dates.[3] Eily O'Horan – then Eilish Dolan – was interned from 17 April until 23 October 1923 after Free State soldiers found arms in her family home.[4] She was fifteen. Her memoirs include a further example of the minimising of possible physical mistreatment evident in women's accounts: even though she writes that she was interrogated in Kilmainham with a revolver to her heart, she prefaces this by stressing that she was 'treated courteously and even kindly' on her initial arrest.[5] Dolan (as she is referred to hereafter) has little to say about the violence or fear experienced by the women prisoners, only that her imprisonment made her certain 'that Ireland would see no real prosperity or peace while such bloodshed and violent deeds held sway on our land'.[6]

Dolan's civil war experience had such profound ramifications for her that, one November morning in 1924, she fled her home in Stoneybatter, Dublin and boarded a mailboat for London with no more than 'a few necessities in a small attaché case, and a few shillings in my pocket, and my wardrobe on my back'.[7] In this, Dolan was one of many revolutionaries who, for various economic, political or personal reasons, sought a home away from Ireland. While Dolan's emigration was far from unique, her motivation for such a sudden flight was unusual. Disillusioned on her release from imprisonment, Dolan followed the 'spiritual revolution' of her Irish-language teacher and future husband, anti-treaty prisoner Pádraig O'Horan (1902–1951).[8] O'Horan had grown so dismayed at the leaders of both the republican movement and Catholic Church during his eighteen-month internment that, on his release, he found a new 'spiritual home' in the Dublin Methodist Mission, hoping to find 'Ireland's healing' in the 'sweet and blessed truth'.[9] He left Ireland to study at Cliff Methodist College in Derbyshire before moving to Belfast in 1926, where he trained for the Methodist ministry at Edgehill Theological College.[10]

Dolan also relocated to what she had known as 'the Black North'.[11] She was appointed a Methodist deaconess-evangelist at Grosvenor Hall in Belfast and attracted crowds across the province of Ulster with her many addresses on topics such as 'Why I left the Church of Rome'.[12] In an unlikely turn, the couple's 'exile' from republicanism led them to start a new life among the northern Protestant community in Belfast, where they married in July 1928. They left Methodism in 1930, however, and joined the Church of England, spending the next twenty years fulfilling various ministries, including in Somerset (1931–2), Nottingham (1932–8), Achill Island (1938–9), Bath (1939–44), Priddy (1944–9) and Sampford (1949–51).

Both Dolan and O'Horan wrote extensively about the civil war from their self-perceived position of exile. Dolan revisited the revolutionary period in two successful religious conversion memoirs, *Through the Gates of Babylon: The Story of a Conversion* (1932) and *No More Foreigners: Impressions of a Spiritual Pilgrimage* (1935), and hinted at her experience of 'exile' in her many short stories and novels.[13] O'Horan, for his part, exploited the testimonial potential of non-fictional, fictional and poetic narrative forms; he produced first-hand essays on his civil war experience in 1927, revisited the same events in an extensive fictionalised account published the same year, and addressed the revolution in poetry throughout his life. For Dolan, writing was both a 'form of escapism' and a vehicle for 'recovery', while O'Horan hinted at his personal urge to 'write to tell of the futility' of the revolutionary project.[14] Their testimonies, like many emigrants' writings, had little impact in post-independence Ireland. If it were not for a notable 2002 article by Rev. Robert P. Roddie, the writings of O'Horan and Dolan could easily be totally forgotten.

This chapter surveys the many veteran testimonies in which the turmoil of revolution coincided with further upheaval through emigration or internal migration. There were, indeed, established narrative templates through which revolutionaries could tease out the traumatic implications of post-civil war displacement due to emigration and partition: they mobilised the longstanding nationalist trope of political exile, but also, in some cases, reappropriated the Anglo-Irish Big House literary tradition in order to grapple with themes of dispossession and change. Female emigrants were less likely to be drawn towards the generally masculine trope of political exile in telling their life stories. This chapter thus teases out the gendered dimensions of emigrant testimonies with a particular focus on the many writings of Pádraig O'Horan and Eily Dolan (aka Eily O'Horan and Elizabeth Brennan), and Kathleen Hoagland's autobiographically based novel *Fiddler in the Sky* (1944).

Moreover, this chapter considers the idea that self-perceived states of 'exile' were not contingent on geographic relocation. Wartime traumatic experience is already a form of displacement that evokes the challenge of return, whether that be the difficulty of homecoming and re-establishing family ties, the challenge of reintegrating into civilian life or the personal desire to reconnect with a nostalgic pre-trauma past (see Chapter One). This is all the more fraught in the aftermath of civil war, as splintered local communities, and even divided families, must learn to co-exist. In his influential study on Spanish writers under the Francoist regime, *Literature and Inner Exile* (1980), Paul Ilie stresses that exile is not necessarily associated with 'physical separation' but rather a 'state of mind whose emotions and values respond to separation and severance as conditions in themselves'.[15] For many veterans of the Irish Civil War, therefore, the feeling of living 'in exile' resulted from 'inner' or 'spiritual' exile, as much as from geographic displacement.

Post-Civil War Displacement and Remembrance

The widespread displacement precipitated by the events of the civil war is by now apparent: Desmond Ryan's reaction to the civil war was to flee 'over the seas from Sion',[16] Patrick Mulloy, author of *Jackets Green*, started a new life in the civil service in London. A number of revolutionary novels end with the protagonist's escape from the newly established Irish Free State. In Jim Phelan's *Green Volcano*, the anti-treaty protagonist Ben Robinson boards a ship from Dublin with his lover Bridget to ensure 'we'll eat when we are hungry'.[17] Meanwhile, Jake Wynne's novel *Ugly Brew* concludes as pro-treatyite Martin O'Neill vomits in the sea (his 'farewell gesture') as he makes for Cape Town (see Chapters One and Three).[18] In a review of Wynne's novel in the short-lived periodical *Ireland To-day*, Seán O'Faoláin was concerned that this 'final touch' would 'enrage our more thin-skinned nationalists'.[19] The reader of my second-hand copy of Wynne's novel certainly did not approve; this concluding passage is accompanied by a '!??!!!' written in the margins.

Emigration was indeed an uncomfortable reminder of the frustrated ambitions of the revolutionary generation. Writing in the American weekly magazine *Life* in 1953, O'Faoláin recalled that many had hoped that a 'native government' would 'soon put a stop to all that'.[20] However, the establishment of the Free State coincided with a renewal of emigration that lasted throughout the 1920s. Thousands of republican activists emigrated. The United States emerged as the most popular destination for revolutionaries, but many relocated to England, Scotland, Australia and indeed across the globe. This phenomenon of emigration has only more recently been addressed within the historiography of the Irish revolution.[21] Partition also led to the forced displacement of thousands of people, as individuals and communities became either minorities or majorities by virtue of which side of the border they found themselves on.[22] This produced a surplus of 'neglected and hidden exodus[es]' which, according to Robert Lynch's estimates, resulted in between 50,000 and 80,000 people becoming refugees.[23] The southern Protestant population also sharply declined, a phenomenon connected to the removal of British administration, but also exacerbated by the burning of Big Houses during the civil war. A number of Protestants from the new Irish Free State resettled in east Ulster, while Catholics from areas north of the border – the 'forgotten northern exodus' – fled south.[24] The riots, sectarian violence and killings in Belfast from 1920–2 also caused massive demographic upheaval. Though figures vary, it is believed that by the end of the civil war, over a quarter of the city's Catholics had been forced from their homes, with many fleeing south or to Scotland (before, in many cases, returning to Belfast).[25] Did these 'moving minorities',[26] which included active revolutionaries, leave fewer testimonial traces?

Furthermore, who was left to remember the events of the revolution in places like Allihies on the Beara Peninsula or West Connemara after nearly all local revolutionaries had emigrated?[27] If the realities of large-scale emigration did indeed 'enrage our more thin-skinned nationalists', leading to the omission of emigration from national histories, such geographic displacement equally problematised revolutionary remembrance at local level. This movement of people disrupts the 'social frameworks' on which, as Maurice Halbwachs has argued, the production of collective memory relies.[28] Emigration also frustrated the sharing of testimony. As addressed in Chapter Two, Mary Manning emigrated to Boston – she never staged Máirín Cregan's Hunger-strike and Manning's novel, Mount Venus, was never published in Ireland for fear of libel. How many civil war prisoners, like Mairéad de Lappe, smuggled their jail journals out from Kilmainham and straight over to Boston?[29] Or how many revolutionaries like Bridie Halpin emigrated to New York, never to broach the topic of her civil war internment with her family?[30]

As much as this scattering of activists problematised revolutionary remembrance, there is nevertheless no shortage of references to emigration in the writings of revolutionaries who remained in Ireland. Drawing attention to continued emigration was a means of protesting against the newly established state. Former anti-treaty prisoner Seosamh Mac Grianna lamented in 1925, 'Is iad na Gaeilgeoirí is mó atá ag imeacht. Anois nuair atá an uile dhuine a bhfuil Gaeilge aige de dhíobháil go crua ar an tír' [It is the Irish speakers who are leaving the most. Now when every Irish speaker is badly needed for the country].[31] Meanwhile, his brother Séamus Ó Grianna – who is rather terse in his autobiographical writings regarding his own civil war internment[32] – addressed the centrality of emigration in rural communities in his fiction; his novel Bean Ruadh de Dhálach (1966), in particular, countered the targeting of potential female emigrants in nationalist anti-emigration propaganda by highlighting the liberation offered to rural women by emigration.[33]

Female revolutionaries, too, tackled post-independence emigration. Kathleen O'Brennan (c. 1876–1948), who carried out a Sinn Féin lecture tour across the USA in 1918–19, addressed the 'Irish-American problem' in her play *Full Measure: A Play in Three Acts*, which appeared in the Abbey in August 1928.[34] The three-act play relates to the outcry caused in a small town in West Kerry when widow Nora Murtagh expresses her intentions to run for the TD nomination in protest against the exploitation of the poor by local 'gombeen' man Batty Quinlan. As Batty exclaims, 'Wild women! In the name of God is Ireland to be governed by them?'[35] Nora's electoral ambitions are frustrated, however, and the play ends as her last remaining son, an anti-treaty republican whose lover had eloped with a Free State soldier, flees Ireland to join another brother who had been selected to run in the Boston legislature. The message was clear: there was more hope for anti-treaty republicans in the diaspora than in rural Ireland. Although the play was well received, this was the last play O'Brennan was successful in staging, pointing once again to the obstacles encountered by women in finding an audience for their works.

Máirín Cregan and Garrett O'Driscoll also confronted the question of emigration. O'Driscoll's short story 'Fair Day', published in *Ireland To-day* in 1937, concludes as a widowed father from a rural republican family accepts that his beloved daughter 'would have to go', as 'the life the land gave wasn't one you would wish to anyone you loved'.[36] The taboo surrounding the realities of emigration is evident from the fact that Cregan's play *Curlew's Call* was rejected by the Abbey in 1939 with the advice that she 'try another subject'.[37] The play, though never performed, was published in the *Capuchin Annual* the following year.[38] The protagonist, Bridgie Riordan, returns from New York to convince her mother, Mary, to come back with her. Thoughts of milk in 'cute little bottles ready for you' are contrasted with the 'life of hardship' in Ireland. Nevertheless, Bridgie's hopes for a new life for her mother in America are thwarted as the natural world – represented by a calling curlew – conspires to prevent emigration: Mary Riordan drowns as she is collecting dillisk seaweed to bring to her pregnant daughter in New York. As in *Hunger-strike*, there is no respite for the female protagonist. The characters cast doubt on the government's relocation of families from the west of Ireland to County Meath, Bridgie loses out on marriage for want of a dowry and her friend Debbie hopes that a new government scheme will enable her to settle down. This commentary on such state relocation initiatives is all the more intriguing given that Cregan's husband, Jim Ryan, was Fianna Fáil Minister for Agriculture from 1932–47.

Exile: Victim Diaspora or Redemptive Trauma?

In contrast to the restrictions on the production of narrative in Ireland, the liminal space of the diaspora was often considered to be a haven for testimony. Ernie O'Malley took advantage of his sojourn in Taos, New Mexico to reflect on his experience during the revolution. In his unpublished short story 'High Seas Piracy', a group of six republicans on New York's Seventh Avenue acknowledge the freedom of expression away from Ireland. They agree that 'sitting at a table three thousand miles away made a difference' and allowed one to 'see things outside of the events themselves'.[39] This narrative device is not unlike the connecting frame story in Dorothy Macardle's short-story collection *Earth-bound* (1924) in which the headquarters of a republican newspaper in Philadelphia provide a refuge for 'exile' testimony. Significantly, also, the collection was published in Worchester, Massachusetts after being rejected by Talbot Press in Dublin.[40]

The idea that the diasporic space facilitated the sharing of testimony may reflect the longstanding situation of the Irish emigrant experience within a narrative of trauma. As Kerby Miller argued, many Irish immigrants in North America from the mid-nineteenth century onwards self-identified as 'exiles'.[41] The pervasiveness of the 'involuntary exile' motif has even led to the characterisation of Irish emigration as a 'victim diaspora', while the proliferation of sorrowful, nostalgic emigrant paeans has been read as a further example of Liam Kennedy's MOPE ('most oppressed people ever') syndrome.[42] The observed overemphasis on the events of the revolution in emigrant testimonies suggests that it was easier to tell life stories through the more affirming nationalist narrative of exile than to address migration in 'drab economic terms'.[43] But this motif of traumatic exile also offered revolutionary veterans a narrative template that facilitated the retelling of traumatic experience.

The tendency of republican emigrants to portray their departure in a 'politicized exilic light'[44] is particularly clear in the handful of memoirs by emigrant IRA veterans that began to emerge from the 1970s. Jeremiah Murphy's memoir, *When Youth Was Mine* (1998), underscores how republican emigrants located the disappointment of their emigration within a larger lineage of political exiles: 'The Flight of the Earls, The Wild Geese and Sarsfield's Irish Brigade all came to mind.'[45] Séamus O'Connor's 1970 account, *Tomorrow Was Another Day*, claimed '[t]hat nostalgia, that longing for, and thinking of Ireland, seemed to be characteristic of all the Irishmen I came across in the US.'[46] The exile trope was equally mobilised by pro-treaty emigrants. In *My Kilkenny Days: 1916–22* (1988), James Comerford drew on the poetry of fellow Kilkenny New York emigrant Fenian John Locke (1632–1704) and recalled that 'Irish exiles retain their inherent love for Ireland.'[47]

This model of exile identity not only permitted the retelling of painful experience, it also helped to counter the culture of shame surrounding emigration, which was exacerbated by the nationalist anti-emigration mandate of the Gaelic League, the First Dáil and the IRA. During the war of independence, the IRA directly targeted potential emigrants by 'reliev[ing]' them of their passports.[48] High rates of female emigration were perceived as a particular threat to the body politic of the new nation; the 'Irish girl emigrant' was warned that she would be rejected in the diaspora for 'running away from your country in her need.'[49] Revolutionary veterans who emigrated in the 1920s thus did so despite the anti-emigration position of the republican movement. De Valera expressed his hope in 1923 that there would be 'no Wild Geese [...] this time' and the anti-treaty leadership denounced emigrants as 'deserters' whose actions were 'worse' than Free State 'murder and executions.'[50] Pro-treaty propaganda anticipated that anti-treaty republicans 'would emigrate out of a sense of shame for having incited unnecessary violence and destruction on their communities.'[51] A contemporary ditty indicates how this shaming was also gendered, as male republican emigrants were bracketed together with the well-established chains of female migrants: 'The colleens of Erin are sailing away, and with them are sailing the Old IRA.'[52]

In the 1938 novel *Dead Star's Light* (see Chapter Five), Elizabeth Connor conveys the tension between emigrants' collective identity as exiles and their perhaps individual sense of shame. As the IRA veteran John Davern exclaims: 'The modern Wild Geese. I never liked that expression ... it sounds all right in the plural, but imagine being called a Wild Goose!'[53] Later commentators also demonstrated a certain scepticism towards republican emigrants' sense of exile. In a chapter perhaps ironically entitled 'The Wild Geese' in Frank O'Connor's novel *Dutch Interior* (1940), it emerges that the character of Gus was not forced to emigrate due to political activities, but rather as he was 'caught with that woman'.[54] In Seán O'Faoláin's *Come Back to Erin* (1940) protagonist Frankie Hannafey, an IRA man who flees to New York in the 1930s, has little time for the republican emigrants he encounters who are still preoccupied with what happened on some night in 1921: 'I didn't come here [...] to be wailing and weeping about what's dead and done with. To hell with all that.'[55]

The shaming of migrants also intersected with ideas of madness, both in Ireland and elsewhere.[56] Anti-emigration propaganda literature routinely drew attention to high rates of Irish immigrants in asylums in the United States. In the early twentieth century, insanity rates in Ireland were attributed to the emigration of 'the best out of the country', while by 1925, increases in 'insanity' at Ballinasloe Mental Hospital were associated with the 'breakdown of Irishmen who emigrated to America'.[57] This uneasy conflation of madness and emigration is hinted at in Peadar O'Donnell's regret that, in his novel *Adrigoole*, he did not allow his fictional character, Hughie Dálach, to emigrate rather than being committed to an asylum (see Chapter One).

The outsourcing of medical patients was indeed a reality. Many revolutionaries suffered due to substandard living conditions on the run, 'wettings', beatings, poor prison conditions or hunger striking – not to mention suffering caused by psychological injury. In the aftermath of the civil war, the IRA aided sick veterans, including those suffering from tuberculosis, to avail of medical treatment abroad, particularly in the United States.[58] This reflects the limited medical services in Ireland and is also indicative of the prescription of 'a change in environment', often to a warmer climate, which was advised for various conditions, including 'nerves'. For example, Cumann na mBan activist Mary Ellen Scullen of Westport, County Mayo, was beaten by the Black and Tans and claimed that she emigrated to Ohio in 1925 on doctor's orders to treat her 'severe shock': '[H]e said the voyage on the ocean & the change may help me but I'm sorry it didn't help a lot.'[59]

However, as much as emigration, couched in the language of 'a change in environment', might have been offered as a 'medical' solution for nervous and other conditions, an 'itinerant lifestyle' could paradoxically be read as indicative of a mental condition itself. In early psychology, the term 'nostalgia' described a nervous disease,[60] while, as already observed, 'hysteria' was symptomatic of a '*wandering* womb' (my emphasis). This might explain why Ernie O'Malley's New York doctor, Frank Murray, associated his nervous condition with his migratory habits: 'As regards question of neurasthenia: his conduct would strike the average individual as strange. He wanders and has been wandering for some years past over the United States and Mexico, going from one job to another, seldom staying in one place long.'[61]

Given the widespread shaming of emigrants, therefore, the forced exile narrative perhaps enabled revolutionary emigrants to rewrite a distressing personal history into a more consolatory shared nationalist narrative; this is a further example of what Dominick LaCapra terms a 'founding trauma' which can paradoxically form 'the valorized or intensely cathected basis of identity for an individual or a group.'[62] One such example is union man J. F. O'Connor's appropriately entitled memoir, *An Irish Civil War Exile* (1989), described somewhat disparagingly by *Books Ireland* as a 'vanity published but interesting-looking autobiography of a now American Irishman.'[63] Though referred to as an 'autobiography', the narrative is written almost as a novel from the self-protective distance of third-person narration; the protagonist is introduced as 'full-fledged soldier' Josie O'Connaire.[64] O'Connor's account opens with an (albeit historically questionable) account of nine rebels who escaped execution for their role in the 1848 rebellion and later went on to achieve huge success in the diaspora. Some were brigadier generals in the US army, another was a member of parliament in Canada and others were attorney generals in Australia. This exile narrative was accompanied by a sense of redemption rather than victimhood. By locating his post-civil war emigration in this larger nationalist narrative, O'Connor was able to claim the identity of an exile, while also pointing to the positive impact such emigrants could wield in their adopted communities. The distancing of third-person narration, as well as the geographic and temporal distance that characterised the production of his 1989 memoir, also enabled O'Connor to address taboo topics such as contentious relations with the Catholic Church, his understanding of homosexuality and other sexual matters, disputes over the Irish Land Commission and anti-Traveller sentiment among the many Irish 'who choose to look down rather than straight ahead'.[65]

Pádraig O'Horan: 'I Must Write to Tell of the Futility'

Not unlike the barely fictionalised persona adopted by O'Connor in *An Irish Civil War Exile*, Pádraig O'Horan's writing hints at a particular understanding of the exile's privileged position to comment on Irish social inequalities – and even redress the material destruction caused by the civil war. One of the earliest casualties of the Battle of Dublin was the historical archive of the Public Records Office: thousands of records dating back to the thirteenth century were destroyed as the Four Courts went up in flames on 30 June 1922. The Irish Genealogical Research Society was founded in 1936 with the ambitious aim of bridging 'the genealogical gap' caused by the burning of these key records.[66] This archival destruction was hardly something the new state wanted to dwell on, and it might not be coincidental, therefore, that the Irish Genealogical Research Society was founded in London's West End. The members of the society were largely made up of British academics and intellectuals – including Robin Flower of the British Museum – but among the founding members was Pádraig O'Horan.[67] In 1938, Mr Herbert Woods, who had been Deputy Keeper of the Public Records Office of Ireland in 1922, addressed the society about seeing thousands of records being 'consigned to the flames'.[68] Woods could not attend the meeting in person, however. His address was read on his behalf by O'Horan.

Whereas Woods attempted to save the records that June day, O'Horan left his home on Essex Quay to join the anti-treaty garrison as soon as he heard the sound of gunfire. His fictionalised writings capture the reverberating soundscape of the destruction:

> Rumble! Rumble—rumble—rumble! Boom!
> Zip-zip-zip-zip-zip-zip-zip! The rifles spoke from the sandbagged windows of the Four Courts.
> R-r-r-r-r-r-r-r-r!
> A baby wailed querulously in a back street. The angry voice of a woman shouted at two bare-footed children shivering in the morning air.
> Boom! Boom! Boom!
> Zip-zip-zip-zip—crash![69]

O'Horan's founding role in the Irish Genealogical Research Society was one of a number of projects he undertook to compensate for the historical damage caused, in his view, by his actions as a member of the anti-treaty IRA. The idealism that drove O'Horan from his home that June morning quickly dissipated. After just a few days defending anti-treaty positions in the city, O'Horan was arrested and interned for eighteen months in Gormanston and Newbridge. Under the influence of a number of Citizen Army internees, he grew appalled at both the abuse of power by republican leaders and the mistreatment of republican activists by the Catholic Church, which had 'failed Ireland in ghastly failure'.[70] Seeing the civil war as an 'outward and visible sign of an inward and spiritual disgrace',[71] he committed himself to an alternative 'spiritual revolution' to 'heal' Ireland's war wounds. Echoing Desmond Ryan's belief in the need to 'rid' ourselves of the past rather than 'harp' on about it, O'Horan exclaimed that '[b]itter brooding upon a tragic past cannot help nor heal the heart of a nation. A spiritual emancipation is the most vital need of the times'.[72]

In addition to genealogical research, O'Horan published two testimonies of his civil war; the first was a series of articles – subtitled 'an incident from the Civil War in Ireland' – which included extracts from his prison diary and was published in the London-based *Methodist Magazine* in 1927 and 1928.[73] Simultaneously, he published a lightly fictionalised testimony, *The Flame of Youth: A Study in Rebel Mentality*, which was serialised in the Belfast weekly newspaper the *Irish Christian Advocate* between November 1927 and October 1928. He also teased out the consequences of his 'spiritual' exile in six poetry volumes, published between 1924 and 1951, as well as in numerous poems, written in both English and Irish, published in journals and newspapers across Britain, Ireland and the United States.[74]

Even though O'Horan's experience of emigration does not comply with established ideas of banishment, he nevertheless located his self-perceived exile within a long tradition of emigration, which he described as 'the tragedy of a dispossessed people'.[75] In his journalistic writings, O'Horan addressed contemporary emigration through the nationalist poetry of Ethna Carbery (1864–1902), who wrote of emigrants who carried 'to the distant land a tear-drop in the eye'.[76] But, as a genealogist, devout Christian and Gaelic scholar, O'Horan also traced nineteenth-century nationalist exile tropes back to the banishment of the 'Wild Geese' in the post-reformation age and further back again to the 'Gaelic exile' of St Patrick and St Colmcille.[77] Once again, this sense of exile could offer some redemption; modern emigrants shared Colmcille's sense that 'in exile', one could 'discover many delightful and nostalgic links of kinship and association'.[78] O'Horan further cites Colmcille's return to Ireland in 575 to the synod of Druim Ceat, near Derry, to negotiate better terms for Ireland's *filí* (poets); this points to his view regarding the ability of the intellectual exile to wield positive influence on the 'home' country.

Inner Exile: Paddy Who Ran

Although O'Horan repeatedly mobilised tropes of exile from the nationalist and Gaelic Christian traditions, his sense of 'spiritual' exile reconfigures traditional conceptions of exile often associated with separation from one's native land. Both he and his wife Eily Dolan experienced multiple inner, and even self-imposed, exiles prior to their geographic relocation. As the title of Dolan's second memoir, *No More Foreigners* (1935), indicates, the O'Horans perceived themselves as 'foreigners' before their conversion to Christ; their 'spiritual pilgrimage' was 'a homecoming after many sad and weary journeyings'.[79] Nonetheless, it was a 'homecoming' which paradoxically 'meant the breaking up of home ties, the misunderstanding and reproach of loved ones'.[80] Nor was it a permanent homecoming, as evident from the fact that the O'Horans exited Methodism suddenly in 1930 and converted to the Church of England. Indeed, O'Horan's Methodist contemporaries disparagingly rendered 'Paddy Horan' as 'Paddy Who Ran'.[81]

This self-exile speaks to the phenomenon of 'inner exile' associated with civil war. As Ilie puts it, 'Inner exile [...] is an emptiness that awaits restoration, much the same way that territorial exile is the absence that compensates itself by nostalgia and hopeful anticipation.'[82] Indeed, the foundation of the Irish Free State and Northern Ireland left behind various pockets of the population who struggled to identify with the new status quo; Francis Carty self-identified as an 'exile from the old county' (Chapter One), while Seán O'Faoláin postulated in 1935 that due to the legacy of the revolution and civil war, '[e]very Irish writer of to-day over thirty is a spiritual *déraciné*'.[83]

Although exile has been considered the 'cradle of nationalism', nationalism can provoke exile too, as 'successful nationalisms', in Edward

Said's view, 'consign truth exclusively to themselves, relegating falsehood to outsiders'.[84] This nationalist insider-outsider discourse appears in O'Horan's writings, as the idealistic Gaelic Leaguer warns others that '[y]ou'll have to learn the Gaelic now or the people will look upon you as an outsider'.[85] The irony, however, is that O'Horan finds that his ability to speak Irish 'like a native', acquired through his studies at the Dublin College of Modern Irish and in the West Cork Gaeltacht, makes him 'an outsider' during his internment.[86] His fellow prisoners used 'fugitive Gaelic phrases', but had little interest in the Language Revival Movement.[87]

O'Horan's self-imposed linguistic exile is indicative of the generational tensions between many revolutionaries and their parents. On joining the anti-treaty side, it appears that O'Horan went against the wishes of his father who supported the treaty.[88] His most bitter exile, however, was arguably not that imposed by his family nor the newly founded state, but his growing sense that he was an 'outsider' even within the republican movement. O'Horan thus found himself 'in prison for Ireland when I don't believe in Ireland'.[89] Return to 'Ireland' did not offer 'non-exile' either. He recalled the prisoners mocking the Irish Free State as a 'place or state of punishment where some souls suffer for a time before they go to America'.[90]

Intersections of Dispossession: From Dublin Tenements, Western Famine to Belfast Refugees

O'Horan's two civil war testimonies reflect the complex succession of exilic states he experienced. His writings also evince a strong sympathy with other displaced groups. Though he published simultaneous fictionalised and standard first-hand testimonies in 1927 and 1928, the fictionalised account, *The Flame of Youth*, is both lengthier and more insightful in terms of the inner turmoil of the author surrogate. The protagonist Páraic Morton is an 18-year-old, 'freckle-faced, tousle-headed, short-trousered boy'.[91] Like the author, he is the son of a Redmondite but the grandson of a Fenian. In the opening pages, Páraic is described as 'Ossianlike'; like Oisín who had returned from a bygone time and place, Páraic lives in a state of semi-exile, pining for a 'vanished' Tír na nÓg, for 'Utopias of native rule'.[92] *The Flame of Youth* opens as Dublin's Parliament Street is 'en fête' after the signing of the Anglo-Irish Treaty. However, it comes with the reminder that 'the Present never lost touch with the Past'.[93] The impending tragedy is set up through the lens of the 'tattered glory' of the memory of the First World War and 1916 Rising:

> Terror and Tragedy – and deserted streets.
> No! No deserted, for see the still forms of the dead.
> Silent streets, do you hear again the echoing footsteps of those who sleep in Flanders' fields?
> Tramp–tramp–tramp. Plunket! [*sic*] Clarke! McBride!
> [...]
> France–France–France, and Easter Week in Dublin.
> And now this.[94]

O'Horan's unsettled fragmented narration suggests the influence of the avant-garde of the First World War poets, but his literary aesthetic is also marked by a distinctly Seán O'Casey-esque flare.[95] Though he chronicles, in both accounts, how he was relocated to a number of buildings across the city during the Battle for Dublin, including Barry's Hotel and in Gardiner's Row, O'Horan's writings bring the civil war into Dublin's tenements. In *The Flame of Youth*, Páraic, along with several fellow volunteers, are taken into a tenement by a number of 'dirty faced, untidy urchins' who urge them to '[c]ome in or yiz'll be shot'.[96] Here they become acquainted with Johnny Murphy, who, drunk on looted alcohol, rowdily sings 'Bold Robert Emmet'. This sense of drunken nationalism directly mimics the characters of Joxer Daly and Jack Boyle in O'Casey's play *Juno and the Paycock* (1924), set during the civil war. Boyle defiantly celebrates that 'if they've taken everything else from us, Joxer, they've left us our memory', to which Joxer's responds that 'mem'ry's the only friend that grief can call its own, that grief – can – call – its own!'.[97] Joxer's response is reiterated verbatim by one of O'Horan's prisoners in *The Flame of Youth*.[98] However, this nationalistic sentiment is undercut by Citizen Army man John Whelan, who rejects Páraic's initial pride at being held in the same cells as the martyrs of 1916: 'We can't eat memories, Páraic, and they don't always make good pillows and are certainly no use for mattresses.'[99] Rather than being roused by the legacies of the republican martyrs, Páraic is instead haunted during his imprisonment by his memories of the shocking sights and sounds of his temporary tenement abode, not being able to stop thinking about the 'little girl with the torn frock and those appealing eyes'.[100]

O'Horan's commitment to documenting the social realities of wartime poverty can be traced back to a distinctly Gaelic League concern for hardship and, particularly, emigration. As civil war loomed in early 1922, O'Horan was busy establishing the 'Western Distress Fund' and spearheading a national campaign to draw attention to the threat of famine.[101] His concern for the impoverished equally applied to Dublin's working classes. While Pearse wrote of '[l]ittle children playing with bare feet on sands in Connacht', O'Horan rebutted that the children of Dublin, too, had bare feet 'but they are not playing on sand'.[102] The ordinary citizens of O'Horan's civil war Dublin care little for the difference between 'the IRA (ah) and th' IRA (ay)'.[103] As Páraic looks at a 'working-class girl dressed in cheap finery' at whom a 'Free State guard glared suspiciously', he cannot help but think: 'What did the Republic mean to her?'[104]

It was not just the locals, with their 'broad Dublinese', who occupied the tenements in O'Horan's civil war Dublin. In his non-fictional account, O'Horan refers to a Catholic woman who 'had fled to Dublin, with many others, during the riots in Belfast'.[105] The new arrival is uneasy about the presence of the rebels and a local woman responds by rushing at her with 'table knife in hand'.[106] O'Horan's inclusion of such tensions between displaced Belfast refugees and impoverished Dubliners is absent from *The Flame of Youth*, his fictionalised account published in Belfast. During this time, O'Horan held a ministerial position at Woodvale Methodist Church, off the Shankill Road in west Belfast, pointing perhaps to a silencing of this aspect of his experience for this particular audience. Nevertheless, in 1927, speaking in Carlisle Methodist Memorial Church in the north of the city, he defended the actions of the IRA: 'The people of the North [...] might have thought of the men of the I.R.A. as murderers, looters and scoundrels, but Jesus did not believe that. He was behind their barricades, in their blasting buildings, lonely cells and internment camps, and He spoke to their hearts.'[107]

O'Horan's unease with recording the experience of the Belfast refugees reflects the general tendency to shirk away from this sectarian conflict. In 1922, a Catholic priest, Fr John Hassan, put together a pseudonymised pamphlet on the events entitled *Facts and Figures of the Belfast Pogrom 1920–1922*. Though Hassan's pamphlet was purportedly commissioned by the Provisional Government, all but eighteen copies published were 'pulped' due to the pro-treaty authorities' concerns that it would incite further unrest and, perhaps, spur on their anti-treaty opposition.[108] This suppression of testimony in newly established Northern Ireland continued after partition: historian Margaret Ward attributes the dearth of post-civil war documentation regarding Belfast Cumann na mBan to the 'hazards of being an active republican in an environment where at least 70 per cent of the population – the unionist majority – was hostile'.[109]

Once again, however, less conventional forms of narrative offered insight into this experience. Michael McLaverty's celebrated autobiographically informed novel *Call My Brother Back* (1939) charts the vicissitudes of sectarian violence in Belfast from summer 1920 to 1922; residents are afraid to talk to neighbours in the street 'for fear their houses would be raided and their sons arrested'.[110] In his posthumous civil war memoir, *The Singing Flame* (1978), Ernie O'Malley documents the occupation of Dublin's Kildare Street Club by the anti-treaty Dublin Brigade in summer 1922 and records that 'Belfast refugees slept in the well-furnished bedrooms and sat somewhat fearfully in the reading rooms' while the IRA men 'played handball and occasionally puffed leisurely at long cigars'.[111] He represented this event in more detail in an unpublished short story, 'Admiral for a Day'. Like O'Horan's account of the distressed Belfast woman, O'Malley's fictionalised account captures a social reality that was 'met with denial' at government level:[112]

> Some of them were dressed in black for they had lost members of their families or relatives through grenades and rifle fire before leaving. Their shabby clothes were a contrast to the subdued splendour of the Club. For months they had expected an attack on their houses; they had lived in a state of siege. In these fine rooms they had put down their clothes tied up in blankets and sheets and some of their household treasures. Some had suitcases or cardboard boxes tied at their bulging middles with rope. [...] They had never dreamt of such splendour – glass chandeliers, lion and bear skins, strange weapons and war clubs from distant and inaccessible parts of the world, soft carpets, oil paintings, lounging chairs that were hard to lift oneself out of and reading lamps. They were impressed and scared. It was beautiful and costly. The bitter memory of the Belfast fighting was in their eyes and faces. These Southern men were kind enough they thought, but they ached for the North, bad enough as it was.[113]

Arresting a Prisoner within a Prison

Echoing Seán O'Casey's socially left-leaning views, O'Horan took issue with the exploitative practices of the leaders of the republican movement whom he viewed as 'scoundrels who try to gratify their own selfish ambitions by sacrificing young boys'.[114] He was particularly bitter that during the fighting in Dublin, he, along with seven other young volunteers, had risked their lives in order 'to keep the Staters back' until the republican leaders got away from the Hammam Hotel.[115] Although the leaders are not named in *The Flame of Youth*, O'Horan publicly denounced Éamon de Valera in 1933, following Fianna Fáil's rise to power, for escaping from the hotel while others risked their lives.[116] O'Horan was also let down by Robert Barton TD who suppressed a potential coup initiated by O'Horan in Portobello Barracks – apparently so that it would not interfere with his own escape plans that same night.[117] During his imprisonment, O'Horan was even disciplined in a republican court by a 'Northern TD' – possibly Seán MacEntee (who was in Gormanston camp at the time) – for being late for a prison parade: 'I felt that it was absurd, in the first instance, to "arrest" a prisoner within a prison. It was a hollow mockery of the law.'[118]

O'Horan was so 'disillusioned' with republican 'principles and policy' that he refused to participate in the mass hunger strike of October 1923 and produced his own anti-hunger strike diary, published in the *Methodist Magazine* in 1928.[119] Author Frank O'Connor was also a 'conscientious objector' to the hunger strike in Gormanston. His autobiographical essay 'A Boy in Prison' (1934) and his short story 'Freedom' (1952) (ostensibly set in a British camp but which clearly reflects the author's internment in Gormanston) both recount how a prisoner refused to do his fatigues, was 'jailed' and resorted to hunger strike in protest against the republican leadership. In both O'Horan's and O'Connor's cases, rebellion against the republican movement was extended through criticism of Catholic convention. O'Connor mocked prisoners who thought they would 'be damned if we don't say the Rosary',[120] while O'Horan lamented that saying the Rosary (with Sinn Féin-coloured beads) 'didn't help me very much when the fighting was on'.[121] For O'Horan, the priestly 'absolution' of confession provided 'no bread for the hunger of souls',[122] while Mass lost its meaning given that 'when bitterness raised her barricades in Dublin City, the Church was inert and inactive'.[123]

O'Horan's writings anticipate the challenge Peadar O'Donnell would make to the Catholic hierarchy in *The Knife* (1930) and *The Gates Flew Open* (1932) – the latter of which O'Horan would refer to in later writings.[124] Jake Wynne also negatively portrayed Catholic priests in *Ugly Brew* (1936), which provoked concern among reviewers, although the author insisted that 'the particular priests of whom I wrote were real ones'.[125] O'Horan, however, took the sentiments of Wynne and O'Donnell even further. He came to believe that the Irish would be better off as loyal citizens of the British Empire, as 'some of the most cruel and vindictive laws made against Ireland were made by Roman Catholic authority'.[126] After the 'tragedy' of civil war, he felt that the Roman Church had failed to provide 'balm for the wounds of the people'.[127] Instead, he found spiritual relief in a copy of the New Testament that an 'oul' wan' 'at th' prison gate' had presented to one of the prisoners.[128] On his release, he sought solace at the Dublin Methodist Mission, alongside his Citizen Army comrade, Liam Phelan, and another anti-treaty prisoner, Seamus McGuinness, who would also convert to Methodism.[129]

The challenge of reintegrating into civilian life faced many released internees and points to a particular case of 'inner exile'. As O'Connor's story 'Freedom' suggests, 'if there was no liberty [...] then equally there was no escape' and 'a man can never really get out of jail'.[130] Sheila Hartnett, who was seventeen when interned alongside Eilish Dolan, reflects in her 1971 memoirs in *The Irish Press* on how the return to civilian life was problematised by the difficulty of reintegrating into her local parish. After her release, Hartnett was refused communion in her local church where, she recalls, 'I so often announced to Jesus "This is Sheila."' Her ostracism from the Church thus evoked a sense of shattered identity, as she could no longer utter the words 'This is Sheila'. Hartnett's poignant account concludes by emphasising her perpetual sense of exile and the impossibility of return: 'Like the butterflies in Reenagross [County Kerry] my celestial flight was over. I want to fly into the clouds of forgetfulness. I never went back.'[131]

However, O'Horan manages to achieve a sense of narrative closure in *The Flame of Youth* by relying on the sense of 'mythical female healing' evident in other veteran testimonies (see Chapter One). Like in the case of Francis Carty, his fictionalised testimony is characterised by a romance narrative absent from his non-fictional account: Páraic Morton writes poetry for Maureen O'Neill '[m]id don and crash of shot and shell'.[132] On his release, Páraic's prime concern is to tell Maureen of the 'strange unrest of his soul', 'his broken dreams' and the 'sordidness and shame'. He hopes that she will join him as they 'share the quest of youth'.[133] After Páraic finds 'healing' in his new Protestant congregation, *The Flame of Youth* closes with the line: 'He would go and tell Maureen.'[134]

Poetry and Exile Testimony

While O'Horan took to both fiction and non-fiction to address his civil war experience, his primary mode of testimony was poetry. Although prose testimony dominates literary and historical study, the genre of poetry strongly speaks to the dialogic nature of testimony, while the layering of metaphor and figurative language can also provide a protected means of testifying and expressing hidden emotions.[135] O'Horan's bilingual corpus of poetry – including six published collections – revisits his childhood and revolutionary experience through the prism of exile. His poetic aesthetic owes much to the influence of Patrick Pearse; in this sense, he was one of a number of poets, including F. R. Higgins and Austin Clarke, who continued with 'Revival poetics' into the early decades of the Free State.

O'Horan's chosen form of poetic expression itself reflected his sense of exile; he located himself within a lineage of Gaelic poets who, abandoned by their patrons, continue their enterprises with the fear of 'singing' but not being listened to.[136] This concern for the plight of poets did not emerge post-independence; it can be traced back to O'Horan's earliest works. O'Horan's poems in English and Irish appeared from 1920 in the 'Irish verse' column of the Sunday *Irish Independent* and were awarded prizes on several occasions.[137] O'Horan was an associate of poet Michael Walsh (1897–1938) who, though now largely forgotten, was widely celebrated for his depiction of the 'quiet of the Irish countryside' and the 'agony of the battlefields' of the First World War.[138] Both Walsh and O'Horan saw it as their duty to serve as 'advocates and defenders of the poets', given the 'average attitude' towards the craft of poetry.[139] From early 1922, O'Horan served as treasurer of the newly established St Enda's Literary Society. The society soon faded out, however, given that, for some like O'Horan, the 'sword was mightier than the pen'.[140] As Walsh reflected, 'The unhappy Civil War was looming. Some of the members shouldered rifles. Then the internment camp, while the skeleton St Enda's that met subsequently in Eustace Street slowly and naturally dissolved.'[141]

Throughout his internment, O'Horan smuggled out short lyric poems that were published in the *Irish Independent*, highlighting how easily transportable snippets of poetry become an essential form of testimony in such prison contexts. Signed off by 'Pádraig Ó hOdhráin, 18 Essex Quay, Dublin', his poems contained no indication of their place of composition. But if his decision to sign off from his family address was a sort of protective shield, his political dismay nevertheless shines through. The poem 'By Night', published in December 1922 when O'Horan was imprisoned in Gormanston, hints at the disillusion and claustrophobia of internment:

> My spirit doth wander far to-night
> Into the realms of starry light,
> Away from the mean desires of Life
> And the clamour of fools for bloody strife.[142]

O'Horan's anger is further apparent in 'Amhrán na Cásga' [Easter Song], published in October 1922, in which the speaker addresses his allegorical lover, 'Róisín':

> Ba mhór é do dhóchas
> Is náireach an smacht
> D'fhág tú gan taoiseach
> Gan tír is gan reacht
>
> [You had high hopes
> But this state brings shame
> It has left you without a leader
> Without country and without aim].[143]

In 'The Song of My Soul', published just months after O'Horan's release, the conventions of the lyric poem are exploited to hint at deep emotional upset:

> The song of my soul is sad
> And the hours pass voicelessly

Ah but all is sad.
Kisses of a Summer's day –
A memory, sad memory.
Joy dies; Hope fails,
All, all is sad, sad.
Dreams shine in purple mists
Softly and tenderly;
Dreams fade oh, dreams fade
All, all is sad, sad.
The gay fields we once knew
Blossom – oh, silently.
And ne'er call to dead Youth;
But days whisper sadly.
We meet Love – the strong one
A little while, wistfully.
Then night falls in darkness
Suddenly, suddenly.[144]

O'Horan's first collection, *Eyes of My Love: Twenty Poems* (1924), was published by Stockwell in London and, as the title suggests, was exclusively made up of romance poems inspired by 'the wonderful eyes of his lady'.[145] Although Terence O'Hanlon lamented the volume's lack of variety, these lyric poems arguably offered O'Horan a means to evoke affective states and once again point to a search for closure, as the female object of desire offers 'healing of the hurt within my heart'.[146] Indeed, the entire collection of love poems could be read as an extended metaphor for the trials and tribulations of revolution and civil war.

The disjunction between a romanticised, remembered past and a disillusioned present evident in 'The Song of My Soul' characterises much of O'Horan's later poetry. His second poetry collection, *Roadways of the Heart: Poems* (1943), was composed of poems previously published in journals across in Ireland, England and the United States.[147] The nostalgia of the earlier poems is arguably augmented in the context of the poet's geographic remove from the homeplace. The speaker of the poem 'Remembering' claims, '[m]y heart is ever longing for the windswept western isle', while a number of poems reflect on youthful jaunts to the countryside when 'our world was so young'.[148] The poem 'A Memory of Kerry' points to the immigrant's difficulties in assimilating into hostile urban environments and the eternal pull towards a restorative Irish countryside:

> For long have I wandered far and wide
> 'Mid the stranger's speech and his noisome mills,
> But my soul goes winging across the tide
> To the Irish roads and the Irish hills.[149]

Such idyllic poems might reflect something of a cliché. But, as widely observed in post-war trauma testimonies, O'Horan's nostalgic sketches enabled him to present the pre-trauma time of his youth in opposition to a more tormented present in which the 'flame of young' is extinguished:

> These simple things. My mother's hand holding mine;
> Her face; the little boy who walked beside her down the festive
>   streets
> And saw displayed the glitter and the gauds of Dublin toy shops.[150]

There is an ethical duty underscoring many of these remembrances. O'Horan's poetry repeatedly reflects on the conviviality of the living and the 'unremembered dead'.[151] Ghosts roam the poet's 'corridors of memory', as recollections of Gaelic League days are disturbed by 'beloved ghosts' who 'peep / Around the corners of the mind'.[152] The poet is driven by the imperative to call to remembrance ('Will you remember?') and equally to be remembered ('will you remember me?').[153] Among O'Horan's elegies for the 'unremembered dead' is a poem dedicated to his fellow poet Michael Walsh, who was a 'flower' 'upon the jewelled cloak / We wove for Cathleen when our days were young'.[154] However, these remembered youthful days are almost always soured, as in the poem 'My Heart is Breathing Memoried Airs':

> Ah, Michael, Matt and Norah now –
> Where are the friends we used to know,
> And where the laughter in the rain,
> And where the fires that mocked the snow?[155]

The idea that the sacrifices of the revolutionary generation were in vain pervades O'Horan's writings. In *The Flame of Youth*, Páraic is utterly distressed on hearing that his Gaelic League comrade Caoimhín has lost his life when transporting a landmine: 'Was it for this that your laughter was stilled? O strong heart of Seán [...] Was it for this that you leaped in your last pulse when a stinging death came? O white soul of Nuala bán [...] Was it for this that you gave your lover the sunshine of your Youth?'[156] That same question – 'Was it for this?' – continues to find expression in O'Horan's poetry.[157] In 'Liffeyside', the speaker brands Dublin the town '[o]f shame and faith and renown' where once the poets stood and the 'light of that building's flame / Made splendid anew your name'.[158]

'Every Generation Goes to the Wars': Second World War

Many emigrant revolutionaries found themselves living in war once again in the 1940s. Josie O'Connor, the 'Irish Civil War exile', survived a U-boat attack on the cargo ship SS *Stone Street* in 1942; John Pinkman, the Liverpool-born Free State army soldier, also survived the Battle of the Atlantic as a marine engineer, while Bridget Dirrane, a Cumann na mBan activist from the Aran islands, joined the Military Airforce in Mississippi and recalled 'drilling the same as I did many years before with Cumann na mBan'.[159] O'Horan's civil war experience, however, compelled him to condemn this 'murderous lust of war' and his anti-war poems merited his inclusion in *English Poetry of the Second World War: A Biobibliography*.[160] The poem 'Every Generation Goes to the Wars' is an indictment of the glorification of war and the failure of transgenerational memory:

> Every generation goes to the wars.
> Marching in the garden; drilling in the park.
> '*All the nice girls love a sailor.*' Isn't it a lark?
> > Laughing and lively go:
> > Limbless and mindless so –
> But who in excited streets will think of the scars,
> For every generation goes to the wars.[161]

Both the 'scars' and 'flags unfurled' of the Second World War are tied to the failed Irish revolutionary ideal. O'Horan's most ambitious poem, 'Let the

Flags Droop', indicates a profound disillusionment with war and revolution, all the more pertinent in light of its publication in 1947. The sense of the futility of the Irish war against the English is captured at the beginning of the poem: the speaker recalls meeting General Frank Percy Crozier of the Auxiliary Division of the RIC – only to discover that his mother was Irish. O'Horan draws on a line from the chorus of the famous song 'The Men of the West': 'Though all the bright dreamings we cherished'. But whereas the original line is followed by a renewed commitment to the national ideal, O'Horan's poem turns into an angry call against overzealous nationalism and militarism:

> *Though all the bright dreaming we cherished* ...
> But that was sung of Ninety Eight.
> O'Connor, O'Higgins, and Collins were
> Its latest rhythm and beat,
> Names that were omens of victory, and desolating defeat.
>
> The bright shining beauty is gone,
> And its ghosts like swirling late leaves
> Go before Gogarty's white swans
> On dark water.
>
> [...]
>
> Here they come – fife and drum
> Down the streets of yesterday.
> Let the pipes loudly cry,
> Let the procession pass by,
> For the rivers overflow,
> And the bright banners go.
> (Is there a lone ghost crying
> Beannacht a's míle beannacht leo?)
>
> *We'll drink the* ... No, let the flags droop
> Depart and decay,
> For this is another, quite different day,
> And our glasses have gone in the Highland way.[162]

O'Horan died suddenly in June 1951.[163] His wife, Eily Dolan, returned to Ireland with their son, Michael, and, in her third religious conversion, turned back to Catholicism. Though she had been 'offered the choice of much material, social and financial benefit in England', Dolan contended that 'Ireland kept on calling me'.[164] This idea of return had preoccupied her writings for years.

Women and Exile in the Writing of Eily Dolan

The O'Horans' literary output was something of a collective endeavour; Dolan's short stories appeared in journals alongside the poems of her husband; biographical notes pointed out that 'fiction is her forte; Pádraig is the poet of the family'.[165] However, unlike her husband's identification with the solitary masculine figure of the exile in the Gaelic Christian or nationalist tradition, Dolan's writings emphasise the experience of return migration and are often motivated towards the undoing of exile. Their writings, considered together, thus point to the gendered experience of emigration that has been explored by various scholars of the Irish diaspora.[166] While some female revolutionary emigrants certainly harnessed the language of exile and self-identified among the 'Wild Geese' (this is particularly evident in pension applications),[167] for many women, the diaspora, and America in particular, offered both personal and economic opportunities.[168] As female activist Bridget Dirrane recounted in her memoirs, her emigration to Boston, to where she had many friends and family, was 'not that traumatic an experience for me'.[169]

Whereas exile is often conceived of as a form of banishment for male political emigrants, women's punishments have historically been connected with 'inner exiles', such as social isolation, containment or institutionalisation. This is particularly clear in Dolan's experience of fleeing from her Stoneybatter home to London. She outlines in her memoirs that her family threatened to give her into 'the hands of the parish priest' if she did not give up on her interest in converting to Methodism.[170] Taking the mailboat to London was less banishment than escape for Dolan.

The threat that Dolan would be passed over to the Catholic Church reflects the institutionalisation of women, including for their political beliefs, which was a feature of the revolutionary period.[171] Whereas Dolan found herself imprisoned in Kilmainham and later in the North Dublin Union,

Cumann na mBan activist Mary Harpur recalled working at the South Dublin Union, which housed another group of female inmates: unmarried women. As she recounted in her unpublished memoir: 'I shudder even now at the shock of it. All those lovely girls, young, fresh looking, from Dublin but from all parts of the county too [...] Non intities [sic] until you got talking to them and they poured out their heartrending stories of running away from home or being sent away from home when "this" happened'.[172] Dolan was aware of these realities. Her story 'The Rustle of Spring' relates to an unmarried mother who returns to her childhood holiday location in Mayo, as 'they tried to take him from me'.[173]

Like the writings of the female revolutionaries explored in Chapter Two, the sophistication and politics of Dolan's writing fluctuates depending on her intended audience – and, indeed, depending on her adopted name. Even though Dolan's novels, published under the name Elizabeth Brennan in the 1960s and 1970s, were recommended 'housewife' reading, her short stories published in The Bell in the 1940s, as Eily O'Horan, have prompted commentary among literary scholars for their challenge to Catholic social and sexual norms; Gerardine Meaney contends that her representation of a mother breastfeeding her child heralded 'an eruption of the female body into mainstream literary discourse'.[174] Indeed, whereas Seán O'Faoláin was sceptical about the civil war novels of Jake Wynne and Patrick Mulloy, Dolan recalled that he 'encouraged her first efforts, printing all her writings in The Bell'.[175] But even her seemingly innocuous romance fiction is autobiographically inflected and offers valuable personal insight into the challenges of migration and return. These literary insights are all the more essential given the dearth of published memoirs by female revolutionary veterans in the diaspora in comparison to their male comrades.[176]

'This Terrible World of Good-by'

Dolan's fictional writings from the 1930s and 1940s (published as Eily O'Horan) testify to a highly complicated relationship to 'home'. In both her memoirs, Dolan recalls visiting her paternal grandparents in Old Bog Road, County Westmeath and laments the 'agony of childish despair at the necessity of leavetaking'.[177] This sense of heartache is re-evoked in her fiction, including in the appropriately entitled story 'The Old Bog Road', in which a male 'exile' finds his mind returning again and again to the 'remote and simple beauty' of Westmeath.[178] A number of other stories reflect on childhood memories of countryside holidays and making soda bread in Grannie's kitchen.[179] This countryside bliss is always shattered, however. This is a 'terrible world of good-by', and the characters must eventually 'go back to the gray dismal streets'.[180] This nostalgic attachment to the rural ancestral home presents the city as a site, therefore, of inner exile for this 'first-generation' Dubliner.[181]

The nostalgic longing for an innocent pre-trauma rural childhood may reflect the fact that Dolan's paternal grandmother was one of the few people who did not 'turn their faces' when she left the Catholic Church.[182] Dolan's relationship with her mother was particularly fraught; she held her mother responsible for agreeing to store guns for the anti-treaty IRA which led to her imprisonment. When the family home was raided and trashed, Dolan accepted responsibility for the guns 'because if I did not my father or mother would be arrested. I was only fifteen at the time but was quite fully-grown and possibly looked somewhat older than I really I was.'[183] This resulted in her internment, first in Kilmainham and subsequently in the North Dublin Union, for six months. Dolan recalls refusing to speak when she was interrogated in the prison with a revolver held to her 'wildly beating heart'.[184] She was 'utterly bewildered and stunned' by the prison environment and stresses in her memoirs the upset caused by the Catholic bishops' refusal of absolution to anti-treaty republicans.[185] She was also acutely aware of the fact that while some of the prisoners were 'very low class', others were 'refined and cultured'.[186] When Dolan and her 19-year-old companion Sheila (perhaps Hartnett), from Kerry, found themselves 'despondent and hungry', a 'little dark lady' who carried Protestant psalms gave them her tea of sandwiches.[187]

Dolan's two memoirs were written as conversion narratives and thus place a strong emphasis on spiritual well-being and her encounters with Protestantism. These 1930s conversion narratives are also characterised by a strong unease with nationalism, as Dolan contends, 'I never could see how civil war and hate could win for Ireland any good.'[188] This rejection of nationalism can be read as protest against her stridently republican mother, who referred to her daughter as a 'shoneen' and whose willingness to store guns resulted in Dolan's imprisonment.[189] However, the repudiation of nationalism in the conversion narratives is somewhat complicated by advertisements for her lectures that indicated that she 'suffered imprisonment for her political conviction'.[190] In a much later interview,

Dolan also suggested that 'as a teenager, [she] fiercely adopted her mother's political views' – before, only later, becoming 'pacifist' like her father.[191]

Remembering the Revolution from the Diaspora

Fiction offered a vehicle for teasing out these conflicting views on nationalism. In 'The Young May Moon' (1937), a young female emigrant in London is haunted by 'a little trail of memories I thought I had forgotten' going back fifteen years. Echoing Dolan's memoirs, the first-person female narrator recalls her early days as a 'shorthand-typist in a stuffy office' in London; she was 'sick for home' and, reflecting established connections between exile and internment, felt her life 'had taken on the nature of *a prison*' (my emphasis).[192] The narrator was saved by the 'faithful friendship' of her future fiancé, an Englishman. However, her loyalty to her fiancé is compromised when she returns to Coologe, County Westmeath, on doctor's advice. This trip coincided with the 'troubled times': 'I recall it now, sitting here in my sedate London home. Guerrilla warfare reared its ugly head in our midst. Every day the newspapers had some fresh story of ambush, murder, and disaster, of executions, of burnings and looting and rioting, to horrify and harass a people already weary and bewildered with war and strife.'[193]

A company of 'young men armed with rifles and revolvers' are granted shelter in the house; this echoes Dolan's description in her memoirs of the 'weary, heartsick-looking' IRA men 'carrying rifles and revolvers' who were harboured by her family in the countryside.[194] The narrator's heart is 'assailed' by a 'queer unaccountable excitement' as she falls for Dublin intellectual Barry McCabe; he offers her a ring under the 'young May moon'.[195] But she never hears again from McCabe and ultimately returns to her English fiancé, finding a 'home' as she lays her head on his shoulder.[196] This could be read as the rejection of the ideals and values of the revolution in favour of a 'home' in Britain. Equally, however, it is the republican cause that abandons the narrator, as her IRA lover, who may or may not have survived, never contacts her.

Return Migration and the Big House Romance

The love triangle thus enabled Dolan to tease out complex allegiances, but romance was also a powerful vehicle for pointing to the possibility of social reintegration. Dolan drew on the established canon of Protestant ascendancy fiction to negotiate the implications of social and personal displacement – as indeed did other IRA writers such as O'Faoláin.[197] Before her emigration, Dolan was a regular at the Abbey theatre. She may have been exposed, therefore, to the work of Abbey director Lennox Robinson (1886–1958) who was one of the earliest writers to address the civil war experience of the ascendancy. His play *The Big House: Four Scenes in Its Life* was staged in 1926 and mocks southern Protestants who identify as 'martyred émigré[s]' in London and carry around pictures of the 'castle before the fire and *after* the fire [...] like an advertisement for a hair restorer or a baby food'.[198] However, the play indicates that even nationalist-minded Protestants were not spared the brunt of the IRA, as the family of the fictional Senator Leger Alcock are burned out of their County Cork home in February 1923.

Elizabeth Bowen's influential novel, *The Last September*, followed in 1929; Dolan records that she read Bowen's family memoir, *Bowen's Court* (1942), in a bomb shelter one night during a 'doodlebug' attack in the Second World War and was 'so enthralled I never heard a bomb'.[199] Bowen's novel draws on autobiographical experience, while Robinson's 1942 memoir hints at the personal experience that inspired his earlier play; he recalls that after Senator Horace Plunkett's home in Foxrock was burnt down in February 1923, he used 'to go to bed and lie awake sweating until the light began to come. I admit I was arrantly cowardly'.[200] Robinson resorts to black humour in his play to both convey the trauma of the event and also to present a more redemptive assessment of the destruction of the Big House; as the curtain closes, Kate Alcock, standing by a 'medley of furniture', remains committed to her own sense of Irishness and pronounces that she 'should like to marry a Republican Catholic curate'.[201]

This idea of mixed marriage pervades Dolan's early fictional writings. Many of her stories address the challenge of return migration, but this dilemma is often resolved as romance develops between returning (economic) emigrants and residents of the Big House. In 'The Old Bog Road' the 'exiled' Séamus Connolly returns to Westmeath and marries Cathleen O'Rourke; Cathleen's family had formerly lived in the Big House but, faced with cold and hunger, they had taken up residence in Connolly's abandoned cottage.[202] In 'Footsteps on the Stairs', the returning 'exile' is finally reunited with his childhood sweetheart after twenty years in the United States.[203] Despite his former hatred for 'all that she stood for', the pair marry and also look forward to raising children of mixed religious heritage. In 'The Proud O'Dempsey's' the returnee is Oliver Eustace; his family had been burned out of Rossmead House during 'the troubles' and vowed 'on their sacred Bibles never to set foot' in Ireland again.[204] On his return, however, Eustace finds Shelagh O'Dempsey and her father residing in his gate lodge. This awkward situation is rectified when Shelagh and Oliver make a match. Shelagh's arrival at the Big House is presented not as a break in tradition but rather as a return, given that the O'Dempsey's had built Rossmead in the thirteenth century before they were dispossessed under the Cromwellian conquest.[205] Dolan thus quite literally marries the plight of the dispossessed Catholics with that of the declining Protestant ascendancy. These reconciled romances are at odds with much fiction of the Big House genre that stresses the 'basic incompatibilities' between the ascendancy class and Catholic Irish.[206]

While a number of Dolan's short stories could be read as supportive of the nationalist anti-emigration agenda,[207] her seemingly conformist writings were loaded with social criticism. Her writings published in the London-based *Chambers's Journal* during the Second World War troubled the Irish nationalist narrative of revolution by highlighting the mobilisation of Irishmen in the British army and suggesting that Irish nationalists 'talk of freedom all their days, yet they would deny you any freedom of thought or action'.[208] Like her husband, she advances a pacifist agenda and, drawing on Yeats' 1919 poem 'An Irish Airman Foresees His Death', presents war, once again, as a 'waste of breath'.[209] Dolan also highlights the immense social pressure placed on women to keep their composure even in wartime; when Noneen's fiancé dies in the Royal Airforce, she is forbidden from acknowledging that she 'wanted to die' or that the language of 'heroic death means nothing to me'. Instead, she wears her pretty dress, silver shoes and Spanish comb – and drinks down a glass of sherry so as not to 'disgrace' 'the Quality' (the ascendancy) of Cooleen Park.[210]

Dolan found it increasingly difficult to secure an audience for her writings after her return to Ireland in 1951. She was employed as a secretary in the editorial department of the *Irish Independent*, recalled that Archbishop McQuaid 'was very good to her during that time of crisis' and managed to repair 'her relationship with her parents'.[211] She was 'intensely' 'annoyed', however, that she had to leave her job on her second marriage to Patrick Brennan in 1954 and was highly critical of RTÉ, for whom

Máiréad Ní Ghráda was a broadcaster, for getting 'rid of women, almost overnight and without any warning'.[212] Though an active member of the Irish Countrywomen's Association (ICA), Dolan expressed her dismay in 1971 that the organisation was 'not allowed to discuss religion, politics, sex, the pill. We are like ostriches with our heads in the sand'.[213]

Like Cregan and Ní Ghráda (see Chapter Two), Dolan's stage work was rejected by the Abbey.[214] She left Dublin in the 1960s and lived in a modest cottage in Sligo, where her interest in the historical daily lives of the Protestant ascendancy developed. The need to write women back into the history of the revolutionary period was central to her one-act play, *The Parting of the Ways: A One-Act Play*, which was broadcast on Raidió Éireann and premiered at the Western Drama Festival at Tubbercurry, County Sligo, in 1969.[215] The play reflects on how Constance Gore-Booth (later the Countess Markievicz) and her sister Eva dissent from their gentry background: they attend political meetings, reject marriage proposals, support the suffrage movement, harbour locals on the run from the Peelers and turn Lissadell into a 'hot-bed of revolution'.[216] Dolan carried out extensive research on the enigmatic figure of Eva Gore-Booth with the intention of producing a biography. It is unclear, however, whether it was ever completed.[217]

Even though Dolan (as Elizabeth Brennan) expressed a preference for writing about 'real people', ultimately romance novels – though not 'great art' – proved more 'lucrative'.[218] Referred to as the 'Mary Stewart of Ireland', Dolan had twelve of her novels published by the UK-based publisher Robert Hale Limited between 1963 and 1984.[219] These romance novels all seem to take place in Ireland, with many featuring returning migrants or second-generation emigrants. They were largely targeted at a US- and UK-based audience. Some, such as *Love's Loom* (1975), were sold for 8p, as part of the *Women's Weekly Library*, and a number were translated into various languages, including Dutch, Italian and Norwegian.[220]

In perhaps the only literary appraisal of Dolan's works, Paul Marchbanks is somewhat dismissive of her 'quickly written' romance novels, in which '[y]oung women in need of male companionship inevitably find their mate in the most "Irish" of geographies, among the cottages and green hills of western, rural Ireland'.[221] However, this criticism does not consider her early writings – and, indeed, confuses her with another Irish novelist also named Elizabeth Brennan.[222] Even if Dolan's novels were 'quickly written', they nevertheless pushed against conventions, as her female protagonists, many of whom 'return' to Ireland from England, navigate the circumstances of their time, aware that it 'took courage to face the disapproval of society'.[223]

Kathleen Hoagland's *Fiddler in the Sky*: Emigration as Escape

Dolan's turn to the Big House narrative template, rather than to the nationalist narrative of exile, indicates the limitations of the exilic motif for conveying women's experiences of emigration. Emigration, for women like Dolan, could be liberating. This escape narrative – due to the strain of revolution – is powerfully addressed in Kathleen Hoagland's (1904–1985) novel *Fiddler in the Sky*, published by Harper & Brothers in the United States. Hoagland was based in New Jersey, where she rubbed shoulders with leading literary figures such as Ernest Boyd, Thomas Wolfe and William Carlos Williams. In 1947, she produced the poetry anthology *1000 Years of Irish Poetry* (1947), which was celebrated as the 'most comprehensive Irish anthology ever compiled'.[224] In her editor's introduction, she lamented that, in light of censorship in Ireland, 'America and England are refuges for the artists nurturing, supporting and giving audience to their songs and stories'.[225] While her poetry anthology addresses revolutionary remembrance through the legacy of the 1916 martyrs, her novel offers a distinctly female perspective on the social and psychological ramifications of revolution – ultimately leading to emigration.

Fiddler in the Sky does not directly address the Irish Civil War of 1922–3: the narrative ends in 1920. But it is, nevertheless, a narrative of 'unacknowledged civil war' characterised by political, family and communal rifts. The novel opens as the protagonist, 13-year-old Pegeen Brendan, watches her maternal grandparents travel to Dublin to see their nephew, Shaun Fitzhugh, who had been released from Lincoln Prison in England following his role in the Rising. Hoagland's prime concern, however, is to document the daily struggles of communities in the west of Ireland during the revolution. The small town of Tirawley – in contrast with its etymology of 'Tír Álainn' [Beautiful Country] – is crippled by social divisions; the district of Bournah is populated by impoverished laundrywomen, 'half-fed' fighting dogs and 'close-cropped' children 'marked with ringworm'.[226] Pegeen's mother organises entertainments for the British soldiers 'to keep them out of harm and away from the servant girls'.[227] The male hierarchy of the town – the priest, bishop, hotelier and organist – speak of the 'docil[ity] of women in bed', while simultaneously making plans to deal with the 'fancy women', 'Bournah sthreels' and 'whores' of the town.[228]

Reflecting the dominance of superstition and prophecies in rural Irish communities to make sense of traumatic events, the locals anticipate the sighting of the 'Black Pig of Connaught' to herald that the time has come 'for Ireland to be free'.[229] But the revolution brings further tension to Tirawley. Pegeen's father, hotelier James Brendan, fears that his wife's revolutionary connections could 'cost him some of his business'.[230] He vents his frustration on the family's black Pekingese dog. This draws on popular analogies between violence against animals and violence against humans (particularly women), and, indeed, foreshadows the domestic violence to come.[231] Brendan resorts to brandy and becomes suddenly overwhelmed by his realisation of the repressed sexuality of his upbringing after seeing a relative in the company of a prostitute.[232] His wife, Elizabeth, spends a few weeks in Dublin to rest her 'nerves' but, ultimately, decides she cannot stay with her husband and finds the community, too, is pitted against her on account of her entertainment of British officers. She makes the decision to flee to the United States with her five children 'in continual fear that politics or the Brendans [her in-laws] might reach out to hinder their departure'.[233]

Emigration, in the opening of the novel, is presented as engendering insanity, as the police 'strapped and manacled' the town's mentally ill, including a woman who 'hasn't been right in the head since Bridgie went to America'.[234] Yet, emigration is also a necessary escape. The novel's concluding passage is characterised by the protagonist's relief as the family catches its final glimpse of the Irish shore:

> 'Thank God, *that's* the last of Ireland, Mamma!' [emphasis in original].
> 'I hope I have done right, pet,' Elizabeth said.
> 'You have, Mamma!'
> Pegeen could not bear to see the green now. She got up and made her way to the prow of the liner. Standing there, alone, she looked into the distance of the ocean; a gray mist was over the water. The ship seemed to shudder with delight as it plowed ahead faster and

faster, leaving the land behind it. The girl's eyes were full of tears, she brushed them away. Tomorrow ... America!'[235]

The backdrop of the First World War in Hoagland's novel certainly resonated on its publication in 1944 given that, once again, war 'thunder[ed] across Europe'.[236] *Fiddler in the Sky* had little impact in Ireland, however. Reviews in the United States were positive, with reviewers questioning the line between fact and fiction, contending that the 'book must be at least partly autobiographical', and there seemed to be 'some parallel between the author's life and that of her protagonist'.[237] Indeed, Kathleen Hoagland – then Kitty Dooher – hailed from Ballina. Many of the minor details in the novel are reflected in official records; immigration records show that, like her protagonist, Dooher fled from Ireland during the revolution with her mother and four siblings.[238] In an interview with a New Jersey newspaper, *The Record*, Hoagland gives ambiguous comments on the family's reasons for emigrating, recounting that her father, '[although] a wonderful man ... got in with a fast crowd, you know, and she [her mother] had to leave [...] It was a lovely life, really, except for that; we had hotels in the country, and my father ran horses ... a lovely life, but ...'[239]

Reporting in *The Record* conveys Hoagland's strong patriotism: she claims that she protested against the Black and Tans in Dublin as a child and recalled that her second cousins, including future Taoiseach Liam Cosgrave (1920–2017), could '[l]ike most Irishmen [...] talk politics in a barroom at three [years old]'.[240] However, the heteroglossia of fiction, like in Dolan's fiction, offers an opportunity to explore far more complex attitudes to nationalism. Pegeen shifts from dreamily claiming she 'always felt like dying for Ireland' to condemning the 'fanatics' of Sinn Féin after the family's fallout with the local nationalist community.[241] Pegeen's cousin Shaun Fitzhugh – who, like Liam's father, the eminent politician W. T. Cosgrave (1880–1965), was sentenced to death for his involvement in the Rising – attempts to persuade Elizabeth from emigrating, asking 'why should you take the boys and money from Ireland? Every boy and every penny will be needed to make Ireland's freedom possible.'[242] Ultimately, the family is chaperoned by British 'Spike Island officers' to the tender to ensure their departure is not thwarted by 'Sinn Féiners'.[243] Even though the family emigrates in the summer of 1920 (both in fiction and real life), Hoagland presents this communal, familial and political schism not as revolution, but as advancing civil war: 'Ireland was divided. One hardly knew what his own brother was thinking. Yes, families were divided, towns were divided; the seeds of civil war were germinating.'[244]

Conclusion

The fact that Hoagland's remarkable testimony, *Fiddler in the Sky*, has yet to receive any scholarly analysis is indicative both of the sidelining of less conventional forms of testimony (including poetry, as evident in this chapter), and also the marginalisation of testimony produced outside Ireland. Yet the diaspora was perceived by many revolutionary veterans as a space that offered enhanced narrative freedom away from the constraints of peer pressure, libel action and censoring in Ireland. The long-established forced exile narrative emerged as a helpful template through which veterans addressed traumatic experience. It was also a template that pointed to the redemptive possibilities of emigration and that went some way towards countering the shaming of emigrants in nationalist discourses – which, indeed, was often associated with questions of mental illness. This collective forced exile narrative was accompanied by the promotion of a sense of solidarity between dispossessed groups – including Dublin's tenement dwellers, Catholic refugees from Belfast, members of the declining Protestant ascendancy and members of the Traveller community. This sense of solidarity further testifies to the desire among those who have endured trauma or oppression to contextualise their suffering across time and space (see Chapter One). However, post-civil war exile was not just associated with geographic displacement or emigration: self-perceived states of exile were often the result of 'spiritual' or 'inner' exiles, as even within Ireland – north and south – veterans were invariably forced to grapple with the post-revolutionary dilemma of returning to civilian life.

The cases of Dolan and Hoagland, nevertheless, underscore that the exile motif concealed the liberating dimensions of emigration. Emigrating, for some, was less banishment than escape; this seems to have been particularly relevant for women, who made up the majority of emigrants from Ireland during much of this period.

Even if emigration was associated with exile and victimhood in the popular imagination, it was also viewed as a means to conceal 'unwanted' elements of society. This was the case during the revolution, too. In his memoir *Remembering Sion*, Desmond Ryan recalls delivering a man named O'Dwyer to a sailor on Dublin's North Wall; the IRA wanted O'Dwyer 'vanished', as he had killed a man with a 'swing of his hurley in rage'. As Ryan recounts, however, America did not provide a solution: 'O'Dwyer is still there, haunted and restless, and a psychoanalyst there had guessed his secret, which left so deep a mark on his mind and character.'[245]

The next chapter moves on to consider the question of perpetrator trauma, as reflected in Ryan's account. It also addresses how veterans managed their urge to tell about perpetrating violence – and how some of the more candid perpetrator testimonies by civil war veterans were produced not in Ireland but in the diaspora.

Chapter Five

'I Killed at Least a Dozen Fellow Irishmen': Perpetrator Testimony

From the mid-1960s, anti-war marches swept across the United States in protest against military involvement in Vietnam. Among the 700 protesters in Rochester, New York, in October 1967 was IRA veteran George Lennon (1900–1991). As he recalled, 'Friends, Hippies, Catholic nuns – we all walk peacefully along the pavements of the city holding lighted candles [...] The flower children lift up their young voices and plaintively sing "All We Are Saying Is Give Peace A Chance".'[1] The IRA veteran's public calls for the United States to withdraw from Vietnam were informed by the 'terror' he had witnessed in Ireland: 'towns were burned, prisoners were mistreated, and thousands put in prisons or internment camps'.[2] This resonated with Lennon's personal experience of severe beatings on his capture by the British military near Kilmacthomas, County Waterford, in May 1921.[3]

By the time of the civil war, Lennon, then in charge of the Waterford anti-treaty IRA, suffered what he referred to as a 'complete breakdown' after the city was sieged by Free State forces.[4] He was treated by Dr W. White for 'severe gastritis + neurasthenia' and was under medical supervision for August and September 1922, before retreating to England for a 'complete change' for three months.[5] With few economic opportunities available to him in Ireland, he emigrated to New York in 1927. For the remainder of his life, Lennon sought various treatments for his recurring 'bad nervous breakdowns';[6] he went to sanatoriums, sought out osteopaths, adopted various diets, took Sanatogen and glucose, and tried open-air and sun treatments. He also searched for spiritual comfort as a member of the Society of Friends (Quakers) and later through Zen Buddhism. In his many correspondences to the Department of Defence seeking financial support on account of his ill health, Lennon emphasised his 'unusually strenuous' service, underscoring that he had taken 'part in seventeen major operations, before my health finally broke down'.[7]

Lennon's testimonial writing points to other traumatic aspects of his service absent from his correspondence with the Pension Board, namely his execution of RIC constable Michael Hickey and his physical rejection of a female revolutionary, referred to as Kathleen of Sleady – both aspects of 'unacknowledged civil war'. Like many veterans, Lennon spoke little of the revolution to his children, preferring to relegate matters such as the 'unmentionable' civil war 'to the dustbin of history'.[8] But he revisited his role as a perpetrator of violence in two separate dramas, the television play *Down by the Glen Side* (1952) and the theatrical sketch 'I and Thou', which is included in his hybridised diary/memoir *Trauma in Time* (c. 1971). This remarkable testimony, written when Lennon was already in his seventies, concludes with an imagined reconciliatory scene in which the protagonist is reunited with his two victims.

This chapter is concerned with testimonies in which the act of perpetrating violence meets with veterans' 'imperative to tell and to be heard'. Despite Joanna Bourke's forceful argument in her foundational study *An Intimate History of Killing* (1991) that 'the characteristic act of men at war is not dying, it is killing',[9] there has been little sustained attention paid to testimonies of perpetrating violence in the historiography of the Irish revolution, even in the cases of the most studied IRA men turned-authors.[10] Within both the popular imagination and scholarly discourse, psychological trauma is routinely conflated with victimhood. The very idea of perpetrator trauma is contested and does not line up with the standard definition of PTSD, according to which the traumatic event is 'outside the range of normal experience'. Only recently has scholarship in the field of trauma studies begun to focus on developing theories of perpetrator trauma. Whereas 'victim trauma' is associated with 'psychological disintegration or disturbing and intrusive memories', Raya Morag suggests that the core of perpetrator trauma is 'the profound moral contradictions challenging the perpetrators'.[11]

Such a rigid dichotomy between victim and perpetrator did not stand, however, during Ireland's revolutionary period. The 'grey zones' between victims, perpetrators and bystanders are ubiquitous throughout this book; revolutionaries, like Patrick Mulloy's protagonist Tim (see Chapter One), could fall victim to severe injustices, yet they could also stand silent as gender-based violence or tortures occurred and equally inflict severe violence themselves. As Primo Levi has argued, the occupants of these grey zones defy easy judgement.[12] Nor does the widely evoked female victim/male perpetrator paradigm hold up in considerations of the Irish revolution. Historian Ann Matthews is one of the few scholars to go against the emphasis on female victimhood in much republican propaganda and historiography, boldly arguing that 'these women were anything but victims'.[13] In light of these many 'grey zones', this chapter explores how violence and its psychological effects on the perpetrator are teased out in the writings of both male and female revolutionary veterans. In particular, it addresses two distinct features of these writings: excessive telling about violence and the foregrounding of empathy between foes, often associated with Frank O'Connor's 1931 short story 'Guests of the Nation'. The chapter then considers how these tropes influenced later testimonial writings, with particular focus on the hybrid fiction/memoir writings of anti-treaty veteran George Lennon and on the novel *He's Somewhere in There* (1975) by Free State army veteran Anthony O'Connor (1907–1983); these testimonies were both produced in the diaspora in the context of the Troubles.

Perpetrator Testimony: The Fantastical and the Consolatory

Bearing witness is generally not associated with perpetrators. Even in a legal context, the accused has a right to remain silent, and audiences are often not accustomed, or willing, to listen to perpetrator confessions. For these reasons, an appreciation of veterans' retreats to less conventional forms of testimony becomes all the more pertinent. In her study of the memoirs of British Second World War veterans, Frances Houghton argues that accounts of perpetrating violence are littered with fantasies, as it was 'far easier to carry out acts of extreme violence when the foe was in some manner dehumanised and mechanised in their imaginations'.[14] The imaginative impulse at the heart of combatant testimonies is also central to Bourke's influential study. As she outlines, '[s]uch forms of dissociation were psychologically useful. By imagining themselves as participating in a fantasy, men could find a language which avoided facing the unspeakable horror not only of dying, but of meting out death.'[15]

The 'contradictory, consolatory and often fantastical'[16] nature of perpetrator testimonies has not been given the consideration it merits in studies of the Irish revolution. In fact, this is already a point of scholarly contention. Anne Dolan's widely cited article on the testimonies of IRA men active on the morning of Bloody Sunday on 21 November 1920 – when thirteen British soldiers and officers were assassinated in their beds – is one of few studies to consider 'killing and its effects on a band of largely untrained young men in a guerrilla war'.[17] However, Eve Morrison is critical of what she sees as narrowly positivist, fact-based interpretations of veteran testimonies and a tendency, as is evident in Dolan's analysis, 'to characterize veterans as mouthpieces for nationalist myths'.[18] Dolan's study does indeed risk judging the men for their 'disturbing' actions, for their mentioning of the colour of the carpet but not 'any blood', and for not admitting 'that mistakes were made, that the wrong men were shot'.[19] As Morrison argues, 'Dolan's decontextualised narrative analysis of the Bureau and O'Malley's Bloody Sunday testimony is original and powerful in its exposition but assumes rather than proves that the explicitness of the men's descriptions of violence provides insight into their emotional psychology (with a lack of gruesome detail read as moral failure or dishonesty).'[20]

The lack of 'gruesome detail' in some men's perpetrator testimonies reflects the active sanitisation of revolutionary violence from the earliest reporting. Newspaper and bulletin reports privileged vague, passive language over any reference to 'killing': policemen 'died from bullet wounds', while IRA men died 'fighting for freedom'.[21] Kitty O'Doherty was purportedly responsible for mellowing Dan Breen's 'bloodthirsty statements' in *My Fight for Irish Freedom* (1924).[22] Serialised newspaper memoirs, such as the *Fighting Story: Told by the Men Who Made It* series, intentionally toned down the violence. Anti-treaty veteran Mossie Hartnett's writings under the name 'Pen Gun' in *The Kerryman* in the 1930s, and later his 1976/1977 articles in *The Limerick Leader*, perpetuate a heroised narrative of unblemished freedom fighters. However, his posthumous memoir *Victory and Woe* (2002) underscores the extent to which these earlier writings were edited to the point, as his editor and son-in-law James J. Joy contends, that they are almost 'unrecognisable'.[23] Hartnett's reference in his posthumous memoir to volunteers' shouts of 'come out ye whores and bastards' is absent from earlier writings, while a reference to the 'sadistic tendency amongst the soldiers guarding their own kith and kin' is also omitted from an earlier account that foregrounds the camaraderie of civil war prison life.[24] As much as there was editing, there was also self-censorship. Dolan speculates that Irish veterans, like conflict veterans internationally, spoke of the violence of 'their comrades' but not of their own and, even if they did speak, 'there were always certain words they would never bring themselves to say'.[25] If a child dared to ask if their parents were responsible for another's death, they could be told 'it was a question one must never ask'.[26]

The Cult of Violence

Once again, this emphasis on silence and omission overlooks the many upfront acknowledgements of committing violence, including during the civil war. Even if civilians, editors and the reading public were willing to exonerate veterans and tone down their violence, Bourke contends that veterans of war are often 'anxious to accept their own agency and to judge and be judged for their deeds'.[27] Indeed, many early non-canonical accounts of Ireland's revolution were steeped in violence. This was less the case in works that formed the canon: for example, Daniel Corkery's influential pre-civil war short-story collection *Hounds of Banba* (1920) emphasises the virtuous patriotism of the volunteers; they show empathy with the poor, with women and with soldiers in the British army, yet there is little mention of the violence they commit. Frank O'Connor's and Seán O'Faoláin's revolutionary writings are similarly restrained in their portrayal of violence. As Paul Delaney outlines, O'Faoláin preferred to shy 'away from depicting the actual moments when the characters are killed and instead chooses to portray death in a distant, oblique or deliberately underdeveloped manner'.[28]

There was a strong counterculture to these celebrated writings, however. As addressed in Chapter One, Patrick Mulloy felt that the 'cult of violence' evident in his novel *Jackets Green* was accepted in Ireland (although not his references to homosexuality and prostitution).[29] Whether conscious or not, veterans understood and represented their combat experience through the lens of their exposure to what has been referred to as the 'masculine pleasure-culture of war'[30] evident in British adventure tales, comic books and Wild West dime novels. One veteran boasted in his witness statement of '[s]napshooting with revolvers [...] in the cowboy fashion'.[31] Francis Carty (see Chapter One), too, recounted a getaway, remembering that 'Buffalo Bill [...] had once escaped from the Indians in a similar way'.[32] Pádraig O'Horan (see Chapter Four) wrote of witnessing the civil war through the lens of 'some blood-curdling novel'.[33] This 'cult of violence' was further inflected by folklore and the Fenian and Ulster mythological cycles. Oral histories gathered by the Irish Folklore Commission (another untapped source) in the 1930s portray violence in literary terms: an enemy Free State soldier is likened to 'a savage beast – awaiting to devour its prey'.[34] In IRB member Eimar O'Duffy's autobiographically informed novel *The Wasted Island* (1919), the protagonist Bernard Lascelle is overcome by the 'battle-lust of the warrior latent within' and, like the warriors of *The Táin*, strangles a soldier before finishing him off with a bayonet.[35]

Graphic violence could, in some cases, be used to detract from internal civil war splits by celebrating the heroic feats of the IRA against the Black and Tans. This reconciliatory aim is clear in anti-treatyite Thomas Irwin's controversial thriller *Benson's Flying Column* (1935), which was dedicated 'to my brother Sam'. Sam Irwin had been a captain in the Free State army and this inscription suggests an attempt to heal 'brother against brother' splits.[36] The novel follows the trajectory of the bloodthirsty IRA leader Davy Benson, who sets out to avenge the death of his girlfriend, Lily O'Neill, a spy for the republican movement in Dublin Castle. Irwin supposedly wrote a sequel, *Murder from Headquarters*, but it seems it never made it to press.[37] This might relate to the outcry over the violence in his first novel: the character of Seán Connor is described as 'the killer; the death-dealing avenger' for whom '[n]othing was a consideration [...] except to kill'.[38] M. J. MacManus, editor of *The Irish Press*, deplored that Irwin's novel gave the impression that 'the men of the IRA enjoyed killing for killing's sake'.[39] A reviewer in the *Irish Independent*, too, felt that it did a 'great disservice to the men of 1919–21', lamenting that '[b]lood gushes in streams from every page [...] Killing is the main theme: I have never before read a book in which there is so much slaughter'.[40]

The characters' violent impulses were all the more troublesome given Irwin's contention in a preface that his characters 'lived [...] and are alive today'.[41] Some didn't doubt it.[42] A letter defending Irwin in the *Irish Independent* argued that he showed 'the old IRA as they really were [...] The very nature of the fight demanded cold-bloodedness, and a quick gunhand'.[43] The editor of Talbot Press, who had already sanitised aspects of the novel, also privately accepted its veracity, foreseeing that with the 'passing of the years, the tendency will be to tone down the lurid aspects of the fighting'.[44]

The debates surrounding the violence in Benson's Flying Column highlight the disjunction between the reluctance among certain sections of the public to accept the realities of revolutionary violence and the willingness of some veterans, at least, to talk about it overtly. Even if editors, journalists and politicians attempted to hush up such brutality, the 'cult of violence' was highly popular. The appeal of these autobiographically based novels was not only connected to the expressed aim to set the record straight, but rather rested on the visceral emotions these war books evoked among readers: Irwin's novel made the bestsellers list and was reissued in 1944, and there were several calls for it to be adapted for the screen.[45]

Telling in Excess

Even though there is a case for reframing the historiography of the Irish revolution through the lens of a 'history of restraint' given that levels of violence were lower than in contemporaneous European conflicts,[46] the cult of violence of the 1920s and 1930s underscores that even 'relatively restrained' warfare could be accompanied by excess in the telling. In his 1928 account 'The Flame of Youth', O'Horan disapprovingly reflects on the tendency of certain anti-treaty prisoners to exaggerate their violent exploits, such as the fictionalised character Hannigan, who is mocked for his ridiculous bragging: 'Landmines! You'd give anyone th' stick t' listen to y' talkin' about blowing up people. Would y' know a landmine from a slot machine, Hannigan?'[47] Frank Gallagher's overlooked civil war diary, serialised in 1924, also refers to a Free State guard who 'boasted that he waited weeks to get that man, and described horribly the killing of him … War is a ghastly thing'.[48] While Dan Breen's memoir was mellowed down, he famously asserted in an 1967 interview that 'I make no apologies for killing, and the only thing that I was ever really sorry for was the number that escaped'.[49] Michael Flannery was similarly known for recounting that although he had not killed anybody during the civil war, he once put a gun to the head of a Free State soldier and regretted to that day 'that it misfired'.[50] John A. Pinkman even recalls meeting 'three different individuals who have "admitted" [...] to having "shot" Cathal Brugha, and I know of one odd character who'd "confessed" to having fired the Lewis gun!'[51]

Such statements might be read to signify that these individuals had no remorse or that killing was even seen as a badge of honour – psychological studies indeed show that not all people who do wrong are negatively affected by their actions.[52] However, in the recent study *Sin Sick: Moral Injury in War and Literature*, Joshua Pederson identifies excessive and hyperbolic telling as the distinguishing feature of perpetrator suffering, as 'moral injury frequently makes evil feel superabundant, hyperpresent and inescapable'.[53] For some, the 'overwhelming urge to keep talking, keep describing', and the exaggeration of the 'reach' and 'efficacy' of the deed, serves in some way as a self-inflicted punishment.[54]

While some testimonial writings reflect bragging about violence, many writings support US historian Drew Giplin Faust's contention that killing, rather than dying, was 'the harder courage' for many combatants.[55] The protagonist in Peadar O'Donnell's novel *Storm* confesses that 'the thought of killing men weighed him down' (a theme less explicitly addressed in his first-hand testimonies).[56] Francis Carty's protagonist in *The Irish Volunteer* offers a rejoinder to Terence MacSwiney's much-cited philosophy that '[i]t is not those who can inflict the most, but those who can endure the most who will conquer'. Instead, Art admits that '[t]he fact is we are killing. Doesn't that put us in the position of inflicting rather than enduring?'[57] This moral dilemma remains a preoccupation of Carty's unpublished writings produced before his death in 1968: the protagonist in the unfinished novel *Blood on the Main St* finds himself facing two RIC officers with a 'bulldog revolver' in his right hand and a Webler in left, but 'his instinct was not to shoot'.[58] These moral dilemmas, informed perhaps by Christian doctrine, also play out in the rationalisation of some forms of violence over others: killing with guns was preferred over stabbings or beatings, snipers were generally maligned and killing with a knife or bayonet was considered to be at odds with the emphasis on respectability within the ranks of the IRA.[59]

Whatever internal doubts volunteers shared regarding committing violence, this was exacerbated during a civil war in which many participated reluctantly. In labour activist Patrick Hogan's autobiographically informed novel *Camps on the Hearthstone*, the protagonist 'never tried to explain his reason for joining the [Free State] army'. He calmly tells his fellow soldiers, 'we must act as if we were engaged against the blackest strangers'.[60] The reality, however, is that both the pro- and anti-treaty sides resisted killing. Many, like anti-treaty veteran Liam Deasy, expressed that they had 'no great enthusiasm to meet former comrades in actual battle'.[61] Anti-treaty commander Dinny Lacey was said to have given the order to 'Fire high lads'.[62] Free State soldiers, too, refused to participate in firing squads; a solution for this, as Séamus MacCall wrote in his novel *Gods in Motley*, was to lock 'them up for the night with half-a-barrel of porter'.[63]

The provision of alcohol to Free State soldiers to ensure that they followed through with executions underscores how the military standard of war demanded the perpetration of violence, with resistance to violence being perceived as a 'form of effeminacy'.[64] This is once again illustrated by the fact that Michael Collins sent any of his men who were 'low in health' to Dr Robert Farnan, a 'ladies' doctor', for some form of talk therapy.[65] Within military and medical discourse, committing violence was not necessarily considered, therefore, to be a trigger of psychic injury. Rather it was the aversion to perpetrating violence that threatened masculinity and could lead to effeminate 'nervous' conditions. This conflicted masculine culture of war forms the basis for the tension in veterans' writings between telling in excess and portraying killing as the 'harder courage'. This was a tension that would play out in the widely evoked sense of 'post-revolutionary disillusion' that characterised cultural production in the decades following the civil war.

The Culture of Disillusion and Frank O'Connor's 'Guests of the Nation' Plot

The term 'disillusion' entered into 'almost every appraisal of Ireland's literary temperament by the Irish writers and critics on the scene in the middle twenties'.[66] It is worth considering how this culture of disillusion speaks to the idea of perpetrator trauma, which, in Alan Gibbs' definition, emerges from '[a]n insidious accretion of guilt coupled with *disillusionment* about the cause being fought' (my emphasis).[67] Indeed, Frank O'Connor's short story 'Guests of the Nation', which is arguably the most influential Irish text of the twentieth century, expressly captures the effects of violence on the perpetrator. The narrator, IRA rebel Bonaparte, and his comrade Noble are irrevocably changed following their role in the execution of two British soldiers with whom they had grown friendly:

Noble says he saw everything ten times the size, as though there were nothing in the whole world but that little patch of bog with the two Englishmen stiffening into it, but with me it was as if the patch of bog where the Englishmen were was a million miles away, and even Noble and the old woman, mumbling behind me, and the birds and the bloody stars were all far away, and I was somehow very small and very lost and lonely like a child astray in the snow. And anything that happened to me afterwards, I never felt the same about again.[68]

O'Connor (real name Michael O'Donovan) did 'odd jobs', as he said, for the IRA and spent the civil war interned as an anti-treaty activist.[69] His writings were regarded at the time as 'successful re-creation[s] of true incidents' and indeed, as discussed in Chapter Four, a number of his stories are autobiographically based.[70] While the actual events that inspired 'Guests of the Nation' are much debated by historians,[71] O'Connor writings, and re-workings of them, point to a certain attempt to process his own experience.[72] Regardless of whether or not O'Connor witnessed or participated in an execution as described in his famous story, there may be a hint of self-implication in the story: O'Connor did, after all, give his surname to cold-hearted IRA leader, Jeremiah Donovan.[73]

The execution plot in 'Guests of the Nation' had a profound influence on subsequent revolutionary remembrance. Though the story is ostensibly set during the war of independence, the idea of killing a friend surely resonated with a public who recalled the high rates of executions during the civil war. Within just three years of its publication, the story was performed as a silent film in 1934, scripted by Mary Manning and directed by Denis Johnston. It also inspired many literary writings, appeared as a play on Broadway and has been evoked in numerous plays, novels and films since.[74]

O'Connor remarked in his posthumous memoir, My Father's Son, that 'Guests of the Nation' had been 'stolen' on countless occasions and he claimed that 'Yeats was the very first to notice the plagiarism'.[75] Indeed, a very similar scenario to the 'Guests of the Nation' plot was replayed in A. P. Fanning's one-act play Vigil performed in the Abbey Theatre on 24 October 1932 and directed by Lennox Robinson. Fanning's acclaimed play reflects on the final hours of three republican prisoners – a poet, a boy and a farmer – who are executed by their Free State captors. The curtain closes as the army sergeant's head 'sinks forward on this arms'.[76]

Not all evocations of the 'Guests of the Nation' plot were plagiarised, however. The construction of 'empathic links with the enemy' at the heart of O'Connor's story is widely identified as a key response to perpetrator trauma, as 'personalising the foe could be crucial to the moral and emotional well-being of combatants and formed a buffer against numbing brutality'.[77] O'Connor was not the first veteran either to invoke such a scenario. For example, reviewers saw the resemblance between IRA veteran Mícheál Ó Siochfhradha's (1900–1986) play *Deire an Chunntais* [End of the Story] and 'Guests of the Nation'.[78] The plot directly mirrors O'Connor's story: two captured Auxiliaries, after over a month as hostages with a friendly band of IRA men, accept the 'bás onórach' [honourable death] of execution over the chance to escape to France.[79] However, Ó Siochfhradha's play was first staged in the Gate Theatre on 22 April 1931 and may thus have been written before the author's exposure to O'Connor's work, which did not appear in print in Ireland until later that year.[80]

The 'Guests of the Nation' plot appeared even earlier again in León Ó Broin's play *An Mhallacht* [The Curse] (1927). Ó Broin was interned for his revolutionary activism and was commissioned as an officer in the Free State army on the outbreak of the civil war. In this play, two friends participate in the execution of British soldiers. Their role in the execution takes a psychological toll and results in a fallout between them, leading to an accidental killing of one friend by the other. The play was ostensibly set during a rising in Warsaw in 1925, but viewers and reviewers saw past the flimsy Polish-name disguises of the characters and speculated that it referred, in fact, to the Irish Civil War.[81] The location was even changed to Dublin in the 1931 print version.[82]

Nevertheless, the cultural currency of the 'Guests of the Nation' motif did directly influence later first-hand veteran testimonies. Perhaps the most famous example is found in Ernie O'Malley's memoir *On Another Man's Wound*, published in 1936, five years after O'Connor's collection. O'Malley was involved in the execution of three British army officers outside Clonmel, County Tipperary, on 19 June 1921: Robert Fisher Bettridge, Walter George Cave Glossop and Alexander Cecil Henry Toogood. O'Malley's tendency to ask veterans about their roles in executing spies during his oral history interviews hints, perhaps, at the impact of this event and his need to contextualise his experience.[83] His autobiographical account of the executions shares many of the features of O'Connor's fictional story:

the officers are treated with dignity, letters are collected to be delivered to their loves ones and O'Malley emphasises his emotional connection with his opponents, as he, too, felt he was in proximity to death: 'My turn might come, too, and soon. It seemed easier to face one's own execution than to have to shoot others.'[84] In O'Connor's story, the unnatural act of burying the bodies is magnified by the disorder reflected in the natural world: 'It was all mad lonely [...] birds hooting and screeching all round disturbed by the guns.'[85] As Nathan Wallace argues, O'Malley's execution scene mimics O'Connor's fictional story, as blunt violence is again followed by the evocation of a poetic, yet potentially menacing, landscape:

> The volley crashed sharply. The three fell to the ground; their arms twitched. The quartermaster put his revolver to each of their foreheads in turn and fired. The bodies lay still on the green grass. We stood to attention. Then slowly we went up the hill across country, making for the centre. None of us spoke until we had crossed a good many fields where wind had snaked the rye grass.[86]

The Brutalisation of War: Perpetrator Trauma

If O'Malley did indeed absorb aspects of O'Connor's fictional story into his retelling of his role in an execution, writings by Irish war veterans were not the only literary influences on a well-travelled and dispersed generation of revolutionaries. O'Malley also took extensive notes on the novels of J. L. Hardy (1894–1958). Hardy, whose father was from the province of Ulster, served as an Auxiliary and was known for practising particularly brutal, psychological torture, which included beatings, burnings with pokers and mock executions – even to the point of death.[87] In the opening of *Never in Vain* (1936), Hardy's protagonist reflects on the impact of committing violence but nevertheless refuses to be consumed by his experiences in Ireland: 'Andrew Kerr wasn't proud of some of the things he had done over there – in fact, some of them wouldn't bear thinking of – but they had been the logical reply to the enemy's methods, and he didn't expect to be dogged over them to the end of his days. Fear! Confound it!'[88] A number of passages refer to Kerr's 'sport of chasing Sinn Féiners' and his knowledge that he could kill 'silently' by pressing the 'muzzle of his gun tight against the man's body and letting drive'.[89] These fictionalised revelations are perhaps all the more arresting given that Hardy was implicated in similar 'noiseless' killings.[90]

Hardy's writings underscore one of the main challenges with perpetrator testimony. Like narratives of sexual violence, the lines between testifying, confessing and extending the violence are always blurred. What might have been, for Hardy, an act of processing his experience could be received by readers as a textual extension of the violence. O'Malley was possibly not the only Irish veteran to page through Hardy's novels, contemplating, perhaps, whether he might recognise any of the fictionalised victims. As a scrawl by O'Malley at the top of his musings read: 'Hardy tortured me in the Castle. These notes show that Hardy is using his Irish experience as a minor background for some of his writings.'[91]

Harding's writings participated in a broader European canon of post-First World War perpetrator confessional literature, as evident in evocatively titled memoirs such as French army veteran Blaise Cendrars' *J'ai tué* [I Killed] (1918) and British Auxiliary commander F. P. Crozier's *The Men I Killed* (1937) which reflected on his time in Ireland.[92] More than any Irish writer of this period, perhaps, Liam O'Flaherty's earlier fiction speaks to the transformative, brutalising effects of the violence of both the First World War and the revolution in Ireland. Even the titles of his writings highlight how the protagonists are stripped of their identities by the deeds they had committed: 'The Sniper' (1922), *Return of the Brute* (1929), *The Informer* (1925), *The Assassin* (1929).[93]

This narrative of psychological brutalisation is well represented, too, in early Irish accounts of the revolution. A. T. Walsh's 1923 novel *Casey of the IRA* was advertised as containing 'a substratum of fact'.[94] The protagonist, Captain Murphy, finds himself in a never-ending cycle of guilt, as '[h]e hated killing, and yet no man in the county had been in more fights than he had'. Even though he 'fall[s] to pieces with nerves for hours' after carrying out a successful job, one 'job' always leads to the planning of another.[95] Mulloy's novel (see Chapter One) documents the gradual brutalisation of an IRA volunteer and later Free State soldier, as does Jake Wynne's *Ugly Brew* (1936) written from the perspective of a pro-treaty soldier. The protagonist of the latter imagines that he might have had a 'nervous breakdown' or have 'gone mad', but that 'fresh incidents were being forced in upon his attention'.[96] In contrast to the profound sense of disillusion that characterises the canon of revolutionary literature and in which killing is presented as the 'harder courage', less canonical texts often equate committing violence not with guilt but with brutalisation and a continuation of the cycle of violence.

The Societal Effects of Perpetrating Violence

The brutalising psychological effects of violence, and the knock-on effect on society, were also a concern for female revolutionaries, particularly those with pacifist commitments. Rosamond Jacob, who was part of the women's peace committee that spoke to the leaders of both sides of the civil war split in July 1922 in an attempt to prevent further violence, includes a passage in her novel *Troubled House* (1938) in which a young IRA activist requires a sort of talk therapy after his involvement in the shootings in Bloody Sunday: 'I can't get away from it – I can't sleep – I can't talk to people – I can't stop walking! Oh, if he'd only been armed – if his wife hadn't been there!'[97] Yet even though Liam suffers emotionally on account of his actions, the modernist artist Nix Ogilvie articulates the established view that it was rather the repulsion of violence that had negative psychological implications: '[I]t's not natural for a young man to have principles against fighting.'[98]

Úna Bean Uí Dhiosca (1880–1958), who was secretary, alongside Jacob, of the Irish section of the Women's International League for Peace and Freedom, more directly confronted the brutalising effects of combat in her autobiographically informed novel *Cailín na Gruaige Duinne* [The Girl with Brown Hair] (1932). The novel, published under the penname 'Breanda', was deceptively advertised by publishers An Gúm as a 'touching little romance'.[99] However, Uí Dhiosca's novel boldly confronts questions of domestic violence, marital breakdown and postnatal depression in the context of the civil war. Born Elizabeth Rachel Leech, Uí Dhiosca came from a Dublin Protestant background, was educated in Switzerland and later learned Irish from Patrick Pearse during her studies at Alexander College. She took Aran native Liam O'Flaherty to task on the pages of *The Irish Statesman* in 1927 for writing in English rather than in Irish, to which he curtly replied, 'I don't write for Úna McC. Dix, and for that reason I'd be pleased if she refrained from drawing my attention to her existence.'[100]

The 'existence' of Bean Uí Dhiosca's remarkable writings have indeed eluded literary scholars and historians alike. If O'Flaherty's preoccupation was with the brutalising effects that war had on men, Uí Dhiosca's *Cailín na*

Gruaige Duinne expressly aimed to underscore the cumulative psychological impact of conflict on women, including those who opposed, or indirectly experienced, the war. Written in arresting first-person narration, protagonist Róisín Ní Bhriain, like the author, perfects her Irish in the Connemara Gaeltacht, where she meets her future husband, Mícheál, an IRA volunteer (Uí Dhiosca met her husband, E. R. Mac Clintock Dix, at Tawin Island, County Galway; he was co-founder of the Irish college there with Éamon de Valera and also an active volunteer).[101] Róisín subsequently travels to Canada where she works as a teacher on the prairies of Saskatchewan (like the author), before returning to Ireland to marry Mícheál and (again like the author) converting to Catholicism. Their marriage is soon disturbed by the shock of the explosion at the Four Courts in June 1922. Reflecting Uí Dhiosca's public opposition to the outbreak of hostilities at the time, Róisín holds both sides to account for the violence: 'Dá ndéanadh na troduidhthe ar gach taobh mar a rinne cúpla fear aca agus a ngunnaí a chaitheamh síos nuair a tugadh an t-ordú sin dóibh sgaoileadh fá Éireannaigh ní bheadh aon chogadh ann' [If the fighters on each side did what some of them did and put their guns down when they were given the order to shoot other Irishmen, there would be no war].[102]

Husband and wife take opposing stances on the treaty and the brutalising effects of civil war splits translates into violence in the home. Róisín's anti-treaty husband attacks her beloved dog, Bran, before tying a stone around its neck and throwing it into the sea.[103] The symbolic meaning was clear to readers familiar with established analogies between animal cruelty and domestic violence (see Chapter Four).[104] Róisín leaves her husband and flees to a YMCA in Belfast where she delivers her first child. She blames her husband's behaviour on 'an [chuma] ina raibh an saoghal Fódlach' [the state of Irish life].[105] Róisín asserts that she, like many women at the time, was not in her '[ciall] cheart' [right mind].[106] In a stark scene that challenges traditional and nationalist conceptions of motherhood, Róisín contemplates killing her child: 'An deamhan a bhí istigh ionam thosuigh sé dom' spocadh – "Tacht é; cuir do dhá láimh fá n-a mhuineál agus bain an anál as, bhéarfaidh sin fuascailt duit"' [The devil inside started taunting me – 'Choke it; put your two hands around its neck and cut off its breathing, that will liberate you'].[107]

While Uí Dhiosca's depiction of her protagonist's deep emotional upset aims to sympathetically underscore the devastating effects of war on women, representations of bloodthirsty republican women who repudiated their reproductive duties to the nation appeared widely in civil war propaganda (see Chapter Three). Whereas men became brutalised by war, contemporary propaganda suggested that war evoked a brutalism in women that was already innate. P. S. O'Hegarty famously decried that these 'gunwomen' 'went more wholeheartedly and more fiercely into the war against the Irish people than ever they had into the war against the Black-and-Tans'.[108] This discourse of violent, murderous women was not reserved for anti-treaty republican women. Anti-treatyite and 'adventurer' Charles John McGuinness (1893–1947) draws on these degrading stereotypes in his unapologetic account of killing a Protestant woman in Derry during the riots of 1920. In his 1934 memoir *Nomad*, McGuinness factually recalls seeing an 'old hag' 'reviling the Pope' and 'kicking and abusing the corpse' of a murdered workman 'with ghoulish glee'. Her barbarism functions as an exculpatory preface to the men's actions:

> 'Let's draw lots and shoot her. That isn't a woman – it's a devil!' I said to my companions.
>
> We drew, and the task fell to me. As a warning to her, I fired several rounds of random shot. My companions did likewise. Then, during a lull, she once more strode into the thoroughfare carrying white strips which, apparently, she was distributing amongst her neighbours as souvenirs of papist blood.
>
> Just as she bent down to dip her rags in the red pool I fired – so did the others, forgetting the lottery in their anger. The hag spun round and fell beside the body she was desecrating.[109]

Representations of active women as savage and unhinged might explain the dearth of women's testimonies of perpetrating violence. The unease regarding female militants – both at the time and up until the present – is most clearly evident in the debates over the allegation that Countess Markievicz shot the unarmed Constable Michael Lahiff during the 1916 Rising and 'delightedly' cried, 'I shot him [...] I shot him.'[110] Countess Markievicz's sister, Eva Gore-Booth defended her sister at the time, rejecting the 'absurd' suggestions of such a 'mad desire to kill soldiers'.[111] Whatever the exact details of Markievicz's militarism, the idea that a woman showed joy in battle was considered to be a particular transgression.

Nell Humphreys, too, initially shared reservations regarding her daughter Síghle's 'unwomanly' attitude and how 'she gloried when the enemy fell'.[112] Such sentiment might explain the caution in Síghle's much later account of the infamous raid on her home in November 1922, in which she makes sure to emphasise her initial reluctance to shoot at the Free State troops: 'I hadn't the heart to fire *until some other soldiers started to come in the gate*' (my emphasis).[113] Indeed, female revolutionaries were accustomed to tactfully exploiting traditional binary conceptions of men as aggressors and women as passive victims to suit their own purposes: Free State soldier John A. Pinkman recalls finding a woman during the Battle for Dublin who exclaimed, 'Don't touch me [...] I'm a Red Cross nurse [...] I'm a woman!' However, when she was searched, Pinkman claims that she was in possession of a revolver that still had a 'wisp of smoke [curling] out of its barrel'.[114]

These gender-based victim/perpetrator conceptions also played out in the civil war split of female revolutionaries. The pro-treaty women's organisation, Cumann na Saoirse, actively aimed to set itself apart from 'the wild women of Cumann na mBan': they 'represented the aspirations of the emerging elite' and promoted more traditional roles for women, such as first aid and nursing.[115] Nevertheless, some pro-treaty women were tasked with military roles and 'Cumann na Saoirse' was famously dubbed 'Cumann na Searchers' on account of the Free State's policy of recruiting female searchers. This was 'sister against sister' war: just as pro-treaty news sources demeaned anti-treaty female activists, anti-treaty women also denounced female searchers as an abomination. In her 1972 memoir, Eithne Coyle deplores the female searchers brought into Kilmainham prison, claiming that they 'fortified themselves with that which produces DUTCH courage' and 'took off their high heeled shoes and banged the prisoners'.[116]

Women's fictionalised writings offer occasional insights into the guilt that women may have felt during the revolutionary period. The protagonist in Máirín Cregan's play *Hunger-strike* (as discussed in Chapter Two) no longer feels pride for encouraging others to 'lend a hand and fight'. By the time of the civil war, she feels compelled to support her husband's hunger strike but has nightmares in which she sees herself killing 'for fun'.[117] Margaret Barrington's (1896–1982) novel *My Cousin Justin* (1939), believed to reflect on her marriage with Liam O'Flaherty, also indicates the guilt experienced by the first-person protagonist narrator. Loulie feels excluded as her husband Egan and cousin Justin bond over the brutalising effects of their wartime experience, an experience which 'lay always at the back of their minds, a dark dream, only released when the fumes of alcohol rose to their heads'.[118] But Loulie also struggles with 'fear' and 'exhaustion' due to her guilt over giving information on Justin's wife, who was then executed as a spy by the IRA.[119] She is haunted in her dreams by the image of Justin, dressed as a judge in court, pointing at her: 'Thou shalt not kill [...] There is no amnesty for the soul'.[120]

This sense of guilt on account of indirect perpetration – in this case, giving information – highlights that the perpetration of revolutionary violence was not just the province of gunmen and gunwomen. Rather, it rested on a broader network of collaborators. While Seán O'Faoláin participated in little direct action – an official dealing with his military service pension application exclaimed that there was 'not any element of military service'[121] – his short story, 'The Bombshop', hints at the unease associated with indirect perpetrator violence. While set in the earlier independence struggle, 'The Bombshop' was understood by readers to reflect on O'Faoláin's work in the chemists' corps during the civil war. In the story, the bombmakers work away unbeknownst to the world – but the indirect violence of their work is brought home when they accidentally shoot the old women harbouring them through the floorboard and are forced to live alongside her corpse.[122]

Perpetrator Silence in Elizabeth Connor's *Dead Star's Light*

Elizabeth Connor's novel *Dead Star's Light* (1938) – and its stage adaptation *The Dark Road* (1947) – also provides perceptive commentary on the nature of perpetrator guilt in the opening decades of the Free State.[123] The novel opens as four respected pillars of the community – a doctor, a solicitor, a banker and his nephew – accidentally run over a 'travelling man from God knows where' on their drive home from a public house in December 1919. They throw the body down a mineshaft and attempt, to little avail, to forget their unwitting complicity in both the killing and the concealment of the body. Connor's novel blends fiction and local history: the plot was reminiscent of the disappearance of postman Larry Griffin in

Stradbally, County Waterford.[124] Furthermore, the nephew character, John Davern, goes on to become the idealistic commander of the local flying column and is believed to be based on the actual figure of Waterford IRA commandant George Lennon (whose fictionalised perpetrator testimonies will be discussed later in this chapter).[125]

Elizabeth Connor was the pen name of Úna Troy, whose husband Joseph C. Walsh served as medical doctor under Lennon in the Déise flying column.[126] Patrick Maume suggests that there 'are hints in Troy's work that her husband's alcoholism originated in a deep misanthropy deriving from civil war experience'.[127] However, though she dedicated *Dead Star's Light* to her husband, Joe, it seems that she chose to base her fictional protagonist on the local column leader, Lennon. Davern, like Lennon, leads the anti-treaty side during the 'battle of Fordtown' (perhaps an evocation of the siege of Waterford in July 1922). Both the fictional and real characters also emigrate to America in the aftermath of the civil war and arouse suspicion on their return due to their socialist and anti-clerical beliefs. Published in the context of the Spanish Civil War, Connor's novel garnered mixed reception, with a reviewer in the *Sunday Independent* lamenting that Davern was 'less a character than a peg on which the author hangs her own savagely disillusioned ideas of present-day Ireland'.[128] Indeed, even though *Dead's Light Star* did not make the censors' list – as Connor's first novel, *Mount Prospect* (1931), had due to its direct allusions to abortion and contraception – it was nevertheless met with backlash. The Walsh family were effectively excommunicated from their parish of Saint Peter and Paul's in Clonmel, County Tipperary, as the local priest was 'truly appalled and grieved by the anti-religious and anti-clerical spirit' of the novel.[129]

Troy, the wife of a doctor, explicitly addresses the embodied consequences of concealed perpetrator trauma in *Dead Star's Light*. Although the guilty men fear that telling their wives about the man they threw down the mineshaft would be too much of a 'shock' to their 'delicate heart[s]',[130] their conspiracy of silence comes to affect them all emotionally as well as physically. Banker Robert Bolger finds 'a constipated mind far more upsetting than a constipated bowel' and suffers a premature stroke, while Dr Mahon takes to drinking 'for life, for sanity' and 'oblivion'.[131] Dr Mahon's wife struggles to come to terms with her husband's drinking and is haunted by her own sense of failure 'as a lover and a comrade' due to infertility.[132] Julia Ross, the wife of solicitor Ignatius Ross, also struggles to sleep beside a man who was 'almost a murderer' and looked at her husband 'like a beaten dog'.[133]

The theme of perpetrator trauma is further teased out in the context of Davern's role in perpetrating violence during the revolution. The novel's title, *Dead Star's Light*, refers to Davern's post-revolutionary disillusion as he realises that he had been guided by 'the light of a dead star'.[134] Although the struggle for independence was 'the happiest [time] of his life',[135] the civil war evoked 'a hate which would endure beyond this generation and take root in the next'.[136] While Davern is implicated in committing violence himself, he gradually disavows violent methods and shrinks away from his comrades who were 'avid with the blood-lust': '[W]hen he saw men blown to limbless trunks, [...] when he saw sprawled bodies whose sightless gaze held an eternal questioning, he loved his enemies with a fierce pity and hated the system that made man slay man.'[137]

The novel points to the possibility of 'working through' such trauma. Davern's emotional baggage eases when he is forced to explain his past misdeeds to his fiancée, Katherine Ross. This brings 'an overwhelming relief, as if the last shadow of that poor tattered ghost had left him forever'.[138] Although the characters try to suppress memory – 'all our talk will never undo what we did'[139] – Davern comes to realise that 'speech was healing'.[140] All the same, his complicity in the violence that he grows to detest forms a key part of Davern's identity:

> Only some things were imprinted on his memory forever, small sharp cameos framed in keener sensation; his first ambush, the jar of the rifle against his shoulder and a figure twisting and falling in the road, while he reloaded with the calm and remote satisfaction of one who has made a successful shy at a coco-nut; hurrying at night behind hedges, from a farmhouse, while the searchlights of a military lorry beat down the lane after him; a shot, and one long, shrill scream, and in a silence that followed, the clear call of a bird, like a mocking echo.[141]

Connor's description of Davern's violent actions once again bears witness to the influence of Frank O'Connor's aesthetic in 'Guests of the Nation': brutal violence is dramatised by emphasising the disorder caused to the natural, all-knowing world.

George Lennon's Perpetrator Re-stagings

George Lennon's experience of perpetrating violence had already been imaginatively teased out in both novel and dramatic form by Elizabeth Connor before, it seems, he began writing about his own experience – and specifically his experience of committing violence. On 18 March 1921, Lennon and the Déise IRA flying column took a number of prisoners, including RIC sergeant Michael Hickey, following an ambush on British military at the Burgery, County Waterford. While the rest of the prisoners were released, Hickey knew the identities of his IRA captors. As a result, he was court-martialled and shot as a 'police spy'.[142] Lennon was acquainted with Hickey and was surely aware of the tragic circumstances of his burial: gravediggers initially refused to bury the body for fear of repercussions from the IRA, and his fiancée ensured the grave was left unmarked to protect it from vandalism.[143]

In Connor's *Dead Star's Light*, the act of disposing of the dead man's body causes Davern to experience a state of dissociation, as though he were an observer to his own wrongdoing: 'The scene before him was an act in a play, a picture thrown on the screen of night, and he must be audience.'[144] Quite intriguingly, Lennon chose to revisit his role as an executioner in two pieces of theatre, rather than in prose fiction or standard autobiography. The first play, *Down by the Glen Side* (1952), was written as a three-act television play, possibly with a US audience in mind. It was never performed or published, though he sent a copy to Úna Troy's daughter, Janet.[145] The play centres on 'Irish Commandant' Henry Rogan who, following the 'Guests of the Nation' motif, strikes up a relationship of mutual respect with English hostage Captain Robert Harley. Rogan hopes to glean insight into imperial military strategy from the captain, but Harley himself is repulsed by war, having experienced those 'ghastly trenches'.[146] Along with his wife, Mildred, Harley hopes to produce and perform an anti-war play at his local parsonage hall. The play will feature an army captain who is due to oversee the gibbeting of a young man but who experiences a change of heart when he hears the cries of the young man's mother. The captain will reject his profession of 'killing', and the play will conclude with the binary gendered anti-war message that 'we need a new kind of courage. More like [a] woman's. Dealing with life not death.'[147]

The plot of *Down by the Glen Side* emulates Harley's planned pacifist production. When Rogan is expected to execute his new companion, he initially feels unable to disobey a military command, lamenting, 'I would give almost anything – but – I cannot ...'[148] However, when the hideout is ambushed, Rogan drops his gun from Harley's temple and flees. His final words are 'Goodbye, English Officer', before he comes under bullet fire from the ambush party. Harley subsequently refuses to give his fellow British soldiers any information on the whereabouts of the Irish soldiers. Rather than acknowledge his intransigence, however, the British officer assumes that he must be 'mentally deranged': 'Get a brandy ration – he is suffering from shock!'[149]

While Yeats may have considered this to be yet another rip-off of O'Connor's 'Guests of the Nation', Lennon's play is, in fact, a subversion of the canonical source text: Rogan goes against the military order, avoids carrying out the execution and saves the life of his hostage. The anti-war propaganda thrust of the play reflects Lennon's developing interests in non-violent philosophies, expressed through his involvement in the American League Against War and Fascism in the 1930s, in the Quakers from the 1940s and in Zen Buddhism from the early 1950s.[150] Through the genre of the theatre, Lennon could re-enact his role as an executioner and imaginatively change the course of history.

Temporal Disorder: 'The Whole of Time Has Already Happened'

But the urge to tell was an 'all-consuming life task' for Lennon. If his 1952 play articulates a counter-history of what could have been, his second theatrical sketch, written almost twenty years later, moves closer to the actual facts of that day in March 1921. The one-act play 'I and Thou' is embedded into his memoir *Trauma in Time*, which was composed, it seems, during a trip to Ireland in 1971 and finalised after Lennon's return to the States. Although never published during his lifetime, his diary/memoir, or drafts of it at least, were circulated. In one photograph, which shows Lennon alongside Paddy Paul, his civil war foe, Paul is holding what is thought to be a draft of Lennon's diary/memoir.[151] *Trauma in Time* has since been transcribed and published by Lennon's son, Ivan.

Lennon's highly experimental testimony offers no security in terms of time or vantage point: the narrative shifts throughout from first-person to third-person to second-person narration. It opens with the writer's arrival in Ireland in the 1930s during the Spanish Civil War, as the narrator wonders, 'What on earth ever brought him back to this place?'[152] Without warning, the narrative then jumps forward in time to Lennon's departure from New York on 15 May 1971. This temporal distortion also occurs when Lennon sees the Rotunda Hospital in Parnell Square during the 1971 visit. This brings Lennon back to his son's birth in the 1940s, but this memory is quickly disrupted by his need to see the site of Vaughan's Hotel, which had adjoined the hospital. It is now 19 September 1920, when he gaily delivered a 'valise full of bombs' into the famous IRA hideout.[153] There is no escape from the memory of the revolution: even celebratory memories of birth are disturbed by the evocation of his youthful folly in the shadow of death.

While Lennon's memoirs have been republished in chronological order,[154] he expressly outlines that his use of non-linear temporal sequences serves a specific purpose:

> Belated Explanation.
> In this journal tenses will be found to be mixed and the dates, seemingly, out of their proper order; but not out of context. The motive is deliberate – the illusion of continuity is the personification of our ignorance. The whole of time has already happened.[155]

This confusion of dislocated time is often viewed as a hallmark of trauma-telling.[156] However, before equating this fragmented narration with the symptomatology of trauma, it is worth considering that Lennon's aesthetic may in fact reflect his interest in Zen Buddhism, according to which time 'is conceived of as cyclic rather than linear: history has no overall direction or purpose, and similar patterns of events may repeat themselves many times over'.[157]

'I and Thou': The Remote Satisfaction of Killing

Just as Lennon's memoir jumps back and forth in time, his narrative switches suddenly into a short one-act play entitled 'I and Thou' which revisits the execution scene represented in the earlier television play. The intimate connection between the killer and his victim, central to so many of these perpetrator narratives, is perhaps ironically evoked in the play's title, 'I and Thou', which refers to Austrian-Jewish philosopher Martin Buber's philosophy of dialogue according to which all human life finds meaning through interpersonal relationships. The production notes outline that the play is set on a 'grey cold morning in Holy Week, Wednesday, *Spy Wednesday*' (my emphasis), notably the day Judas betrayed Jesus. Four cast members are listed: a partisan officer, a constabulary sergeant, a priest and a firing squad. Although the cast members are unnamed, the dialogue refers to 'George' and thus betrays the autobiographical tenets of the play:

> Police Sergeant (pleadingly): George, I knew you as a child, you used to play with the head constable's children in the barracks.
> Partisan Officer (almost inaudibly): Yes.
> Police Sergeant (intimately): You are the one person in the world that can save me.
> Partisan Officer (pity is choking him): *I would give anything ... anything in the world to save you ... but I cannot –* [my emphasis][158]

The words of the partisan officer directly mimic Rogan's exclamation in the earlier play that: 'I would give almost anything – but – I cannot ...' However, unlike *Down by the Glen Side*, there is no sudden change of heart in the second play. The partisan officer places the label of 'Police Spy' on the prisoner's tunic, ties a bandage over his eyes and calls 'fire'. To ensure the job is complete, the partisan officer 'draws his Luger, bends down and fires into the man's temple'.[159]

While Lennon was a committed pacifist, his writings suggest that the adrenaline of killing can bring relief: the partisan officer looks down at the dead enemy officer and finds that his 'turmoil is calmed'.[160] This sense of relief and even unexplainable pleasure evoked by warfare emerges in other writings: Connor's novel *Dead Star's Light* hints at the protagonist's 'calm and remote satisfaction' after shooting on target, while Ernie O'Malley, in his civil war memoir *The Singing Flame*, acknowledges the 'momentary pleasure that I had in hitting a mark'.[161]

Lennon takes these remarks a step further by explicitly linking the pleasure of killing with sexual gratification, such as in his description of his role in an attack on Kilmallock police station: 'What a strangely satisfying, almost wild, sensation it was to push forward the bolt, feeling the round slide smoothly out of the magazine and into the breach. *You* snuggled the butt voluptuously into *your* shoulder, took careful aim and pulled the trigger. The crash of the rifle was orgiastic' (my emphasis).[162] In this, Lennon's testimony supports Bourke's observation, based on extensive analysis of soldiers' testimonies, that, for some combatants, killing seemed to 'resemble spiritual enlightenment or sexual eroticism' and could be described as 'an orgasmic, charismatic experience'.[163] The expression of such taboo emotion is mellowed in Lennon's case, however, by his resort to second-person address rather than the first-person voice that characterises much of his memoir. Not only does this shift in vantage point place distance between the author and the transgressive subject matter, the second-person 'you' also invites the reader to step into his shoes, to see for themself the strength of such contradictory emotion.

Lennon's jump away from first-person narration generally coincides with descriptions of particularly painful events, such as an occasion on which he contemplated consuming a 'slim tube of morphine tablets' for fear he could be captured and tortured, and an episode during which a 'young Tan' from Liverpool died in his arms.[164] These difficult memories are both told through third-person voice. While this displaced subjectivity can be a helpful distancing strategy for addressing traumatic or contentious experience, it serves a key function in perpetrator testimony. As Gibbs outlines in his study of memoirs by US military personnel involved in the Gulf War, these shifts in narrating persona establish a break from 'the writer now and the soldier then' and thus separate the speaker from 'the uncomfortable inescapability of his individual violent past'.[165]

Kathleen of Sleady: Confessions of Gender-based Violence

The retreat to third-person narration emerges once again in Lennon's description of his physical rejection of a young female revolutionary near Sleady, County Waterford. Lennon recounts that he was accustomed to stopping at a cottage where a girl would lay out food and play Jacobite melodies on the accordion as he nodded off to sleep. One night, the girl's younger sister was also present, never taking 'her eyes off him'.[166] What followed would occupy an incredibly painful place in Lennon's memories, as described in a passage marked by an ellipsis:

> It happened as he passed through the castle garden. The girl appeared as if from nowhere, flung her arms about him and clung to him frantically. Quite overcome by surprise and a brutal ignorance he pulled her arms away and flung her from him ... but he had not progressed very far down the road when he was overtaken by such a feeling of disgust for himself that he had to lean weakly against the ditch. Why had he been so cruel, and why inflict such hurt on another person? An inner instinct told him that he lacked something true and something natural. The memory would remain with him forever.[167]

Although violence against women is widely acknowledged in popular literature (as discussed in Chapter Three), Lennon offers a rare account from the perspective of the perpetrator. His guilt over this incident is heightened by the fact that he was never 'permitted to make amends'.[168] As he recounts in *Trauma in Time*, he went back to Sleady to see his 'little friend' when the truce was announced.[169] By the time he returned, however, 'they would not tell me the circumstances of her lonesome death'.[170] Looking for answers years later, he asked an old comrade, Seamus Phelan, 'Why was she buried in unconsecrated ground?' Phelan deftly changed the subject, suggesting that, 'Ah now, such things are best forgotten, best forgotten.'[171]

Yet Lennon could not forget his ambiguously described encounter with Kathleen. In fact, his earlier television play, too, presents the mistreatment of women as a consequence of the inexplicable cruelty of war. Rogan is mocked for 'hating' a girl – who, significantly, also bears the name Kathleen:

2ND IRISH SOLDIER [...] *TO ROGAN*
Little Kathleen was there, her eyes shone when she heard Henry Rogan was back in the glen with the column. She's a grand little girl!

ROGAN *IMPATIENTLY*
That will do!

2ND IRISH SOLDIER *CONFIDENTIALLY TO HARLEY*
He hates wimmen!

ROGAN *ANGRILY*
I said that will do!

2ND IRISH SOLDIER *EXPLAINING TO HARLEY*
Sure, we all love our country so much we have no time to be loving the wimmen.[172]

Unlike Charles Nomad McGuinness' stark and unapologetic description of killing a woman in Derry (Lennon corresponded with McGuinness and was presumably aware of the memoir),[173] Lennon's acknowledgement of men's mistreatment of women had a specific aim: it reflected his anti-war agenda which was expressly tied to the dismantling of hypermasculine military aggression and the advocation of a 'new kind of courage' that was 'more like [a] woman's'. Lennon clearly did not approve of the masculine glorification of war in much revolutionary remembrance, and his writings should be understood as part of his expressed aim to counteract dominant remembrance of the 'tuppence ha'penny' revolution which he felt was made up of 'lies'.[174] There was also a reconciliatory aim behind his personal project of remembrance: he wrote in 1934 of his wish to 'bring together again old comrades-in-arms' in order to 'heal the bitterness that has so seriously retarded national progress'.[175]

If Lennon advocated for reconciliation in the 1930s, the urgency of his personal therapeutic writing project was perhaps exacerbated by the 'explosions being set off in the North' which formed a backdrop to the 1971 diary/memoir.[176] The final entry in *Trauma in Time* is dated 27 September 1971 and powerfully reflects on the inescapable consequences of Lennon's perpetrator guilt. Once again, Lennon surrenders to his imagination in an effort to undo history: the third-person protagonist finds himself on a 'pilgrimage that seemed to have no end' until he is reunited with both his victims:

> Kathleen and the constabulary sergeant were some way off beckoning him on. Leaving her companion she came to meet him and this time he did not repulse her. Kathleen no longer looked sad and they smiled happily at each other. The three of them walked hand in hand towards the source of the mountain stream.[177]

Anthony O'Connor's *He's Somewhere in There* – a 'Victim of History'?

Lennon was not the only veteran to attempt to make amends in the context of escalating violence in Northern Ireland. Anthony O'Connor's autobiographical novel *He's Somewhere in There* appeared in print in 1975 and is one of the most remarkable testimonial novels to emerge from the revolutionary period. The opening pages include what is surely one of the starkest confessions of perpetrating violence from the pen of a civil war veteran:

> But for this war I should be in America doing a decent job of work – maybe Johnny too – but, here I was, a sergeant in the Free State Army, having killed at least a dozen fellow Irishmen in the wild country road skirmishes that were a feature of the National Army and the Republicans and I not yet twenty years of age.[178]

Presented in the foreword as a 'factual account of the Western Sector during the Irish Civil War 1922/23', the novel opens in January 1923 as the novel's teen narrator, Steve Corrigan, a soldier in the Free State army, looks on 'through a mist of tears' as six anti-treaty prisoners are executed.[179] Among the executed is the narrator's childhood friend and Athlone neighbour Johnny Costello. The novel subsequently jumps back in time to trace the circumstances that placed Steve and Johnny on opposite sides of the civil war split.

Though O'Connor takes strong artistic license, *He's Somewhere in There* was certainly informed by his own experience. Irish Army census records confirm that O'Connor, like his protagonist, enlisted at the Custume Barracks, Athlone, in June 1922 at the age of eighteen.[180] He later emigrated to Canada in 1925, where he worked on the National Railways before relocating to London in 1927. During the Second World War, he served in the Royal Air Force as a squadron leader and later made a career as a manager in some of west London's most celebrated gentlemen's social clubs. He exposed the underbelly of this gentlemanly world in his tongue-and-cheek memoir *Clubland: The Wrong Side of the Right People* (1976), published just a year after *He's Somewhere in There*. In perhaps the only critical appraisal of the novel, Fintan O'Toole, in an essay on O'Connor's nephew and namesake, billionaire Tony O'Reilly, asserts that the civil war was 'a personal burden' for O'Connor that was 'too painful to be told bluntly and was wrapped in a thin layer of fiction'.[181]

If *He's Somewhere in There* demonstrates the dynamics of therapeutic writing, the novel is also remarkable both for its detail of social and military life and for its industrious deployment of a range of narrative strategies to present the narrator as powerless against the force of military command. For example, Robert Nye, reviewing the novel in *The Guardian*, praised its honesty and referred to the narrator as 'a victim of history'.[182] Even Steve's hard-hitting, albeit ambiguous, confession that he 'killed at least a dozen fellow Irishmen' is strategically prefixed by a reference to his own sense of being 'trapped' in the Free State army and his hopes of emigrating. Steve's contention that he could be working in America with Johnny, but for this war, provides yet another example of the empathic links with the enemy motif central to the 'Guests of the Nation' plot. Like the 1930s novels of Wynne, Mulloy and others, O'Connor's account emphasises the gradual brutalisation of the Free State soldier as a means to explain his actions.

'To Johnny': Empathetic Links with the Foe

The panicky nature of the execution of the six prisoners at the opening of the novel reflects the historical realities: Johnny refuses his blindfold, round target markers are pinned over the prisoners' hearts and, after the line-up shooting, the provost fires 'a single shot' into each of the prisoners' heads.[183] But there is even stronger factual resonance: the fictional execution scene is dated January 1923, which corresponds with the execution of five anti-treaty combatants in Athlone Barracks on 20 January 1923.[184] The executed men were attached to the North Galway IRA Brigade and hailed from Connaught – all except for Thomas Hughes, who was from a farm of seven acres in Bogginfin, a short distance outside Athlone.[185]

The fact that the Hughes family, who lived locally, were not informed of their son's execution caused national outcry. As Seán Ó Laidhin TD lamented in Dáil Éireann at the time:

> His parents live one and a half miles from Athlone. His mother was
> in town at the market, and was going home when she was overtaken
> by some person in authority, who told her about the execution. As

this was the first time in the history of Ireland that an execution took place in Athlone, and this man's people live within a mile of the town, surely it was the duty of the Government to notify them before executing him.[186]

In *He's Somewhere in There*, the executed prisoner's mother comes to the barracks looking for information on Johnny, but Steve cannot bring himself to tell her the truth and denies that Johnny is 'somewhere in there' [the barrack].[187] These details suggest that the character of Johnny might be based, however loosely, on Thomas Hughes. Whether or not O'Connor was acquainted with Hughes, he fictionally recreates an incredibly intimate bond between his protagonist Steve and the executed republican Johnny. The novel is even dedicated 'TO JOHNNY'. Like the foreword which describes the novel as a 'factual account', this dedication *seems* to confirm the authenticity of the testimony. Indeed, O'Toole's discussion of *He's Somewhere in There* reads the novel as a true story of O'Connor's 'own intimate betrayal of his friend Johnny'.[188] However, although *He's Somewhere in There* gives testimony of O'Connor's first-hand experience and captures an emotional truth, it is important to avoid any overly literal readings of these fictionalised testimonies. The fact/fiction line is almost always impossible to make out. In the case of *He's Somewhere in There*, it could be the fictional narrator, Steve Corrigan, speaking through the dedication rather than O'Connor, the author.

As evident in other testimonial writings, Johnny and Steve's innocent, pre-trauma childhood is set up as a contrast to their subsequent corruption. As a child, Johnny abhors violence and is almost angelic in nature: Steve recalls that '[t]he fish always seemed to like Johnny's worm better than mine'.[189] Gradually, however, the boys are dragged into the militarisation around them: in Athlone during the First World War, 'it wasn't hard to come by the odd Lee Enfield rifle and .303 ammunition'.[190] After the arrival of the Black and Tans, Johnny joins the IRA in targeting a number of RIC men and British officers. Steve works as a chemist's assistant until the truce and only unwittingly gets wrapped up in the escalating violence when he informs undertaker and IRA intelligence officer Jim Bailey that RIC officer Sergeant Craddock had raided the Costello home. Three nights later Craddock is assassinated by the IRA, causing Steve 'to reflect on the wisdom of my visit to Jim Bailey':

> A burst of machine-gun-fire – said to have come from the lock-up
> shop of Foley's the greengrocers – shattered the lives of Sergeant
> Craddock and Constable Tom Healy – Craddock's death was no
> surprise but there was grief in my home for young Tom Healy who
> came from Crossmalina, my mother's birthplace. On posting to
> Athlone he had called often and they talked about the people they
> knew in the area.[191]

This is clearly a reference to the assassination of the Athlone-based RIC
officer of the same name, Sergeant Thomas Craddock, on 22 August 1920.
A Roman Catholic and a native of County Donegal, Craddock had served
in the Boer War and was widely disliked for his brutal tactics.[192] He was
assassinated as he was leaving the Comrades of the Great War Club on King
Street – the street on which O'Connor lived.[193]

If Steve had little remorse about the assassination of 'rebel hunter'
Craddock, his grief at the death of 'young Tom Healy' from 'Crossmalina'
illustrates that many RIC officers were valued members of the community.[194]
This may relate to the fact that O'Connor's own father, John, was an RIC
constable until his resignation in July 1920, after which time he resettled
in Dublin.[195] Indeed, RIC officers in the Midlands region came under great
pressure during this period: Patrick Shea, whose father served in the RIC
in Athlone, recalled that a 'feeling of an approaching siege grew', as the RIC
became 'isolated from the townspeople'.[196] Perhaps this 'unacknowledged'
civil war was too complicated to incorporate into the novel: the author's
RIC family connections are not explicitly addressed and the fathers of Steve
and Johnny work in retail and insurance.

The Road to Brutalisation

Steve's implication in Craddock's assassination underscores his
powerlessness in the face of spiralling warfare. When he joins the Free
State army in June 1922, he finds himself stationed at Athlone barracks,
'issued with a Lee Enfield rifle and 150 rounds of ammunition, with a stern
warning to hold on to them at all costs or I'd be bloody well shot if I lost
them!'[197] Meanwhile, Johnny, already active in the IRA, takes the anti-treaty
side. Johnny's girlfriend, Maureen – in line with the stereotype – cautions
Steve that 'any man who wears the Free Staters' uniform is a traitor to the

Cause!'[198] Steve soon regrets his decision to enlist and counts down the days until he can emigrate. He finds himself trapped, however, as he fears that deserting from the army would harm his chances of getting on the quota to Boston.

O'Connor portrays Steve's betrayal of his friend Johnny's trust by drawing on the well-established civil war love triangle. Rather unwittingly, Steve is seduced by Johnny's girlfriend, Maureen, who – reflecting the cliché of sexualised female revolutionaries – invites him to spend the night with her. Perhaps more informed by the sexual revolution of the 1970s than attitudes in the 1920s, Maureen denounces the inequalities between men and women in terms of attitudes towards extramarital sex: 'Why did God make it so enjoyable if he wanted us to avoid it? You will have twenty girls, maybe more, before you marry. I will have Johnny, and the memory of you, thank God, to content me through the years. Why is it all right for a man to sleep around before marriage and not a woman?'[199] A reviewer in *The Irish Press* denounced the novel as 'bandwagon writing' and felt that '[t]he exemplification of the whole split in the fate of two friends on opposite sides is trite enough but to have them share the same girlfriend and have the Free State one serve on the execution squad of the other is too much'.[200] Nevertheless, O'Connor's use of the well-tested romance plot – 'bandwagon writing' or not – serves to heighten Steve's sense of guilt on account of being a 'traitor to Johnny'.[201]

The novel also offers insight into the poor conditions for soldiers in Athlone, who had to make do with limited weapons, 'bits and pieces' of 'shaggy' uniforms and delayed payments.[202] Of particular interest is O'Connor's description of the arrival of ex-British army officers, many of whom had mutinied as part of the Connaught Rangers uprising in India in July 1920. This brings a renewed sense of army discipline to the barracks – but military order is also accompanied by heavy drinking and boasting about the soldiers' commercial relationships with women. Steve hears that in India, Pershore, Rawalpindi and Karachi, 'the wimmin there have tits as long as yer arms. They're untouchable until ye give 'em a couple o' bob ... then they're all right'.[203] He also witnesses first-hand the emotional turmoil endured by the Connaught Rangers, as one soldier, Gallagher, re-enacts an incident when his friends were marched away by military policemen in Pershore. In his distress, Gallagher lashes out at a colleague for no particular reason: 'He grabbed a bayonet from its scabbard and, in a maniacal fury, began to lunge at all and sundry. There was no doubt his intentions to drive it in someone.'[204]

This connection between what could be described as post-traumatic stress disorder and a propensity towards violence underlies the spiral of violence that characterises the rest of the novel. Steve's early activities consist of attempts to challenge anti-treaty columns in the rural outskirts of Athlone, as well as Sligo, Birr and Roscommon; this reflects the military presence of the Western Command during this early civil war period.[205] His first cycling expedition is disastrous: Steve and ten others are caught off guard by machine-gun fire and seven of the party of soldiers are 'dead or badly wounded'.[206] Steve finds himself bending over the body of his roommate who is 'lying in a pool of black liquid ... An only child with a widowed mother. It was so obscene.'[207] While the death toll is an exaggeration, the Western Command Free State army did experience losses in these early civil war days; among the deceased was 16-year-old John McCormack, shot in an ambush outside Glasson, Athlone.[208] This is the first of a series of events that gradually lead to Steve's brutalisation; over the course of the novel, the innocent, and perhaps foolish, 19-year-old chemist's assistant is converted into something of a killing machine.

'I Had Carried Out Orders': Limited Agency

Although initially apprehensive, Steve joins a flying column tasked with 'destroy[ing] [...] all rebels in the west of Ireland' which, he feels, is preferable 'to staying in a barrack room with the Connaught Rangers'. [209] Life on the road, however, came with its own dangers – including from the soldiers' superiors. The column was to be led by a Colonel Lawson, formerly a major in the British army; he is described as being 'one of Michael Collins' right-hand men' and threatens that 'if any man is not in cover when we next make a sudden stop, I will personally shoot him'.[210] Steve is particularly impacted by his participation in an ambush on the Galway/Mayo border which resulted in the deaths of a number of men in both the Free State and republican camps. Steve struggles to comprehend his actions and emphasises his limited agency due to military structures: 'I had carried out orders. I had shot, pulled, tugged, lifted and buried in an atmosphere of hate and viciousness that would seem impossible in the men who, a few months earlier, had been side by side in Ireland's problems.'[211]

Steve's brutalisation occurs in gradual steps. At first, he tries to aim off target, but his superior Madigan threatens that 'you're going to get a couple of them or I'll want to know why!'[212] Forced into killing, he then justifies (and rationalises) his shooting by attempting to objectify his targets: 'As I aimed, I tried to make believe it was only a dark object and there was nothing at the end of it.'[213] Steve's relative innocence is also highlighted through comparisons between himself and other more sadistic officers – these 'negative referents' are indeed a feature of perpetrator testimony as a means to lessen culpability.[214] For example, Colonel Lawson is 'ruthless' in his 'bloody manhunt' for rebels, and other officers enjoy 'mowing the prisoners down'.[215] Only after Steve's comrade Madigan is killed does he come to fully deride his opponents, claiming, '[t]hey looked so "enemy" – strong and rugged in their shaggy jackets and cloth caps. They couldn't be Irish, these men who could blast the life out of Madigan and a dozen others.'[216]

By the final ambush of the novel, Steve empties 'the magazine of my Lee Enfield' without hesitancy and watches how the 'staccato splatter ended when a man hurled sideways from the bush'.[217] When Johnny, his childhood friend, is arrested, Steve's numbing is complete to the extent that he cannot save his friend's life – even though Johnny intervened to ensure Steve's safety previously in the novel. He watches on as Johnny is executed and finds that his natural instinct is to hold his gun closer: 'I felt very alone and held tight to the Lee Enfield rifle that was now as much part of me as an arm or a leg.'[218] Mechanised and numb, Steve becomes part of a conspiracy of silence, aware that there would be no 'mantle of martyrdom' for the civil war dead and that the 'dead poor were seldom mentioned, remembered or lamented'.[219] O'Connor's novel, published over fifty years later, is written, therefore, to counter the silence in which the fictional Steve is complicit.

Despite such a reparative aim, O'Connor's explicit representations of violence, like many such accounts, nevertheless produce an uneasy tension between educating and perpetuating a 'pleasure culture of war', whereby war and killing are honoured. His memoir, *Clubland*, sheds further light on this enigma. After the civil war, O'Connor served in the Royal Air Force and was enveloped in military culture for the rest of his life. Unlike the graphic violence in *He's Somewhere in There*, O'Connor only briefly reflects on his Second World War experience in *Clubland* and rather mocks the bravado of the military-medal-wearing clients of the gentlemen's clubs he manages. He ridicules Lord Branton for his fear of cockroaches, commenting that 'I knew that although he had shot *a dozen something or others* in East Africa, one of our little speedsters landing on his head would scare the daylight out of him' (my emphasis).[220] The reference to the number of deaths committed by Branton echoes the key line in *He's Somewhere in There*, as Steve confesses: 'Here I was, a sergeant in the Free State Army, having killed *at least a dozen* fellow Irishmen' (my emphasis).[221] In both cases, the men are characterised by the death toll they were responsible for, suggesting that military and social stature, in this hypermasculine *Clubland* world, was determined by killing. In this context, could O'Connor's fictionalised confession in *He's Somewhere in There* indulge in some sort of trophy-collecting? Does his novel and its exaggerated death toll play into this problematic military culture?

However, O'Connor also expresses a genuine scepticism of the glorification of war through his support of the 1969 feature film *Oh What a Lovely War*, co-produced by his nephew, photographer Brian Duffy. The film criticises British generals for their over-eagerness in sacrificing young soldiers and O'Connor's comment that '[General] Haig had destroyed a generation of young men' even caused club members to call for his resignation. Furthermore, *Clubland* hints at another context underpinning the production of *He's Somewhere in There*. On 11 December 1974, the IRA shot up the front of the Cavalry Club. Sardonic as ever, O'Connor attributes this to an awful attempt at '*agneau irlandais*' [Irish lamb] in the club in the days preceding the attack: '[T]he general feeling was that someone must have tipped off the IRA about this treasonable affront to a national dish. The next day they shot up the Club with a machine-gun, luckily harming nothing but the facade. They couldn't even hit the window.'[222]

Despite this blasé account, this instance is integral for appreciating the context in which *He's Somewhere in There* emerged. In the foreword to the novel, O'Connor celebrates the election of Erskine Childers in 1973 as a demonstration by 'Southern Ireland' of their 'distaste and boredom with the happenings in Ulster'. That Childers was Protestant, had an English accent and was born in Chelsea to an American mother and English father was evidence for O'Connor of 'the best traditions of the Anglo-Irish', which were central to paving a path of peace essential for a 'united Ireland'.[223] Childers' election, too, was perhaps seen as reparation for the death of his father, also Erskine Childers, who was famously executed by Free State troops when found in possession of a gun given to him by Michael Collins.[224] Not only that, but Childers had made his 16-year-old son, the future president, promise that he would seek out each one of the men who had signed his father's death sentence and offer them forgiveness.

If the context of the Troubles was a motivation for the publication of *He's Somewhere in There*, the conflict also detracted from O'Connor's testimony, as neither publishers nor the public, it would appear, had a particular desire to review the earlier civil war during the 1970s. Assessed through the criterion of literature rather than as life writing, *He's Somewhere in There* garnered little critical attention, with one reviewer advising the author to study 'the techniques of the historical novel, as expounded by Stendhal, Tolstoy, or di Lampedusa'.[225] The neglect of O'Connor's remarkable novel, another 'unlistened-to story' from the pen of a Free State army soldier, further illustrates the scholarly disregard of fictionalised testimony and points to the limited appeal of perpetrator narratives, regardless of the many self-protective and self-justifying narrative strategies mobilised by O'Connor.

Conclusion

Even if violence during Ireland's revolutionary period was restrained by comparison to other conflicts, the experience of enacting violence nevertheless provoked numerous, often contradictory, attempts to explain it. The consequences of killing – and, significantly, of killing acquaintances – is at the core of the culture of post-revolutionary disillusion that emerged following the civil war period, as epitomised in Frank O'Connor's influential short story 'Guests of the Nation'. The theme of empathetic links between perpetrator and victim had a significant influence on subsequent cultural production and veteran writings.

While the writings in the canon present what Seán O'Faoláin endorsed as a 'brutalism' that was 'essentially romantic' (see Chapter One), popular narratives outside the canon offer a far cruder sense of revolutionary violence – and, indeed, had a large and eager readership. These popular fictionalised writings by veterans can tend towards excessive telling – death tolls are exaggerated, bloodiness is expansive, violence is sexualised and the psychological impacts presented as far-reaching. Excessive telling could nevertheless conceal an unease or even a sense of guilt. Many testimonies suggest that killing, rather than dying, demanded the 'harder courage' in wartime and particularly in civil war.

If men's writings reflect on the brutalisation of war and their powerlessness to curb the spiral of violence, female revolutionaries had to contend with cultural representations of women as innately violent and bloodthirsty 'furies' and 'diehards'. From as early as 1916, the idea of women not only participating in warfare but actually being animated by the experience was received as a particular obscenity. This, in turn, plays out in women's testimonies, as they cede to the social expectation to self-represent according to conventional models of femininity, gloss over their experience of committing violence or recall this experience with hesitancy. Even if female revolutionaries were less likely than men to take up arms, they nevertheless were involved in a range of activities – from passing information, to gathering intelligence and raising funds – that formed the networks of war. This indirect implication in violence provoked moral doubts for some. The realities of committing violence also affected those with no direct military involvement. Úna Bean Uí Dhiosca and Elizabeth Connor were both married to IRA activists; their writings speak to the psychological knock-on effects of men's perpetration of violence in the domestic sphere.

The enduring influence of early popular narratives of perpetrator trauma is abundantly clear in the later writings of anti-treaty veteran George Lennon and pro-treaty veteran Anthony O'Connor. Produced in the diaspora in the context of the Troubles, their remarkable fictionalised testimonies underscore that their urge to tell about their experience of perpetrating violence required the adoption of numerous self-protective narrative strategies in order to make their testimonies consumable to the public and also bearable to themselves. These testimonies demonstrate the absolute necessity of broadening historical scholarship to include less conventional forms of life writing. The literary self-protective strategies were essential to enabling these testimonies of perpetrating violence; veterans drew on preceding literary tropes, re-enacted their experience through fiction, experimented with temporal disjunction and displaced subjectivities, and deployed a range of distancing and exculpatory strategies to facilitate their trauma telling, and, in O'Connor's case, to downplay personal responsibility. Reading perpetrator writing, too, evokes unease, as evident in both the contemporary outcry regarding 'killing for killing's sake' in certain popular narratives and the relative neglect of the subject in academic scholarship. It may have been easier to dismiss O'Connor's novel as crude amateur fiction than to grapple with the starkness of his confessions.

The writings of Lennon and O'Connor contributed to a broader outpouring of testimony from the 1960s as veterans felt an increased urge to tell before it was too late. Kerry anti-treaty veteran Billy Mullins was urged by friends and family to write his memoirs because '[i]t should be written, it must be written and you are the only one left to do it'.[226] Niall Harrington, who had been in the Free State army, hoped when writing his posthumously published civil war memoir 'that the telling of the story now, even at this late stage, will clear the air'.[227] Earlier commitments to forget in the name of the common good developed over time into endeavours to remember. Civil war writings have since been found in attics and archives, handwriting has been decoded and transcribed, narratives have been published, self-published and posted online by family members. Not all testimonies have found such attentive receivers, however. Published civil war testimonies only constitute a small portion of the many narratives by veterans who had stories to tell and retell – and who wanted to be heard.

Afterword

Acts of Reparation

My jail experience is written in letters of fire across my brain, never to be effaced.[1]

Polly Cosgrove, Kilmainham Jail internee, 19 July 1923

[The] civil war [...] wounded Irish family relationships so deeply that it could still hardly be spoken of in the Ireland in which I grew up. In that silence wounds festered, scar tissue distorted the body politic, and the idea that lies were safer than truth became the norm.[2]

Felicity Hayes-McCoy (b. 1954)

The above statements capture the complexities of remembering the Irish Civil War: they sum up the tension between veterans' inability to forget and the obstacles to remembering especially felt by subsequent generations. This book underscores that, for many veterans, the desire to remain silent had to contend with the urge to tell. Despite the prevailing emphasis on the silence engendered by the Irish Civil War, the many voices that broke the silence can no longer be overlooked. Civil wars engender vibrant bodies of competing discourses; the Irish Civil War is no exception. And if civil war is universally deemed to be 'uniquely traumatic',[3] the experience of trauma generates attempts to find meaning, as much as it represses memory.

Cultural, social and medical understandings of trauma constantly evolve over time. But what does not change is the common urge among those who have lived through traumatic events to somehow unburden themselves of negative emotions and share their story through a testimonial act. Traumatic memories from the Irish Civil War were often articulated in narratives that moved away from conventional autobiographical forms; veterans creatively carved out liminal narrative spaces for themselves in order to facilitate their breaking of silence. Popular, seemingly artless, middlebrow or lowbrow fiction was one of the preferred models of self-expression for many veterans. This endorsement of popular realist forms – more so than modernist techniques – reflects the literary practice of the time. Fictionalised testimonies abounded in the aftermath of the First World War and readers were willing to read fiction through an autobiographical lens. The Gothic, too, allowed for the exploration of unknown, repressed emotion, while romance fiction, and even children's fiction, provided a sturdy cover for the explorations of transgressive themes at odds with official remembrance. Poetry also played an important testimonial role; it was a genre that facilitated the exploration of intense inner emotions, often in first-person narration. In light of a strong culture of litigation, these less conventional narrative forms offered a sense of protection against both official and social censure.

Literary forms of expression are also particularly relevant in the study of civil war representation: tried-and-tested civil war motifs – such as the brother-against-brother metaphor, the love triangle plot or the accidental killing narrative – offered helpful templates for veterans to mobilise. For many revolutionaries, these fictional veils and plots did not undermine their projects of truth-telling: Anthony O'Connor's novel was presented as a 'factual account of the Western Sector', Annie M. P. Smithson referred her readers to her novel for an account of her civil war experience, and Patrick Mulloy claimed his 'entire story' was 'based on a series of true incidents'.[4]

How is it that these writings have been subject to outright neglect in scholarship to date? On discovering the writings of Garrett O'Driscoll, Jody Allen-Randolph marvelled at the fact that a woman 'who inscribed female characters into revolutionary events in her fiction [...] [was] erased from the national canon'.[5] Yet the same shock and outrage can be applied to almost all the testimonies introduced in this book. The occlusion of these remarkable writings can be attributed to a range of influences. It reflects official reluctance to receive civil war writing, as 'amnesia', for many, was seen as necessary for reconciliation. It highlights the strength of the formation of the revolutionary canon, spearheaded by writers and critics like Seán O'Faoláin, who adopted very specific ideas of what the canon of the 'brutal literature of despair' written by veterans of the revolution should look like. It points to the marginalisation and trivialisation of women's writings – even when their works were bestsellers. The omission of many of these testimonies from literary studies illustrates the neglect of popular and less easily categorisable literary narratives. Middlebrow, perhaps sub-literary, testimonial writings – as well as folklore and oral interviews – have been overlooked despite their commanding testimonial functions.

The omission of these testimonies is not merely indicative of a narrow focus within literary studies. It highlights a major blind spot in twentieth-century Irish historiography, characterised by a distrust of popular culture, a refusal to follow Hayden White's destabilisation of the dichotomy between fiction and history (which gained ground in the 1970s), and a continued stress on a disjuncture between (official) History and memory.[6] The wealth of civil war testimony written in the Irish language underscores the need for a bilingual, even multilingual, approach to the study of Irish history. This neglect is hardly surprising, however. As Vincent Morley recently argued, 'the inability of so many historians of Ireland to read primary sources in the indigenous language of the country is the most striking example of the profession's failure to adapt its techniques to meet the challenges posed by the raw materials of Irish history'.[7]

For historian Robert Fanning, '[t]he many voices of those who became the cannon fodder of the revolution and of the civil war must for the most part remain forever inaccessible', because '[h]owever diverse the range of written sources, they can, of course, only shed light on the motivations of the lettered and of the literate'.[8] Rather than yield to the inaccessibility of certain aspects of everyday experience in revolutionary Ireland, this book builds an alternative archive of testimony with which to grapple with the experience of ordinary people. During his imprisonment, Pádraig O'Horan wrote letters home on behalf of an illiterate dock worker; his writings testify to the experience of the 'unremembered dead' and those who are not found in official histories: the people of Dublin's tenements, Belfast refugees contending with layers of civil wars, Citizen Army volunteers who were being written out of a civil war narrative that focused on two perspectives: pro- or anti-treaty. For Mary Manning, it was Kenneth Sarr's autobiographically inflected novel *Somewhere to the Sea* (1936) that offered an insight into the 'great solid mass of quiet people who went on living and eating and laughing and sleeping or trying to sleep, during those years'.[9] Patrick Mulloy endeavoured to offer 'a tale of plain people caught in the mad whirl of revolution'.[10] Martin T. Henry's novel *Ambushed Lovers* was concerned with the 'rank and file' and not 'the leaders'.[11]

These writings challenge many firmly held convictions within Irish historiography. They show that fictionalised veteran narratives were amongst the earliest testimonial accounts of the Irish revolution and that fiction interacted with, and informed, first-hand testimony. They illustrate how women used fiction to take ownership of revolutionary remembrance and to reclaim the subject of women's pain from reductive stereotypes. Fiction enabled women both to secure an audience and to overcome the self-effacement often evident in first-hand accounts by female revolutionaries. While some women mediated and consolidated the masculine commemorative narrative of the revolutionary period in non-fiction writings, such as school textbooks or history writing, fiction by the same women authors could complicate and even contest those narratives.

Despite a widespread emphasis on the culture of sexual prudery ushered in by the new state, autobiographically informed narratives hint at a more liberal, inquisitive attitude to changing gender roles and non-heterosexual relations connected to the shifting sexual landscape during wartime. Literary representations of the volunteers' relations with prostitutes also complicate the supposed piety of IRA combatants, which, it has been suggested, ensured the 'relative scarcity' of sexual violence in revolutionary Ireland. Violence, including sexual violence, is explicitly addressed in many of these writings. These taboos were not as hidden as often perceived.

Veterans went to huge lengths to testify and publicly air their stories. They faced rejection from theatres and publishing houses. Their writings were hidden behind pen names, sent to publishers abroad and self-published at the authors' own expense. In some cases, successful publication was followed by censorship or libel cases. The lengths taken to share these writings may reflect the fact that many of these testimonies were self-acknowledged projects of therapeutic writing, or 'scriptotherapy' to use Suzette Henke's term; this is either acknowledged by the author or metafictionally incorporated into the narrative. However, the cathartic compensation of writing was often a never-ending task, offering respite, rather than resolution. These writings, nevertheless, offer an indispensable archive for understanding the experience and treatment of trauma and mental health beyond the narrowly defined parameters of political and medical authorities. The works of George Lennon and Garrett O'Driscoll even challenge the conventional medical management of such conditions by suggesting that medical diagnoses were exploited as a means of controlling those who threatened the status quo.

Although these testimonies shed light on individual psychological pain, they are nevertheless directed outwards as much as inward. The various self-protective narrative strategies adopted by veterans are ultimately indicative of the lengths taken to reach a public audience and find confirming witnesses for their stories. Audiences, too, shaped what was not said. This was particularly challenging when presenting perpetrator trauma or sexual trauma, topics readerships were less accustomed to receiving. Telling was thus always accompanied by the need to conceal; even if Desmond Ryan advocated 'blow[ing] off steam once and for all', he nevertheless acknowledged he 'threw some of the less welcome into the wastepaper basket'.[12]

The avid readers of these testimonies ensured that autobiographically informed novels like *Jackets Green, Ugly Brew, Benson's Flying Column, The Marriage of Nurse Harding* and *Somewhere to the Sea* found themselves on the bestseller list. These readers included IRA veteran Mike Quill, who could not 'stop reading'; for him, and for many others, reading the accounts of others may have functioned as a means to remember his own revolutionary days vicariously. These imagined communities of engaged witnesses are addressed in nearly all of the testimonies considered; in dedications, paratexts or introductory prefaces. The collaboration of testimonial storytelling is most powerfully addressed in Dorothy Macardle's *Earth-bound,* in which the narrators are surrounded by a group of attentive respondents who validate their stories. In receiving these stories, it is the readers who facilitate the translation of personal narratives into public testimonies. It is also the interaction of the texts and their readers that facilitated a counter-memory of the civil war that existed in the shadow of state and socially sanctioned 'silence'.

While readers empathetically identified with the stories of others – as evident in critics' reviews and personal letters to authors – the release of painful stories into the public domain also exposed veterans to backlash. Ryan wrote in the knowledge that his writing might be dismissed as 'bilge' by the 'professional critics'.[13] Reviewers could dismiss Smithson's novel as 'naïve pages', Mulloy's *Jackets Green* was considered 'revolting' and O'Connor's *He's Somewhere in There* was scorned for its 'low level of intelligence and sensibility'.[14] For some, the act of speaking, but not being listened to, proved incredibly painful. Mulloy's story was censored and proved financially ruinous due to an unsuccessful defamation case. Even after the ban was lifted, the novel was never reprinted, despite his lifelong efforts.

If the reception of these testimonies by contemporary readers is critical in bringing the stories to testimonial resolution, what is the role of the researcher as an active witness, albeit at a historical remove? Historian Dominick LaCapra outlines that working with testimony 'raises the issue of the way in which the historian or other analyst becomes a secondary witness, undergoes a transferential relation, and must work out an acceptable subject-position with respect to the witness and his or her testimony'.[15] Dori Laub likens the role of readers and listeners to 'the blank screen on which the event comes to be inscribed for the first time'.[16] However, this model has been criticised for privileging the expertise of the analyst/reader over the agency of the testifying subject. As Kalí Tal strongly objects, 'the survivor's experience has been replaced by the experience of those who come in contact with the survivor's testimony – an appropriative gambit of stunning proportion'.[17]

In addition, the concept of the reader as a 'blank screen' entails a denial of the researcher's subjectivity.[18] This emphasis on the detachment of the researcher is perhaps indicative of the dominance of positivism and empirical inquiry which underwrites much historical study – even more so, perhaps, in the Irish context. As Anne Karpf outlines:

> Historians rarely reflect on their own affective investment in the material they study; indeed, there is often an inverse relationship between the traumatic intensity of the event being studied and their readiness to discuss their own emotional involvement or the affective sources which led them to take up that research field in the first place [...] [A]ny leakage of feeling into research often still seems to be a source of shame, a transgression of the ideal type researcher. What appears to be demanded of the historian, in such cases, is the blank canvas of the psychoanalyst, upon which history itself can project its own feelings.[19]

This project evoked a succession of affective experiences and unsettling encounters. The sense of responsibility at the heart of a project that seeks to revoice muffled, dissenting voices of trauma was brought home to me as I first read Kathleen Hoagland's autobiographical novel, *Fiddler in the Sky*, published in the United States in 1944.[20] The only copy available in Ireland was in the National Library. As I read Hoagland's arresting testimony, I had to physically separate the pages, some of which, due to a printing error, were still uncut. I was this copy's first reader. Once again, it might be asked how an autobiographical novel that addressed the intersection between revolutionary politics, alcoholism, domestic violence and emigration could be omitted from all scholarly consideration? How did Hoagland's account go unread in Ireland, though it was well received in the United States? And how, in historical research, does the researcher become 'not only a secondary witness but in some sense also a surrogate one, charged with speaking on behalf of those who no longer can'?[21]

The role of the secondary or surrogate witness also entails a burden of responsibility. While there is a tendency to assume that any projects that seek to recover stories of pain are unquestionably 'ethically valuable', Colin Davis has recently argued that this 'uninterrogated commitment to the ethical value of secondary witnessing is the founding blind spot of trauma studies'.[22] As Davis further contends, 'we like – perhaps we *need* – to believe that we are doing something ethically valuable when we immerse ourselves within, listen to, talk and write about, stories of unspeakable trauma'.[23] If many of the subjects included in this book exist in grey zones between victims, perpetrators and bystanders, it is worth considering that the researcher, too, exists in this grey terrain of implication. To use Michael Rothberg's terms, might the historian also be an 'implicated subject' who occupies a position 'aligned with power and privilege without being themselves direct agents of harm'?[24]

Maintaining distance as a researcher became even more challenging on other occasions. When checking page numbers for Máirín Cregan's *Hunger-strike* (1932), again in the National Library of Ireland, I found a handwritten inscription on the opening page: 'To Mrs. Davin and Maudie wishing them a Happy Christmas, from Máirín Cregan, 1932.' I could easily have incorporated this into the discussion of Cregan's play: the dedication is another reminder of the audacity of Cregan, who published her remarkable autobiographically informed play at her own expense. The play documents the deep psychological implications of the revolution in the domestic world and her confirming witnessing audience was made up of her fellow revolutionaries: Maudie Davin, a Dublin musician, also probably transported messages in her violin case. On Good Friday 1916, Cregan sent a coded telegraph to Maudie's sister Mina – 'Delighted to assist at concert' – to inform the Dublin Volunteers that she had gained assistance in Tralee to transport arms.[25] Cregan shared her play as a Christmas present with an audience that she knew would be attuned to her story, an intimate audience who could readily validate the sentiment of her play.

However, this encounter with such an intimate personal message stretched beyond the question of the text's reception. Maudie Davin is also my great-grandmother. I had already written about Cregan's play as I held this copy in front of me, with no idea how Maudie's copy of *Hunger-strike* had ended up in the National Library. This was just one of numerous encounters that highlight the impossibility of the 'noble dream' of objectivity in historical research.[26]

It was also in Máirín Cregan's and Jim Ryan's home in Greystones that Maudie Davin met her future husband: Frank Aiken. Perhaps more than any Irish statesman of the twentieth century, Frank was known for his unease with the memory of the civil war. As head of the Fourth Northern Division IRA, he attempted to remain neutral on the outbreak of hostilities, reciting an old priest in a now widely cited quote: 'War with the foreigner brings to the fore all that is best and noblest in a nation – civil war all that is mean and base.'[27] He sided with the republican camp after being arrested and imprisoned in Dundalk by members of the pro-treaty Fifth Northern Division. After their escape from Dundalk Gaol, his division played no significant part in the conflict. Not long after Frank was appointed IRA chief of staff – following the death of Liam Lynch – in April 1923, he gave a 'dump arms' order, effectively ending the civil war.

I was often reminded of his words that 'dreadful things happen in war and worse in civil war' – although I knew little, if anything, about the events in question. Frank was highly reticent about his revolutionary experience, never speaking to his family about his own actions as a perpetrator or of the suffering inflicted on those close to him. The release of archival materials in the early 2000s led to the family's discovery of his division's role in the atrocity in the Protestant village of Altnaveigh on 17 June 1922.

These silences abound. They are also gendered. When transcribing an interview Ernie O'Malley collected from Michael O'Hanlon in 1950, I was haunted for months by a fleeting comment that 'one of the girls was accidentally shot'. She was aiding a band of republicans who had escaped from the Curragh in December 1922.[28] Unable to stop thinking of the unnamed 'girl' who was 'accidentally shot', I set myself the painstaking task of trailing through the Kildare death records. I discovered the deceased was an 18-year-old female revolutionary, Annie Cardwell – and a first cousin of my great-grandfather, Frank. Her tragic death did not feature in family or national histories. Nor did I know about the revolutionary background of my New York-based great-grandaunt, Nellie Stuart, whom I discovered in the Cumann na mBan nominal rolls as I compiled data on post-civil war female emigrants.

When I visited Francis Carty's son, Francis Xavier Carty, in Ballsbridge in December 2019, he presented me with an old newspaper cutting proving Frank's frequently evoked stubborn silence: the article was an *attempt* by Carty, then editor of *The Irish Press*, to interview Frank on his retirement from political life in 1969. Even if Carty's mother, Margaret, had harboured Frank when he was on the run in 1923, it was no good. As Carty wryly wrote, 'when Frank Aiken wishes to say nothing he smiles in a friendly way, shakes his head from time to time, uses practically no words at all'.[29] That same summer Frank had a 'great bonfire' in his office, burning all his civil war papers. He is remembered as something of a 'historian's worst nightmare'.[30] Perhaps this book, to use Frank O'Connor's words, is its own 'act of reparation'.

Rather than deny one's implication in the research undertaken, therefore, it is perhaps more productive to address these 'affective investments' – and the risks involved. LaCapra outlines two extremes in terms of responses to testimony: 'full identification, whereby you try to relive the experience of the other' and 'pure objectification, which is the denial of transference, the blockage of affect as it influences research'.[31] While the blockage of affect seems to be the preferred model of the two, this positivist refusal to address the researcher's own emotional responses may prove to be as problematic as over-identification. As Marla Morris contends:

> Without at least the awareness of what defence mechanisms are and what they do, the historian is at the mercy of her own repressions. These repressions and resistances will determine, to a certain extent, what it is the historian chooses to write about or not write about.

> What gets excluded from history, then, has as much to do with what
> it is historians can psychically handle.[32]

Working on this book has highlighted a tendency among scholars to avoid writing about topics which might be both psychically challenging and defy straightforward empathic identification. The experience of perpetrators hardly emerges in scholarship of the revolution and when it does, there can be a tendency towards moral judgement. Sexual violence still causes unease, evident in the tendency to downplay its occurrence. Women's writing that is more difficult to understand from a feminist perspective is less likely to be recovered. The relative scholarly neglect, and even trivialisation, of the refugee crisis provoked by partition and of high post-civil war emigration hints at the exclusion from history of uncomfortable historical realities that have lingering legacies in the present.

If the code of silence erected around the Irish Civil War is socially constructed, we might also address how researchers, past and present, have been implicated in its making and its preservation. Furthermore, while there have been many calls during this decade of commemorations for 'ethical remembrance', spearheaded by President Michael D. Higgins, it is hard to imagine how such might be achieved, if at all, without first acknowledging the subjectivity and biases of the researcher. Holocaust survivor Saul Friedländer suggested that the historian should include metafictional self-reflexivity in their works, contending that 'the voice of the commentator must be clearly heard' in order to 'disrupt the facile linear progression of the narration, introduce alternative interpretations, question any partial conclusions'.[33] It might be time thus to develop a self-reflective model of history writing which would address the implicated subjectivity of the researcher and cultivate discussion on what we choose to 'write about or not write about'.

If this book highlights the subjectivity of the testimonial writings under analysis, it also, therefore, acknowledges that any historical writing is the product of a 'ratio of subjectivities' made up of 'that of the witness and that of the historian'.[34] The selection of the texts for analysis within this study is perhaps most evidently subjective. There are many more civil war testimonies deserving of study. For the purpose of this book, I have attempted to incorporate as broad a range of perspectives as possible. Following Desmond Ryan's recognition of the writings of O'Donnell,

Carty and Mulloy for their evocation of the 'spiritual wounds' of civil war, I have endeavoured to represent various outlooks on the question of the Anglo-Irish Treaty in each chapter. In a number of cases, I also selectively chose narratives, not only for thematic and formulaic purposes, but also for the extent of the contextualising information available. The selection of testimonies of those who were directly involved and whose testimonies could be corroborated with other 'official' sources was part of an attempt to prove the validity of these less conventional writings and make the strongest case possible for their inclusion in historical study. However, that is not to say that imaginary testimonies, written by those with no first-hand experience, do not contribute to social memory as much as accounts by veterans based on direct experience. The consideration of civil war writings by non-veterans also opens up possibilities for the study of civil war narratives by later generations. There is no shortage of such narratives. In fact, the paradoxically vocal silence of the civil war continues to be a central theme in popular historical fiction and family memoirs.[35]

The unsatisfied urge 'to tell and to be heard' about the Irish Civil War will produce another crop of competing narratives during the centenary commemorations of 2022–3. There are many more books to be written about the persistent legacies of Ireland's acknowledged and unacknowledged civil war(s). As Desmond Ryan presciently warned, 'we should always be Still Remembering Sion'.[36]

ENDNOTES

Introduction

1   'Display Ad: The Unspeakable War', *The Irish Times*, 17 September 1958, p. 6.
2   Begoña Aretxaga, *Shattering Silence: Women, Nationalism, and Political Subjectivity in Northern Ireland* (Princeton, NJ: Princeton University Press, 1997), p. 15; Diarmaid Ferriter, 'Irish Civil War Has Its Own Contentious Monuments', *The Irish Times*, 26 August 2017; Fearghal McGarry, 'Revolution, 1916–1923', in Thomas Bartlett (ed.), *The Cambridge History of Ireland. Volume 4: 1880 to the Present* (Cambridge: Cambridge University Press, 2018), p. 292.
3   Nicholas Allen, *Modernism, Ireland and Civil War* (Cambridge: Cambridge University Press, 2009), p. 2; Philip O'Leary, *Gaelic Prose in the Irish Free State: 1922–1939* (University Park, PA: Penn State Press, 2010), p. 331.
4   See https://www.decadeofcentenaries.com (accessed 20 October 2021).
5   Guy Beiner, 'Memory Too Has a History', *Dublin Review of Books*, 1 March 2015. Available at https://www.drb.ie/essays/memory-too-has-a-history (accessed 9 February 2020).
6   Anne Dolan, *Commemorating the Irish Civil War: History and Memory, 1923–2000* (Cambridge: Cambridge University Press, 2003), p. 4.
7   *Irish Independent*, 7 September 1927, p. 5; *The Irish Times*, 10 June 1943, p. 3.
8   This quote is taken from Gavin Foster's research on intergenerational civil war memory, see Foster, 'Local and Family Memory of the Irish Civil War', Queen's University Belfast, 12 June 2017. Available at https://soundcloud.com/history-hub/gavin-foster-local-family-memory-irish-civil-war (accessed 11 June 2019), 19.28.
9   Deputy T. J. O'Connell, Dáil Éireann debates, vol. 40, no. 3, 16 October 1931.
10 Elisa Adamia, 'The Truth of Fiction: Some Stories of the Lebanese Civil War', in Karine Deslandes, Fabrice Mourlon and Bruno Tribout (eds), *Civil War and Narrative: Testimony, Historiography, Memory* (New York: Palgrave Macmillan, 2017), p. 111. See Anne Heimo and Ulla-Maija Peltonen, 'Memories and Histories, Public and Private: After the Finnish Civil War', in Katharine Hodgkin and Susannah Radstone (eds), *Contested Pasts: The Politics of Memory* (Abingdon: Routledge, 2003), pp. 42–56.
11 Frances Flanagan, *Remembering the Revolution: Dissent, Culture, and Nationalism in the Irish Free State* (Oxford: Oxford University Press, 2015), p. 9; P. K. Horan, 'The Flame of Youth: A Study in Rebel Mentality', *Irish Christian Advocate*, 4 May 1928, p. 209.
12 Roger Luckhurst, *The Trauma Question* (Abingdon: Routledge, 2013), p. 79.
13 Dori Laub, 'An Event without a Witness: Truth, Testimony and Survival', in Shoshana Felman and Dori Laub, *Testimony: Crises of Witnessing in Literature, Psychoanalysis and History* (Milton Keynes: Taylor & Francis, 1992), p. 78.

14 Síghle Humphreys interviewed by Helen Ní Shé, 22 March 1987, *Glórtha na Réabhlóide*, RTÉ Raidió na Gaeltacha. Available at: http://140.203.202.64/items/show/725 (accessed 11 June 2020). Mary O'Connor (née Harpur), unpublished memoir, p. 29; Frank O'Connor, *An Only Child* (Macmillan & Company, 1961 [1971]), p. 239. My thanks to Caitríona Nic Mhuiris for sharing a copy of Harpur's memoir. Mary Harpur was active in Cumann na mBan and later married Seán O'Connor, who was attached to the First Battalion of the Irish-speaking unit of the Free State army. All translations my own.

15 Desmond Ryan, *Unique Dictator: A Study of Eamon de Valera* (London: A. Barker, 1936), p. 205; P. S. O'Hegarty, *The Victory of Sinn Féin: How It Won It and How It Used It* (Dublin: Talbot Press, 1924), p. 147; C. S. Andrews, *Dublin Made Me: An Autobiography* (Cork: Mercier Press, 1979), p. 306.

16 Michael Hopkinson, *Green Against Green: The Irish Civil War* (Dublin: Gill & Macmillan, 1988), p. 274; Charles Townshend, *The Republic: The Fight for Irish Independence, 1918–1923* (London: Penguin, 2013), p. 450; Roy Foster, "'Old Ireland and Himself": William Orpen and the Conflicts of Irish Identity', *Estudios Irlandeses*, 2005, p. 46.

17 For an insightful consideration of civil war memory, see Gavin Foster, 'Remembering and Forgetting in Public and Private: Reflections on the Dualities of Irish Civil War Memory in the Decade of Commemoration', *The Old Athlone Society* (2015), pp. 31–50. Notable book-length studies of the civil war in recent years include: Gemma Clark, *Everyday Violence in the Irish Civil War* (Cambridge: Cambridge University Press, 2014); Gavin Foster, *The Irish Civil War and Society: Politics, Class, and Conflict* (Basingstoke: Palgrave Macmillan, 2015); Pádraig Yeates, *A City in Civil War: Dublin 1921–1924* (Dublin: Gill & Macmillan, 2015); John Dorney, *The Civil War in Dublin: The Fight for the Irish Capital, 1922–1924* (Dublin: Merrion Press, 2017); Seán Enright, *The Irish Civil War: Law, Execution and Atrocity* (Dublin: Merrion Press, 2019).

18 F. S. L. Lyons, *Ireland Since the Famine* (London: Weidenfeld and Nicolson, 1971), p. 460; David Fitzpatrick, *Politics and Irish Life 1913–1921: Provincial Experience of War and Revolution* (Dublin: Gill & Macmillan, 1977), p. 231.

19 Hopkinson, *Green Against Green*; Eoin Neeson, *The Civil War in Ireland* (Cork: Mercier Press, 1966); Calton Younger, *Ireland's Civil War* (London: Frederick Muller, 1968).

20 See Foster, 'Local and Family Memory'; Guy Beiner, *Remembering the Year of the French: Irish Folk History and Social Memory* (Madison, WI: University of Wisconsin Press, 2007), p. 13.

21 Joseph Valente, 'Ethnostalgia: Irish Hunger and Traumatic Memory', in Oona Frawley (ed.), *Memory Ireland. Volume 3: The Famine and the Troubles* (Syracuse, NY: Syracuse University Press, 2014), p. 177.

22 See Joseph J. Lee, *Ireland, 1912–1985: Politics and Society* (Cambridge: Cambridge University Press, 1989), p. 527; Bill Kissane, *The Politics of the Irish Civil War* (Oxford: Oxford University Press, 2005); Timothy Wilson, *Frontiers of Violence: Conflict and Identity in Ulster and Upper Silesia, 1918–1922* (Oxford: Oxford University Press, 2010); Clark, *Everyday Violence in the Irish Civil War*; Townshend, *The Republic*, p. 452; Anne Dolan, 'Killing in "the Good Old Irish Fashion"? Irish Revolutionary Violence in Context', *Irish Historical Studies* 44, no. 165 (May 2020), p. 12.

23 Liam Kennedy, *Unhappy the Land: The Most Oppressed People Ever, the Irish?* (Dublin: Irish Academic Press, 2015).

24 Anne Dolan, 'Writing the History of the Irish Civil War', UCD College of Arts and Humanities, 12 October 2018, 12:45. Available at: https://www.youtube.com/watch?v=d6164yPQj3w (accessed 20 August 2020).

25 Cathy Caruth, *Unclaimed Experience: Trauma, Narrative, and History* (Baltimore, MD: Johns Hopkins University Press, 1996), p. 4.

26 Kai T. Erikson, *Everything in Its Path: Destruction of Community in the Buffalo Creek Flood* (New York: Simon and Schuster, 1976), p. 153.

27 Jeffrey C. Alexander, 'Toward a Theory of Cultural Trauma', in Jeffrey C. Alexander et al. (eds), *Cultural Trauma and Collective Identity* (Oakland, CA: University of California Press, 2004), p. 76. Opponents warn of the danger of conflating individual trauma with public trauma, see Wulf Kansteiner, 'Genealogy of a Category Mistake: A Critical Intellectual History of the Cultural Trauma Metaphor', *Rethinking History* 8, no. 2 (June 2004), pp. 193–221.

28 For example, Lily McManus wrote in her diary on 24 July 1922: 'Darkness and fear over the land. All is weird, unnatural. Men's eyes filled with scales; men's hearts hardening. Hatred and malice and lies abroad. Children learning to be spies. Suspicion everywhere. This is the awful Civil War.' Meanwhile, writing to John J. Hearn, Mary MacSwiney wrote in August 1922 that 'our situation is heartbreaking'. Newspaper reports too lamented the 'unspeakable hardships on women and children [...] to an extent unheard of in the worst days of the British regime'. Lily MacManus, *White Light and Flame: Memories of the Irish Literary Revival and the Anglo-Irish War* (Dublin: Talbot Press, 1929), p. 223; John J. Hearn Papers, National Library of Ireland (hereafter NLI) Ms 15,989; *Irish Independent*, 16 November 1922, p. 7.

29 *Donegal Democrat*, 3 February 1922, p. 6; *The Freeman's Journal*, 22 May 1922, p. 4; *Kilkenny People*, 15 April 1922, cited in Hopkinson, *Green Against Green*, p. 274.

30 *The Freeman's Journal*, 18 May 1918, p. 4. See Deasy's evocation of the civil war through the lens of the Treaty of Limerick in 1691. Liam Deasy, *Brother Against Brother* (Cork: Mercier Press, 1982), p. 30.

31 Guy Beiner, *Forgetful Remembrance: Social Forgetting and Vernacular Historiography of a Rebellion in Ulster* (Oxford: Oxford University Press, 2018), p. 78.

32 David Armitage, 'Ideas of Civil War in 17th-Century England', *Annals of the Japanese Association for the Study of Puritanism* 4 (2009), p. 6, cited in Nicholas McDowell, 'Civil Wars of Words: From Classical Rome to the Northern Ireland Troubles', *Global Intellectual History* 4, no. 3 (September 2019), p. 296.

33 P. K. Horan, 'The Flame of Youth: Chapter I – When the Sun Arose', *Irish Christian Advocate*, 25 November 1927.

34 Frank Gallagher, *The Four Glorious Years* (Dublin: Irish Press, 1953).

35 Joseph McGarrity, 'Introduction', in Dan Breen, *My Fight for Irish Freedom* (Dublin: Talbot Press, 1924), p. xi.

36 David Armitage, 'Three Narratives of Civil War: Recurrence, Remembrance and Reform from Sulla to Syria', in Deslandes et al. (eds), *Civil War and Narrative*, p. 8.

37 Rev. Fr Aloysius Travers, Bureau of Military History Witness Statement (hereafter BMH WS) 200, pp. 18–19. Originally delivered as a lecture to the Irish Transport and General Workers' Union; see 'Easter Week 1916/Personal Recollections', *Capuchin Annual* 1942, pp. 211–20.

38 Kissane, *The Politics of the Irish Civil War*, p. 1.

39 Kennedy, *Unhappy the Land*, p. 35.

40   Peter Hart, *The I.R.A. and Its Enemies: Violence and Community in Cork, 1916–1923* (Oxford: Oxford University Press, 1998), p. 293.

41   Máire Comerford, 'Chapter entitled Sisters', unpublished memoir, UCD Archive, LA18/10.

42   Séan O'Faoláin, *Vive Moi! An Autobiography* (Boston, MA: Little Brown, 1964 [1993]), p. 176.

43   Ibid., p. 181.

44   Stef Craps et al., 'Decolonizing Trauma Studies Round Table Discussion', *Humanities* 4(4), 2015, p. 907.

45   J. Roger Kurtz, 'Introduction', in J. Roger Kurtz (ed.), *Trauma and Literature* (Cambridge: Cambridge University Press, 2018), p. 1; Colin Davis and Hanna Meretoja, 'Introduction to Literary Trauma Studies', in idem (eds), *The Routledge Companion to Literature and Trauma* (Milton: Taylor & Francis, 2020), p. 1.

46   Cited in Kalí Tal, *Worlds of Hurt: Reading the Literatures of Trauma* (Cambridge: Cambridge University Press, 1996). Revised online edition, Chapter 2.

47   Luckhurst, *The Trauma Question*, p. 24.

48   Ibid., p. 1.

49   For insightful criticism of the dominant model of trauma theory, see Susannah Radstone, 'Trauma Theory: Contexts, Politics, Ethics', *Paragraph* 30, no. 1 (2007), pp. 9–29; Ruth Leys, *Trauma: A Genealogy* (Chicago, IL: University of Chicago Press, 2010); Graham Dawson, 'The Meaning of "Moving On": From Trauma to the History and Memory of Emotions in "Post-Conflict" Northern Ireland', *Irish University Review*, vol. 47, iss. 1, pp. 82–102.

50   Michelle Balaev, 'Trends in Literary Trauma Theory', *Mosaic: An Interdisciplinary Critical Journal* 41, no. 2 (2008), p. 156; Stef Craps, *Postcolonial Witnessing: Trauma Out of Bounds* (Basingstoke: Palgrave Macmillan, 2012); Luckhurst, *The Trauma Question*. For a discussion of the application of trauma theory to early modern Ireland, see Naomi McAreavey, 'Reading Conversion Narratives as Literature of Trauma: Radical Religion, the Wars of the Three Kingdoms and the Cromwellian Re-Conquest of Ireland', in David Coleman (ed.), *Region, Religion and English Renaissance Literature* (Abingdon: Routledge, 2016), p. 167.

51   Craps, *Postcolonial Witnessing*, p. 31. See Laura S. Brown, 'Not Outside the Range: One Feminist Perspective on Psychic Trauma', *American Imago* 48, no. 1 (1991), pp. 119–33.

52   See George A. Bonanno, 'Loss, Trauma, and Human Resilience: Have We Underestimated the Human Capacity to Thrive After Extremely Aversive Events?', *American Psychologist* 59, no. 1 (2004), pp. 20–8.

53   See David Durnin, *The Irish Medical Profession and the First World War* (Basingstoke: Palgrave Macmillan, 2019); David Durnin and Ian Miller (eds), *Medicine, Health and Irish Experiences of Conflict 1914–45* (Manchester: Manchester University Press, 2017); Brendan D. Kelly, *'He Lost Himself Completely': Shell Shock and Its Treatment at Dublin's Richmond War Hospital, 1916–19* (Dublin: Liffey Press, 2014); Michael Robinson, *Shell-shocked British Army Veterans in Ireland, 1918–39: A Difficult Homecoming* (Manchester: Manchester University Press, 2020).

54   Clark, *Everyday Violence in the Irish Civil War*, p. 104. The reluctance of the Military Service Pensions Board to address nervous disease is apparent in the case of Charles Dalton. As late as 1940, the Board was willing to process Dalton's claim for an injury to his hand; however, internal notes indicated 'Of course, we could not touch the question of the disease aspect

of his disability'. Note by JJH, 5 June 1940. Military Service Pension Collection (hereafter MSPC), 24SP1153.

55 For example, in her witness statement, Cumann na mBan's Aoife de Búrca dismisses 'a number of golfers' who 'appeared to be of the West British type', characterising them by their 'delicate nerves'. Aoife de Búrca, BMH WS 359, undated, pp. 1–2.

56 Elaine Showalter, *The Female Malady: Women, Madness, and English Culture, 1830–1980* (New York: Pantheon Books, 1985).

57 An Army Pension memo dated 14 February 1934 outlined that 'in certain types of cases [of] women applicants, the Pensions Board will occasionally require that an examination and report by a gynaecological specialist may be necessary'. MSPC, Administrative Files, Army Pensions Board, 1/M/47. See Alice O'Rourke, MSPC, MSP34REF17007.

58 See Síobhra Aiken, '"The Women Who Had Been Straining Every Nerve": Gender-Specific Medical Management of Trauma in the Irish Revolution (1916–1923)', in Melania Terrazas Gallego (ed.), *Trauma and Identity in Contemporary Irish Culture* (Bern: Peter Lang, 2020), pp. 133–58.

59 Foster, *The Irish Civil War and Society*, pp. 44–5.

60 Dorothy Macardle, 'The Kilmainham Tortures: Experiences of a Prisoner', *Éire*, 1 May 1923; 'Free State Hysteria: Hare Park Camp', *Éire*, 7 April 1923; Dorothy Macardle, *Tragedies of Kerry, 1922–1923* (Dublin: Emton Press, 1924); 'The NDU Invincible' [booklet written by female internees in the North Dublin Union, 14 May 1923], Kilmainham Gaol Archive, 20MS-1B43-08.

61 Quotes from P. S. O'Hegarty, the Bishop of Elphin and President W. T. Cosgrave, cited in Foster, *The Irish Civil War and Society*, pp. 33–4.

62 Papers of Síghle Humphreys, UCD Archive, UCDA P106/979 (1). Transcripts available at: 'Síghle's Account of her first years in prison 1922–23' [written either in 1928 or more likely in 1931]. Available at: https://humphrysfamilytree.com (accessed 10 August 2020).

63 Ibid.

64 As Kacandes contends, texts 'can perform trauma, in the sense that they can fail to tell the story, by eliding, repeating, and fragmenting components of the story'. Irene Kacandes, 'Narrative Witnessing as Memory Work: Reading Gertrud Kolmar's A Jewish Mother', in Mieke Bal, Jonathan V. Crewe and Leo Spitzer (eds), *Acts of Memory: Cultural Recall in the Present* (Lebanon, NH: University Press of New England, 1999), p. 56.

65 See Judith Lewis Herman, *Trauma and Recovery* (New York: BasicBooks, 1992); Louise A. DeSalvo, *Writing as a Way of Healing: How Telling Our Stories Transforms Our Lives* (Boston, MA: Beacon Press, 2000); Judith Harris, *Signifying Pain: Constructing and Healing the Self through Writing* (Albany, NY: SUNY Press, 2003); Bessel van der Kolk, *The Body Keeps the Score: Mind, Brain and Body in the Transformation of Trauma* (London: Penguin, 2014).

66 Meg Jensen, 'Testimony', in Davis and Meretoja (eds), *The Routledge Companion to Literature and Trauma*, p. 73.

67 David Fitzpatrick, 'Commemoration in the Irish Free State: A Chronicle of Embarrassment', in Ian McBride (ed.), *History and Memory in Modern Ireland* (Cambridge: Cambridge University Press, 2001), pp. 184–203.

68 Dolan, *Commemorating the Irish Civil War*, p. 124.

69 Flanagan, *Remembering the Revolution*, p. 12.

70   Frank Aiken, Dáil Éireann debates, vol. 85, no. 12, 4 February 1942. See Donal Ó Drisceoil, *Censorship in Ireland, 1939–1945: Neutrality, Politics, and Society* (Cork: Cork University Press, 1996), p. 107.

71   Hopkinson, *Green Against Green*, p. xii.

72   Ernie O'Malley, *The Singing Flame* (Tralee: Anvil Books, 1978); Liam Deasy, *Brother Against Brother* (Cork: Mercier Press, 1982); Niall C. Harrington, *Kerry Landing – August 1922: An Episode of the Civil War* (Tralee: Anvil Books, 1992); John A. Pinkman, *In the Legion of the Vanguard* (Cork: Mercier Press, 1998).

73   Peter Costello, *The Heart Grown Brutal: The Irish Revolution in Literature from Parnell to the Death of Yeats, 1891–1939* (Dublin: Gill & Macmillan, 1977), p. 193.

74   P. C. Trimble, 'A Current Commentary (announcing Frank O'Connor's *Guests of the Nation*)', *The Irish Book Lover*, July/August 1931, p. 112.

75   Herman, *Trauma and Recovery*, p. 1.

76   Max Saunders, *Self Impression: Life-Writing, Autobiografiction, and the Forms of Modern Literature* (Oxford: Oxford University Press, 2010), p. 18.

77   Leonard V. Smith, *The Embattled Self: French Soldiers' Testimony of the Great War* (Ithaca, NY: Cornell University Press, 2014), p. 150.

78   Ronan Crowley, 'Revivalism à Clef, Revivalism sans Clef: Writing the Renaissance in James Stephens, Brinsley MacNamara, and Eimar O'Duffy', *New Hibernia Review* 23, no. 3 (2019), p. 130.

79   Ibid. Flanagan's study *Remembering the Revolution* underscores that Eimar O'Duffy, George Russell and Desmond Ryan 'all wove their critiques into semi-fictional disguises', p. 198.

80   'Two Rising Catholic Novelists', *Universe (London)*, 7 September 1934; Letter to Mr Hern Paul Hempel, 20 November 1934. National Archives of Ireland (hereafter NAI), Talbot Press Archive, 1048/1/134.

81   Claudia Gronemann, 'Autofiction', in Martina Wagner-Egelhaaf (ed.), *Handbook Autobiography/Autofiction* (Berlin: De Gruyter, 2019), p. 241.

82   Saunders, *Self Impression*, p. 7.

83   Anna Richardson, 'Mapping the Lines of Fact and Fiction in Holocaust Testimonial Novels', in Louise Olga Vasvári and Steven Tötösy de Zepetnek (eds), *Comparative Central European Holocaust Studies* (West Lafayette, IN: Purdue University Press, 2009), p. 53.

84   See Smith, *The Embattled Self*, p. 13, p. 195.

85   Laub, 'Foreword', in Felman and Laub, *Testimony: Crises of Witnessing*, p. xvii.

86   See Beiner, 'Memory Too Has a History'; Maurice Halbwachs, *On Collective Memory* (Chicago, IL: University of Chicago Press, 1992).

87   Hayden White, 'The Historical Text as Literary Artifact', *Tropics of Discourse: Essays in Cultural, Criticism* (Baltimore, MD: Johns Hopkins University Press, 1978), p. 82.

88   For example, Colm Ó Gaora's application for a military service pension indicates that he was unwell during the ambush of four RIC men in Clifden on 16 March 1921; this event is described in his memoir. See Colm Ó Gaora, *Mise* (Baila Átha Cliath: Oifig an tSoláthair, 1943); Colm Ó Gaora, MSP34REF4434. See also Mossie Hartnett, *Victory and Woe: The West Limerick Brigade in the War of Independence* (Dublin: UCD Press, 2002).

89   David Armitage, *Civil Wars: A History in Ideas* (New Haven, CT: Yale University Press, 2017), pp. 31–90.

90   McDowell, 'Civil Wars of Words', p. 297.

91   *Meath Chronicle*, 4 July 1925, p. 1.

92   Janet Pérez, 'Behind the Lines: The Spanish Civil War and Women Writers', in Janet Pérez and Wendell M. Aycock (eds), *The Spanish Civil War in Literature* (Lubbock, TX: Texas Tech University Press, 1990), p. 171.

93   Clair Wills, *Dublin 1916: The Siege of the GPO* (Cambridge, MA: Harvard University Press, 2009), p. 236.

94   Examples include Alice Mulligan's poem, 'Till Ferdia Came', Séamus Ó Grianna's story 'Cogadh na gCarad', and the novel, *Buaidh na Treise: Cogadh Gaedheal re Gallaibh* (1932) by Mícheál Ó Gríobhtha. See Alan Titley, *An tÚrscéal Gaeilge* (Baile Átha Cliath: An Clóchomhar, 1992), pp. 358–9.

95   Richard Thomas, '"My Brother Got Killed in the War": Internecine Intertextuality', in Brian Breed, Cynthia Damon and Andreola Rossi (eds), *Citizens of Discord: Rome and Its Civil Wars* (Oxford: Oxford University Press, 2010), p. 293.

96   Philip O'Leary, 'Presenting a Challenging Past: Piaras Béaslaí's play *An Danar* (1928)', 39th California Celtic Conference – UC Berkeley, March 2017. My thanks to Professor O'Leary for sharing this conference paper. Other examples of temporally concealed civil war writings include: León Ó Broin's play *An Mhallacht*, which was set in Warsaw in 1925 on its first performance (but in civil war Dublin in the print edition) (Baile Átha Cliath: Oifig Díolta Foillseacháin Rialtais, 1931); Seán Ó Tuama's play *Gunna Cam agus Slabhra Óir* (Baile Átha Cliath: Sáirséal agus Dill, 1964), ostensibly set in sixteenth-century Ireland; and David Martin's novel, *The Road to Ballyshannon* (London: Abacus, 1983), advertised as being set during the seventeenth-century English Civil War.

97   As Peadar O'Donnell wrote, 'the news from Spain [...] rekindled the antagonisms of our own Civil War'. Peadar O'Donnell, *Salud!: An Irishman in Spain* (London: Methuen, 1937), p. 9.

98   Costello, *The Heart Grown Brutal*, p. 221.

99   Joe Good, *Inside the GPO 1916: A First-Hand Account* (Dublin: O'Brien Press, 2015), p. 187.

100   Breandán Ó hEithir, 'An Lasair a Múchadh Nach Mór', *Comhar* 37, no. 6 (1978), p. 17.

101   Ivan Lennon, *Lennons in Time* (self-published, *c.* 2017), p. 7. Available at: https://www.academia.edu/32727560/LENNONS_IN_TIME (accessed 20 August 2020).

102   Mícheál Breathnach, *Cuimhne an tSeanpháiste* (Baile Átha Cliath: Oifig an tSoláthair, 1966), p. 216. See O'Leary, *Gaelic Prose in the Irish Free State*, p. 332. For a similar declaration of reticence, see Breen, *My Fight for Irish Freedom* (1924 edition), p. 255.

Chapter 1

1   Desmond Ryan, *Remembering Sion: A Chronicle of Storm and Quiet* (London: A. Barker, 1934), p. 276.

2   'This sad business of looking back', *Irish Independent*, 22 May 1934, p. 4.

3   Ryan, *Remembering Sion*, p. 301; Desmond Ryan, 'Still Remembering Sion', *University Review* 5, no. 2 (1968), p. 252.

4   Ryan, 'Still Remembering Sion', p. 248.

5   Flanagan, *Remembering the Revolution*, p. 186.

6   Kit Ó Céirín and Cyril Ó Céirín (eds), *Women of Ireland: A Biographic Dictionary* (Kinvarra: Tír Eolas, 1996), p. 111.

7   Frank O'Connor, *The Big Fellow: A Life of Michael Collins* (London: T. Nelson, 1937), p. ix.

8   O'Faoláin, *Vive Moi!*, p. 146.

9   Ryan, *Unique Dictator*, p. 205.

10   Ryan's father, W. P. Ryan, took a strong interest in alternative educational theories and in the ideas of the spiritualist philosophy (anthroposophy) advanced by the Austrian philosopher Rudolf Steiner. Steiner put forward a model of psychology which would take 'into account both the soul's hidden powers and the complex connections between psychological and organic, bodily processes'. See Flanagan, *Remembering the Revolution*, p. 176.

11   Rudolf Steiner, 'Psychoanalysis in the Light of Anthroposophy', delivered at the Goetheanum in Dornach, Switzerland, 10 November 1917. Available at: https://wn.rsarchive.org/GA/GA0178/19171110p01.html (accessed 10 August 2020).

12   See Jill L. Matus, *Shock, Memory and the Unconscious in Victorian Fiction* (Cambridge: Cambridge University Press, 2009).

13   Undated diary [1916–17], Ryan papers, UCD LA10/J 3, cited in Flanagan, *Remembering the Revolution*, p. 168.

14   Ryan, *Remembering Sion*, p. 278.

15   Ibid., p. 276.

16   Undated diary [1916–17], cited in Flanagan, *Remembering the Revolution*, p. 170.

17   Flanagan, *Remembering the Revolution*, p. 170.

18   Desmond Ryan, *The Man Called Pearse* (Dublin: Maunsel and Company, 1919); Desmond Ryan, *James Connolly : His Life, Work & Writings* (Dublin: Talbot Press, 1924); Desmond Ryan, *The Invisible Army: A Story of Michael Collins* (London: A. Barker, 1932).

19   For example see O'Connor, *The Big Fellow*; Ernie O'Malley, *Rising Out: Seán Connolly of Longford (1890–1921)* (Dublin: UCD Press, 2007); Florence O'Donoghue, *No Other Law: The Story of Liam Lynch and the Irish Republican Army, 1916–1923* (Dublin: Irish Press, 1954).

20   Ryan, *The Invisible Army*, p. 228.

21   Ryan, *Remembering Sion*, p. 301.

22   Ryan, 'Still Remembering Sion', p. 245.

23   Ibid., p. 248.

24   Richard Kearney, 'Narrating Pain: The Power of Catharsis', *Paragraph* 30, no. 1 (2007), p. 51.

25   Leigh Gilmore, *The Limits of Autobiography: Trauma and Testimony* (Ithaca, NY: Cornell University Press, 2001), p. 7.

26   Suzette A. Henke, *Shattered Subjects: Trauma and Testimony in Women's Life-Writing* (New York: St. Martin's Press, 1998), p. xii.

27   See Alexandra Bacopoulos-Viau, 'From the Writing Cure to the Talking Cure: Revisiting the French "Discovery of the Unconscious"', *History of the Human Sciences*, 32(1), 2009, pp. 41–65.

28   Rosamond Jacobs documents the practice of automatic writing in her diary, 24 November 1919, NLI Ms 3582/36. Available at: http://jacobdiaries.ie/2019/11/24/week-107-24th-30th-november-1919/ (accessed 10 August 2020).

29   Brendan Kelly, *Hearing Voices: The History of Psychiatry in Ireland* (Dublin: Irish Academic Press, 2016), p. 143.

30   James Knowlson, *Damned to Fame: The Life of Samuel Beckett* (New York: Bloomsbury, 1996), p. 167.

31   Leeann Lane, *Rosamond Jacob: Third Person Singular* (Dublin: UCD Press, 2010), location 5006 [Kindle edition].

32   During a particularly bad bout, Mac Grianna was charged with terrifying his neighbour. As reported, '[Prof. Green] placed against the partition wall and climbed up to look through the glass portion, from which position he made faces at her and uttered loud groaning noises.' *Evening Herald*, 5 December 1941, p. 1, cited in Brian Ó Conchubhair, 'Seosamh Mac Grianna: A Bhealach Féin', in John Walsh and Peadar Ó Muircheartaigh (eds), *Ag Siúl an Bhealaigh Mhóir: Aistí in Ómós don Ollamh Nollaig Mac Congáil* (Baile Átha Cliath: LeabhairCOMHAR, 2016), pp. 138–9.

33   'The Papers of Seosamh Mac Grianna', James Hardiman Library, NUI Galway, G42/ 1–7, cited in Fionntán de Brún, *Seosamh Mac Grianna: An Mhéin Rúin* (Baile Átha Cliath: An Clóchomhar, 2002), p. 168. See also Pól Ó Muirí, *A Flight from Shadow: The Life & Works of Seosamh Mac Grianna* (Belfast: Lagan Press, 1999); Pól Ó Muirí, *Seosamh Mac Grianna: Míreanna Saoil* (Indreabhán: Cló Iar-Chonnachta, 2007); Gearóidín Uí Laighléis, *Gallán an Ghúim* (Baile Átha Cliath: Coiscéim, 2017).

34   Seosamh Mac Grianna, *Dá mBíodh Ruball ar an Éan* (Baile Átha Cliath: Oifig an tSoláthair, 1940), p. 231.

35   *Dá mBíodh Ruball ar an Éan* was published in incomplete form with the concluding line, 'Thráigh an tobar sa tsamhradh, 1935. Ní sgríobhfaidh mé níos mó. Rinne mé mo dhícheall, agus is cuma liom.' [The well dried up in summer 1935. I will not write anymore. I did my very best, and I don't care.]

36   Letter from Frank Saurin to Commandant P. J. Paul, Department of Defence, 19 June 1941. Charlie Dalton, MSPC, 24SP1153.

37   Note from JJH, 5 May 1940, Charlie Dalton, MSPC, 24SP1153.

38   Carol Mullan, interview. The 1916 Rising Oral History Collections, Irish Life & Lore. Available at: https://www.irishlifeandlore.com (accessed 30 August 2020).

39   'Fighting with the Dublin Brigade, IRA', *Kilkenny People*, 7 December 1929, p. 7.

40   Ryan, 'Still Remembering Sion', p. 248.

41   Sigmund Freud, 'Remembering, Repeating and Working-Through (Further Recommendations on the Technique of Psycho-Analysis II', in James Strachey (ed.), *The Standard Edition of the Complete Psychological Works of Sigmund Freud*, Volume XII (1911–1913) (London: Hogarth Press and the Institute of Psycho-analysis, 1958), pp. 145–56.

42   Dominick LaCapra, *Writing History, Writing Trauma* (Baltimore, MD: Johns Hopkins University Press, 2001), p. 21.

43   Ibid., p. 42.

44   Ryan, 'Still Remembering Sion', p. 252.

45   Ibid., p. 246.

46   'The War of Irish Freedom: A Review of a Book of the Week', *The Irish Press*, 19 September 1932, p. 9.

47   D. B., 'Review of Desmond Ryan's *The Invisible Army: A Story of Michael Collins*', *The Irish Book Lover*, vol. XX, 1932, p. 118. See also Flanagan, *Remembering the Revolution*, p. 185.

48   Ryan, 'Still Remembering Sion', p. 245.

49   Cited in Eileen Battersby, 'Nothing but Doubts', *The Irish Times*, 14 November 1996.

50   Francis Stuart, *Pigeon Irish* (London: Macmillan, 1932), p. 260; Francis Stuart, *The Coloured Dome* (London: V. Gollancz, 1932), p. 63.

51   Francis Stuart, *Things to Live For: Notes for an Autobiography* (London: Macmillan, 1935), p. 96.

52   Francis Stuart, *Black List, Section H* (Carbondale, IL: Southern Illinois University Press, 1971).

53   Whitehead's influential book *Trauma Fiction*, for example, considers 'mimicking' strategies employed by authors to reflect the symptoms of trauma; in particular, she emphasises 'intertextuality, repetition and a dispersed or fragmented narrative voice'. Anne Whitehead, *Trauma Fiction* (Edinburgh: Edinburgh University Press, 2004), p. 84.

54   Margaret R. Higonnet, 'Authenticity and Art in Trauma Narratives of World War I', *Modernism/Modernity* 9, no. 1 (January 2002), pp. 91–107.

55   Luckhurst, *The Trauma Question*, p. 83.

56   Craps, *Postcolonial Witnessing*, p. 42; Susana Onega, 'Affective Knowledge, Self-Awareness and the Function of Myth in the Representation and Transmission of Trauma. The Case of Eva Figes', *Journal of Literary Theory* 6, no. 1 (20 February 2012), p. 84.

57   *Evening Echo*, 16 September 1932, p. 6.

58   Terence Brown, *The Literature of Ireland: Culture and Criticism* (Cambridge: Cambridge University Press, 2010), p. 99.

59   Michael Rothberg, *Multidirectional Memory: Remembering the Holocaust in the Age of Decolonization* (Stanford, CA: Stanford University Press, 2009), p. 100. Mark Quigley also contends that Seán O'Faoláin's espousal of realism 'constitutes at once a critique of mainline modernism and an alternative late-modernist practice'. See Mark Quigley, *Empire's Wake: Postcolonial Irish Writing and the Politics of Modern Literary Form* (New York: Fordham University Press, 2013), p. 68.

60   On the connection between less 'recognizably autobiographical forms' and trauma testimony, see Gilmore, *The Limits of Autobiography*.

61   James J. Comerford, *My Kilkenny Days: 1916–22* (Kilkenny: Dinan Pub, 1980), p. 929.

62   Lord Banbury, 'With the Dublin Brigade (1917–1921)', House of Lords, vol. 80 cc1036-44, 6 May 1931. Available at: https://api.parliament.uk/historic-hansard/lords/1931/may/06/with-the-dublin-brigade-1917-1921 (accessed 20 August 2020).

63   Allen, *Modernism, Ireland and Civil War*, p. 199.

64   Patrick Mulloy, *Jackets Green: A Novel* (London: Grayson & Grayson, 1936), p. 5.

65   Francis Plunkett, *As the Fool* (London: Wishart, 1935). The biographical sketch of the author on the inside cover of the novel notes that: 'Francis Plunkett claims to have graduated as a writer from the famous Dublin academic institution, Mountjoy Prison, where he spent some time on account of his political activities.' The author's full name was Myles Francis Mordaunt Plunkett; Mountjoy prison records show that he was indeed interned as a military prisoner on 7 July 1922. Irish Prison Registers 1790–1924. Available at: findmypast. ie (accessed 30 August 2020).

66 See *The All England Law Reports: (Incorporating the Law Times Reports and the Law Journal Reports) of Cases Decided in the House of Lords, the Privy Council, All Divisions of the Supreme Court, and Courts of Special Jurisdiction* (London: Butterworth, 1936), p. 3.

67 William O'Brien's copy of Dalton's *With the Dublin Brigade*, which was donated to the NLI in 1968, is just one example, NLI AA15133.

68 W. D., 'Review of *Miss Rudd and Some Lovers*, by Eimar O'Duffy', *Studies: An Irish Quarterly Review* 13, no. 50 (1924), pp. 332–4.

69 Selskar Kearney, *The False Finger Tip: An Irish Detective Story* (Dublin: Maunsel & Roberts, 1921).

70 *The Charlotte News*, 22 March 1936.

71 *Irish Independent*, 12 May 1936, p. 4.

72 M. Ní M., 'Review of John Brophy's *The Rocky Road*', *The Irish Book Lover*, vol. XXI, Jan./Feb. 1933, p. 21.

73 Ryan, 'Still Remembering Sion', p. 252.

74 Shirley Quill, *Mike Quill, Himself: A Memoir* (Greenwich, CT: Devin-Adair, 1985), p. 221.

75 E. Ann Kaplan, *Trauma Culture: The Politics of Terror and Loss in Media and Literature* (New Brunswick, NJ: Rutgers University Press, 2005), p. 90.

76 Sidonie Smith and Julia Watson, *Reading Autobiography: A Guide for Interpreting Life Narratives* (Minneapolis, MN: University of Minnesota Press, 2001), p. 157.

77 Ryan, 'Still Remembering Sion', p. 249.

78 Ibid.

79 Other testimonies that document civil war imprisonment include: Margaret Buckley's *The Jangle of the Keys* (Dublin: J. Duffy & Company, 1938), Séamus O'Connor's *Tomorrow Was Another Day: Irreverent Memories of an Irish Rebel Schoolmaster* (Tralee: Anvil, 1970) and Ernie O'Malley's *The Singing Flame*. A number of unpublished civil war prison diaries have been made available in more recent years, such as Joseph Campbell's '*As I was among the Captives': Joseph Campbell's Prison Diary*, edited by Eileán Ní Chuileanáin (Cork: Cork University Press, 2001) and Seán a' Chóta's *Dialann Phríosúin*, edited by Micheál Ó Catháin (unpublished PhD thesis, NUI Maynooth, 2012). Two further serialised (and overlooked) prison accounts are those of Frank Gallagher and P. K. Horan, published in *Éire* and *Sinn Féin* (1924) and in *The Methodist Magazine* and *Irish Christian Advocate* (1927, 1928) respectively.

80 P. de. B., 'The Gates Flew Open: A Bitter, Vulgar Book', *Irish Independent*, 1 February 1932, p. 4.

81 *The Guardian*, 9 February 1932, p. 5.

82 Peadar O'Donnell, *Storm: A Story of the Irish War* (Dublin: Talbot Press, 1926); Peadar O'Donnell, *Islanders* (London: J. Cape, 1928); Peadar O'Donnell, *Adrigoole* (London: J. Cape, 1929); Peadar O'Donnell, *The Knife* (London: J. Cape, 1930).

83 See Donal Ó Drisceoil, '"My Pen Is Just a Weapon": Politics, History and the Fiction of Peadar O'Donnell', *The Irish Review*, no. 30 (2003), pp. 62–70.

84 Colm Ó Lochlainn, 'Review of Peadar O'Donnell's *The Gates Flew Open*', *The Irish Book Lover*, vol. XX, March–April, 1932, p. 46.

85 Peadar O'Donnell, 'To the Editor', *Irish Independent*, 6 February 1932, p. 10; *The Kerryman*, 11 June 1932, p. 19.

86 Donal Ó Drisceoil, *Peadar O'Donnell* (Cork, Cork University Press, 2001), p. 68.

87 Avishai Margalit defines a 'moral witness' as a witness who has witnessed 'the combination of evil and the suffering it produces' and whose testimony has a 'moral purpose'. Avishai Margalit, *The Ethics of Memory* (Boston, MA: Harvard University Press, 2002), pp. 148–51. See also Jay Winter, *Remembering War: The Great War Between Memory and History in the Twentieth Century* (New Haven, CT: Yale University Press, 2006).

88 Peadar O'Donnell, *The Gates Flew Open* (London: J. Cape, 1932), p. 194.

89 Ibid., p. 48.

90 Johann A. Norstedt, 'Peadar O'Donnell', in Denis Lane and Carol McCrory Lane (eds), *Modern Irish Literature* (New York: Ungar, 1988), p. 488.

91 Alexander Gonzalez, *Peadar O'Donnell: A Reader's Guide* (Chester Springs, PA: Dufour Editions, 1997), p. 85.

92 O'Donnell, *The Knife*, p. 220. On semi-hangings and mock crucifixions see O'Donnell, *The Gates Flew Open*, p. 91.

93 Richard English, *Ernie O'Malley* (Oxford University Press, 1998), p. 25.

94 O'Donnell, *The Knife*, p. 280; p. 246.

95 Ibid., p. 244.

96 Ibid., p. 264; O'Donnell, *The Gates Flew Open*, p. 169.

97 Peadar O'Donnell, *There Will Be Another Day* (Dublin: Dolemen Press, 1963), p. 24. Frank Gallagher noted in his prison diary that O'Donnell felt that 'unity between Ulster Specials and [the] IRA on national freedom is not impossible'. Cited in Richard English, 'Green on Red: Two Case Studies in Early Twentieth Century Irish Republican Thought', in D. George Boyce, Robert Eccleshall and Vincent Geoghegan (eds), *Political Thought in Ireland Since the Seventeenth Century* (Abingdon: Routledge, 2008). p. 180.

98 O'Donnell, *The Gates Flew Open*, p. 183.

99 Ibid., p. 67.

100 Ibid., pp. 164–5.

101 Ibid., p. 226.

102 Bonanno, 'Loss, Trauma, and Human Resilience', pp. 20–8; D. Keltner and G. A. Bonanno, 'A Study of Laughter and Dissociation: Distinct Correlates of Laughter and Smiling during Bereavement', *Journal of Personality and Social Psychology* 73, no. 4 (October 1997), p. 687.

103 O'Donnell, *The Gates Flew Open*, p. 81.

104 O'Donnell, *The Knife*, p. 234.

105 E. L. (Ethel Lillian) Voynich, *The Gadfly* (New York: Henry Holt and Co., 1897).

106 Rothberg, *Multidirectional Memory*, p. 2.

107 Tal, *Worlds of Hurt*, p. 74.

108 Guy Beiner, 'Between Trauma and Triumphalism: The Easter Rising, the Somme, and the Crux of Deep Memory in Modern Ireland', *Journal of British Studies* 46, no. 2 (2007), p. 375.

109 LaCapra, *Writing History, Writing Trauma*, p. 23.

110 Dominick LaCapra, *History in Transit: Experience, Identity, Critical Theory* (Ithaca, NY: Cornell University Press, 2018), p. 57.

111 LaCapra, *Writing History, Writing Trauma*, p. 22.

112 O'Donnell, *The Gates Flew Open*, p. 86.

113 *An Phoblacht*, 22 November and 6 December 1930, cited in Ó Drisceoil, *Peadar O'Donnell*, p. 56; O'Donnell, *The Gates Flew Open*, p. 5 (this dedication is omitted in later editions).

114 O'Donnell notes in *The Gates Flew Open* that he escaped 'wearing Dr Comer's brown boots'. Dr Comer insisted that he had ordered the boots from Arnott's specifically for Jack Keogh. See 'Jack Comer [interview]', in Cormac O'Malley and Cormac Ó Comhraí (eds), *The Men Will Talk to Me: Galway Interviews* by Ernie O'Malley (Cork: Mercier Press, 2013), p. 250.

115 Séamus Mac Cosgair, Dáil Éireann debates, vol. 15, no. 3, 22 April 1926.

116 Cited in Peter Hegarty, *Peadar O'Donnell* (Cork: Mercier Press, 1999), p. 160.

117 Ó Drisceoil, '"My Pen Is Just a Weapon"', p. 63; Grattan Freyer, *Peadar O'Donnell* (Lewisburg, PA: Bucknell University Press, 1973), p. 38.

118 See Peadar O'Donnell in Uinseann Mac Eoin (ed.), *Survivors: The Story of Ireland's Struggle as Told through Some of Her Outstanding Living People* (Dublin: Argenta Publications, 1980), p. 21.

119 O'Donnell, *Storm*, p. 128.

120 Ibid., p. 85.

121 Ibid.; O'Donnell, *Adrigoole*, pp. 235–6.

122 O'Donnell, *Adrigoole*, p. 328.

123 Freyer, *Peadar O'Donnell*, p. 46.

124 Cited in Hegarty, *Peadar O'Donnell*, p. 199.

125 Tom Boylan, 'Peadar O'Donnell: A Rebellious Relative', in Ciara Boylan, Sarah-Anne Buckley and Pat Dolan (eds), *Family Histories of the Irish Revolution* (Dublin: Four Courts Press, 2018), p. 188.

126 'Priest-Editor Tells of Receipt of Manuscript; Mr. O'Donnell Questioned as to His Continental Visits; Closing Stages of Libel Action', *The Irish Press*, 15 June 1932, p. 5.

127 Allen, *Modernism, Ireland and Civil War*, p. 200.

128 Desmond Clarke and Stephen J. Brown (eds), *Ireland in Fiction. Volume 2: A Guide to Irish Novels, Tales, Romances and Folklore* (Cork: Royal Carbery Books, 1985), p. 42.

129 Francis Carty, *The Irish Volunteer* (London: J. M. Dent & Sons, 1932), p. 56.

130 Niall Montgomery, '"Who's Who Anyway?" Essays on Well-known Irish Figures', undated [*c.* 1930s], NLI Ms 50,118/4/4.

131 Smith, *The Embattled Self*, p. 150.

132 Ciaran Carty, *Intimacy with Strangers: A Life of Brief Encounters* (Dublin: Lilliput Press, 2013), p. 11.

133 Francis Xavier Carty, *Bruises, Baws and Bastards: Glimpses into a Long Life Passing* (Able Press, 2017), p. 158; 'Margaret Carty' [obituary], *The Irish Press*, 12 June 1946, p. 9; 'Selskar' [Francis Carty], 'A Fianna Fáil View', *The Echo*, 7 February 1931.

134 Montgomery, 'Who's Who Anyway?'.

135 'Editor Retires', *The Irish Press*, 30 July 1968, p. 3.

136 Carty read on behalf of the South Wexford Deputation before an advisory committee on 3rd February 1936. Military Archive, IRA Nominal Rolls, RO/546.

137 Carty was also interviewed for Calton Younger's 1968 study *Ireland's Civil War*. Carty's sons – Ciaran and Francis Xavier – have produced memoirs which reflect on their father's experience. See Ciaran Carty, *Confessions of a Sewer Rat: A Personal History of Censorship & the Irish Cinema* (Dublin: New Island Books, 1995); C. Carty, *Intimacy with Strangers*; F. X. Carty, *Bruises, Baws and Bastards*.

138 Francis Carty, *Legion of the Rearguard* (London: J. M. Dent & Sons, 1934).

139 'Ireland's Fight: Legion of the Rearguard', *Natal Mercury* [Durban, South Africa], 14 December 1934. It was also considered 'rather the work of a reporter than of a novelist', 'Two Rising Catholic Novelists', *Universe* (London), 7 September 1934. From the personal papers of F. X. Carty.

140 Owen Regan, 'Looking at Ireland', *Sunday Dispatch* [Irish edition], 22 July 1934.

141 Francis Carty, Letter to the editor, *Kilkenny People*, 5 May 1931. From the personal papers of F. X. Carty.

142 Sylvia Lynd, 'New Novels', *The Observer*, 12 August 1934, p. 5. From the personal papers of F. X. Carty.

143 Carty, *Legion of the Rearguard*, p. 7.

144 Ibid., p. 180, p. 192.

145 Carty, *The Irish Volunteer*, p. 158; Carty, *Legion of the Rearguard*, p. 135, p. 201.

146 Carty, *The Irish Volunteer*, p. 14, p. 126.

147 See Graham Greene, 'Impressions of Dublin', *Reflections* (London: Reinhardt Books, 1990), pp. 1–3.

148 Graham Greene, 'Fiction', *The Spectator*, 13 July 1934.

149 'Modern Irish Novels, Dependence Upon Outside Readers, Lecture by Mr. Frank Carty', *The Irish Times*, 3 December 1934, p. 8.

150 Michael L. Storey, *Representing the Troubles in Irish Short Fiction* (Washington, D.C.: Catholic University of America Press, 2004), p. 27.

151 Francis Carty, BMH WS 1040, 20 November 1954, p. 6.

152 Carty, *The Irish Volunteer*, p. 105.

153 Francis Carty, *Two and Fifty Irish Saints: With a Foreword by John Ryan* (Dublin: Duffy, 1941); Francis Carty, *Irish Saints in Ten Countries* (Dublin: Duffy, 1942).

154 Montgomery, 'Who's Who Anyway?'.

155 Carty, BMH WS 1040, p. 33.

156 Carty, *Legion of the Rearguard*, p. 133.

157 Ibid., p. 135.

158 Carty, BMH WS 1040, p. 32.

159 O'Malley, *The Singing Flame*, p. 135.

160 Carty, *Legion of the Rearguard*, p. 136.

161 Ibid.

162 Ibid., p. 139.

163 Paul Fussell, *The Great War and Modern Memory* (Oxford: Oxford University Press, 2000), p. 30.

164 Carty, *Legion of the Rearguard*, p. 138.

165 Ibid., p. 137.

166 Ibid., p. 138.

167 Hartnett, *Victory and Woe*, p. 71. For another striking evocation of women's suffering, see Frank O'Connor, 'A Boy in Prison', *Life and Letters*, August 1934, pp. 525–35.

168 See Younger, *Ireland's Civil War*, p. 350.

169 Carty, *Legion of the Rearguard*, p. 185.

170 Ibid., p. 247.

171 Ibid., p. 262.

172 Ibid., p. 268.

173 Ibid., p. 270.

174   Ibid., p. 271.

175   See Evelyn Cobley, 'Narrating the Facts of War: New Journalism in Herr's *Dispatches* and Documentary Realism in First World War Novels', *The Journal of Narrative Technique* 16, no. 2 (1986), pp. 97–116.

176   M. J. MacManus, 'An Irish War Novel', *The Irish Press*, 17 July 1934, p. 2.

177   Carty, *Legion of the Rearguard*, p. 25.

178   Patrick Hogan, or Pádraig Ó hÓgáin (1885–1969), was a native of Kilmaley, County Clare. He was active in the 1913 strike and lockout in Dublin and was interned in 1921 for his volunteer activities in Limerick. Elected to the Dáil in 1923 as a Labour Party TD, Hogan went on to serve as Ceann Comhairle from 1961 to 1967. Patrick Hogan, *Camps on the Hearthstone* (Dublin: C. J. Fallon, 1956).

179   Patrick Colm Hogan, 'Revolution and Despair: Allegories of Nation and Class in Patrick Hogan's *Camps on the Hearthstone*', *The Canadian Journal of Irish Studies* 25, no. 1/2 (1999), p. 185.

180   Ibid., p. 183.

181   Carty, *Legion of the Rearguard*, p. 181.

182   Ibid., p. 203.

183   Ibid., pp. 185–6.

184   Records suggest there were, in fact, only three Free State casualties: two Free State soldiers during the ambush, Corporal Thomas McMahon and Private Maurice Quirke, and 17-year-old Private Michael Campion, who died from injuries sustained some days later. See Aaron Ó Maonaigh, 'The Killurin Ambush and the Outbreak of Civil War in County Wexford', *The Past: The Organ of the Uí Cinsealaigh Historical Society*, no. 33 (2019), pp. 52–67.

185   Carty, BMH WS 1040, p. 35.

186   F. X. Carty, *Bruises, Baws and Bastards*, p. 132.

187   Carty, *Legion of the Rearguard*, p. 121; Carty, BMH WS 1040, p. 31.

188   D. S., 'Story of Irish Civil War: Mr Carty's Novel', *Irish Independent*, 24 July 1934, p. 3.

189   Carty, *Legion of the Rearguard*, p. 272.

190   Tal, *Worlds of Hurt*, p. 103.

191   Ibid.

192   *The Irish Press*, 18 December 1935, p. 7. Carty also pitched a third novel to Dent press entitled 'Man Without Guile'. The publishers felt, however, it could not be 'profitably published'; this novel related to Carty's father's hair salon and newsagent shop at 2a North Main Street, Wexford. J. M. Dent & Sons Records at Wilson Special Collections Library, 6 January 1938.

193   F. X. Carty, *Bruises, Baws and Bastards*, p. 169.

194   A de B., 'As Others Wish to See Us', *The Irish Press*, 3 October 1934, p. 8.

195   Colm, 'Review of *Shake Hands with the Devil*', *The Irish Book Lover*, July–August 1934, p. 99.

196   'Modern Irish Novels, Dependence Upon Outside Readers, Lecture by Mr. Frank Carty', *The Irish Times*, 3 December 1934, p. 8.

197   Military Archives, IRA Nominal Rolls, RO/546.

198   Carty, BMH WS 1040, p. 24.

199   Carty, *Legion of the Rearguard*, p. 102.

200   Carty, BMH WS 1040, p. 29.

201 Carty was awarded a Silver Medal at the 1932 Tailteann Literary Awards for a novel entitled *The Volunteer*. On its publication, *The Irish Volunteer* was considered 'one of the best pictures of the Irish revolution that has yet appeared'; it was reissued in a cheaper edition due to high sales and serialised in *The Irish Press* from December 1935. *The Irish Press*, 1 July 1932; Letter from J. M. Dent & Sons to Messrs. Curtis Brown, 22 November 1933, Dent Press Archive.

202 Seán O'Faoláin, 'The Re-Orientation of Irish Letters', *The Irish Times*, 21 September 1935, p. 7.

203 Seán O'Faoláin, 'A Letter to the Editor', *Sinn Féin*, 20 September 1924, p. 7, cited in Paul Delaney, *Seán O'Faoláin: Literature, Inheritance and the 1930s* (Dublin: Irish Academic Press, 2014), p. 19.

204 Francis Carty, 'Is Nationality to be Taken for Granted? Author Reply to Seán O'Faoláin', *Sinn Féin*, 1924 [undated]. From the personal papers of F. X. Carty.

205 English, *Ernie O'Malley*, p. 164.

206 Helen Gosse, 'Review of *The Irish Volunteer*', *Fortnightly Review*, April 1932, p. 542. From the personal papers of F. X. Carty.

207 Montgomery, 'Who's Who Anyway?'.

208 'Jackets Green', Typescript of a Novel by Fionn O'Malley (Pseud., i.e. Patrick Mulloy)', NLI Ms 2142.

209 Seán O'Faoláin, 'Books of the Week: The Re-Orientation of Irish Letters', *The Irish Times*, 21 September 1935, p. 7.

210 Seán O'Faoláin, 'Fiction', *The Spectator*, 6 March 1936, vol. 156, p. 414.

211 Seán O'Faoláin, 'Book Section', *Ireland To-day*, June 1936, p. 75.

212 Ibid., July 1936, p. 72.

213 Ibid.

214 Dolan, *Commemorating the Civil War*, p. 3.

215 'Jackets Green', Typescript of a Novel'.

216 *Irish Independent*, 9 December 1936, p. 8; 'An Irishman in London', *Ulster Herald*, 23 December 1950, p. 7; Liam Ó Duibhir, 'Appendix 2; List of Internees in Ballykinlar No. 2 Compound: Dublin', *Prisoners of War: Ballykinlar, An Irish Internment Camp 1920–1921* (Cork: Mercier Press, 2013), p. 307.

217 National Army Census, Military Archive of Ireland, 12–13 November 1922. Mulloy is registered under Joseph Mulloy at his address of 106 Lr George St, Dún Laoghaire.

218 Des Hickey, 'How Colonels Almost Took Over!', *Sunday Independent*, 22 September 1974, p. 13.

219 'Irish Author Engaged', *Irish Independent*, 9 December 1936, p. 8.

220 'An Irishman in London', *Ulster Herald*, 23 December 1950, p. 7.

221 *Irish Examiner*, 21 January 1978, p. 9.

222 'Jackets Green', Typescript of a Novel'.

223 Herman, *Trauma and Recovery*, p. 1.

224 Erich Maria Remarque, *All Quiet on the Western Front* (English translation of *Im Westen nichts Neues* by A. W. Wheen) (Boston, MA: Little, Brown, 1929).

225 Cobley, 'Narrating the Facts of War', p. 100.

226 Mulloy, *Jackets Green*, p. 311.

227 Seán Ó'Faoláin, 'Fiction', *The Spectator*, 6 March 1936, vol. 156, p. 414; Francis Mac Manus, 'Review of *Jackets Green*', *The Irish Press*, 10 March 1936, p. 6.

228 Michael Rothberg, *Traumatic Realism: The Demands of Holocaust Representation* (Minneapolis, MN: University of Minnesota Press, 2000), p. 406.

229 Gerd Bayer, 'Trauma and the Literature of War', in J. Roger Kurtz (ed.), *Trauma and Literature* (Cambridge: Cambridge University Press, 2018), p. 213.

230 Norah Hoult, 'Review of *Jackets Green* and *Benson's Flying Column*', *The Dublin Magazine: A Quarterly Review of Literature, Science and Art*, April–June 1936, p. 101.

231 A. O'R, 'Mr. Pat Mulloy: An Appreciation', *The Irish Press*, 30 January 1978, p. 7.

232 Mulloy, *Jackets Green*, p. 10.

233 Ibid., p. 54.

234 Ibid., p. 57, p. 54.

235 On Belfast confetti, see William Murphy, *Political Imprisonment and the Irish, 1912–1921* (Oxford: Oxford University Press, 2014), p. 205.

236 Eugene Igoe was a Mayo-born RIC officer who coordinated the Igoe gang, a group of Irish-born RIC officers who patrolled Dublin in plain clothes on the lookout for wanted IRA men.

237 As outlined by Francis O'Duffy, 'There were a number of persons among the prisoners who had been active Volunteers and were wanted by the British on serious charges, e.g. Dublin Volunteers who had taken part in the Mount Street attack on the British Intelligence Officers. The principal plan adopted in Camp II to safeguard these prisoners was to get them to change identity with other prisoners, if possible, persons who resembled them in appearance. In some cases, a double exchange was made: A became B, B became C, and C became A.' Francis O'Duffy, BMH WS 665, 1 April 1952, p. 5.

238 Mulloy, *Jackets Green*, pp. 154–5.

239 O'Duffy recalls that a group of escaping men crossed the recreation field, but were 'accidentally discovered' in the long grass. The alarm was raised at once and the 'powerful search-lights were turned on'. O'Duffy, BMH WS 665, p. 16.

240 Mulloy, *Jackets Green*, p. 122.

241 Joanna Bruck, '"A Good Irishman Should Blush Every Time He Sees a Penny"': Gender, Nationalism and Memory in Irish Internment Camp Craftwork, 1916–1923', *Journal of Material Culture*, 20(2), p. 162.

242 Mulloy, *Jackets Green*, p. 139.

243 See Patrick Hannifin, 'Rewriting Desire: The Construction of Sexual Identity in Legal and Literary Discourse in Postcolonial Ireland', in Didi Herman and Carl Stychin (eds), *Sexuality in the Legal Arena* (London: A&C Black, 2000), p. 52.

244 Mulloy, *Jackets Green*, p. 159.

245 Ó Duibhir, *Prisoners of War: Ballykinlar*, p. 90.

246 Louis J. Walsh, *On My Keeping and in Theirs: A Record of Experiences 'on the Run', in Derry Gaol, and in Ballykinlar Interment Camp* (Dublin: Talbot Press, 1921), pp. 76–9. As William Murphy notes, 'Barry was killed by Private A. Barrett, a sentry, who claimed to have fired because he believed Barry was about to make a dash for freedom through the compound gate. A guard at the gate supported Barrett's account, but it was rejected by internee witnesses.' Murphy, *Political Imprisonment and the Irish*, p. 223.

247 Mulloy, *Jackets Green*, p. 158.

248 Ibid., p. 168.

249 Ibid., p. 178.

250 Ibid., p. 188, p. 232, p. 246.

251   Ibid., p. 225.

252   Ibid., p. 220.

253   Ibid., p. 282.

254   Ibid., p. 282, p. 284.

255   Ibid., p. 283.

256   Ibid., p. 282.

257   Ibid., p. 285.

258   Ibid., p. 182.

259   Ibid., p. 171.

260   Ibid., p. 227.

261   Ibid., p. 261, p. 317.

262   Ibid., p. 213.

263   Ibid., p. 309.

264   Ibid., p. 246.

265   Ibid., p. 257.

266   Ibid., p. 291.

267   Ibid., p. 319.

268   Ibid., p. 171.

269   Ibid., p. 293.

270   Ibid., p. 314.

271   Ibid., p. 301.

272   Ibid., p. 307.

273   Ibid., p. 305.

274   Ibid., p. 308.

275   Allen, *Modernism, Ireland and Civil War*, p. 196.

276   Mulloy, *Jackets Green*, p. 317.

277   See O'Leary, *Gaelic Prose in the Irish Free State*, p. 196.

278   Mulloy, *Jackets Green*, p. 330; Allen, *Modernism, Ireland and Civil War*, p. 176.

279   Margaret R. Higonnet, 'Civil Wars and Sexual Territories', in Helen M. Cooper, Adrienne Munich and Susan Merrill Squier (eds), *Arms and the Woman: War, Gender, and Literary Representation* (Chapel Hill, NC: University of North Carolina Press, 1989), p. 95.

280   Mulloy, *Jackets Green*, p. 322.

281   Ibid., p. 331.

282   'Irishman's Diary: Abbey Actor for U.S.A', *The Irish Times*, 29 April 1936, p. 4; 'What Dublin Is Reading', *The Irish Times*, 29 February 1936, p. 7; 'Wants His Banned Book Back in Print', *Independent*, 26 May 1968, p. 3.

283   'Banned Books', *The Irish Times*, 10 June 1936, p. 5.

284   Primo Levi cited in Dori Laub, 'Bearing Witness, or the Vicissitudes of Listening', in Shoshana Felman and Dori Laub, *Testimony: Crises of Witnessing in Literature, Psychoanalysis and History* (Milton Keynes: Taylor & Francis, 1992), p. 68.

285   'Bang Startles Court: Incident in Libel Action', *The Irish Times*, 27 May 1937, p. 4.

286   *Sunday Independent*, 22 September 1974, p. 13.

287   Seán O'Faoláin, *Midsummer Night Madness: And Other Stories* (London: J. Cape, 1932); John Brophy, *The Rocky Road* (London: J. Cape, 1932); Liam O'Flaherty, *The Martyr* (London: Gollancz Limited, 1933); Rearden Conner, *Shake Hands with the Devil: A Novel* (London: Dent, 1934); Francis Plunkett, *As the Fool* (London: Wishart, 1935); Jim Phelan,

Lifer (London: Peter Davies, 1938). See Dónal Ó Drisceoil, 'Appendix A', in Clare Hutton and Patrick Walsh (eds), *The Oxford History of the Irish Book. Volume V: The Irish Book in English, 1891–2000* (Oxford: Oxford University Press, 2011), pp. 644–9.

288   Danine Farquharson, 'Liam O'Flaherty's *The Martyr* and the Risks of Satire', *The Canadian Journal of Irish Studies* 25, no. 1/2 (1999), p. 386.

289   Séamus MacCall, *Gods in Motley* (London: Constable, 1935), p. 10.

290   Letter to Séamus MacCall, 21 November 1934. NAI, Talbot Press Archive, 1048/1/134. MacCall's novel was published by Constable Press in London.

291   'Author's Libel Action: *Jackets Green* Verdict', *The Irish Times*, 28 May 1937, p. 7.

292   'Author's Libel Action, Newspaper Wins, Judge Ruling on Comment', *The Guardian*, 17 June 1937, p. 19.

293   'Jackets Green', *The Irish Times*, 1 October 1945, p. 3.

294   'Irish Author's Appeal', *The Irish Times*, 2 April 1938, p. 12; 'Irish Novelist's Appeal: Security to Be Given for Costs', *The Irish Times*, 19 October 1937, p. 5.

295   'London Letter', *The Irish Times*, 20 September 1945, p. 3. See Mulloy's response: '[Letter to the Editor]: *Jackets Green*', *The Irish Times*, 1 October 1945, p. 3.

296   'Book Prohibited in Free State: Author's Libel Action against Newspaper', *The Guardian*, 25 May 1937, p. 7.

297   'Jackets Green, Typescript of a Novel'.

298   'Wants His Banned Book Back in Print', *Irish Independent*, 26 May 1968, p. 3.

299   My thanks to Gareth Mulloy for providing me with a copy of *Harvest of the Wind*. Other works by Mulloy include the play *Here We Dwell*, which was performed at Rudolf Steiner Theatre, London in 1950 and which evoked 'a strong nationalist atmosphere'. His 1964 play, *The Treadmill*, won first prize in a competition sponsored by the Scottish Community Drama Association. The play represents Mulloy's concerns for the social conditions of the London Irish. Set in Hampstead, the play was described by the author as 'a thriller with a difference'. *Irish Independent*, 28 August 1964, p. 14.

300   Patrick Mulloy, *Harvest of the Wind* (unpublished play, 1964), p. 79.

301   *The Irish Press*, 27 March 1950, p. 6.

302   *Sunday Independent*, 22 September 1974, p. 13.

303   P. D. K., 'Review of *Mutiny without Malice*', *An Cosantóir*, vol. 35, no. 8, August 1975.

304   Brendan Behan, 'Advice from an Emigrant', *The Irish Press*, 23 July 1955, p. 6.

305   Patrick Mulloy, *Andy Tinpockets* (London: Thames Publishing Co, 1950).

306   Deputy T. J. O'Connell, Dáil Éireann debates, vol. 40, no. 3, 16 October 1931.

307   Ryan, *The Invisible Army*, p. 224.

Chapter 2

1   Kenneth Sarr was the pen name of Kenneth Reddin (1895–1967). The novel was a bestseller in Hodges Figgis, Fred Hanna and Sign of the Three Candles, while Mulloy's novel topped the sales in W. J. Humphries and Easons & Son. 'What Dublin is Reading', *The Irish Times*, 29 February 1936, p. 7.

2   M. J. M, 'A Fine First Novel', *The Irish Press*, 3 March 1936, p. 8.

3   Mary Manning, 'Backdrop for a Troubled Stage (Review): *Somewhere to the Sea*, by Kenneth Reddin', *The Saturday Review*, 5 September 1936, p. 18.

4   Ibid.

5   Michael Hopkinson, 'Introduction', in Frank Henderson, *Frank Henderson's Easter Rising: Recollections of a Dublin Volunteer*, edited by Michael Hopkinson (Cork: Cork University Press, 1998), p. 10.

6   An exception is the character of Nuala Godfrey Dhu in *The Knife*. As Ó Drisceoil observes, O'Donnell's female characters are 'at least as active as men, and often more so'. Ó Drisceoil, *Peadar O'Donnell*, p. 129.

7   One case is that of Elizabeth MacCurtain, who prematurely gave birth to stillborn twins after witnessing her husband, Lord Mayor of Cork Tomás MacCurtain, being shot by Crown forces in his bedroom. Another is Mrs Brennan of Belfast, who purportedly died a number of days after giving birth due to the 'shock' of a house raid. A further case is that of Mrs Luke Quinn who delivered twins, one of whom was stillborn and the other who died shortly after birth. This was associated with the shock caused by the death of her brother-in-law. See Caoimhe Nic Dháibhéid, 'Fighting Their Fathers' Fight: The Post-Revolutionary Generation in Independent Ireland', in Senia Pašeta (ed.), *Uncertain Futures: Essays about the Irish Past for Roy Foster* (Oxford: Oxford University Press, 2016), p. 151; G. B. Kenna, *Facts and Figures of the Belfast Pogrom 1920–1922* (Belfast: O'Connell Publishing Company, 1922), p. 106; Patrick Quinn, MSPC DP3352.

8   On the gendered dynamics of wartime reviews, see Tal, *Worlds of Hurt*, p. 69.

9   Mary Manning, *Mount Venus* (Boston, MA: Houghton Mifflin Company, 1938); see Leo Keohane, *Captain Jack White: Imperialism, Anarchism and the Irish Citizen Army* (Dublin: Merrion Press, 2014).

10 Manning, *Mount Venus*, p. 2, p. 6, p. 8.

11 Paul Lerner and Mark S. Micale, 'Trauma, Psychiatry, and History', in idem (eds), *Traumatic Pasts: History, Psychiatry, and Trauma in the Modern Age, 1870–1930* (Cambridge: Cambridge University Press, 2001), p. 22; Lisa Dietrich, 'PTSD: A New Trauma Paradigm', in J. Roger Kurtz (eds), *Trauma and Literature* (Cambridge: Cambridge University Press, 2018), p. 88.

12 On gendered commemoration internationally, see James E. Young, 'Regarding the Pain of Women: Questions of Gender and the Arts of Holocaust Memory', *PMLA* 124, no. 5, 2009, p. 1779; John R. Gillis, *Commemorations: The Politics of National Identity* (Princeton, NJ: Princeton University Press, 2018).

13 See Foster, *The Irish Civil War and Society*, pp. 33–4.

14 Jensen, 'Testimony', p. 73.

15 Elaine Showalter, 'Feminist Criticism in the Wilderness', *Critical Inquiry* 8, no. 2 (1981), p. 193.

16 Foster, *The Irish Civil War and Society*, p. 45.

17 *The Irish Independent*, 12 January 1922, p. 5; see Jason K. Knirck, *Women of the Dáil: Gender, Republicanism and the Anglo-Irish Treaty* (Dublin: Irish Academic Press, 2006).

18 Hannah Sheehy-Skeffington, 'Letters from Abroad: The Irish Electorate', *The Freeman*, 10 May 1922, p. 206.

19 Cal McCarthy, *Cumann na mBan and the Irish Revolution* (Cork: Collins Press, 2014), p. 227; Ann Matthews, *Dissidents: Irish Republican Women, 1923–1941* (Cork: Mercier, 2012), p. 257; Sinéad McCoole, *No Ordinary Women: Irish Female Activists in the Revolutionary Years, 1900–1923* (Dublin: O'Brien Press, 2003 [2015]), pp. 244–65. Future research is required on women prisoners held in Armagh Gaol.

20   Louise Ryan, 'Splendidly Silent: Representing Irish Republican Women, 1919–1923',
      in Ann-Marie Gallagher, Cathy Lubelska and Louise Ryan (eds), *Re-Presenting the Past:
      Women and History* (London: Longman, 2001), p. 39. See Linda Connolly (ed.), *Women and
      the Irish Revolution* (Dublin: Irish Academic Press, 2020); Oona Frawley (ed.), *Women and
      the Decade of Commemorations* (Bloomington, IN: Indiana University Press, 2021).

21   O'Hegarty, *The Victory of Sinn Féin*, p. 75.

22   See Aiken, '"The Women Who Had Been Straining Every Nerve"', pp. 133–58.

23   Siobhán Lankford, *The Hope and the Sadness: Personal Recollections of Troubled Times in
      Ireland* (Cork: Tower Books, 1980) p. 250.

24   Ibid.

25   Colonel Eamon Broy, BMH WS 1285, 17 November 1955, p. 86.

26   Michael Scot, *Three Tales of the Times* (Dublin: Talbot Press, 1921).

27   15 November 1921, NAI, Talbot Press Archive, 1048/1/68. See Joanna Wydenbach, 'Emily
      Ussher and *The Trail of the Black & Tans*', *Revue LISA/LISA e-Journal. Littératures, Histoire
      Des Idées, Images, Sociétés Du Monde Anglophone – Literature, History of Ideas, Images and
      Societies of the English-Speaking World*, January 2000, pp. 22–38.

28   29 May 1922, NAI, Talbot Press Archive, 1048/1/72.

29   Senia Pašeta, *Irish Nationalist Women, 1900–1918* (Cambridge: Cambridge University
      Press, 2013), p. 1.

30   8 February 1934, NAI, Talbot Press Archive, 1048/1/132.

31   Buckley, *The Jangle of the Keys*.

32   Eithne Coyle, 'Reminiscences of Eithne O'Donnell (née Coyle)', 12 July 1972 [unpublished
      memoir], Kilmainham Gaol Archive, 20MS-1B33-19; Síghle Humphreys, 'Account of Her
      First Years in Prison 1922–23'. UCDA P106/978 (1). Transcription available at: https://
      humphrysfamilytree.com/Humphrys/sighle.papers.html (accessed 20 August 2020).

33   Leigh Gilmore, *Tainted Witness: Why We Doubt What Women Say About Their Lives* (New
      York: Columbia University Press, 2017), p. 2.

34   See Conrad Balliett, 'The Lives – and Lies – of Maud Gonne', *Éire–Ireland*, vol. 13, no. 3 (Fall
      1979); Margaret Ward, 'Review of Adrian Frazier, *The Adulterous Muse*', *Women's History
      Association of Ireland* (blog), 7 March 2017. Available at: https://womenshistoryassociation.
      com/book-reviews/review-of-adrian-frazier-the-adulterous-muse-by-dr-margaret-ward/
      (accessed 18 August 2020).

35   *Rebel Cork's Fighting Story, 1916–1921* (Tralee: Kerryman, 1947); *Kerry's Fighting Story,
      1916–21* (Tralee: Kerryman, 1947); *Dublin's Fighting Story, 1913–1921* (Tralee: Kerryman,
      1948); *Limerick's Fighting Story, 1916–21* (Tralee: Kerryman, 1948).

36   See Eve Morrison, 'The Bureau of Military History and Female Republican Activism, 1913–
      23', in Maryann Gialanella Valiulis (ed.), *Gender and Power in Irish History* (Dublin: Irish
      Academic Press, 2008), pp. 59–83.

37   Rogers highlights that Seán MacEntee's account *Episode at Easter* (1966) does not name the
      female messenger, Angela Mathews, nor mention her gender. See Ailbhe Rogers, 'Cumann
      na mBan in Co. Louth, 1914–1921', in Donal Hall and Maguire Martin (eds), *County Louth
      and the Irish Revolution: 1912–1923* (Dublin: Irish Academic Press, 2017), p. 42. Similarly,
      Charles Dalton notes in *With the Dublin Brigade* (1929) that the men of the squad met in
      a restaurant which was 'owned by a supporter of ours'. William O'Brien's annotated copy of
      the memoir held in the NLI suggests that the unnamed supporter was none other than Mrs
      Jennie Wyse Power.

38   Lucy McDiarmid, *At Home in the Revolution: What Women Said and Did in 1916* (Dublin: Royal Irish Academy, 2015), p. 38, p. 133.

39   Karen Steele, 'When Female Activists Say "I": The Veiled Rebel and Counterhistories of Irish Independence', in Gillian McIntosh and Diane Urquhart (eds), *Irish Women at War: The Twentieth Century* (Dublin: Irish Academic Press, 2010), p. 51.

40   Síghle Humphreys, 'Account of Her First Years in Prison 1922–23'. UCDA P106/978 (1). Transcription available at: https://humphrysfamilytree.com/Humphrys/sighle.papers.html (accessed 20 August 2020).

41   Mairéad and Siobhán de Paor, 'Blaze Away With Your Gun', *The Kerryman*, 21 December 1968; December 1968; 3 January 1969. See the joint witness statement of the Cooney sisters, Mrs Denis O'Brien and Mrs Lily Curran, BMH WS 805, 17 February 1953.

42   See Eithne Coyle, 'Manuscript drafts and covering letter by Eithne Coyle [relating to Maud Gonne MacBride]', UCDA P61/1; Nadia Claire Smith, 'From Dundalk to Dublin: Dorothy Macardle's Narrative Journey on Radio Éireann', *The Irish Review*, no. 42 (2010), p. 31.

43   Kathleen McKenna, *A Dáil Girl's Revolutionary Recollections* (Dublin: Original Writing, 2014), p. 228.

44   Michael Kevin O'Doherty, *My Parents and Other Rebels: A Personal Memoir* (Donegal: Errigal Press, 1999), p. 102; Margaret O'Callaghan, 'Women and Politics in Independent Ireland, 1921–68', in Angela Bourke et al. (eds), *The Field Day Anthology of Irish Writing V: Irish Women's Writing and Traditions* (New York: New York University Press, 2002), p. 123.

45   See MacManus, *White Light and Flame*.

46   Margaret O'Callaghan, 'Women's Political Autobiography in Independent Ireland', in Liam Harte (ed.), *A History of Irish Autobiography* (Cambridge: Cambridge University Press, 2018), p. 135.

47   Alice M. Cashel, *The Lights of Leaca Bán: A Story of Recent Times in Ireland* (Dublin: Browne and Nolan, 1935), p. 29.

48   Lily M. O'Brennan, 'Annotated Typescript Draft of Novel *Leading a Dog's Life in Ireland*', NLI Ms 41,502/1.

49   Esther Graham, *The Call to Arms: A Tale of the Land League Days* (Dublin: Browne and Nolan, 1929).

50   See Rosamond Jacob, *The Rebel's Wife* (Tralee: Kerryman, 1957); 'Women in the News', *The Irish Press*, 17 June 1936, p. 5.

51   Karen Steele, 'Revolutionary Lives in the Rearview Mirror: Memoir and Autobiography', in Marjorie Elizabeth Howes (ed.), *Irish Literature in Transition, 1880–1940*, Volume 4 (Cambridge: Cambridge University Press, 2020), p. 115.

52   *Offaly Independent*, 19 May 1923, p. 8; *Westmeath Independent*, 19 May 1923, p. 8.

53   Listed as 'Maighréad Kelly' in the membership rolls of the Ardchraobh of Cumann na mBan, Irish Military Archives, Cumann na mBan Nominal Rolls, MAI, MSPC, CMB/126.

54   As listed in 1911 census. See http://www.census.nationalarchives.ie (accessed 15 October 2021).

55   David Fitzpatrick, *Harry Boland's Irish Revolution* (Cork: Cork University Press, 2004), p. 221.

56   Jody Allen-Randolph, '"If No One Wanted to Remember": Margaret Kelly and the Lost Battalion', in Tina O'Toole, Gillian McIntosh and Muireann O'Cinnéide (eds), *Women Writing War: Ireland 1880–1922* (Dublin: UCD Press, 2016), p. 135.

57   Ibid.

58 Ibid., pp. 133–49.

59 Ibid., p. 136.

60 Garrett O'Driscoll, 'The Blind Man: A Story', *Green and Gold: A Magazine of Fiction, Etc.* V, no. 20 (November 1925), pp. 133–40; Garrett O'Driscoll, 'The June Babies: A Story', *Green and Gold: A Magazine of Fiction, Etc.* IV, no. 16 (November 1924), pp. 223–34; Garrett O'Driscoll, 'The Lacklander: A Story', *Green and Gold: A Magazine of Fiction, Etc.* V, no. 18 (1925), pp. 1–11.

61 Garrett O'Driscoll, 'Those of the Lost Battalion', *The Irish Press*, 2 July 1934, p. 8.

62 Garrett O'Driscoll, *Noreen* (London: George Roberts 1929), p. 44.

63 Ibid., p. 50.

64 Allen-Randolph, 'If No One Wanted to Remember', p. 143.

65 O'Driscoll, *Noreen*, p. 277.

66 'Prize-Winning Novel by Local Author: *Noreen* by Garrett O'Driscoll', *Nenagh Guardian*, 15 March 1930, p. 1.

67 British poet Alice Meynell (1847–1922) was highly celebrated at the turn of the century and her work appeared in Irish suffrage journal, *The Irish Citizen*.

68 O'Driscoll, *Noreen*, p. 94.

69 Ibid., p. 97.

70 See Garrett O'Driscoll, 'Are the Irish Cruel to Animals?', *The Irish Press*, 26 January 1934, p. 6.

71 O'Driscoll, *Noreen*, p. 151.

72 Ibid., p. 54.

73 Ibid., p. 14.

74 Ibid., p. 93.

75 Ibid., p. 131.

76 Ibid., p. 172.

77 Ibid., p. 174.

78 Ibid., p. 106.

79 Higonnet, 'Civil Wars and Sexual Territories', p. 95.

80 O'Driscoll, *Noreen*, p. 259, p. 235.

81 Ibid., p. 202.

82 Ibid.

83 Ibid., p. 231, p. 245.

84 Ibid., p. 202, p. 233.

85 Ibid., p. 182, p. 34, p. 194, p. 224, p. 226.

86 Garrett O'Driscoll, 'Mettle: A Story', *Green and Gold: A Magazine of Fiction, Etc.* V, no. 21 (December 1925), p. 265.

87 O'Driscoll, *Noreen*, p. 256.

88 Garrett O'Driscoll, 'A Flippant Young Man: A Story', *Green and Gold: A Magazine of Fiction, Etc.* II, no. 8 (November 1922), pp. 167–76.

89 Allen-Randolph, 'If No One Wanted to Remember', p. 140.

90 O'Driscoll, 'A Flippant Young Man', p. 173, p. 169.

91 Ibid., p. 173.

92 O'Driscoll, *Noreen*, p. 90, p. 98, p. 62.

93 Ibid., p. 107.

94 Ibid., p. 245.

95   Ibid., p. 275.

96   Ibid., p. 107.

97   Ibid., p. 313.

98   Jean-Michel Ganteau and Susana Onega, 'Introduction', in idem (eds), *Trauma and Romance in Contemporary British Literature* (Abingdon: Routledge, 2013), p. 5.

99   Martin Henry, *Ambushed Lovers: A Tale of The Troubled Times in Ireland* (Dublin: Talbot Press, 1929); 'Obituary Mr. Martin Henry', *The Irish Press*, 19 September 1931, p. 15.

100   Peadar Ó Dubhda, *Brian* (Baile Átha Cliath: Oifig Díolta Foillseacháin Rialtais, 1937); Éamonn Mac Giolla Iasachta, *Toil Dé* (Baile Átha Cliath: Oifig Díolta Foillseacháin Rialtais, 1933). Philip O'Leary contends that *Brian* 'shift[s] in emphasis from a novel dealing with political and military issues to a love story [which] coincides with the approach of the Truce in July 1921', while *Toil Dé* is also 'primarily concerned with political and cultural ideas in the chapters leading up to the Irish Civil War, but then focuses on personal and romantic concerns'. O'Leary, *Gaelic Prose in the Free State*, p. 319; Philip O'Leary, 'The Irish Renaissance, 1890–1940: Literature in Irish', in Margaret Kelleher and Philip O'Leary (eds), *The Cambridge History of Irish Literature*, Volume 2 (Cambridge: Cambridge: Cambridge University Press, 2006), p. 254.

101   Sheila Hartnett, 'There is a Great Loneliness on Me', *The Irish Press*, 29 December 1971, p. 9. See also Pinkman, *In the Legion of the Vanguard*, p. 151.

102   Robert Jay Lifton, 'Interview', in Cathy Caruth (ed.), *Trauma: Explorations in Memory* (Baltimore, MD: Johns Hopkins University Press, 1995), p. 128.

103   O'Driscoll, *Noreen*, p. 319.

104   Ibid., p. 326.

105   Garrett O'Driscoll, 'The Bean-a-Tighe Looks Back', *The Meath Chronicle*, 7 September 1935, p. 8.

106   Allen-Randolph, 'If No One Wanted to Remember', p. 145.

107   O'Driscoll, *Noreen*, p. 176.

108   Jody Allen-Randolph, *Eavan Boland* (Washington, D.C.: Rowman & Littlefield, 2013), p. 10.

109   O'Driscoll, 'The Lacklander', pp. 1–11.

110   Ibid., p. 2.

111   Ibid., p. 9.

112   Ibid., p. 11.

113   Allen-Randolph, 'If No One Wanted to Remember', p. 144.

114   T. Deevy, 'Just Yesterday: A Story', *Green and Gold: A Magazine of Fiction*, etc., vol. IV, no. 17 December 1924–March 1925, pp. 268–76; Shelley Troupe, 'TSI: Teresa Deevy, or What Do We Know about *The Reapers*?', Teresa Deevy Archive; NUI, Maynooth, 2014. Available at: https://www.academia.edu/7135600/_TSI_Teresa_Deevy_or_What_do_we_know_about_The_Reapers_ (accessed 20 August 2020).

115   See Oonagh Walsh, '"Her Irish Heritage": Annie M. P. Smithson and Autobiography', *Études Irlandaises* 23, no. 1 (1998), pp. 27–42.

116   Valerie Coughlan 'Writing for Children', in Heather Ingman and Clíona Ó Gallchóir (eds), *A History of Modern Irish Women's Literature* (Cambridge: Cambridge University Press, 2018), p. 155.

117   S. T., 'Her Irish Heritage', *An Lóchrann*, Eanáir 1918.

118 Eimar O'Duffy, 'Review of *The Walk of a Queen* by Annie M. P. Smithson', *The Irish Review*, 6 January 1923, pp. 70–1, cited in Flanagan, *Remembering the Revolution*, p. 69.

119 Marie Bashford-Synnott, 'Annie M. P. Smithson Romantic Novelist, Revolutionary Nurse', *Dublin Historical Record* 64, no. 1 (2011), p. 47.

120 '*The Walk of a Queen*, by Annie M. P Smithson', *Irish Independent*, 11 December 1922, p. 3.

121 Linda Kearns; Annie M. P. Smithson (ed.), *In Times of Peril: Leaves from the Diary of Nurse Linda Kearns from Easter Week, 1916, to Mountjoy, 1921* (Dublin: Talbot Press, 1922). Letter to Smithson, 25 May 1922, NAI, Talbot Press Archive, 1048/1/72.

122 Walsh, '"Her Irish Heritage"', p. 28.

123 Bashford-Synnott, 'Annie M. P. Smithson', p. 49.

124 Annie M. P. Smithson, *Myself – and Others: An Autobiography* (Dublin: Talbot Press, 1944), p. 100.

125 Ibid., p. 203.

126 Cumann na mBan Nominal Rolls, MSPC, MAI, CMB/85.

127 Annie M. P. Smithson, 'Hills o' Home', *Green and Gold: A Magazine of Fiction, etc.*, vol. I, no. 4, September 1921, pp. 255–60.

128 Smithson, *Myself – and Others*, p. 201.

129 Ibid., p. 248.

130 Cited in Bashford-Synnott, 'Annie M. P. Smithson', p. 67.

131 Smithson, *Myself – and Others*, p. 200.

132 Letter to Annie P. Smithson, 25 May 1922, NAI, Talbot Press Archive, 1048/1/72.

133 Smithson, *Myself – and Others*, p. 268.

134 See Danae O'Regan, 'Representations and Attitudes of Republican Women in the Novels of Annie M. P. Smithson (1873–1948) and Rosamond Jacob (1888–1960)', in Louise Ryan and Margaret Ward (eds), *Irish Women and Nationalism: Soldiers, New Women and Wicked Hags* (Dublin: Irish Academic Press, 2004), pp. 80–95.

135 See R. F. Foster, *Vivid Faces: The Revolutionary Generation in Ireland, 1890–1923* (London: Penguin, 2014), pp. 142–3.

136 Whereas Liam's mother urges him to 'rest and eat', he is more relaxed after the visit of a mysterious IRA man who convinces him to 'tell me about it and see if you don't feel better'. Rosamond Jacob, *The Troubled House: A Novel of Dublin in the 'Twenties* (Dublin: Browne and Nolan, 1938), p. 88.

137 Annie M. P. Smithson, *The Walk of a Queen* (Dublin: Talbot Press, 1922 [1989]), p. 72.

138 O'Regan, 'Representations and Attitudes', p. 94.

139 Smithson, *The Walk of a Queen*, p. 53.

140 Ibid., p. 26.

141 Ibid., p. 13, p. 25.

142 McAreavey, 'Reading Conversion Narratives as Literature of Trauma', p. 167.

143 Smithson, *The Walk of a Queen*, p. 65.

144 Ibid., p. 89.

145 Ibid.

146 Ibid., p. 213.

147 Ibid., p. 242.

148 Smithson, *Myself – and Others*, p. 255.

149 Smithson does not name the sergeant. However, records suggest that the incident occurred on 7 July 1922 and that deceased was James McNamee, Sergeant Major, 1st Midland

Division, National Forces. Available at: http://www.irishmedals.ie/National-Army-Killed. php (accessed 20 April 2020).

150 Letter to Smithson, 29 January 1935, NAI, Talbot Press Archive, 1048/1/135.

151 *The Irish Press*, 10 December 1935, p. 10.

152 Smithson, *Myself – and Others*, p. 252.

153 'Some of the New Novels: Romantic Tales by Irish Authors', *Irish Independent*, 19 November 1935, p. 4; L. K., 'Review of *The Marriage of Nurse Harding*', *The Irish Book Lover*, vols 24–25, March–April 1936, p. 46.

154 Smithson, *Myself – and Others*, p. 93.

155 Ibid., p. 250.

156 Steele, 'When Female Activists Say "I"', p. 54.

157 Annie M. P. Smithson, *The Marriage of Nurse Harding* (Dublin: Talbot, 1935 [1989]), p. 103.

158 Carty, *Legion of the Rearguard*, p. 120.

159 Smithson, *Myself – and Others*, p. 258.

160 Smithson, *The Marriage of Nurse Harding*, p. 103.

161 Ibid., p. 110, p. 134.

162 See Richard J. McNally, *Remembering Trauma* (Boston, MA: Harvard University Press, 2005).

163 Smithson, *Myself – and Others*, p. 252.

164 Smithson, *The Marriage of Nurse Harding*, p. 101.

165 Smithson, *Myself – and Others*, p. 260.

166 Smithson, *The Marriage of Nurse Harding*, p. 111.

167 Ibid., p. 116.

168 Smithson, *Myself – and Others*, p. 203; Smithson, *The Marriage of Nurse Harding*, p. 109.

169 Smithson, *Myself – and Others*, p. 256.

170 Smithson, *The Marriage of Nurse Harding*, p. 95.

171 Ibid., p. 111.

172 Smithson, *Myself – and Others*, p. 262.

173 Gerardine Meaney, 'Fiction, 1922–1960', in Clíona Ó Gallchoir and Heather Ingman (eds), *A History of Modern Irish Women's Literature* (Cambridge: Cambridge University Press, 2018), p. 193.

174 Maria Beville, 'Gothic Memory and the Contested Past: Framing Terror', in Lorna Piatti-Farnell and Maria Beville (eds), *The Gothic and the Everyday: Living Gothic* (London: Palgrave Macmillan, 2014), pp. 64–5.

175 Siobhán Kilfeather, 'The Gothic Novel', in John Wilson Foster (ed.), *The Cambridge Companion to the Irish Novel* (Cambridge: Cambridge University Press, 2006), p. 81.

176 Annie M. P. Smithson, 'The Guide: A Story', *Green and Gold*, vol. I, no. 2, March 1921, pp. 81–5; Annie M. P. Smithson, *The Guide* (London: Catholic Truth Society, 1923).

177 4 October 1923, NAI, Talbot Press Archive, 1048/1/80.

178 Letter to Dorothy Macardle, 30 November 1923, NAI. Talbot Press Collection, 1048/1/81.

179 Dorothy Macardle, *Tragedies of Kerry 1922–1923* (Dublin: Emton Press, 1924).

180 Irina Ruppo Malone, 'Spectral History: The Ghost Stories of Dorothy Macardle', *Partial Answers: Journal of Literature and the History of Ideas* 9, no. 1 (2011), p. 95.

181 Nadia Clare Smith, *Dorothy Macardle: A Life* (Dublin: Woodfield Press, 2007), p. 57.

182 Dorothy Macardle, *The Unforeseen* (Garden City, NY: Doubleday 1946), p. 206.

183 Dorothy Macardle, *Earth-bound: Nine Stories of Ireland* (Worchester, MA: Harrigan Press, 1924), p. 8.

184 Ibid., p. 46.

185 Ibid., p. 102.

186 Ibid., p. 50.

187 See Dorothy Macardle, 'Letter from Kilmainham', *Éire*, 12 May 1923, p. 5; Macardle, 'The Kilmainham Tortures', p. 4; Macardle, 'Thoughts in a Hospital', *Éire*, 20 Oct. 1923, pp. 4–5. For a more personal reflective account of the impact of Erskine Childer's death on Macardle, see 'A Year Ago', *Éire*, 14 July 1923, p. 2.

188 See Dorothy Macardle, BMH WS 457, 4 Dec 1950 and Macardle, 'Living with Maud Gonne', RTÉ Radio Scripts, UCDA P260/672, 15 September 1956. See Nadia Clare Smith, 'From Dundalk to Dublin: Dorothy Macardle's Narrative Journey on Radio Éireann', *The Irish Review*, no. 42 (2010), pp. 27–42.

189 See, for example, Dorothy Macardle, 'The Prisoner' [poem], *Éire*, 30 June 1923, p. 2. See Leeann Lane, *Dorothy Macardle* (Dublin: UCD Press, 2019), p. 112.

190 Dorothy Macardle, *The Irish Republic: A Documented Chronicle of the Anglo-Irish Conflict and the Partitioning of Ireland, with a Detailed Account of the Period 1916–1923* (Dublin: Irish Press, 1937), p. 24.

191 Lane, *Dorothy Macardle*, p. 230.

192 Clarke and Brown (eds), *Ireland in Fiction*, p. 154.

193 Lane, *Dorothy Macardle*, p. 112.

194 See Jennifer Molidor, 'Dying for Ireland: Violence, Silence, and Sacrifice in Dorothy Macardle's *Earth–Bound: Nine Stories of Ireland* (1924)', *New Hibernia Review* 12, no. 4 (2008); Abigail L. Palko, 'Queer Seductions of the Maternal in Dorothy Macardle's *Earth-Bound*', *Irish University Review* 46, no. 2 (25 October 2016), pp. 287–308.

195 Sandra M. Gilbert and Susan Gubar, *The Madwoman in the Attic: The Woman Writer and the Nineteenth-Century Literary Imagination* (New Haven, CT: Yale University Press, 1980), p. 73.

196 Molidor, 'Dying for Ireland', p. 44.

197 Macardle, *Earth-bound*, p. 49.

198 Ibid., p. 47.

199 Ibid.

200 Gerardine Meaney, 'Identity and Opposition: Women's Writing', in Angela Bourke et al. (eds), *The Field Day Anthology of Irish Writing V: Irish Women's Writing and Traditions* (Cork: Cork University Press), p. 978.

201 Susan Lanser, *Fictions of Authority: Women Writers and Narrative Voice* (Ithaca, NY: Cornell University Press, 1992), p. 92.

202 See Molidor, 'Dying for Ireland', pp. 43–61; Palko, 'Queer Seductions'.

203 de Paor, Mairéad and Siobhán, 'Blaze Away With Your Gun', *The Kerryman*, 21 December 1968, December 1968 and 3 January 1969, p. 9.

204 Coyle, 'Reminiscences of Eithne O'Donnell, pp. 17–18.

205 Ibid., p. 18.

206 Buckley, *The Jangle of the Keys*, p. 15; see Laura McAtackney, 'Gender, Incarceration and Power Relations during the Irish Civil War (1922–1923)', in Victoria Sanford, Katerina Stefatos and Cecilia M. Salvi (eds), *Gender Violence in Peace and War: States of Complicity* (New Brunswick, NJ: Rutgers University Press, 2016), p. 56.

207 Dorothy Macardle, 'The Prisoners: 1798–1923', *Éire*, 13 September 1924, pp. 1–2.

208 Macardle refused food for some time in November 1922 and participated in a week-long hunger strike from 23 March 1923. Palko highlights that the only other story in the collection signed off from Kilmainham, 'The Return of Niav', also addresses the question of hunger striking, albeit less openly so, as the figure of Neoineen refuses to take food in a protest against her mother's absence. Lane, *Dorothy Macardle*, p. 68; Palko, 'Queer Seductions', p. 294.

209 Malone, 'Spectral History', p. 100.

210 Lane, *Dorothy Macardle*, p. 71.

211 Macardle, *Earth-bound*, p. 104.

212 Ibid.

213 Ibid., p. 105.

214 Ibid., p. 106, p. 108.

215 Malone, 'Spectral History', p. 102.

216 Nora Connolly O'Brien, BMH WS 286, 21 July 1949, p. 54.

217 Diary entry for 7 February 1923, cited in Lane, *Dorothy Macardle*, p. 79. See also Connolly's discussion of her 'nerves' 'giving way'. Nora Connolly O'Brien, *We Shall Rise Again* (London: Mosquito Press, 1981), pp. 54–5.

218 O'Brien, *We Shall Rise Again*, p. 52.

219 Dorothy Macardle, 'Mountjoy', *Éire*, 2 June 1923.

220 O'Donnell, *The Gates Flew Open*, p. 194.

221 Caoilfhionn Ní Bheacháin, 'Seeing Ghosts: Gothic Discourses and State Formation', *Éire-Ireland* 47, no. 3 (2012), p. 37.

222 Ó Nualláin, B. [Myles na gCopaleen], 'Books in Irish', *The Irish Times*, 31 August 1940, p. 5. There is no name listed with this review, but it has been attributed to Brian Ó Nualláin, see Breandán Ó Conaire, *Myles na Gaeilge: Lámhleabhar ar Shaothar Gaeilge Bhrian Ó Nualláin* (Baile Átha Cliath: An Clóchomhar: 1986), p. 246.

223 O'Leary, *Gaelic Prose in the Irish Free State*, p. 326.

224 Ní Ghráda married Civic Guard Risteard Ó Ciosáin at the Church of St Mary's, Haddington Rd, Dublin on 1 July 1923. Available at: Civil Records, irishgenealogy.ie (accessed 20 August 2020).

225 Ernest Blythe, BMH WS 939, 12 April 1954, p. 117.

226 See Lil Conlon, *Cumann na mBan and the Women of Ireland, 1913–25* (Kilkenny: Kilkenny People Ltd, 1969) and McKenna, *A Dáil Girl's Revolutionary Recollections*.

227 Newspaper reporting suggests that eight women were brought to court: five at the Police Court and three at Southern Police Court. Mountjoy prison records list four prisoners committed on 3 November 1919: Margaret O'Grady (clerk), Johanna O'Loane (student), Mary O'Brien (clerk), Mary McCarthy (shop assistant). Irish Prison Registers 1790–1924. Available at findmypast.ie (accessed 30 August 2020).

228 Máiréad Ní Ghráda, 'Interview [with Aedín Ní Chaoimh]', *Dá bhFaighinn Mo Rogha*, RTÉ Radio, 28 March 1969. RTÉ Sound Archive, AA3326.

229 Éamon Ó Ciosáin, 'Máiréad Ní Ghráda agus a Saothar Liteartha', in Mairéad Ní Ghráda, *Breithiúnas: Dráma Dhá Ghníomh* (Baile Átha Cliath: Oifig an tSoláthair, 1978), p. 175.

230 'Girls Arrested: Gaelic League Flag Day', *Irish Independent*, 2 November 1919, p. 8; 'Names in Irish Only: Flagsellers to go to Jail Rather than Pay Fine', *Irish Independent*, 5 November

1919, p. 3; 'Mountjoy Visitors: Flagsellers Demand Money Held by Police', *The Freeman's Journal*, 7 November 1919, p. 6.

231   'Lady Flagsellers Sent to Jail', *Leitrim Observer*, 8 November 1919, p. 3; 'Police Station Windows Smashed', *The Irish Times*, 4 November 1919, p. 7.

232   Eileen Morgan, '"Unbroken Service": Máiréad Ní Ghráda's Career at 2RN, Ireland's First Broadcasting Station, 1927–35', *Éire-Ireland* 37, no. 3–4 (2002), p. 56, p. 75.

233   Morgan, '"Unbroken Service"', pp. 74–5.

234   I could not get access to the original textbook due to restrictions during the COVID-19 pandemic. This quote is taken from an article in the *Evening Herald*, 28 March 1984, p. 23.

235   Pádraig Ó Siadhail suggests the play was rejected by the Abbey in 1939 (these files are currently under embargo). *Stailc Ocrais* was finally produced and published over twenty years later; it won a £50 Art Council prize in 1960, was performed in An Damer theatre in 1962, published in 1966 and produced by various amateur theatre groups during the fifty-year commemorations of the Rising. Máiréad Ní Ghráda, *Stailc Ocrais: Tragóid Stairiúil, Dráma Aonghmímh* (Baile Átha Cliath: Oifig an tSoláthair, 1966). See Siobhán Ní Bhrádaigh, *Máiréad Ní Ghráda: Ceannródaí Drámaíochta* (Indreabhán: Cló Iar-Chonnachta, 1996); Philip O'Leary, *An Underground Theatre: Major Playwrights in the Irish Language 1930–80* (Dublin: UCD Press, 2017).

236   The play was initially accepted on 7 August 1936. This decision was overturned a week later and 'detailed criticism' returned to the 'authoress' 'so as to enable her if she so wished, to improve the play and make it possible to produce'. Abbey Minute Books, Special Collections, NUI Galway.

237   Ní Bhrádaigh, *Máiréad Ní Ghráda*, p. 51.

238   Máiréad Ní Ghráda, *An Bheirt Dearbhráthar agus Scéalta Eile* (Baile Átha Cliath: Oifig an tSoláthair, 1939), p. 27.

239   See for example Ní Ghráda, 'Comhrac', *An Bheirt Dearbhráthar*.

240   C. Ó N., 'Leabhar do na Gaedhilgeoirí', *The Irish Independent*, 21 May 1940, p. 4.

241   Ní Ghráda, *An Bheirt Dearbhráthar*, p. 172. The reference to Kilmichael most likely refers to the much-debated ambush of an auxiliary patrol by Tom Barry's IRA flying column on 28 November 1920.

242   Ibid., p. 175.

243   Ibid., p. 180.

244   Ibid., p. 40.

245   Ibid., p. 220.

246   Ibid., p 118.

247   Ibid., p. 126.

248   *Irish Ecclesiastical Record* (Dublin: Browne and Nolan, Limited, 1961), p. 136.

249   See *National Collection of Children's Books*. Available at: https://nccb.tcd.ie (accessed 30 August 2020).

250   Máirín Cregan, *Old John* (New York: Macmillan, 1936); Máirín Cregan, *Rathina* (New York: Macmillan, 1942); Susan Cahill, '"Far Away from the Busy World": Máirín Cregan's Children's Literature', in John Countryman, J. and Kelly Matthews (eds), *Country of the Young: Interpretations of Youth and Childhood in Irish Culture* (Dublin: Four Courts Press: 2013), p. 71.

251 Cahill, "'Far Away from the Busy World'", p. 71. See also Fiona Brennan, 'Máirín Cregan: Author and Playwright', *Killorglin's River of Memories* (Kerry: Killorglin Archive Society, 2020), pp. 20–9.

252 'Dr. Jim Ryan, T.D.', *Éire*, 1 December 1923.

253 Máirín Ryan, BMH WS 416, 28 Iúil 1950, p. 4.

254 J. G. Ryan, 'Máirín Cregan', *Kerry Magazine*, iss. 23, 2013, p. 50.

255 Máirín Ryan, BMH WS 416, p. 16.

256 Sworn Evidence Given Before the Referee on 28 November 1940, by Mrs Maureen Ryan, Kindlestown House, Delganey, Co. Wicklow. MSPC MAI MSP34REF52148, p. 3.

257 Máirín Cregan, 'The Rush to Meet the Arms-Ship', *The Irish Press*, 24 April 1933, p. 6.

258 Máirín Cregan, 'Carrying the Message in Easter Week: A Courier's Thrilling Story', *The Irish Press* (Christmas Supplement), 25 December 1934, pp. 13 and 36; 'Recruiting in 1914: Seán MacDermott's Part: Broadcast on Life of Great Patriot', *The Meath Chronicle*, 18 January 1936, p. 9; Máirín Cregan, 'James Connolly: An Incident', *The Capuchin Annual*, 1936, p. 226.

259 Máirín Ryan, interview with Ernie O'Malley, Ernie O'Malley Papers, UCDA p17b/103 [undated].

260 Letter to Máirín Cregan from Abbey Theatre, Dublin, 12 June 1931, NLI Ms 50,423/1.

261 Letter to Mrs Ryan from Patrick T. Keohane, M. H. Gill, 2 November 1932, NLI Ms 50, 423/1.

262 Ibid.

263 Letter to Máirín Cregan from James Carty, 17 March 1933, NLI Ms 50,423/1.

264 Letter to Máirín Cregan from James Carty, 24 July 1933, NLI Ms 50,423/1.

265 Máirín Cregan, *Hunger-strike: A Play in Two Acts* (Dublin: M. H. Gill, 1932), p. 23.

266 Letter to Máirín Cregan from D. Ó Corcora, 15 April 1934, NLI Ms 50,423/1.

267 É[ibhlín] Nic G[hráinne], 'Review of *Hunger-strike: A Play in Two Acts*, by Máirín Cregan', *Dublin Magazine*, vol. VIII, no. 2, April–June 1933, p. 87.

268 'Review of *Hunger-strike*', *The Catholic Bulletin*, March 1933, p. 218.

269 Cregan, *Hunger-strike*, p. 3.

270 Ibid., p. 26.

271 Ibid., p. 27.

272 O'Hegarty, *The Victory of Sinn Féin*, p. 102.

273 Cregan, *Hunger-strike*, p. 23.

274 See Olga Glebova, 'Trauma, Female Identity and the Trope of Splitting in Lessing, Figes, Tennant and Weldon', in Sonya Andermahr and Silvia Pellicer-Ortín (eds), *Trauma Narratives and Herstory* (London: Palgrave Macmillan UK, 2013), p. 59.

275 Cregan, *Hunger-strike*, p. 23.

276 Ibid., p. 34.

277 Ibid., p. 32.

278 Ibid., p. 26, p. 18.

279 Ibid., p. 37.

280 'Women on Hunger-strike', *The Freeman's Journal*, 21 April 1923, p. 7.

281 Mary McAuliffe, "'An Idea Has Gone Abroad that All the Women Were Against the Treaty'": Cumann na Saoirse and Pro-treaty Women, 1922–3', in Mícheál Ó Fathartaigh and Liam Weeks (eds), *Debating and Establishing the Irish State* (Dublin: Irish Academic Press 2018), p. 164; Aidan Seery and Karin Bacon, 'Auto/Biographical Research and the Family',

in Julie M. Parsons and Anne Chappell (eds), *The Palgrave Handbook of Auto/Biography* (Basingstoke: Palgrave Macmillan 2020), pp. 143–56.

282 Patrick Maume, 'Ryan, Mary Kate ('Kit', 'Cáit')', *Dictionary of Irish Biography*, 2015.

283 Cregan, *Hunger-strike*, p. 48.

284 Ibid.

285 Ibid.

286 Mary McWhorter, 20 June 1936, untitled newspaper extract, NLI Ms 50,423/1.

287 UCD Archive, James Ryan papers, P88/72.2.

288 'Radio Programmes', *The Irish Press*, 5 May 1936, p. 5.

289 Letter from Tomás Ó Maoileoin to Radio Athlone, 6 May 1936, NLI Ms 50,423/1.

290 Letter from Mary Manning to Máirín Cregan, 21 February 1933, NLI Ms 50,423/1.

Chapter 3

1 Lindsey Earner-Byrne, 'The Rape of Mary M.: A Microhistory of Sexual Violence and Moral Redemption in 1920s Ireland', *Journal of the History of Sexuality* 24, no. 1 (2015), p. 87.

2 Éamon de Valera referred to women as the most 'unmanageable of revolutionaries', while Shaw Desmond branded women the 'Amazons of Sinn Féin'. See Margaret Ward, *Unmanageable Revolutionaries: Women and Irish Nationalism* (London: Pluto Press, 1983); Shaw Desmond, *The Drama of Sinn Féin* (New York: C. Scribner's Sons, 1923), p. 401.

3 See Sarah Benton, 'Women Disarmed: The Militarization of Politics in Ireland 1913–23', *Feminist Review*, no. 50 (1995), pp. 148–72; Louise Ryan, '"Drunken Tans": Representations of Sex and Violence in the Anglo-Irish War (1919–21)', *Feminist Review*, no. 66 (2000), pp. 73–94; Ann Matthews, *Renegades: Irish Republican Women 1900–1922* (Cork: Mercier, 2010); Matthews, *Dissidents*; Earner-Byrne, 'The Rape of Mary M.'; Marie Coleman, 'Violence against Women in the Irish War of Independence, 1919-1921', in Diarmaid Ferriter and Susannah Riordan (eds), *Years of Turbulence: The Irish Revolution and Its Aftermath* (Dublin: UCD Press, 2015), pp. 137–56; Gabrielle Machnik-Kekesi, 'Gendering Bodies: Violence as Performance in Ireland's War of Independence (1919–1921)' (Concordia University: unpublished thesis, 2017); Justin Dolan Stover, 'Families, Vulnerability and Sexual Violence During the Irish Revolution', in Jennifer Evans and Ciara Meehan (eds), *Perceptions of Pregnancy from the Seventeenth to the Twentieth Century* (Basingstoke: Palgrave, 2017), pp. 57–75; Linda Connolly, 'Towards a Further Understanding of the Violence Experienced by Women in the Irish Revolution', *Maynooth University Social Sciences Institute*, Working Paper Series, no. 7 (Maynooth University, January, 2019); Linda Connolly, 'Sexual Violence in the Irish Civil War: A Forgotten War Crime?', *Women's History Review*, 6 March 2020, pp. 1–18; Susan Byrne, '"Keeping Company with the Enemy": Gender and Sexual Violence against Women during the Irish War of Independence and Civil War, 1919–1923', *Women's History Review* 2, March 2020, pp. 1–18; Clark, *Everyday Violence*; Gemma Clark, 'Violence against Women in the Irish Civil War, 1922-3: Gender-Based Harm in Global Perspective', *Irish Historical Studies* 44, no. 165 (May 2020), pp. 75–90; Mary McAuliffe, 'The Homefront as Battlefront: Women, Violence and the Domestic Space during War in Ireland, 1919-1921', in Linda Connolly (ed.), *Women and the Irish Revolution* (Dublin: Irish Academic Press, 2020), pp. 164–82;

Gerri O'Neill, "'Looting and Overtures and Acts of Indecency by Black and Tans": The Pursuit of Justice for Acts of Sexual Violence during Ireland's War of Independence (1919–21)', *Studia Hibernica* 47, no. 1 (September 2021), pp. 89–106.

4   Coleman, 'Violence against Women in the Irish War of Independence', p. 154; Clark, 'Violence against Women', p. 90; Connolly, 'Sexual Violence in the Irish Civil War', p. 1, p. 5.

5   Connolly, 'Towards a Further Understanding', p. 2, p. 24; Clark, 'Violence against Women', p. 75.

6   There are many examples; these are from the promotional material for Diarmaid Ferriter's *A Nation and Not a Rabble: The Irish Revolution 1913–23* (London: Profile Books, 2015) and *Between Two Hells: The Irish Civil War* (London: Profile Books, 2021).

7   Beiner, 'Memory Too Has a History'.

8   Tom Inglis, 'Origins and Legacies of Irish Prudery: Sexuality and Social Control in Modern Ireland', *Éire-Ireland*, vol. 40: 3 and 4, Fall/Winter 2005, p. 11.

9   Shani D'Cruze, 'Approaching the History of Rape and Sexual Violence: Notes towards Research', *Women's History Review* 1, no. 3 (September 1992), p. 379, cited in Connolly, 'Towards a Further Understanding', p. 6.

10   Sabine Sielke, *Reading Rape: The Rhetoric of Sexual Violence in American Literature and Culture, 1790–1990* (Princeton, NJ: Princeton University Press, 2009), p. 11.

11   Lynn A. Higgins and Brenda R. Silver's study of literary representations of sexual violence also contends that 'the politics and aesthetics of rape are one'; while Sarah Projansky, in considering sexual violence on the screen, asserts that 'rape discourse is part of the fabric of what rape is'. See Lynn A. Higgins and Brenda R. Silver, *Rape and Representation* (New York: Columbia University Press, 1993), p. 1; Sarah Projansky, *Watching Rape: Film and Television in Postfeminist Culture* (New York: NYU Press, 2001), p. 2; Jody Freeman, 'The Disciplinary Function of Rape's Representation: Lessons from the Kennedy Smith and Tyson Trials', *Law & Social Inquiry* 18, no. 3 (1993), p. 520.

12   I have taken the term 'gatekeeper' from Rachel Sarah Jo Macreadie, 'Politicizing the Personal: Reading Gender-Based Violence in Rape Survivor Discourse' (unpublished PhD thesis, University of Melbourne, 2014), p. 10.

13   Higgins and Silver, *Rape and Representation*; Sorcha Gunne and Zoe Brigley Thompson (eds), *Feminism, Literature and Rape Narratives: Violence and Violation* (Abingdon: Routledge, 2012).

14   See Earner-Byrne, 'The Rape of Mary M.'; Connolly, 'Towards a Further Understanding'.

15   Pinkman, *In the Legion of the Vanguard*, p. 109.

16   Kathleen Behan, *Mother of All the Behans: The Story of Kathleen Behan as Told to Brian Behan* (London: Hutchinson, 1984), p. 52.

17   For O'Mahony's and Healy's testimonies, see 'Outrages on Irish Women', *Irish Bulletin*, 14 April 1921; for Kelly's account, see 'We Have Done Nothing to Them', *Irish Bulletin*, 4 May 1921.

18   Marie Coleman, *The Irish Revolution, 1916–1923* (Abingdon: Routledge, 2013), p. 93; Clark, *Everyday Violence in the Irish Civil War*, p. 192.

19   Available at Alfred O'Rahilly Papers, University College Cork, Boole Library. Thanks to Ciara Hyland, director of *Cogadh ar Mhná* (TG4/RTÉ, 2020), for sharing this information. For a reference to Healy see Séamus Fitzgerald, BMH WS 1737, 24 June 1958, p. 30.

20 A statement from Nellie O'Mahony dated 25 January 1921 suggests more severe mistreatment than the published testimony in the *Irish Bulletin*. In the published statement, Nellie recounts that an armed Auxiliary Cadet raised her nightdress 'above my waist and kept it in that position for several minutes. All this time he was going through the actions of searching me, putting his hand under the blouse and all round my body'. However, in this other statement, Nellie claims that the cadet 'forced' her to take off her nightdress and 'kept me *naked* about 10 minutes while searching me' (my emphasis). 'Letter from 1st Southern Division IRA to General Headquarters IRA Society of Irish Revolutionary History and Militaria', Society of Irish Revolutionary History and Militaria, 12 April 2019. Available at: https://sirhm.com/2019/04/12/letter-from-1st-southern-division-ira-to-general-headquarters-ira/ (accessed 20 August 2020).

21 Earner-Byrne, 'The Rape of Mary M', p. 86.

22 Dara Kay Cohen, *Rape During Civil War* (Ithaca, NY: University Press, 2016), p. 10; Sielke, *Reading Rape*, p. 8.

23 See Kim Murphy, *I Had Rather Die: Rape in the Civil War* (Batesville, VA: Coachlight Press, 2014).

24 See Sonja Maria Hedgepeth and Rochelle G. Saidel (ed.), *Sexual Violence Against Jewish Women During the Holocaust* (Lebanon, NH: University Press of New England, 2010); see Maud Joly, 'Las Violencias Sexuadas de la Guerra Civil Española: Paradigma para una Lectura Cultural del Conflicto', *Historia Social*, no. 61 (2008), pp. 89–107.

25 Kathleen Clarke, *Revolutionary Woman: Kathleen Clarke, 1878–1972: An Autobiography*, edited by Helen Litton (Dublin: O'Brien Press, 1991), p. 90.

26 Clarke, *Revolutionary Woman*, p. 90. See also Kristine A. Byron, *Women, Revolution, and Autobiographical Writing in the Twentieth Century: Writing History, Writing the Self* (New York: Edwin Mellen, 2007).

27 McAtackney, 'Gender, Incarceration and Power Relations during the Irish Civil War (1922–1923)', p. 56.

28 Gina Herrmann, '"They Didn't Rape Me": Traces of Gendered Violence and Sexual Injury in the Testimonies of Spanish Republican Women Survivors of the Franco Dictatorship', in Nanci Adler and Selma Leydesdorff (eds), *Tapestry of Memory: Evidence and Testimony in Life-Story Narrative* (New Brunswick, NJ: Transaction, 2013), p. 84, p. 93.

29 Peg Broderick-Nicholson, BMH WS 1682, 27 September 1957, p. 4.

30 Eithne Coyle, BMH WS 750, 10 Mí na Samhna 1952, p. 5.

31 Ibid., p. 20; Letter from Frank Simons, 26 November 1945, Eithne O'Donnell, MSPC MAI MSP34REF60256.

32 'Donegal Amazon's Exploit', *The Freeman's Journal*, 27 April 1922, p. 2; Lucy Noakes, '"A Disgrace to the Country They Belong to": The Sexualisation of Female Soldiers in First World War Britain', *Revue LISA/LISA e-Journal*, vol. VI – n°4 (September 2008). Available at: https://doi.org/10.4000/lisa.951 (accessed 20 August 2020).

33 Eithne Coyle, BMH WS 750, 10 Mí na Samhna 1952; Eithne Coyle, 'Reminiscences of Eithne O'Donnell (née Coyle)', 12 July 1972 [unpublished memoir], Kilmainham Gaol Archive, 20MS-1B33-19. UCD holds both a handwritten and typed version of this memoir, 'Manuscript draft and typescript accounts by Eithne Coyle', UCDA P61/2. The Eithne Coyle O'Donnell papers catalogue (UCDA P61) suggests that the memoir may be from the 1940s, given, perhaps, that the narrative refers to Coyle's activities until her resignation from

Cumann na mBan in 1941. However, given the memoir is written in biro pen, it may be from a later period. For sake of clarity, I refer here to the '1972 memoir' as the version of the memoir held in Kilmainham was signed by Coyle on that date.

34   Coyle, 'Reminiscences', p. 15.

35   Coyle, BMH WS 750, p. 14.

36   Ibid., p. 18.

37   Coyle, 'Reminiscences', p. 15. See also MSPC MSP34REF60256. In her statement to the pension board (circa 1945), Coyle does not mention the presentation of the revolver by the IRA and mentions just one attack at Clady.

38   Coyle, BMH WS 750, p. 20.

39   Coyle, 'Reminiscences', p. 18.

40   Coyle, BMH WS 750, p. 6.

41   Ibid.

42   Coyle, 'Reminiscences', p. 5.

43   Ibid.

44   Ibid., p. 7.

45   Diarmaid Ferriter, *Occasions of Sin: Sex and Society in Modern Ireland* (London: Profile Books, 2010), p. 95.

46   Cited in Ferriter, *Occasions of Sin*, p. 96; Foster, *Vivid Faces*, p. 116. The 'moral rearmament' of the IRA is illustrated in a number of studies by citing the following quote from Todd Andrews (with ellipsis): 'We didn't drink. We respected women and [...] knew nothing about them.' However, the full quote is: 'We didn't drink. We respected women and, *except for the amorous Earle*, knew nothing about them.' The reference to 'the amorous Earle', surely troubles the revolutionaries' supposed sexual innocence. Tom Garvin, *Nationalist Revolutionaries in Ireland 1858–1928: Patriots, Priests and the Roots of the Irish Revolution* (Oxford: Clarendon Press, 1987), p. 68; Maria Luddy, *Prostitution and Irish Society, 1800–1940* (Cambridge: Cambridge University Press, 2007), p. 2.

47   Clark, 'Violence against Women', p. 85.

48   Louise Ryan, '"In the Line of Fire": Representations of Women and War (1919–1923) through the Writings of Republican Men', in Ryan and Ward (eds), *Irish Women and Nationalism*, p. 58.

49   Michael Cronin, *Impure Thoughts: Sexuality, Catholicism and Literature in Twentieth-Century Ireland* (Manchester: Manchester University Press, 2012), pp. 4–5.

50   Foster, *Vivid Faces*, p. 115.

51   Nicholas Allen, 'Reading Revolutions, 1922–39', in Clare Hutton and Patrick Walsh (eds), *The Oxford History of the Irish Book. Volume V: The Irish Book in English, 1891–2000* (Oxford: Oxford University Press, 2011), p. 95.

52   Carty, *The Irish Volunteer*, p. 56.

53   Carty, *Legion of the Rearguard*, p. 111; Mulloy, *Jackets Green*, p. 28.

54   Andrews, *Dublin Made Me*, p. 299.

55   Clark, 'Violence against Women', p. 75, pp. 84–5.

56   Foster, *The Irish Civil War and Society*, p. 61.

57   See Timothy Hanson Ellis, 'Visual Culture and Visuality in the Politics of the Irish Free State, 1921–1939' (unpublished PhD thesis, Teesside University, 2020).

58   Foster, *The Irish Civil War*, p. 61.

59   Clark, 'Violence against Women', p. 84.

60 Des Hickey, 'How Colonels Almost Took Over!', *Sunday Independent*, 22 September 1974, p. 13.

61 Una Crowley and Rob Kitchin, 'Producing "Decent Girls": Governmentality and the Moral Geographies of Sexual Conduct in Ireland (1922–1937)', *Gender, Place and Culture* 15, no. 4 (2008), p. 364.

62 John Borgonovo, '"Exercising a Close Vigilance over Their Daughters": Cork Women, American Sailors, and Catholic Vigilantes, 1917–18', *Irish Historical Studies* 38, no. 149 (2012), p. 93.

63 Ibid.

64 Dan Breen, BMH WS 1739, 13 February 1959, p. 36.

65 Conner, *Shake Hands with the Devil*, p. 10.

66 Ibid.

67 Ibid., p. 77.

68 Ibid., p. 10.

69 In the 1959 film version, the character of Kitty Brady is presented as a barmaid rather than a prostitute. However, the author refused to change passages in the novel for the sake of making it 'acceptable to the Irish censor' on its serialisation in the Irish edition of the *Sunday Dispatch*. He further lamented that '[s]everal Irish people, including those who should know better, have tried to tell me that no such character existed in Ireland. I disagree.' Rearden Conner, 'Shake Hands With the Devil [Letter to the Editor]', *The Irish Times*, 27 May 1959, p. 7.

70 Rearden Conner, *A Plain Tale from the Bogs* (London: J. Miles, 1937), p. 241.

71 Ernest Boyd, 'Joyce and the New Irish Writers', *Current History (1916–1940)* 39, no. 6 (1934), p. 704.

72 Dorothy Elliott, 'A Novel of the Irish Civil War Days Literary Guild Selection for February', *The Post-Crescent*, 3 February 1934, p. 13.

73 Patrick Maume, 'Louis d'Alton', *Dictionary of Irish Biography*.

74 *El Paso Times*, 12 June 1938, p. 6.

75 Louis d'Alton, *Death is So Fair* (London: William Heinemann, 1936), p. 119.

76 Ibid., p. 260.

77 Aodh de Blácam, 'As Others Wish to See Us', *The Irish Press*, 15 September 1936, p. 6. Aodh de Blácam (1890–1951) was the son of W. G. Blackham, a Newry-born Protestant MP. He was a member of the London Gaelic League, converted to Catholicism and was imprisoned for his Sinn Féin activism during the struggle for independence. A prolific journalist, he was a strong voice for Catholic-nationalist opinion throughout the 1930s.

78 Jason Crouthamel, 'Male Sexuality and Psychological Trauma: Soldiers and Sexual Disorder in World War I and Weimar Germany', *Journal of the History of Sexuality* 17, no. 1 (2008), pp. 62–3.

79 Ibid., p. 61.

80 *The Irish Book Lover*, January 1936–December 1937, p. 91; *Montrose Review (Scotland)*, 19 June 1936.

81 Jake Wynne, *Ugly Brew* (London: Chatto & Windus, 1936).

82 Letter from Jake Wynne to John Green (literary agent), 3 June 1936, Chatto and Windus Archive, University of Reading, CW_67-17.

83 'The "Career" of a Gunman', *Belfast Newsletter*, 13 May 1937, p. 13.

84 *The Observer*, 21 June 1936, p. 6.

85   Seán O'Faoláin, 'Book Section', *Ireland To-day*, June 1936, p. 72.

86   Wynne, *Ugly Brew*, p. 4.

87   Ibid., p. 106.

88   Ibid., p. 12.

89   Ibid.

90   Anthony Keating, 'Sexual Crime in the Irish Free State 1922–33: Its Nature, Extent and Reporting', *Irish Studies Review* 20, no. 2 (May 2012), pp. 135–55.

91   Wynne, *Ugly Brew*, p. 296.

92   Ibid., p. 306.

93   Ibid., p. 308.

94   Ibid., p. 310.

95   Cited in Allen, 'Reading Revolutions, 1922–39', p. 95.

96   'What Dublin Is Reading', *The Irish Times*, 11 July 1936, p. 7.

97   Wynne, *Ugly Brew*, p. 307.

98   Mulloy, *Jackets Green*, p. 307.

99   Cited in Philip Howell, 'Venereal Disease and the Politics of Prostitution in the Irish Free State', *Irish Historical Studies* 33, no. 131 (2003), p. 331.

100 Wynne, *Ugly Brew*, p. 312.

101 Mulloy, *Jackets Green*, p. 203.

102 Larry Nelson, Ernie O'Malley Interview, UCDA, P17b/89. Thanks to Aaron Ó Maonaigh for sharing this.

103 Patrick McLogan, 'Interview', in Síobhra Aiken et al. (eds), *The Men Will Talk to Me: Ernie O'Malley's Interviews with the Northern Divisions* (Dublin: Merrion Press, 2018), p. 17.

104 Cited in Philip Howell, 'Venereal Disease', p. 331.

105 Wynne, *Ugly Brew*, p. 312.

106 Mulloy, *Jackets Green*, p. 203.

107 'Jackets Green, Typescript of a Novel'.

108 Mulloy, *Jackets Green*, p. 308.

109 Byrne, 'Keeping Company with the Enemy', p. 1.

110 Ryan, '"Drunken Tans"', p. 15; 'Girls Painted Over', *Irish Independent*, 14 September 1922, p. 5; *Belfast Newsletter*, 14 September 1922, p. 5. See also letter from Eta Horgan to Sheila Humphreys *c.* 1968, Sheila Humphreys Papers, UCDA, 106/1389; Kenna, *Facts and Figures of the Belfast Pogrom 1920–1922*, p. 146.

111 Machnik-Kekesi, 'Gendering Bodies', p. 64.

112 Ernie O'Malley, 'High Seas Piracy', Ernie O'Malley Papers, Archives of Irish America #060, Box 2, Folder 15, NYUL. My thanks to Cormac O'Malley for sharing a typed version of this story.

113 Máirtín Ó Cadhain, *Barbed Wire* (Baile Átha Cliath: Coiscéim, 2002), p. 433.

114 Emma V. Miller, 'Trauma and Sexual Violence', in J. Roger Kurtz (ed.), *Trauma and Literature* (Cambridge: Cambridge University Press, 2018), p. 227.

115 Monk Gibbons, 'Introduction', in Michael Farrell, *Thy Tears Might Cease* (New York: Knopf, 1964), p. xv.

116 Farrell, *Thy Tears Might Cease*, p. 418.

117 d'Alton, *Death is So Fair*, pp. 185–6.

118 Colm Ó Gaora, 'An Díoghaltas', in *As na Ceithre h-Áirdibh: Cnuasach Gearr-scéal* (Baile Átha Cliath: Oifig an tSoláthair, 1938); O'Leary, *Gaelic Prose in the Irish Free State*, p. 323.

119 d'Alton, *Death is So Fair*, p. 201.

120 Ibid., p. 202.

121 Ibid.

122 Machnik-Kekesi, 'Gendering Bodies', p. 61.

123 Elizabeth Bowen, *The Last September* (Constable, 1929 [2015]), p. 61.

124 O'Leary, 'The Irish Renaissance', p. 245.

125 Tomás Bairéad, *Gan Baisteadh* (Baile Átha Cliath: Sáirséal agus Dill, 1972), p. 154.

126 Tomás Bairéad, *An Geall a Briseadh* (Baile Átha Cliath: Oifig Díolta Foillseacháin Rialtais, 1938), p. 129.

127 Ibid., p. 138.

128 Aingeal Ní Chualáin (ed.), 'Tomás Bairéad, 1893–1973', *Tomás Bairéad: Rogha Scéalta* (Conamara: Cló Iar-Chonnacht, 2010), p. 18.

129 'Award for Irish Journalist: Stories in Gaelic', *Irish Independent*, 21 August 1939, p. 6.

130 'What Dublin is Reading', *The Irish Times*, 2 July 1938, p. 7.

131 Jim Phelan, *Green Volcano* (London: Peter Davies, 1938), p. 223.

132 Patrick Maume, 'Jim Phelan', *Dictionary of Irish Biography*, February 2016.

133 A. J. Lees, 'Jim Phelan's Liverpool Home', George Garrett Archive. Available at: https://www. georgegarrettarchive.co.uk/component/content/article/2-uncategorised/73-jim-phelan-s-liverpool-home.html (accessed 18 April 2020).

134 Jim Phelan, *The Name's Phelan: The First Part of the Autobiography of Jim Phelan* (Belfast: Blackstaff Press, 1948 [1993]), p. 121.

135 Ibid., p. 109.

136 George Orwell, 'Review of *Jail Journey* by Jim Phelan', *Horizon: A Review of Literature and Art* (London: Faber & Faber, 1940), reprinted in George Orwell, *The Complete Works of George Orwell: A Patriot After All, 1940–1941* (London: Secker & Warburg, 1998), p. 171.

137 Phelan, *Green Volcano*, p. 224.

138 Connolly, 'Towards a Further Understanding', p. 33.

139 Ryan, '"Drunken Tans"', p. 80.

140 Phelan, *Green Volcano*, p. 224.

141 Manning, *Mount Venus*, p. 6.

142 Noakes, '"A Disgrace to the Country They Belong To"' [online].

143 O'Faoláin, *Midsummer Night Madness: And Other Stories*, p. 166.

144 MacCall, *Gods in Motley*, p. 80.

145 Conner, *Shake Hands with the Devil*, p. 101.

146 Conner, *A Plain Tale from the Bogs*, p. 83.

147 *Donegal Democrat*, 20 November 1937, p. 9.

148 Carty, *Legion of the Rearguard*, pp. 7–8.

149 Phelan, *Green Volcano*, pp. 160–1.

150 Stuart, *The Coloured Dome*, p. 90.

151 Ibid., p. 136.

152 Ibid., p. 223.

153 Plunkett, *As the Fool*, p. 252; Liam O'Flaherty, *The Assassin* (London: J Cape, 1928), p. 37.

154 O'Flaherty, *The Martyr*, p. 148.

155 Mulloy, *Jackets Green*, p. 140.

156 Frank O'Connor, 'September Dawn', *Dublin Magazine*, vol. IV, no. 3, July 1929, pp. 7–20; Frank O'Connor, *Guests of the Nation* (London: Macmillan, 1931), p. 98.

157 O'Connor, *Guests of the Nation*, p. 97, p. 90.

158 Michael Brennan, *The War in Clare, 1911–1921: Personal Memoirs of the Irish War of Independence* (Dublin: Four Courts Press, 1980), p. 100, cited in Louise Ryan, 'In the Line of Fire', p. 51.

159 Síghle Bean Uí Dhonnchadha in Mac Eoin (ed.), *Survivors*, p. 345.

160 Broderick-Nicholson, BMH WS 1682, p. 5.

161 Cumann na mBan Nominal Rolls, MAI, MSPC, CMB/72.

162 O'Flaherty, *The Martyr*, p. 133.

163 Sharon Crozier-De Rosa, *Shame and the Anti-Feminist Backlash: Britain, Ireland and Australia, 1890–1920* (Abingdon: Routledge, 2017), p. 233.

164 Noakes, '"A Disgrace to the Country They Belong To"' [online].

165 Nicolas Allen, 'Frank O'Connor and Critical Memory', in Hilary Lennon (ed.), *Frank O'Connor: Critical Essays* (Dublin: Four Courts Press, 2007), p. 30.

166 Tadhg Ó Dúshláine, 'Scéal Úrscéil: *Fánaí*, Seán Óg Ó Caomhánaigh, 1927', *Léachtaí Cholm Cille*, 19 (1989), pp. 93–128.

167 Seán Óg Ó Caomhánaigh, *Fánaí* (Baile Átha Cliath: Oifig an tSoláthair, 1927 [1989]), p. 74.

168 Ó Dúshláine, 'Scéal Úrscéil', p. 124.

169 Seán Óg Ó Caomhánaigh, 'Dialann Phríosúin Sheáin a' Chóta', edited by Mícheál Ó Catháin (unpublished PhD thesis, NUI Maynooth, 2012), p. 60.

170 Ibid., p. 177.

171 Ibid., p. 105.

172 Ibid., p. 218.

173 Campbell, '*As I Was Among the Captives*', p. 10.

174 Ó Caomhánaigh, 'Dialann Phríosúin Sheáin a' Chóta', pp. 61–2.

175 Ibid., p. 118.

176 Ibid.

177 Ó Caomhánaigh, *Fánaí*, p. 15.

178 A., 'Recent Books in Irish: Two Novels and Some Short Stories', *The Irish Times*, 20 January 1928, p. 3.

179 S. A., 'A Hobo in Irish/ Public Funds and Private Censorship', *Irishman*, 18 February 1928, cited in Ó Dúshláine, 'Scéal Úrscéil', p. 119.

180 *Sinn Féin*, 22 July 1911, cited in Ó Dúshláine, 'Scéal Úrscéil', p. 104.

181 Anthony O'Connor, *He's Somewhere in There* (London: Foxgate, 1975), p. 74.

182 Ibid., p. 76.

183 Phelan, *Green Volcano*, p. 188.

184 Cohen, *Rape during Civil War*, p. 10.

185 O'Donnell, *The Knife*, pp. 164–5.

186 Ibid., p. 211.

187 P. C. Trimble, 'Review of *The Knife*', *The Irish Book Lover*, November/December 1930, p. 183.

188 Liam O'Flaherty, *Shame the Devil* (London: Grayson & Grayson, 1934), pp. 119–20.

189 Farquharson, 'Liam O'Flaherty's *The Martyr*', p. 379.

190 Wilbur Needham, 'Is This a Burlesque?', *The Los Angeles Times*, 25 June 1933, p. 29.

191 O'Flaherty, *The Martyr*, p. 181.

192 Ibid., pp. 181–2.

193   Ibid., p. 182.

194   Ibid., p. 183.

195   Diana Scully and Joseph Marolla, 'Convicted Rapists' Vocabulary of Motive: Excuses and Justifications', *Social Problems* 31, no. 5 (1984), p. 534.

196   O'Flaherty, *The Martyr*, p. 178.

197   Emy Koopman, 'Ethical Challenges When Reading Aesthetic Rape Scenes', in Nate Hinerman and Matthew Lewis Sutton (eds), *On Suffering: An Interdisciplinary Dialogue on Narrative and Suffering* (Leiden: Brill, 2020), p. 83.

198   *New York Herald Tribune*, Books, vol. 9, iss. 2, 1933.

199   Phelan, *Green Volcano*, p. 63.

200   See Ryan, '"Drunken Tans"', p. 76.

201   Meg Samuelson, 'The Disfigured Body of the Female Guerrilla: (De)Militarization, Sexual Violence, and Redomestication in Zoë Wicomb's *David's Story*', *Signs* 32, no. 4 (2007), p. 833.

202   Phelan, *Green Volcano*, p. 63.

203   Ibid., p. 42.

204   Ibid., p. 46.

205   Phelan, *The Name's Phelan*, p. 268.

206   F[rancis] MacM[anus], 'Review of *The Troubled House; Green Volcano*, by Rosamond Jacob and Jim Phelan', *The Irish Monthly*, vol. 66, no. 785, 1938, pp. 805–6.

207   Forrest Reid, 'Fiction', *The Spectator*, 2 September 1938, p. 30.

208   'New Novels', *The Irish Times*, 17 September 1938, p. 7.

209   Phelan, *Green Volcano*, p. 95.

210   Ibid., p. 96.

211   Nicola Henry, *War and Rape: Law, Memory, and Justice* (Abingdon: Routledge, 2011), p. 117.

212   See Mary Kostsonouris, *Retreat from Revolution: The Dáil Courts, 1920–24* (Dublin: Irish Academic Press, 1994).

213   See Byrne, 'Keeping Company with the Enemy'; Connolly, 'Sexual Violence in the Irish Civil War', pp. 11–14.

214   Phelan, *Green Volcano*, p. 47.

215   Ibid., p. 49.

216   Ibid., p. 107.

217   Ibid., p. 224.

218   Ibid.

219   Joanna Bourke, 'Sexual Violence, Bodily Pain, and Trauma: A History', *Theory, Culture & Society* 29, no. 3 (May 2012), pp. 25–31.

220   Ibid., p. 36.

221   O'Flaherty, *The Martyr*, pp. 181–2.

222   Macreadie, 'Politicizing the Personal', p. 10.

223   Phelan, *Green Volcano*, p. 172.

224   'In one prison in the southwest castration was regularly employed as a method of torture', James Mackay, *Michael Collins: A Life* (Edinburgh: Mainstream Publishing Company, 1996), p. 266. 'In Kerry […] interrogations were conducted with the aid of a hammer and men went mad or were found to be castrated', Tim Pat Coogan, *The IRA* (London: Palgrave Macmillan 2002), p. 40.

225   Lady Gregory, *Lady Gregory's Journals: Book One to Twenty-Nine, 10 October 1916–24 February 1925* (Oxford: Oxford University Press, 1978), p. 276.

226   Ó Caomhánach exploits his description of the men's showering to assert his own masculinity, contending: 'níor bheag é mo bhród asam féin ar feicsint suim gach aon'ne im chneas geal agus im dheunamh. B'é mé an t-aon duine ar ár líon nár órduig an dochtúir do ball áirighthe do bhearradh.' [I was proud of myself when I saw everyone's interest in my bright skin and appearance. I was the only one of us who the doctor didn't order to shave a certain part], 'Dialann Phríosúin Sheáin a' Chóta', p. 24.

227   Mulloy, *Jackets Green*, p. 33.

228   Ibid., p. 291.

229   James M. Cahalan, *Great Hatred, Little Room: The Irish Historical Novel* (Syracuse, NY: Syracuse University Press, 1983), p. 110.

230   J. J. H., 'Review of Dermot Barry's *Tom Creagan: A Novel*', *The Irish Book Lover*, vol. XIX, September–October 1931, pp. 149–50.

231   Dermot Barry, *Tom Creagan: A Novel* (Dublin: At the Sign of the Three Candles, 1931), p. 51.

232   Ibid., p. 173.

233   Ibid., p. 186.

234   *The Age* (Melbourne), 5 December 1931, p. 4.

235   D. 'Tales of the Troubles', *The Guardian*, 24 December 1931, p. 5.

236   Tadhg Gahan, MSPC, MSP34REF1127.

237   Ibid., 8 June 1928.

238   Ibid., 9 June 1928.

239   Denis Barry, 'New Hope and Remembrance', *Capuchin Annual* 1942, p. 196.

240   Barry, *Tom Creagan*, p. 136.

Chapter 4

1   Nicola Ryan, 'Elizabeth Brennan: I'm Only Happy When I'm Writing', *Sligo Champion*, 29 June 1984, p. 12.

2   'A Light Romance from the Housewife in Clondalkin', *Sunday Independent*, 31 March 1963, p. 9.

3   *Irish Examiner*, 23 February 1939, p. 7.

4   Eilish Dolan was also known as Eily Horan, Eily O'Horan and Elizabeth Brennan. For the purpose of clarity, I refer to Dolan by her maiden name throughout this chapter. Robert P. Roddie, 'Pádraig and Eily O'Horan: A Story of Rebellion and Redemption', *Dublin Historical Record* 55, no. 1 (2002), pp. 75–87; Pat Dolan and Michael Dolan, 'Our Aunt Eilish's Untold Story of Rebellion, Romance and Religion', in Ciara Boylan, Sarah-Anne Buckley and Pat Dolan (eds), *Family Histories of the Irish Revolution* (Dublin: Four Courts Press, 2018), pp. 37–48.

5   Eily Horan, *Through the Gates of Babylon: The Story of a Conversion* (London: Christian Irishman, 1932), p. 34.

6   Eily Horan, *No More Foreigners. Impressions of a Spiritual Pilgrimage* (London: Lutterworth Press, 1935), p. 32. I am grateful to Pat and Michael Dolan for their collaboration on research for this chapter.

7   Horan, *Through the Gates*, p. 55.

8   'Methodist Clergyman who Fought in 1916', *Fermanagh Herald*, 3 December 1927, p. 9.

9   Horan, 'Hills of Morning', *Irish Christian Advocate*, 28 September 1928, p. 469.

10   P. K. Horan, 'An IRA Lad at Cliff College', *Methodist Magazine*, 1927.

11   Horan, *Through the Gates*, p. 61.

12   *Ballymena Observer*, 18 May 1928.

13   Dolan's conversion testimonies were published under the name: Horan, *Through the Gates of Babylon* and Horan, *No More Foreigners*. Her short stories appeared in various literary journals under the name Eily O'Horan, including *Chambers's Journal*, *My Garden*, *The Bell*, *Catholic Magazine*, *Irish Examiner*, *Irish Weekly Independent* and *The Irish Home*. Her later novels, published under the name Elizabeth Brennan, include: *His Glamorous Cousin* (London: Hale, 1963); *Her Lucky Mistake* (London: Hale, 1966); *Retreat from Love* (London: Hale, 1967); *Love in the Glade* (London: Hale, 1968); *Patrick's Woman* (London: Hale, 1969); *Mountain of Desire* (London: Hale, 1970); *Innocent in Eden* (London: Hale, 1971); *No Roses for Jo* (London: Hale, 1972); *Love's Loom* (London: Hale, 1973); *A Girl Called Debbie* (London: Hale, 1975); *Sweet Love of Youth* (London: Hale, 1978); *Girl on an Island* (London: Hale, 1984). It is likely that she wrote under other pen names also.

14   *The Sligo Champion*, 29 June 1984, p. 12; these are the words of O'Horan's fictional surrogate, Páraic Morton: P. K. Horan, 'The Internment Camp', *Irish Christian Advocate*, 17 August 1928, p. 398.

15   Paul Ilie, *Literature and Inner Exile: Authoritarian Spain, 1939-1975* (Baltimore, MD: Johns Hopkins University Press, 1980), p. 2.

16   Ryan, *Remembering Sion*, p. 276.

17   Phelan, *Green Volcano*, p. 280.

18   Wynne, *Ugly Brew*, p. 328.

19   Seán O'Faoláin, 'Fiction', *Ireland To-day*, vol. 1, no. 2, July 1936, p. 72.

20   Seán O'Faoláin, 'Love Among the Irish', *Life*, 16 March 1953, p. 140.

21   See Brian Hanley, *The IRA, 1926–1936* (Dublin: Four Courts Press, 2002); Brian Hanley, 'Irish Republicans in Interwar New York', *IJAS Online*, no. 1 (2009), pp. 48–61; Gavin Foster, '"No 'Wild Geese' This Time"?: IRA Emigration after the Irish Civil War', *Éire-Ireland* 47, no. 1 (2012); Gavin Wilk, *Transatlantic Defiance: The Militant Irish Republican Movement in America, 1923–45* (Manchester: Manchester University Press, 2014); Síobhra Aiken, '"Sinn Féin Permits ... in the Heels of Their Shoes": Cumann na mBan Emigrants and Transatlantic Revolutionary Exchange'. *Irish Historical Studies* 44, no. 165 (May 2020), pp. 106–30.

22   Robert Lynch, *The Partition of Ireland: 1918–1925* (Cambridge: Cambridge University Press, 2019), p. 169.

23   Ibid., p. 196.

24   See Peter Leary, *Unapproved Routes: Histories of the Irish Border, 1922–1972* (Oxford: Oxford University Press, 2016); Eunan O'Halpin, 'Ulster Says Go: The Forgotten Exodus of Northern Nationalists', *The Irish Times*, 17 June 2015.

25   See Eamon Phoenix, *Northern Nationalism: Nationalist Politics, Partition and the Catholic Minority in Northern Ireland, 1890–1940* (Belfast: Ulster Historical Foundation, 1994), p. 251.

26   Lynch, *The Partition of Ireland*, p. 161.

27   See Foster, 'No Wild Geese', p. 110.

28   Halbwachs, *On Collective Memory*; Beiner, *Forgetful Remembrance*, p. 124.

29   Proinsias Mac Aonghusa, 'Forty-seven Years Later, Proinsias Mac Aonghusa Recalls the Ladies' Jail Journal – Kilmainham 1923', *The Irish Press*, 20 January 1971, p. 8.

30   On Bridie Halpin, see Íde B. O'Carroll, *Models for Movers: Irish Women's Emigration to America* (Cork: Attic Press, 1990); McCoole, *No Ordinary Women*.

31   Cited in Aisling Ní Dhonnchadha and Máirín Nic Eoin, 'Ar an gCoigríoch: Migration and Identity in Twentieth-Century and Contemporary Irish-Language Literature', *The Irish Review*, 44 (2012), p. 67.

32   Ó Grianna claims in his memoirs, published in 1945, that he had forgotten most of the men with whom he was imprisoned and that he would hardly recognise one out of one hundred of them. His short stories written in English in the 1960s refer more directly to the civil war. Séamus Ó Grianna, *Saoghal Corrach* (Baile Átha Cliath: An Press Náisiúnta, 1945), p. 178. See Nollaig Mac Congáil, 'Scéalta Béarla Mháire', *Feasta*, Meitheamh & Iúil 2002; Séamus Ó Grianna, Nollaig Mac Congáil (ed.), *The Sea's Revenge and Other Stories* (Cork: Mercier, 2003).

33   See Máirín Nic Eoin, *Trén bhFearann Breac: An Díláithriú Cultúir agus Nualitríocht na Gaeilge* (Baile Átha Cliath: Cois Life, 2005), p. 153.

34   *Irish Independent*, 6 August 1928, p. 8. Kathleen O'Brennan, *Full Measure: A Play in Three Acts*, NLI Ms 15,601.

35   O'Brennan, *Full Measure*.

36   Garrett O'Driscoll, 'Fair Day', *Ireland To-day*, vol. II, no. 8, August 1937, p. 57.

37   Abbey Theatre Minute Book, 10 February 1939, p. 198.

38   Máirín Cregan, 'Curlew's Call', *Capuchin Annual* 1940, pp. 177–89.

39   AIA#060, Box 2, Folder 15, NYU Library. Thanks to Cormac O'Malley for sharing this.

40   Letter to Dorothy Macardle, 30 November 1923, NAI. Talbot Press Collection, 1048/1/81.

41   Kerby A. Miller, *Emigrants and Exiles: Ireland and the Irish Exodus to North America* (Oxford: Oxford University Press, 1985).

42   Jennifer Redmond, *Moving Histories: Irish Women's Emigration to Britain from Independence to Republic* (Oxford: Oxford University Press, 2019), p. 2.

43   Angela McCarthy, *Personal Narratives of Irish and Scottish Migration, 1921–65: 'For Spirit and Adventure'* (Manchester: Manchester University Press, 2007), p. 45.

44   Foster, 'No Wild Geese', p. 117.

45   Jeremiah Murphy, *When Youth Was Mine – A Memoir of Kerry 1902–1925* (Dublin: Mentor Books, 1998 [2018]), p. 316.

46   O'Connor, *Tomorrow Was Another Day*, p. 129.

47   Comerford, *My Kilkenny Days*, p. 948.

48   Patrick G. Daly, BMH WS 814, 21 March 1953.

49   'The Irish Girl Emigrant', *Fermanagh Herald*, 20 August 1921. See Aiken, '"Sinn Féin Permits … in the Heels of Their Shoes".

50   *Irish Independent*, 'To Work Openly – Mr. De Valera's Attitude', 24 July 1923; UCDA Aiken Papers, PiO4/i326(i), both cited in Foster, 'No Wild Geese', p. 1, p. 105.

51   *United Irishman*, 14 April 1923, cited in Foster, 'No Wild Geese', p. 116, fn 119.

52   The ditty concludes with the lines 'While Tim [Healy] sits as gay as a cock on the gate, representing King George in the Irish Free State', cited in Edward O'Malley, *Memories of a Mayoman* (Baile Átha Cliath: Foilseacháin Náisiúnta Teoranta, 1981), p. 67.

53 Elizabeth Connor, *Dead Star's Light* (London: Methuen & Company, 1938), p. 169.

54 Frank O'Connor, *Dutch Interior* (London: Macmillan, 1940), p. 159.

55 Seán O'Faoláin, *Come Back to Erin* (New York: Viking Press, 1940), p. 183.

56 For example, Michel Foucault, in his study of *Madness and Civilization*, identified 'the madman' as 'the Passenger par excellence that is, the prisoner of the passage'. Michel Foucault, *Madness and Civilization: A History of Insanity in the Age of Reason* (New York: Vintage Books, 1988), p. 11. This is also reflected in the Irish mythological figure of Suibhne mac Colmáin, referred to as Mad Sweeney.

57 *Irish Daily Independent*, 21 September 1904, p. 2; 'Emigration: A Cause of Lunacy', *Connacht Tribune*, 31 October 1925, p. 9.

58 See Gavin Wilk, '"No Hope for Him Unless He Can Be Got Out of the Country": Disabled Irish Republicans in America, 1922–1935', *New Hibernia Review / Iris Éireannach Nua* 18, no. 1 (2014), pp. 106–19.

59 Mary Ellen Scullen, MSP34REF52788, 27 November 1936.

60 Madelaine Hron, 'The Trauma of Displacement', in J. Roger Kurtz (ed.), *Trauma and Literature* (Cambridge: Cambridge University Press, 2018), p. 288.

61 Letter from Dr Frank Murray, 19 September 1934, Ernie O'Malley, MSPC, 34A6, DP 2760.

62 LaCapra, *Writing History, Writing Trauma*, p. 23.

63 'A Hundred Books Received', *Books Ireland*, no. 137 (1989), p. 226.

64 J. F. O'Connor, *Irish Civil War Exile* (New York: Vantage Press, 1989), p. 14.

65 Ibid., p. 21, p. 22, p. 175.

66 'London Notes and Comments', *Yorkshire Post and Leeds Intelligencer*, 20 January 1939, p. 8.

67 O'Horan claimed to be a founding member. Other early members included the Hon. George Bellew, Somerset Herald, Mr T. B. Butler, Mr Robin Flower, Mr Theobald Matthew, Sir Michael O'Dwyer, John O'Reilly, Mr Aubrey Toppin and Mr Herbert Wood. *Sunderland Daily Echo and Shipping Gazette*, 13 November 1936; 'Tracing Lost Records', *Belfast Telegraph*, Friday 23 July 1937; 'London Notes and Comment', *Yorkshire Post and Leeds Intelligencer*, 20 January 1939.

68 'Our London Letter', *Irish Independent*, 17 January 1938, p. 7.

69 Horan, 'The Attack', *Irish Christian Advocate*, 27 January 1928, p. 44.

70 Horan, 'The Internment Camp', *Irish Christian Advocate*, 17 August 1928, p. 398.

71 Horan, 'Letter', *Irish Christian Advocate*, 9 November 1928, p. 539.

72 Pádraig Kevin Horan, *In the Crown of a Stranger. An Irish Historical Review, with Special Reference to the Papacy* (Belfast: Christian Irishman, 1933), p. 84.

73 My thanks to Robin P. Roddie of the Methodist Historical Society of Ireland for providing me with transcribed copies of these articles.

74 Pádraig Kevin Horan, *Eyes of My Love: Twenty Poems* (London: Stockwell, 1924); Pádraig O'Horan, *Roadways of the Heart: Poems* (London: Fortune Press, 1943); Pádraig O'Horan, *The Bright-winged Piper: Poems* (London: Fortune Press, 1945); Pádraig O'Horan, *The Proud and Lovely: Poems* (London: Fortune Press, 1946); Pádraig O'Horan, *Wheat and a Rose: Poems* (London: Fortune Press, 1946); Pádraig O'Horan, *Gabriel Was a Troubadour: Poems of the Nativity* (London: A. R. Mowbray, 1948).

75 'A Sweet Gaelic Singer: Poetess of Nationality and Culture', *Irish Examiner*, 16 April 1938, p. 13.

76 Ibid.

77 P. K. O'Horan, 'St. Patrick, First of the Exiles', St Patrick's Day Number, *The Cork Examiner*, 1937; P. K. O'Horan, 'St. Patrick's Sceptred Isle', St Patrick's Day Number, *Cork Weekly Examiner*, 1938; O'Horan, 'Patrick at Tara', *The Bright-winged Piper. Poems*, p. 21.

78 P. K. O'Horan, 'Saintly Exile and Historic Foundation – Columcille of Iona', *The Cork Examiner*, 3 July 1937.

79 Horan, 'Hills of Morning', *Irish Christian Advocate*, 5 October 1928, p. 479.

80 Horan, *No More Foreigners*, p. 42.

81 *Belfast Newsletter*, 22 March 1929, p. 7; Roddie, 'Pádraig and Eily O'Horan', p. 85.

82 Ilie, *Literature and Inner Exile*, p. 14.

83 Seán O'Faoláin, 'Irish Letters: To-day and To-morrow', *The Fortnightly* 138, September 1935, p. 370, cited in Delaney, *Seán O'Faoláin: Literature, Inheritance and the 1930s*, p. 31.

84 Edward W. Said, *Reflections on Exile and Other Essays* (Cambridge, MA: Harvard University Press, 2000), p. 176.

85 Horan, 'The Former Generation', *Irish Christian Advocate*, 30 December 1927, p. 1287.

86 *Western People*, 13 May 1939, p. 7; Catherine W. Reilly (ed.), *English Poetry of the Second World War: A Biobibliography* (Boston, MA: G. K. Hall, 1986), p. 247; *The Cork Examiner*, 2 December 1938, p. 1.

87 Horan, 'Prisoners in Portobello: An Incident from the Civil War in Ireland', *Methodist Magazine*, 1928, pp. 434–8; Horan, 'Christmas in Prison: An Incident from Civil War in Ireland', *Methodist Magazine*, 1927, pp. 720–4.

88 See Horan, 'The Former Generation', *Irish Christian Advocate*, 23 December 1927, p. 1255.

89 These are the words of Páraic Morton. Horan, 'Chapter the Tenth', *Irish Christian Advocate*, 18 May 1928, p. 221.

90 Horan, 'Christmas in Prison', pp. 720–4.

91 Horan, 'The Former Generation', *Irish Christian Advocate*, 2 December 1927.

92 Ibid.

93 Ibid.

94 Horan, 'When the Sun Arose', *Irish Christian Advocate*, 25 November 1927.

95 Dolan recalls seeing O'Casey plays in the Abbey. 'Elizabeth Brennan – Prolific Novelist', *Western People*, 30 October 1976, p. 20.

96 Horan, 'Thro' Red Days', *Irish Christian Advocate*, 16 March 1928, p. 125.

97 Seán O'Casey, *Two Plays: Juno and the Paycock; The Shadow of a Gunman* (London: Macmillan, 1925), p. 32

98 Horan, 'Thro' Red Days', *Irish Christian Advocate*, 18 May 1928, p. 238.

99 Ibid.

100 Ibid.

101 *Irish Independent*, 9 February 1922, p. 6.

102 This is a reference to Pearse's poem 'The Wayfarer'. Horan, 'The Surrender', *Irish Christian Advocate*, 23 March 1928, p. 137.

103 Horan, 'Prisoners in Portobello: An Incident from the Civil War in Ireland', *Methodist Magazine*, 1928, pp. 434–8.

104 Horan, 'Chapter the Tenth', *Irish Christian Advocate*, 11 May 1928, p. 221.

105 Horan, 'The Flail of Death', *Methodist Magazine*, 1927, pp. 617–21.

106 Ibid.

107 *Fermanagh Herald*, 3 December 1927, p. 9.

108 See Kieran Glennon, *From Pogrom to Civil War: Tom Glennon and the Belfast IRA* (Cork: Mercier Press, 2013).

109 Margaret Ward, 'Gendered Memories and Belfast Cumann na mBan, 1917–1922', in Linda Connolly (ed.), *Women and the Irish Revolution* (Dublin: Irish Academic Press, 2020), pp. 47–67.

110 Michael McLaverty, *Call My Brother Back: A Novel* (London: Longmans, Green & Co., 1939 [1970]), p. 215.

111 O'Malley, *The Singing Flame*, p. 75.

112 Lynch, *The Partition of Ireland*, p. 180.

113 Ernie O'Malley, 'Admirals for a Day', Ref: Ernie O'Malley Papers, NYU Library, AIA#060, Box 1, Folder 4. My thanks to Cormac O'Malley for providing a typed copy of this story.

114 Horan, 'The Former Generation', *Irish Christian Advocate*, 2 December 1927.

115 Horan, 'Thro' Red Days', *Irish Christian Advocate*, 9 March 1928, p. 116.

116 'Former I.R.A. Man Rev. P. K. Horan and Some Facts from Irish History Converted in Prison', *Belfast Newsletter*, 24 January 1933.

117 Horan, 'Prisoners in Portobello', *Methodist Magazine*, 1928, pp. 434–8.

118 Horan, 'Christmas in Prison', pp. 720–4.

119 Horan, 'From a Prison Diary: Incidents of the Irish Civil War', *Methodist Magazine*, 1928, pp. 676–83.

120 Frank O'Connor, 'A Boy in Prison', *Life and Letters*, August 1934, p. 527.

121 Horan, 'Chapter the Tenth', *Irish Christian Advocate*, 1 June 1928, p. 262.

122 Horan, 'Chapter the Tenth', *Irish Christian Advocate*, 22 June 1928, p. 291.

123 Horan, 'The Internment Camp', *Irish Christian Advocate*, 10 August 1928, p. 387.

124 In his pamphlet *Crown of a Stranger*, Horan refers back to O'Donnell's reference in *The Gates Flew Open* that 'Cromwell is not dead; his spirit is tabernacled in Maynooth'. Horan remarks that though the association between the Puritan Cromwell and the Catholic Church might seem like a paradox, O'Donnell's account demonstrates that the 'Gael is fond of harking back to the past'. Horan, *In the Crown of a Stranger*, p. 27.

125 Letter from Jake Wynne to John Green (literary agent), 3 June 1936, Chatto and Windus Archive, University of Reading, CW_67-17.

126 'Former I.R.A. Man Rev. P. K. Horan', *Belfast Newsletter*, 24 January 1933.

127 Horan, 'The Rearguard Action'.

128 Horan, 'St. Patrick's Day in Ballygorman', *Irish Christian Advocate*, 14 September 1928, p. 441.

129 Dubliner Cornelius W. Whelan/Phelan joined the Irish Citizen's Army in 1913 and supported the Worker's Republican Party over the nationalist movement. Phelan shared O'Horan's interest in the Gaelic League. Census records suggest that his parents were both bilingual Irish-English speakers and that his father was a springmaker on the locomotives. Phelan relocated to Liverpool after the civil war and O'Horan notes that he brought up his family according to Protestant values.

130 O'Connor, 'Freedom', p. 109.

131 Sheila Hartnett, 'Once Upon a Time in Kenmare', *The Irish Press*, 31 December 1971, p. 17.

132 Horan, 'Behind the Barricades', *Irish Christian Advocate*, 24 February 1928, p. 91.

133 Horan, 'The Internment Camp', *Irish Christian Advocate*, 17 August 1928, p. 398.

134 Horan, 'Hills of Morning', *Irish Christian Advocate*, 5 October 1928, p. 479–80.

135 See Meg Jensen, *The Art and Science of Trauma and the Autobiographical: Negotiated Truths* (London: Palgrave Macmillan, 2019), p. 162.

136 O'Horan, 'O Where are Now the Patrons of the Poets?', *The Bright-winged Piper*, p. 17.

137 See *Sunday Independent*, 24 September 1922, p. 8; *Sunday Independent*, 7 May 1922, p. 3; *Sunday Independent*, 26 February 1922, p. 7.

138 Michael Walsh, *The Heart Remembers Morning* (Dublin: Talbot Press, 1931), p. 45.

139 Michael Walsh, 'Dublin Literary Memories', in Patrick Walsh (ed.) *Along My Father's Hills: A Miscellany by Michael and William Walsh* (Dublin: Colour Books, 1997), p. 12.

140 Members included poet Lilian Mary Nally, playwright M. M. Brennan, writer Máirín Ní Chinnéide and novelist Eilís Ní Riain, better known as Deirdre O'Brien.

141 Walsh, 'Dublin Literary Memories', p. 13.

142 Pádraig Ó hOdhráin, 'By Night', *Sunday Independent*, 10 December 1922, p. 9.

143 Pádraig Ó hOdhráin, 'Amhrán na Cásga', *Sunday Independent*, 1 October 1922, p. 8.

144 Pádraig Ó hOdhráin, 'Song of My Soul', *Sunday Independent*, 2 March 1924, p. 11.

145 *Nationalist and Leinster Times*, 5 July 1924, p. 6.

146 Pádraig O'Horan, 'I Walked Alone', *Roadways of the Heart*, p. 14.

147 O'Horan's poems were published in the *Irish Independent*, *The Irish Press*, *The Cork Examiner* and in English periodicals such as *Chambers's Journal*, *Homes and Gardens* and *Poetry Quarterly*.

148 Pádraig O'Horan, 'A Memory of Kerry', 'At the Gates (A Memory of Cork)', 'Remembering', *Roadways of the Heart*, p. 26, p. 19, p. 28.

149 O'Horan, 'A Memory of Kerry', p. 27.

150 O'Horan, 'These Simple Things', *The Bright-winged Piper*, p. 20.

151 O'Horan, 'Walk Gently Thro' The World', *The Proud and Lovely*, p. 31.

152 O'Horan, 'These Simple Things'.

153 O'Horan, 'Will You Remember?', *Roadways of the Heart*, p. 14.

154 Pádraig O'Horan, 'For a Young Irish Poet', *Poetry Quarterly*, 1939–1940, p. 46.

155 Pádraig O'Horan, 'My Heart Is Breathing Memoried Airs', *New Catholic World*, August 1947, p. 394.

156 Horan, 'St. Patrick's Day in Ballygorman', *Irish Christian Advocate*, 7 September 1928, p. 433.

157 See O'Horan, 'After the Raids: Bath, April, 1942', *Roadways of the Heart*, p. 23.

158 O'Horan, 'The Liffeyside', *The Bright-winged Piper*, p. 23.

159 O'Connor, *Irish Civil War Exile*, p. 52; Pinkman, *In the Legion of the Vanguard*, p. 195; Bridget Dirrane, Rose O'Connor and Jack Mahon, *A Woman of Aran: The Life and Times of Bridget Dirrane* (Dublin: Blackwater Press, 1997), p. 61.

160 Reilly, *English Poetry of the Second World War*.

161 O'Horan, 'Every Generation Goes to the Wars', *The Proud and the Lovely*, p. 48.

162 O'Horan, 'Let the Flags Droop', *Wheat and a Rose*, p. 41.

163 *The Irish Times*, 21 June 1951, p. 9.

164 *Western People*, 30 October 1976, p. 20.

165 Eily O'Horan, 'The Proud O'Dempseys', *Catholic World*, January 1950, p. 252.

166 See Hasia R. Diner, *Erin's Daughters in America: Irish Immigrant Women in the Nineteenth Century* (Baltimore, MD: JHU Press, 1983); Janet A. Nolan, *Ourselves Alone: Women's*

Emigration from Ireland, 1885-1920 (Lexington, KY: University Press of Kentucky, 1986); Margaret Lynch-Brennan, *The Irish Bridget: Irish Immigrant Women in Domestic Service in America, 1840-1930* (Syracuse, NY: Syracuse University Press, 2009); Breda Gray, *Women and the Irish Diaspora* (London: Psychology Press, 2004); Bernadette Whelan, 'Women on the Move: A Review of the Historiography of Irish Emigration to the USA, 1750–1900', *Women's History Review* 24, no. 6 (2 November 2015), pp. 900–16.

167 See Hannah O'Connor, MSPC, MSP34REF18859. For further discussion, see Síobhra Aiken, '"Sick on the Irish Sea, Dancing Across the Atlantic": (Anti-)Nostalgia in Women's Diasporic Remembrance of the Irish Revolution', in Oona Frawley (ed.), *Women and the Decade of Commemorations* (Bloomington, IN: Indiana University Press, 2021), pp. 88–106.

168 Whelan, 'Women on the Move', p. 910.

169 Dirrane, *A Woman of Aran*, p. 46.

170 Horan, *Through the Gates of Babylon*, p. 52.

171 In her study of the Richmond Asylum casebooks, Bridget Keown illustrates how one patient, Nora (a pseudonym), was admitted to the asylum in 1916 by her brother because she was 'moody', 'did not care to go out', 'declined walks' and hallucinated. Significantly, Nora's condition was attributed to her overzealous work in 'organizing for [the] Gaelic League, the United Irishwomen, and the Comogie Association [sic]', of which Nora contended her brother did not approve. Bridget Keown, '"I Would Rather Have My Own Mind": The Medicalization of Women's Behavior in Ireland, 1914–1920', *Nursing Clio*, 25 October 2017. Available at: https://nursingclio.org/2017/10/25/i-would-rather-have-my-own-mind-the- medicalization-of-womens-behavior-in-ireland-1914-1920/ (accessed 18 May 2018).

172 Mary Harpur, memoir, p. 42.

173 Eily O'Horan, 'The Rustle of Spring, a Story', *The Bell*, vol. XIII, no. 5, February 1947, pp. 28–39.

174 Gerardine Meaney, *Gender, Ireland and Cultural Change: Race, Sex and Nation* (Abingdon: Routledge, 2010), p. 10. See also Kalene Nix-Kenefick, 'The Woman, the Body and *The Bell*: the Female Voice in the Bell's Short Fiction by Women, 1940–1954', in Ruth Connolly and Ann Coughlan (eds), *New Voices in Irish Criticism 5* (Dublin: Four Courts, 2005), p. 116.

175 Ida Grehan, 'Writing Woman', *The Irish Times*, 21 November 1967; 'Space and Solitude', *The Irish Press*, 23 November 1971, p. 6.

176 I am aware of only two published memoirs by female revolutionary emigrants: Dirrane, *A Woman of Aran*; Anne Crowley Ford, Daniel Ford (ed.), *When I Am Going: Growing Up in Ireland and Coming to America, 1901–1927* (Scotts Valley, CA: CreateSpace Independent Publishing Platform, 2012).

177 Horan, *No More Foreigners*, p. 8.

178 See *The Guardian*, 8 October 1937, p. 9.

179 Eily O'Horan, 'The Bend of the Road', *Catholic World*, July 1949, pp. 263–8; see also, Eily O'Horan, 'Ripe Gooseberries', *My Garden*, August 1949, pp. 135–8.

180 Eily O'Horan, 'The Bend of the Road', *Catholic World*, July 1949, p. 268, p. 264.

181 *Western People*, 30 October 1976, p. 20.

182 Horan, *No More Foreigners*, p. 9.

183 Horan, *Through the Gates of Babylon*, p. 32.

184 Ibid., p. 34.

185 Horan, *No More Foreigners*, p. 33.

186 Horan, *Through the Gates of Babylon*, p. 36.

187 Horan, *No More Foreigners*, p. 35.

188 Horan, *Through the Gates of Babylon*, p. 22.

189 Ibid., p. 24.

190 'Former IRA Man to Preach in Assembly Hall Northern', *Northern Whig*, 21 January 1933.

191 *Western People*, 30 October 1976, p. 20.

192 Eily O'Horan, 'The Young May Moon', *Chambers's Journal*, vol. VI, January 1937–December 1937, p. 356.

193 Ibid., p. 357.

194 Ibid.; Horan, *Through the Gates of Babylon*, p. 19.

195 O'Horan, 'The Young May Moon', p. 358.

196 Ibid., p. 360.

197 See Denis Sampson, 'The Big House in Seán O'Faoláin's Fiction', in Jacqueline Genet (ed.), *The Big House in Ireland: Reality and Representation* (New York: Barnes & Noble, 1991), pp 179–90.

198 Lennox Robinson, *The Big House: Four Scenes in Its Life* (London: Macmillan, 1928), pp. 82–3.

199 *The Irish Times*, 21 November 1967, p. 6.

200 Lennox Robinson, *Curtain Up: An Autobiography* (London: M. Joseph, 1942), p. 135.

201 Robinson, *The Big House*, p. 188, p. 197. The recourse to humour to convey the trauma of burning out a Big House is also evident in Patrick Campbell's account of his home being burnt out on Christmas Eve 1922. First published in *The Spectator* 1959, cited in Helen Litton, *The Irish Civil War: An Illustrated History* (Dublin: Wolfhound Press, 1995), p. 113.

202 Eily O'Horan, 'The Old Bog Road', *Chambers's Journal*, vol. VI, 1937, pp. 738–41. Also published in St Patrick's Edition of the *Irish Independent*, March 1937.

203 Eily O'Horan, 'Footsteps on the Stairs', *Chambers's Journal*, vol. VIII, 1939, pp. 938–44.

204 Eily O'Horan, 'The Proud O'Dempseys', *Catholic World* 170, no. 1018 (January 1950), p. 252.

205 O'Horan, 'The Proud O'Dempseys', p. 255.

206 Otto Rauchbauer, 'The Big House in the Irish Short Story after 1918: A Critical Survey', in idem (ed.), *Ancestral Voices: The Big House in Anglo-Irish Literature: A Collection of Interpretations* (New York: Georg Olms Verlag, 1992), p. 168.

207 For stories that could be assimilated into the anti-emigration agenda, see Eily O'Horan, 'Lady of My Delight', *Chambers's Journal*, vol. VII, 1938, pp. 539–44; Eily O'Horan, 'Oh, Come All Ye Faithful', *Cork Holly Bough and Weekly Examiner*, Christmas 1936, p. 7; Eily O'Horan, 'Christmas Hamper', *Cork Holly Bough and Weekly Examiner*, Christmas 1937, p. 10.

208 Eily O'Horan, 'The Tower', *Chambers's Journal*, vol. X, 1941, p. 658.

209 Eily O'Horan, 'Tryst at Sheelin', *Chambers's Journal*, vol. XII, 1943, pp. 355–7.

210 Eily O'Horan, 'The Quality', *Chambers's Journal*, vol. XIII, 1944, pp. 649–51.

211 *Sligo Champion*, 29 June 1984, p. 12. Dolan and Dolan, 'Our Aunt Eilish's Untold Story of Rebellion, Romance and Religion', p. 44.

212 As Brennan claimed: 'A great friend of mine, a radio personality, was informed of her dismissal by reading it on a notice board. The awful part is [that] RTÉ got away with it as not enough women got together to make a fuss about it,' *The Irish Press*, 23 November 1971, p. 6.

213 *The Irish Press*, 23 November 1971, p. 6.

214 *The Irish Times*, 21 November 1967, p. 6.

215 Elizabeth Brennan, *The Parting of the Ways: A One-Act Play*, RTÉ Written Archives, Radio Drama Scripts, UCDA p261/254; *Irish Examiner*, 12 March 1969, p. 28; *Sligo Champion*, 21 March 1969, p. 9.

216 Brennan, *The Parting of the Ways*, p. 25.

217 'Elizabeth Brennan – Prolific Novelist', *Western People*, 30 October 1976, p. 20.

218 Ryan, 'Elizabeth Brennan', *Sligo Champion*, 29 June 1984, p. 12; *The Irish Times*, 21 November 1967, p. 6.

219 *Western People*, 30 October 1976, p. 20.

220 *Sunday Independent*, 6 June 1971, p. 4; Elizabeth Brennan, *Wacht niet liefste* (Amsterdam: N.V. Uitg. Mij. Mundus, 1971); Elizabeth Brennan, *Kom tilbake, Peter* (Oslo, 1978).

221 Paul Marchbanks, 'Elizabeth Brennan', in Alexander G. Gonzalez (ed.), *Irish Women Writers: An A-to-Z Guide* (Santa Barbara, CA: Greenwood Publishing Group, 2006), p. 49.

222 The author Elizabeth Brennan (*c.* 1903–1995) of Abbeyfield, Killester published a number of popular novels, including *Out of the Darkness* (Dublin: Metropolitan Publishing Company, 1945) and *Am I My Brother's Keeper?* (Dublin: Metropolitan Publishing Company, 1946).

223 Brennan, *Her Lucky Mistake* [cover blurb].

224 Clayton Hoagland and Kathleen Hoagland, *Thomas Wolfe, Our Friend, 1933–1938: A Dated Record from the Journal of Clayton Hoagland, Rutherford, New Jersey* (Virginia: Croissant, 1979); *The Irish Press*, 13 June 1946, p. 7.

225 Kathleen Hoagland, *1000 Years of Irish Poetry: The Gaelic and Anglo-Irish Poets from Pagan Times to the Present* (Old Greenwich, CT: Devin-Adair Company, 1947), p. liii.

226 Kathleen Hoagland, *Fiddler in the Sky* (New York: Harper & Brothers, 1944), p. 5.

227 Ibid., p. 62.

228 Ibid., p. 53, p. 253, p. 55.

229 Ibid., p. 63.

230 Ibid., p. 39.

231 Ibid., p. 11; see Lisa Anne Surridge, *Bleak Houses: Marital Violence in Victorian Fiction* (Athens, OH: Ohio University Press, 2005).

232 Hoagland, *Fiddler in the Sky*, p. 55.

233 Ibid., p. 285.

234 Ibid., p. 7.

235 Ibid., p. 294.

236 Ibid., p. 55.

237 *The Cincinnati Enquirer*, 10 June 1944, p. 5; *Fort Worth Star Telegram*, 21 May 1944, p. 17.

238 Official records further elucidate numerous similarities between the protagonist and the novelist; 1911 census records confirm that the Dooher children lived in a separate house from their parents, that their father, a hotelier, was significantly older than his wife. Like

the fictional parents, Hoagland's mother hailed from Dublin city, while the father was native to the west of Ireland. See www.census.nationalarchives.ie (accessed 15 October 2021).

239   *The Record*, 28 October 1982, p. C1, p. C19.

240   *The Record*, 4 March 1973.

241   Hoagland, *Fiddler in the Sky*, p. 63.

242   Ibid., p. 227.

243   Ibid., p. 290.

244   Ibid., p. 164.

245   Ryan, *Remembering Sion*, p. 246.

Chapter 5

1   George Lennon, *Trauma in Time: (An Irish Itinerary)* (unpublished: c. 1971), p. 3. Available at: https://www.academia.edu/6362572/GGL_TRAUMA_IN_TIME; see also 'Memoirs of George Lennon'. Available at: http://www.waterfordmuseum.ie/exhibit/web/Display/article/317/Memoirs_Of_George_Lennon_.html (accessed 8 August 2020).

2   'Ex-Rebel Holds Viet War Futile', *Democrat and Chronicle*, 21 October 1967, p. 16.

3   George Lennon, Application for Military Service Pension, MSPC, MSP34REF11591.

4   Statement of George Lennon, Military Service Pension, MSPC, MSP34REF11591, 24 September 1938.

5   William White, 15 December 1936; 'George Lennon: Detailed Statement', MSPC, MSP34REF11591, 27 August 1937.

6   George Lennon MSPC, MSP34REF11591, 27 August 1937.

7   Ibid., Letter to Secretary, 6 December 1943.

8   Lennon, *Lennons in Time*, p. 177, p. 105. Available at: https://www.academia.edu/32727560/LENNONS_IN_TIME (accessed 20 August 2020).

9   Joanna Bourke, *An Intimate History of Killing: Face-to-Face Killing in Twentieth-Century Warfare* (London: Granta Books, 2000 [1991]), p. 1.

10   For example, Stephen Hopkins observes that 'the fact that [Ernie] O'Malley had killed a fellow Irishman during the civil war has not been much discussed, either in his own memoir or in the critical analysis of his work'. Stephen Hopkins, '"Irish History Unidealised": The Politics of Republican Memoir and Narratives of the Defeated and Defiant', in Deslandes et al. (eds), *Civil War and Narrative*, p. 74.

11   Raya Morag, *Waltzing with Bashir: Perpetrator Trauma and Cinema* (New York: Bloomsbury, 2013), p. 6.

12   See Primo Levi, *The Drowned and the Saved* (New York: Summit Books, 1988). See also Breandán Mac Suibhne, *The End of Outrage: Post-Famine Adjustment in Rural Ireland* (Oxford: Oxford University Press, 2017), p. 17.

13   Ann Matthews, 'Internment and Women during the Civil War 1922–23', *The Old Athlone Society* (2015), p. 141.

14   Frances Houghton, *The Veterans' Tale: British Military Memoirs of the Second World War* (Cambridge: Cambridge University Press, 2019), p. 166.

15   Bourke, *An Intimate History of Killing*, p. 28.

16   Ibid., p. 10.

17   Anne Dolan, 'Killing and Bloody Sunday, November 1920', *The Historical Journal* 49, no. 3 (2006), p. 791.

18   Eve Morrison, 'Witnessing the Republic: The Ernie O'Malley Notebook Interviews and the Bureau of Military History Compared', in Cormac O'Malley (ed.), *Modern Ireland and Revolution: Ernie O'Malley in Context* (Dublin: Irish Academic Press, 2016), p. 139.

19   Ibid.; Dolan, 'Killing and Bloody Sunday', p. 792, p. 809, p. 791.

20   Morrison, 'Witnessing the Republic', p. 139.

21   Flanagan, *Remembering the Revolution*, p. 17.

22   Terry Clavin (Michael) Kevin O'Doherty, 'Dictionary of Irish Biography'.

23   See James H. Joy, 'Victory and Woe: Mossie Harnett and the West Limerick Brigade in the Irish War of Independence, 1915–1923' (unpublished PhD thesis, George Mason University, 2000), p. 4.

24   For example, compare the account of the Brosna Barrack attacks in *Limerick's Fighting Story* and in Hartnett, *Victory and Woe*. See also Hartnett, 'Truce, Civil War, Prison and then My Release', *Limerick Leader*, 26 March 1977, p. 7.

25   Dolan, 'Killing in "the Good Old Irish Fashion"?', p. 18.

26   Jody Allen-Randolph, '"If No One Wanted to Remember"', p. 140.

27   Bourke, *An Intimate History of Killing*, p. 8.

28   Delaney, *Sean O'Faolain*, p. 157.

29   Des Hickey, 'How Colonels Almost Took Over!', *Sunday Independent*, 22 September 1974, p. 13.

30   On the 'pleasure-culture of war', see Graham Dawson, *Soldier Heroes: British Adventure, Empire and the Imagining of Masculinities* (Abingdon: Routledge, 2013), p. 4.

31   Edward Moane, BMH WS 896, 30 September 1953, p. 18.

32   Carty, *The Irish Volunteer*, p. 115.

33   Pádraig O'Horan, 'Behind the Barricades', *Irish Christian Advocate*, 10 February 1928, p. 65.

34   Tom Casey, 'Civil War in Kerry', National Folklore Collection UCD, gathered in 1931, Iml 1271, l. A 124–51.

35   Eimar O'Duffy, *The Wasted Island* (Dublin: Martin Lester, 1919), pp. 481–2.

36   Thomas Irwin, the son of a Liberties' trade union leader born in 1901, was active in the IRA Dublin Brigade from 1918 to 1923. He was an adjutant on the anti-treaty side during the battle of Dublin and engaged in a twelve-day hunger strike during his imprisonment. He later worked for forty years as a Dublin Corporation maintenance foreman and also wrote television plays. He was involved with the Executive Committee of the Old Dublin Brigade of the IRA and issued a statement supporting Irishmen who joined the republican fight during the Spanish Civil War. *The Irish Press*, 17 December 1936, p. 5. On Sam Irwin, see MSPC 24SP3894.

37   Clarke and Brown (eds), *Ireland in Fiction*, p. 125.

38   Thomas P. Irwin, *Benson's Flying Column* (Dublin: Talbot Press, 1935), pp. 125–6.

39   M. J. M., '*Benson's Flying Column* by Thomas P. Irwin', *The Irish Press*, 7 January 1936, p. 8.

40   'Raw Meat', *Irish Independent*, 24 December 1935, p. 2.

41   Irwin, *Benson's Flying Column*, p. 8.

42   Irwin was praised for writing 'with exact knowledge of his subject' and it was suggested that his book would be 'precious to many whose own memory of those days can corroborate his narrative'. L. K., 'Review of Thomas P. Irwin's *Benson's Flying Column*', *The Irish Book Lover*, vol. XXIV, p. 21, January–February 1936.

43   Book-worm, 'To the Editor', *Irish Independent*, 31 December 1935, p. 3.

44   Letter to M. J. MacManus, 9 December 1935, NAI, Talbot Press Archive, 1048/1/139.

45   'What Dublin Is Reading', *The Irish Times*, 11 January 1936, p. 5; *Evening Herald*, 14 December 1961, p. 14; 'Letter to Editor', *Evening Herald*, 18 March 1965, p. 16.

46   Dolan, 'Killing in "the Good Old Irish Fashion"?'

47   P. K. Horan, 'The Flame of Youth', *Irish Christian Advocate*, 24 August 1928, p. 408.

48   Proinnsias Ó Gallchobhair, 'Leaves from a Prison Diary', *Éire*, 12 July 1924, p. 1.

49   Cited in *Bóthar na Saoirse – My Fight for Irish Freedom, Scéal Dan Breen*, TG4, 12 January 2011.

50   Cited in Patrick Maume, 'Michael Flannery', *Dictionary of Irish Biography*.

51   Pinkman, *In the Legion of the Vanguard*.

52   Joshua Pederson, *Sin Sick: Moral Injury in War and Literature* (Ithaca, NY: Cornell University Press, 2021) [Kindle edition].

53   Ibid.

54   Ibid.

55   Drew Gilpin Faust, *This Republic of Suffering* (New York: Knopf Doubleday, 2008), p. 32.

56   O'Donnell, *Storm*, p. 48.

57   Carty, *The Irish Volunteer*, p. 168.

58   Francis Carty, *Blood on the Main St* [unpublished manuscript]. My thanks to Francis Xavier Carty for sharing a copy of this manuscript.

59   See Dolan, 'Killing in "the Good Old Irish Fashion"?', p. 23.

60   Hogan, *Camps on the Hearthstone*, p. 234.

61   Deasy, *Brother Against Brother*, p. 58.

62   Billy Mullins, *Memoirs of Billy Mullins: Veteran of the War of Independence* (Tralee: Kenno, 1983), pp. 61–2.

63   MacCall, *Gods in Motley*, p. 25.

64   Joanna Bourke, 'Effeminacy, Ethnicity and the End of Trauma: The Sufferings of "Shell-Shocked" Men in Great Britain and Ireland, 1914–39', *Journal of Contemporary History* 35, no. 1 (2000), p. 60.

65   Colonel Eamon Broy, BMH WS 1285, 17 November 1955, p. 86.

66   John Zneimer, *The Literary Vision of Liam O'Flaherty* (Syracuse, NY: Syracuse University Press, 1970), p. 19.

67   Alan Gibbs, *Contemporary American Trauma Narratives* (Edinburgh: Edinburgh University Press, 2014), p. 169.

68   O'Connor, *Guests of the Nation*, p. 19.

69   Anthony Whittier, 'Frank O'Connor', in Malcolm Cowley (ed.), *Writers at Work: The Paris Review Interviews* (New York: The Viking Press, 1958), p. 149.

70   P. C. Trimble, 'Review of Frank O'Connor's *Guests of the Nation*', *The Irish Book Lover*, vol. XIX, November–December 1931, pp. 179–80.

71   Morrison speculates that 'Guests of the Nation' could be based on the West Cork IRA's execution of two captured Essex Regiment soldiers, Percy Taylor and Thomas Watling, in December 1920, or the execution of John Steer and George Motley of the East Lancashire Regiment in July 1921 by the IRA in east Kerry. However, if the story is indeed based on an account O'Connor heard in Gormanston, it may equally have come from the folkloric tradition and predate the revolution. As Matthews notes, the story may reflect rumours about the execution of two English detectives ordered by Fenian leader Jeremiah O'Donovan

Rossa. See James H. Matthews, *Voices: A Life of Frank O'Connor* (New York: Atheneum, 1983), p. 70; Eve Morrison, 'Hauntings of the Irish Revolution: Veterans and Memory of the Independence Struggle and Civil War', in Marguerite Corporaal, Christopher Cusack and Ruud van den Beuken (eds), *Irish Studies and the Dynamics of Memory: Transitions and Transformations* (Bern: Peter Lang: 2017), p. 99.

72 For example, 'Ambush' relates to an occasion during which the author, Seán O'Faoláin, Seán Hendrick and Vincent O'Leary tried to ambush a Free State army convoy. Matthews, *Voices: A Life of Frank O'Connor*, p. 69.

73 Paul Delaney, '"Rising Again": Revision, Trauma, and Frank O'Connor's "Guests of the Nation"', *New Hibernia Review* 23, no. 3 (6 December 2019), p. 47. This may also be a reference to the Fenian leader, Jeremiah O'Donovan Rossa.

74 More renowned adaptations included Brendan Behan's play *An Giall/The Hostage* (1958), Ken Loach's film *The Wind That Shakes the Barley* (2006) and Neil Jordan's *The Crying Game* (1992).

75 Frank O'Connor, *My Father's Son* (Syracuse, NY: Syracuse University Press, 1968 [1999]), p. 34.

76 A. P. Fanning, *Vigil: A Play in One Act* (Dublin: P. J. Bourke, 1961), p. 19.

77 Bourke, *An Intimate History of Killing*, p. 7. See also Gibbs, *Contemporary American Trauma Narratives*, p. 183; Houghton, *The Veterans' Tale*, p. 7.

78 'New Gaelic Books', *The Irish Times*, 9 December 1933, p. 4. Ó Siochfhradha, a native of Kerry, served in the 3rd Tipperary Brigade, see Michael Sugrue, MAI, Service (1917–1921) Medal application, MD6040.

79 Mícheál Ó Siochfhradha, *Deire an Chunntais: Dráma Aon-Mhire* (Baile Átha Cliath: Oifig Díolta Foillseacháin Rialtais, 1932), p. 25.

80 O'Connor's story was first published in the US-based magazine *Atlantic Monthly* in January 1931, but the collection did not appear in Ireland until the autumn of that year.

81 'Dráma Nua-Cheaptha i n-Amharclainn na Mainistreach', *Evening Herald*, 8 November 1927, p. 6.

82 Ó Broin, *An Mhallacht agus Drámaí Eile*.

83 My thanks to John Borgonovo for sharing insight on this topic.

84 Ernie O'Malley, *On Another Man's Wound* (Dublin: At the Sign of the Three Candles, 1936 [2001]), p. 371.

85 O'Connor, *Guests of the Nation*, p. 18.

86 O'Malley, *On Another Man's Wound*, p. 374; Nathan Wallace, 'The Importance of Being Ernie O'Malley in Ken Loach's *The Wind That Shakes the Barley*', in O'Malley, *Modern Ireland and Revolution*, p. 72.

87 O'Malley, *On Another Man's Wound*, p. 271.

88 J. L., Hardy, *Never in Vain* (London: Collins, 1936), p. 4.

89 Ibid., p. 94, p. 277.

90 Gardiner connects Hardy to the murders of Limerick Sinn Féin councillor John Lynch in the Exchange Hotel in September 1920 and of shopkeeper Peter O'Carroll on Manor St in October 1920. Eamonn T. Gardiner, 'An Examination of the Auxiliary Division, Royal Irish Constabulary, Exploring Possible Links between Conduct and Conflict-Related Injury, Traumatic Experiences and Stress' (unpublished PhD thesis, NUI Galway, 2017), p. 304.

91 'Notes and Extracts Taken from Various Books by Captain J. L. Hardy, who Tortured Ernie O'Malley in Dublin Castle', undated, NLI Ms 10,973/5.

92   Frank Percy Crozier, *The Men I Killed* (London: Joseph, 1937).

93   Liam O'Flaherty, *The Informer* (London: Jonathan Cape, 1925); O'Flaherty, *The Assassin*; Liam O'Flaherty, *Return of the Brute* (London: Mandrake Press, 1929).

94   'Review of *Casey of the I.R.A.*', *The Irish Monthly*, vol. 52, 1924, p. 168. Walsh was a schoolteacher from Swinford, County Mayo and achieved a reputation as an author of revolutionary sketches in *The Freeman's Journal* and *An tÓglach* (said to be based on anecdotes the author 'heard or came across firsthand'). A. T. Walsh, *Casey of the I.R.A.* (Dublin: Talbot Press, 1923); *An tÓglach*, 21 June 1924, p. 6; *Evening Herald*, 30 June 1923, p. 5.

95   A. T. Walsh, 'The Stuff of Dreams: A Story of the Anglo-Irish War of 1920–21', *An tÓglach*, 20 October 1923.

96   Walsh, *Casey of the I.R.A.*, p. 138.

97   Jacob, *The Troubled House*, pp. 86–9.

98   Ibid., p. 115.

99   Cited in Erin Ní Eaghra, 'Ní Sciath ar bith Arm ach Tuar Tubaiste Géire – Saighdiúr Stuachach ar son na Síochána: Úna Bean Uí Dhiosca' (unpublished MA thesis, NUI Galway, 2007), p. 62.

100   Liam O'Flaherty, *The Letters of Liam O'Flaherty*, edited by A. A. Kelly (Dublin: Wolfhound Press, 1996), p. 207.

101   SÓD, 'An Mhuintir Seo Againn: Úna Bean Uí Dhiosca', *The Irish Press*, 14 December 1957, p. 2.

102   Úna Uí Dhiosca opposed the use of force in a letter in *The Separatist*, September 1922. See O'Leary, *Gaelic Prose in the Irish Free State*, p. 338; Úna Uí Dhiosca, *Cailín na Gruaige Duinne* (Baile Átha Cliath: Oifig Díolta Foillseacháin Rialtais, 1932), p. 84.

103   The dog's name may be a reference to Fionn mac Cumhaill's much-loved dog, Bran.

104   Uí Dhiosca, *Cailín na Gruaige Duinne*, pp. 88–9; Surridge, *Bleak Houses*.

105   Uí Dhiosca, *Cailín na Gruaige Duinne*, p. 91.

106   Ibid.

107   Ibid., pp. 93–4.

108   O'Hegarty, *The Victory of Sinn Féin*, p. 103.

109   Charles John McGuinness, *Nomad: Memoirs of an Irish Sailor, Soldier, Pearl-Fisher, Pirate, Gun-Runner, Rum-Rummer, Rebel and Antarctic Explorer* (London: Methuen, 1934), p. 140.

110   Max Caulfield, *The Easter Rebellion* (London: Four Square, 1965 [1975]), p. 88.

111   Letter from Eva-Gore Booth to Katharine Tynan Hickson, November 1916, cited in Sonja Tiernan, *Eva Gore-Booth: An Image of Such Politics* (Manchester: Manchester University Press, 2012), p. 205.

112   Extract from letter from Nell Humphreys, UCDA P106/384. Transcription available at: https://humphrysfamilytree.com/Humphrys/sighle.papers.html (accessed 20 August 2020).

113   Sighle's Account of the Raid from the 1970s, UCDA, P106/1991. Transcription available at: https://humphrysfamilytree.com/Humphrys/sighle.papers.html (accessed 20 August 2020).

114   Pinkman, *In the Legion of the Vanguard*, p. 129.

115   Ward, *Unmanageable Revolutionaries*, p. 173.

116   Eithne Coyle, 'Reminiscences of Eithne O'Donnell (née Coyle)', 12 July 1972, [unpublished memoir] Kilmainham Gaol Archive, 20MS-1B33-19, p. 22.

117   Cregan, *Hunger-strike*, p. 27.

118   Margaret Barrington, *My Cousin Justin* (London: J. Cape, 1939), p. 248.

119   Ibid., p. 244.

120 Ibid., p. 252.

121 See Seán O'Faoláin, MSPC, MSP34REF49115.

122 O'Faoláin, *Midsummer Night Madness: And Other Stories.*

123 Connor, *Dead Star's Light;* Elizabeth Connor, 'Typescript *The Dark Road,* a Play in Three Acts with Prologue and Epilogue', NLI, Úna Troy Papers, Ms 35,687. The successful stage adaption, *The Dark Road,* ran in the Abbey from 12–31 May 1947. The plot of *The Dark Road* faithfully retraces that of the novel, although, as Terence O'Reilly notes, the anti-clerical opinions of the characters are omitted from the play. Furthermore, the stage version concludes differently from the novel. The novel ends on a note of optimism: Ross' death, while bringing financial ruin on his own family, brings relief to his accomplices who feel they can finally move on. Davern and Katherine descend towards Kilvane from Slievcrag to start a new life. In the final act of the play, the four accomplices revisit the site of their crime, the Slievcrag mineshaft, hoping to confront Ross with evidence of his fraud. However, Ross throws himself into the mineshaft, escaping financial disgrace and leaving his accomplices '[i]n the same bloody mess as where we started'. See Terence O'Reilly, *Rebel Heart: George Lennon: Flying Column Commander* (Cork: Mercier Press, 2009).

124 Postman Larry Griffin disappeared in Stradbally, County Waterford on Christmas Day, 1929, and his body was purportedly discarded in a mineshaft near Bunmahon. See Fachtna Ó Drisceoil, *The Missing Postman: What Really Happened to Larry Griffin?* (Cork: Mercier Press, 2011).

125 Troy's biographer Brady argues that 'Davern is undoubtedly a character from the creative pen of Úna Troy'. Nevertheless, the fictional and real characters share a number of features. George Lennon also believed that the book reflected on his own activities. See Donal Brady, *Úna Troy 1910–1993: Her Life and Work* (Waterford: Copper Coast Geopark, 2012), p. 20.

126 Ann. M. Butler, 'Úna Troy – Author', Copper Coast Geopark, 17 April 2017. Available at: https://coppercoastgeopark.com/una-troy-author/ (accessed 20 August 2020).

127 Patrick Maume, 'Úna Troy', *Dictionary of Irish Biography.*

128 Philip Rooney, 'Caricature of Irish Life', *Sunday Independent,* 13 March 1938, p. 5.

129 W. Byrne, SS Peter and Paul's, Clonmel, 18 March 1938, Úna Troy Papers, NLI Ms 35,686 (2).

130 Connor, *Dead Star's Light,* p. 9.

131 Ibid., p. 29, p. 93.

132 Connor, *The Dark Road,* p. 21.

133 Connor, *Dead Star's Light,* p. 23, p. 40.

134 Ibid., p. 239.

135 Ibid., p. 77.

136 Ibid., p. 127.

137 Ibid., p. 78.

138 Ibid., p. 318.

139 Connor, *The Dark Road,* p. 24.

140 Connor, *Dead Star's Light,* p. 318.

141 Ibid., p. 78.

142 Pat McCarthy, *The Irish Revolution, 1912–23: Waterford* (Dublin: Four Courts Press, 2015), pp. 80–1.

143 Lennon, *Lennons in Time,* p. 143.

144 Connor, *Dead Star's Light*, p. 7.
145 George Lennon, 'Television Play Manuscript, *Down by the Glen Side*: An Original Television Play "Live", September, 1952 (To Janet)', NLI, Úna Troy, Ms 35,699 (1).
146 Ibid., p. 37.
147 Ibid., p. 41.
148 Ibid., p. 53.
149 Ibid., pp. 57–8.
150 Lennon, *Lennons in Time*, p. 223.
151 Ibid., p. 231.
152 Lennon, *Trauma in Time*, p. 2.
153 Ibid.
154 See 'Memoirs of George Lennon'. Available at: http://www.waterfordmuseum.ie/exhibit/web/Display/article/317/Memoirs_Of_George_Lennon_.html. (accessed 8 August 2020).
155 Lennon, *Trauma in Time*, p. 3.
156 See Whitehead, *Trauma Fiction*.
157 Damien Keown, *Buddhism: A Very Short Introduction* (Oxford: Oxford University Press, 2013), p. 34.
158 Lennon, *Trauma in Time*, p. 32.
159 Ibid.
160 Ibid.
161 Connor, *Dead Star's Light*, p. 78; O'Malley, *The Singing Flame*, p. 183.
162 Lennon, *Trauma in Time*, p. 15.
163 Bourke, *An Intimate History of Killing*, p. 15.
164 Lennon, *Trauma in Time*, p. 30, p. 15.
165 Gibbs, *Contemporary American Trauma Narratives*, p. 171, p. 178.
166 Lennon, *Trauma in Time*, p. 33.
167 Ibid.
168 Ibid.
169 Ibid., p. 34.
170 Ibid.
171 Ibid., p. 22.
172 Lennon, 'Television Play Manuscript, *Down by the Glen Side*', p. 27.
173 Two letters from Charles J. McGuinness to George Lennon, 1931, 1932, Úna Troy papers, NLI Ms 35,699.
174 Lennon, *Lennons in Time*, p. 122.
175 George Crolly, 'An Irish Volunteer', *The Irish Review* [New York], vol. 1, no. 2, 1934. Here Lennon, writing under a pen name, is supporting the establishment of an Irish Volunteer force under Fianna Fáil in 1934.
176 Lennon, *Trauma in Time*, p. 5.
177 Ibid., p. 46.
178 O'Connor, *He's Somewhere in There*, p. 11.
179 Ibid., p. 7.
180 'Anthony O'Connor; Custume Barracks (Westmeath); Age 18', 20 June 1922, Irish Army Census Collection 1922, Irish Military Archives, p. 122. O'Connor's Christian name, on census records, was Stephen Joseph Anthony. He thus shared his first name with the novel's narrator, Steve Corrigan.

181 Fintan O'Toole, *The Ex-Isle of Erin* (Dublin: New Island Books, 1997), p. 32.

182 Robert Nye, 'Bread and Butter and a Bit of Jam', *The Guardian*, 16 January 1975, p. 11.

183 O'Connor, *He's Somewhere in There*, p. 10. For discussion of simultaneous executions during the civil war, see Enright, *The Irish Civil War*, p. 34.

184 Nollaig Ó Gadhra, *Civil War in Connacht* (Cork: Mercier Press, 1999), p. 63.

185 The men executed were Martin Bourke (Caherlistrane, County Galway); Thomas Hughes (Athlone); Stephen Joyce, Herbert Collins and Michael Walsh (from Derrymore, Caherlistrane, County Galway). General Tom Maguire TD evaded execution.

186 Seán Ó Laidhin, Dáil Éireann debates, vol. 2, vo. 22, 30 January 1923. See also Thomas Hughes, MSPC, DP4571; 'The Late Mr. Thos Hughes', *Westmeath Independent*, 27 January 1923, p. 7.

187 O'Connor, *He's Somewhere in There*, p. 216.

188 O'Toole, *The Ex-Isle of Erin*, p. 32.

189 O'Connor, *He's Somewhere in There*, p. 19.

190 Ibid., p. 35.

191 Ibid., p. 53.

192 Phil Tomkins, *Twice A Hero: From the Trenches of the Great War to the Ditches of the Irish Midlands 1915–1922* (Cirencester: Memoirs Publishing, 2013), p. 116. For a description of Craddock's methods, see Thomas Costello, BMH WS 1296.

193 John Burke, *Athlone 1900–1923: Politics, Revolution & Civil War* (Dublin: History Press, 2015), p. 195. For address see 'Anthony O'Connor', Irish Army Census Collection 1922.

194 O'Connor, *He's Somewhere in There*, p. 47.

195 Royal Irish Constabulary Service Records 1816–1922. Available at: findmypast.ie (accessed 20 August 2020); Matt Cooper, *The Maximalist: The Rise and Fall of Tony O'Reilly* (Dublin: Gill & Macmillan, 2015), p. 29.

196 Cited in Burke, *Athlone 1900–1923*, p. 182.

197 O'Connor, *He's Somewhere in There*, p. 56.

198 Ibid., p. 61.

199 Ibid., p. 106.

200 'Novel Notes', *The Irish Press*, 19 April 1975, p. 7.

201 O'Connor, *He's Somewhere in There*, p. 63.

202 Ibid., p. 127. This is reflective of the realities. As Burke outlines, 'Athlone had 720 troops in the garrison, yet just 249 rifles, 100 grenades and eighty-seven revolvers'. See Burke, *Athlone 1900–1923*, p. 237.

203 O'Connor, *He's Somewhere in There*, p. 109.

204 Ibid., p. 110.

205 See Burke, *Athlone 1900–1923*, p. 239.

206 O'Connor, *He's Somewhere in There*, p. 86.

207 Ibid., p. 84.

208 Ibid., p. 239.

209 Ibid., p. 112, p. 113.

210 Ibid., p. 114.

211 Ibid., pp. 117–18.

212 Ibid., p. 248.

213 Ibid., pp. 119–20.

214   See Clare Bielby, 'Scripting the Perpetrating Self: Masculinity, Class and Violence in German Post-Terrorist Autobiography', in Clare Bielby and Jeffrey Stevenson Murer (eds), *Perpetrating Selves: Doing Violence, Performing Identity* (Cham: Springer International Publishing, 2018), pp. 95–6.

215   O'Connor, *He's Somewhere in There*, p. 132.

216   Ibid., p. 133.

217   Ibid., p. 182.

218   Ibid., p. 11.

219   Ibid., p. 10, p. 13.

220   Anthony O'Connor, *Clubland: The Wrong Side of the Right People* (London: Martin Brian & O'Keefe, 1976), p. 95.

221   O'Connor, *He's Somewhere in There*, p. 11.

222   O'Connor, *Clubland*, p. 83.

223   O'Connor, *He's Somewhere in There*, p. 8.

224   O'Connor notes in the preface that Childers was executed by 'a firing squad, commanded by my cousin, Rory, at Portobello Barracks in Dublin'. This seems to have led reviewers to believe that O'Connor was a cousin of Rory O'Connor, the Dublin-born anti-treaty leader who was executed in Mountjoy Gaol in December 1922. This reference to 'cousin Rory' is unclear, however, and may, indeed, be a fabrication; the leader of the firing squad which was in command of Childers' execution was Free State officer, Paddy O'Connor, of Limerick.

225   Gabriel Rosenstock, 'Little Lines of Ireland', *Irish Independent*, 25 January 1975, p. 8.

226   Mullins, *Memoirs of Billy Mullins*, p. 203.

227   Harrington, *Kerry Landing*, p. 132.

Afterword

1   Letter from Polly Cosgrove to Bridie Halpin on NDU paper, 19 July 1923, Kilmainham Jail Archive, OBJ0027.

2   Felicity Hayes-McCoy, *A Woven Silence* (Dublin: Gill & Macmillan, 2015), p. 163.

3   McDowell, 'Civil War of Words', p. 298.

4   'Jackets Green, Typescript of a Novel'; Smithson, *Myself – and Others*, p. 252; O'Connor, *He's Somewhere in There*, p. 7.

5   Allen-Randolph, '"If No One Wanted To Remember"', p. 144.

6   See Beiner, *Forgetful Remembrance*, p. 5.

7   Vincent Morley, *The Popular Mind in Eighteenth-Century Ireland* (Cork: Cork University Press, 2017), p. 1.

8   Robert Fanning, 'Vivid Faces: The Revolutionary Generation in Ireland 1890–1923', *History Ireland* (blog), 3 March 2015; see also Fearghal Mac Bhloscaidh, 'Objective Historians, Irrational Fenians and the Bewildered Herd: Revisionist Myth and the Irish Revolution', *Irish Studies Review* 28, no. 2 (2 April 2020), p. 208.

9   Mary Manning, 'Backdrop for a Troubled Stage (Review): *Somewhere to the Sea*, by Kenneth Reddin', *The Saturday Review*, 5 September 1936, p. 18.

10   'Jackets Green, Typescript of a Novel.'

11   Henry, *Ambushed Lovers*, p. 192.

12   Ryan, 'Still Remembering Sion', p. 245.

13   Ibid., p. 246.

14   Eimar O'Duffy, 'Review of *The Walk of a Queen* by Annie M. P. Smithson', *The Irish Review*, 6 January 1923, pp. 70–1, cited in Flanagan, *Remembering the Revolution*, p. 69; 'Book Prohibited in Free State: Author's Libel Action Against Newspaper', *The Guardian*, 25 May 1937, p. 7; Gabriel Rosenstock, 'Little Lines of Ireland', *Irish Independent*, 25 January 1975, p. 8.

15   Dominick LaCapra, *History and Memory after Auschwitz* (Ithaca, NY: Cornell University Press, 1998), p. 11.

16   Laub, 'Bearing Witness', p. 57.

17   Tal, *Worlds of Hurt*, p. 21.

18   See Craps, *Postcolonial Witnessing*, p. 42; Tal, *Worlds of Hurt*, p. 58.

19   Anne Karpf, 'Chain of Testimony: The Holocaust Researcher as Surrogate Witness', in Nicholas Chare and Dominic Williams (eds), *Representing Auschwitz: At the Margins of Testimony* (London: Palgrave Macmillan, 2013), p. 86.

20   Hoagland, *Fiddler in the Sky*.

21   Karpf, 'Chain of Testimony', p. 87.

22   Colin Davis, 'Trauma, Poststructuralism and Ethics', in Colin Davis and Hanna Meretoja (eds), *The Routledge Companion to Literature and Trauma* (Milton Keynes: Taylor & Francis Group, 2020), p. 41.

23   Ibid

24   Ibid.; Michael Rothberg, *The Implicated Subject: Beyond Victims and Perpetrators* (Stanford, CA: University Press, 2019), p. 1.

25   Máirín Ryan, BMH WS 416, 28 Iúil 1950, p. 4.

26   See Peter Novick, *That Noble Dream: The 'Objectivity Question' and the American Historical Profession* (Cambridge: Cambridge University Press, 1988).

27   Frank Aiken first employed this proverb in a letter to the Provisional Government on 3 August 1922. Hopkinson, *Green Against Green*; Armitage, *Civil Wars*, p. 9.

28   Michael O'Hanlon, 'Interview' in Síobhra Aiken et al. (eds), *The Men Will Talk to Me*, p. 145.

29   Francis Carty, 'Frank Aiken: Some Personal Impressions', *The Irish Press*, 8 July 1969, p. 8.

30   Frank Aiken Jnr, 'Preface', in Bryce Evans and Stephen Kelly (eds), *Frank Aiken: Nationalist and Internationalist* (Dublin: Merrion Press, 2014), p. xvi.

31   LaCapra, *Writing History, Writing Trauma*, p. 147.

32   Marla Morris, *Curriculum and the Holocaust: Competing Sites of Memory and Representation* (Abingdon: Routledge, 2001), p. 51; cited in Karpf, 'Chain of Testimony', p. 4.

33   Cited in LaCapra, *History and Memory after Auschwitz*, p. 107.

34   Beiner, *Remembering the Year of the French*, p. 22.

35   See Síobhra Aiken, 'The Silence and the Silence Breakers of the Irish Civil War 1922–2022', *Éire-Ireland*, edited by Sara Dybris McQuaid and Fearghal McGarry, Spring/Summer 2022.

36   Ryan, 'Still Remembering Sion', p. 252.

BIBLIOGRAPHY

1. MANUSCRIPT AND ARCHIVAL SOURCES

All England Law Reports
Cases Decided in the House of Lords, the Privy Council, All Divisions of the Supreme Court, and Courts of Special Jurisdiction (London: Butterworth, 1936).

Dictionary of Irish Biography
Available at: https://www.dib.ie (accessed 30 August 2020).

National Folklore Collection, University College Dublin

Kilmainham Gaol Archive
Eithne Coyle, 'Reminiscences of Eithne O'Donnell (née Coyle)', 12 July 1972 [unpublished memoir], 20MS–1B33–19.
Letter from Polly Cosgrove to Bridie Halpin on NDU paper, 19 July 1923, OBJ0027.

House of Commons Hansard Archives
Available at: https://hansard.parliament.uk; https://api.parliament.uk/historic-hansard/index. html.

Military Archives, Cathal Brugha Barracks, Military Rd, Rathmines
Bureau of Military History.
Cumann na mBan Nominal Rolls.
Irish Army Census Collection, 1922.
Military Service Pensions Collection.
1916 Medal and the Service (1917–21) Medals Series.

Mountjoy Prison, General Register of Prisoners
Superintendent Registrar's District of Dublin. Available at: findmypast.ie.

National Archives Dublin
Talbot Press Archive, 1048/1.
Census of Ireland 1901/1911 [online].

National Library of Ireland

Éamonn and Áine Ceannt, and Kathleen and Lily O'Brennan Papers, Mss 13,069–13,070; 41, 478–41,522.

Jackets Green, Typescript of a Novel by Fionn O'Malley (Pseud., i.e. Patrick Mulloy), Ms 2142.

John J. Hearn Papers, Mss 15,985–15,996.

Máirín Cregan Papers, Ms 50,423.

Niall Montgomery Papers, Ms 50,118.

Robert Brennan Papers, Ms 49,686.

Rosamond Jacob Papers, Mss 33,107–33,146; Ms 32,582.

Úna Troy Papers, Ms 35,683–35,699.

National Collection of Children's Books

Available at: https://nccb.tcd.ie.

National University of Ireland, Galway

Abbey Theatre Minute Books, Special Collections, NUI Galway.

The Papers of Seosamh Mac Grianna, G42/1–7.

New York University Archive

Ernie O'Malley Papers.

Online Sources

'Letter from 1st Southern Division IRA to General Headquarters IRA Society of Irish Revolutionary History and Militaria', Society of Irish Revolutionary History and Militaria, 12 April 2019. Available at: https://sirhm.com/2019/04/12/letter-from-1st-southern-division-ira-to-general-headquarters-ira/.

Royal Irish Constabulary Service Records 1816–1922

Available at: findmypast.ie.

RTÉ Radio Archives

Agallamh le Síghle Humphreys (Helen Ní Shé), 22 Márta 1987, Glórtha na Réabhlóide ar RTÉ Raidió na Gaeltachta. Available at: http://www.reabhloid.ie/items/show/46.

Máiréad Ní Ghráda, Interview [with Aedín Ní Chaoimh], Dá bhFaighinn Mo Rogha, RTÉ Radio, 28 March 1969. RTÉ Sound Archive. AA3326.

Tithe an Oireachtais – Dáil Éireann Debates

TG4

Bóthar na Saoirse – My Fight for Irish Freedom, Scéal Dan Breen, TG4, 12 January 2011.

The 1916 Rising Oral History Collections
Mullan, Carol. Interview [undated], *Irish Life & Lore*. Available at: https://www.irishlifeandlore. com.

University of Reading, Special Collections
Chatto & Windus Papers.

University College Dublin
Papers of Desmond Ryan, UCDA LA10.
Papers of Eithne Coyle O'Donnell, UCDA P61.
Papers of Ernie O'Malley, UCDA P17.
Papers of James Ryan, UCDA P88.
Papers of Máire Comerford, UCDA LA18.
Papers of Sighle Humphreys, UCDA P106.

Wilson Special Collections Library, University of North Carolina at Chapel Hill
J. M. Dent & Sons Records.

2. PRINTED PRIMARY SOURCES

a. Newspapers and Literary Journals
An Lóchrann
An tÓglach
Ballymena Observer
Belfast Newsletter
Capuchin Annual
Catholic Bulletin
Catholic World
Chambers's Journal
Democrat and Chronicle
Donegal Democrat
Dublin Magazine
Éire
El Paso Times
Evening Echo
Evening Herald
Fermanagh Herald
Fortnightly Review
Fort Worth Star Telegram
Ireland To-day
Irish Bulletin

Irish Christian Advocate (Belfast)
Irish Examiner
Irish Independent
Irishman
Kilkenny People
Leitrim Observer
Meath Chronicle
Methodist Magazine (London)
Montrose Review (Scotland)
My Garden
Natal Mercury (Durban, South Africa)
New York Herald Tribune
Northern Whig
Offaly Independent
Sligo Champion
Sunday Dispatch
Sunday Independent
Sunderland Daily Echo and Shipping Gazette
The Age (Melbourne)
The Bell
The Capuchin Annual
The Charlotte News (North Carolina)
The Cincinnati Enquirer
The Freeman's Journal
The Guardian
The Irish Book Lover
The Irish Home
The Irish Monthly
The Irish Press
The Irish Review (Dublin)
The Irish Review (New York)
The Irish Times
The Los Angeles Times
The Meath Chronicle
The New York Times
The Observer
The Post-Crescent (Wisconsin)
The Record (New Jersey)
The Saturday Review (Boston)
The Spectator
Universe (London)
Western People
Westmeath Independent
Yorkshire Post and Leeds Intelligencer

b. Testimony (Fiction and Non-fiction)

Andrews, C. S., *Dublin Made Me: An Autobiography* (Cork: Mercier Press, 1979).

— *A Man of No Property* (Cork: Mercier Press, 1981).

Bairéad, Tomás, *An Geall a Briseadh* (Baile Átha Cliath: Oifig Díolta Foillseacháin Rialtais, 1938).

— *Gan Baisteadh* (Baile Átha Cliath: Sáirséal agus Dill, 1972).

— *Tomás Bairéad: Rogha Scéalta*, edited by Aingeal Ní Chualáin (Indreabhán: Cló Iar-Chonnacht, 2010).

Barrington, Margaret, *My Cousin Justin* (London: J. Cape, 1939).

Barry, Dermot, *Tom Creagan: A Novel* (Dublin: At the Sign of the Three Candles, 1931).

Behan, Kathleen, *Mother of All the Behans: The Story of Kathleen Behan as Told to Brian Behan* (London: Hutchinson, 1984).

Bowen, Elizabeth, *The Last September* (London: Constable, 1929 [Random House, 2015]).

Breathnach, Mícheál, *Cuimhne an tSeanpháiste* (Baile Átha Cliath: Oifig an tSoláthair, 1966).

Breen, Dan, *My Fight for Irish Freedom* (Dublin: Talbot Press, 1924).

Brennan, Elizabeth, *His Glamorous Cousin* (London: Hale, 1963).

— *Her Lucky Mistake* (London: Hale, 1966).

— *Retreat from Love* (London: Hale, 1967).

— *Love in the Glade* (London: Hale, 1968).

— *The Parting of the Ways: A One-Act Play*, RTÉ Written Archives, Radio Drama Scripts, UCDA p. 261/254 [1969].

— *Patrick's Woman* (London: Hale, 1969).

— *Mountain of Desire* (London: Hale, 1970).

— *Innocent in Eden* (London: Hale, 1971).

— *Wacht niet liefste* [Dutch translation] (Amsterdam: N.V. Uitg. Mij. Mundus, 1971).

— *No Roses for Jo* (London: Hale, 1972).

— *Love's Loom* (London: Hale, 1973).

— *A Girl Called Debbie* (London: Hale, 1975).

— *Kom tilbake, Peter* [Norwegian translation] (Oslo, 1978).

— *Sweet Love of Youth* (London: Hale, 1978).

— *Girl on an Island* (London: London: Hale, 1984).

Brennan, Michael, *The War in Clare, 1911–1921: Personal Memoirs of the Irish War of Independence* (Dublin: Four Courts Press, 1980).

Brennan, Robert, *The Toledo Dagger* (London: John Hamilton, 1926).

— *Allegiance* (Dublin: Browne and Nolan, 1950).

— *The Man Who Walked Like a Dancer* (London: Rich and Cowan, 1951).

Briscoe, Robert, *For the Life of Me* (Boston, MA: Little, Brown, 1958).

Brophy, John, *The Rocky Road* (London: J. Cape, 1932).

Buckley, Margaret, *The Jangle of the Keys* (Dublin: J. Duffy & Company, 1938).

Campbell, Joseph, *'As I Was Among the Captives': Joseph Campbell's Prison Diary, 1922–1923*, edited by Eilean Ní Chuilleanáin (Cork: Cork University Press, 2001).

Carty, Francis, *Léigheacht Ar Ghéibheann Shasana Indiu: Deis Éireann: Lecture on England's Difficulties To-day and Ireland's Opportunity* (Baile Átha Cliath: Sinn Féin Árd-Chomhairle, 1922).

— *The Irish Volunteer* (London: J. M. Dent & Sons, 1932).

— *Legion of the Rearguard* (London: J. M. Dent & Sons, 1934).

— *Two and Fifty Irish Saints: With a Foreword by John Ryan* (Dublin: Duffy, 1941).

— *Irish Saints in Ten Countries* (Dublin: Duffy, 1942).

— *Blood on the Main St* [unpublished novel draft], undated.

Cashel, Alice M., *The Lights of Leaca Bán: A Story of Recent Times in Ireland* (Dublin: Browne and Nolan, 1935).

Clarke, Kathleen, *Revolutionary Woman: Kathleen Clarke, 1878–1972: An Autobiography*, edited by Helen Litton (Dublin: O'Brien Press, 1991).

Collins, Michael, *The Path to Freedom* (Dublin: Talbot Press, 1922).

Collis, John Stewart, *The Sounding Cataract* (London: Cassell, 1936).

Comerford, James J., *My Kilkenny Days: 1916–22* (Kilkenny: Dinan Publishing, 1980).

Comerford, Máire, *Lasamar ár dTinte*, translated by Diarmaid Ó Murchú, *Agus* [journal] (Corcaigh), 1981–90.

Conlon, Lil, *Cumann na mBan and the Women of Ireland, 1913–25* (Kilkenny: Kilkenny People Ltd, 1969).

Conner, Rearden, *Shake Hands with the Devil: A Novel* (London: J. M. Dent & Sons, 1933).

— *A Plain Tale from the Bogs* (London: J. Miles, 1937).

Connor, Elizabeth, *Dead Star's Light* (London: Methuen & Company, 1938).

— 'Typescript *The Dark Road*, a Play in Three Acts with Prologue and Epilogue', NLI, Úna Troy Papers, Ms 35,687.

Corkery, Daniel, *Hounds of Banba* (Dublin: Talbot Press, 1920).

Cregan, Máirín, *Hunger-strike: A Play in Two Acts* (Dublin: M. H. Gill, 1932).

— 'The Rush to Meet the Arms-Ship', *The Irish Press*, 24 April 1933, p. 6.

— 'Carrying the Message in Easter Week: A Courier's Thrilling Story', *The Irish Press*, 25 December 1934, pp. 13 and 36.

— 'James Connolly: An Incident', *The Capuchin Annual*, 1936, p. 226.

— *Old John* (New York: Macmillan, 1936).

— 'Curlew's Call', *The Capuchin Annual* 1940, pp. 177–89.

— *Rathina* (New York: Macmillan, 1942).

— Máirín Ryan, Interview, Ernie O'Malley Papers, UCDA p17b/103 [undated].

Crowley Ford, Anne, *When I Am Going: Growing Up in Ireland and Coming to America, 1901–1927*, edited by Daniel Ford (Scotts Valley, CA: CreateSpace Independent, 2012).

Crozier, Frank Percy, *The Men I Killed* (London: Joseph, 1937).

D'Alton, Louis, *Death Is So Fair* (London: William Heinemann, 1936).

Dalton, Charles, *With the Dublin Brigade (1917–1921)* (London: Peter Davies, 1929).

de Paor, Mairéad and Siobhán, 'Blaze Away With Your Gun', *The Kerryman*, 21 December 1968, December 1968 and 3 January 1969.

Deasy, Liam, *Brother Against Brother* (Cork: Mercier Press, 1982).

Deevy, Teresa, 'Just Yesterday: A Story', *Green and Gold: A Magazine of Fiction, etc.*, vol. IV, no. 17 December 1924–March 1925, pp. 268–76.

Dirrane, Bridget, Rose O'Connor and Jack Mahon, *A Woman of Aran: The Life and Times of Bridget Dirrane* (Dublin: Blackwater Press, 1997).

Dublin's Fighting Story, 1913–1921 (Tralee: Kerryman, 1948).

Fanning, A, P., *Vigil: A Play in One Act* (Dublin: P. J. Bourke, 1961).

Farrell, Michael, *Thy Tears Might Cease* (London: Hutchinson, 1964).

Gallagher, Frank, *Days of Fear* (London: John Murray, 1928).

— *The Four Glorious Years* (Dublin: Irish Press, 1953).

Gonne, Maud, *A Servant of the Queen: Reminiscences* (London: Victor Gollancz, 1938).

Good, Joe, *Inside the GPO 1916: A First-hand Account* (Dublin: O'Brien Press, 2015).

Graham, Esther [Lily O'Brennan], *The Call to Arms: A Tale of the Land League Days* (Dublin: Browne and Nolan, 1929).

Greene, Graham, *Reflections*, edited by Judith Adamson (London: Reinhardt, 1990).

Gregory, Lady, *Lady Gregory's Journals: Book One to Twenty-Nine, 10 October 1916–24 February 1925* (Oxford: Oxford University Press, 1978).

Hardy, J. L., *Everything is Thunder* (London: Doubleday, 1935).

— *Never in Vain* (London: Collins 1936).

— *Recoil: A Mystery Novel* (London, Doubleday, 1936).

Harpur, Mary (O'Connor), Memoir (unpublished, undated).

Harrington, Niall C., *Kerry Landing – August 1922: An Episode of the Civil War* (Tralee: Anvil Books, 1992).

Hartnett, Mossie, *Victory and Woe: The West Limerick Brigade in the War of Independence* (Dublin: UCD Press, 2002).

Hartnett, Sheila, 'There is a Great Loneliness on Me', 'Comradeship in Kilmainham', 'Once Upon a Time in Kenmare', *The Irish Press*, 29, 30 and 31 December 1971, p. 9, p. 17, p. 17.

Henderson, Frank, *Frank Henderson's Easter Rising: Recollections of a Dublin Volunteer*, edited by Michael Hopkinson (Cork: Cork University Press, 1998).

Henry, Martin, *Ambushed Lovers: A Tale of The Troubled Times in Ireland* (Dublin: Talbot Press, 1929).

Hoagland, Clayton and Kathleen, *Thomas Wolfe, Our Friend, 1933–1938: A Dated Record from the Journal of Clayton Hoagland* (Virginia: Croissant, 1979).

Hoagland, Kathleen, *Fiddler in the Sky* (New York: Harper & Brothers, 1944).

— *1000 Years of Irish Poetry: The Gaelic and Anglo-Irish Poets from Pagan Times to the Present* (New York: Devin-Adair Company, 1947).

Hogan, David, *The Challenge of the Sentry and Other Stories of the Irish War* (Dublin: Talbot Press, 1928).

— *Dark Mountain, and Other Stories* (London: Harold Shaylor, 1931).

Hogan, Patrick, *The Unmarried Daughter and Other Stories* (Dublin: George Roberts, 1928).

— *Camps on the Hearthstone* (Dublin: C. J. Fallon Limited, 1956).

Horan, Eily, *Through the Gates of Babylon: The Story of a Conversion* (Belfast: Christian Irishman, 1932).

— *No More Foreigners: Impressions of a Spiritual Pilgrimage* (London: Lutterworth Press, 1935).

Horan, Pádraig Kevin, *Eyes of My Love: Twenty Poems* (London: Stockwell, 1924).

— 'The Flame of Youth: A Study in Rebel Mentality', *Irish Christian Advocate*, November 1927– October 1928.

— 'Incident[s] from the Civil War in Ireland' [series], *Methodist Magazine*, 1927–8.

— *In the Crown of a Stranger. An Irish Historical Review, with Special Reference to the Papacy* (Belfast: Christian Irishman, 1933).

Irwin, Thomas P., *Benson's Flying Column* (Dublin: Talbot Press, 1935).

Jacob, Rosamond, *The Troubled House: A Novel of Dublin in the 'Twenties* (Dublin: Browne and Nolan, 1938).

— *The Rebel's Wife* (Tralee: Kerryman, 1957).

Kearney, Selskar, *The False Finger Tip: An Irish Detective Story* (Dublin: Maunsel & Roberts, 1921).

Kearns, Linda and Annie M. P. Smithson (eds), *In Times of Peril: Leaves from the Diary of Nurse Linda Kearns from Easter Week, 1916, to Mountjoy, 1921* (Dublin: Talbot Press, 1922).

Kenna, G. B., *Facts and Figures of the Belfast Pogrom 1920–1922* (Belfast: O'Connell Publishing Company, 1922).

Kerry's Fighting Story, 1916–21 (Tralee: Kerryman, 1947).

Lankford, Siobhán, *The Hope and the Sadness: Personal Recollections of Troubled Times in Ireland* (Cork: Tower Books, 1980).

Lennon, George, 'Television Play Manuscript, *Down by the Glen Side*: An Original Television Play "Live", September, 1952 (To Janet)', NLI Ms 35,699 (1).

— *Trauma in Time: (An Irish Itinerary)* (unpublished: *c.* 1971). Available at: http://www.waterfordmuseum.ie/exhibit/web/Display/article/317/Memoirs_Of_George_Lennon_.html; https://www.academia.edu/6362572/GGL_TRAUMA_IN_TIME (accessed 8 August 2020).

Limerick's Fighting Story, 1916–21 (Tralee: Kerryman, 1948).

Lloyd, Nora, *The Young May Moon* (London: Nelson, 1936).

Macardle, Dorothy, 'The Kilmainham Tortures: Experiences of a Prisoner', *Éire*, 1 May 1923, p. 4.

— 'Letter from Kilmainham', *Éire*, 12 May 1923, p. 5.

— 'Mountjoy', *Éire*, 2 June 1923.

— 'The Prisoner' [poem], *Éire*, 30 June 1923, p. 2.

— 'A Year Ago', *Éire*, 14 July 1923, p. 2.

— 'Thoughts in a Hospital', *Éire*, 20 October 1923, pp. 4–5.

— 'The Prisoners: 1798–1923', *Éire*, 13 September 1924, pp. 1–2.

— *Earth-bound: Nine Stories of Ireland* (Worchester, MA: Harrigan Press, 1924).

— *Tragedies of Kerry 1922–1923* (Dublin: Emton Press, 1924).

— *The Irish Republic: a Documented Chronicle of the Anglo-Irish Conflict and the Partitioning of Ireland, with a Detailed Account of the Period 1916–1923* (Dublin: Irish Press, 1937).

— *Uneasy Freehold* (London: Peter Davies, 1941).

— *The Unforeseen* (Garden City, NY: Doubleday, 1946).

— *The Dark Enchantment* (Garden City, NY: Doubleday, 1953).

MacCall, Séamus, *Gods in Motley* (London: Constable, 1935).

McDonnell, Kathleen Keyes, *There is a Bridge at Bandon: A Personal Account of the Irish War of Independence* (Cork: Mercier Press, 1972).

MacEntee, Séan, *Episode at Easter* (Dublin: Gill, 1966).

Mac Eoin, Uinseann (ed.), *Survivors: The Story of Ireland's Struggle as Told through Some of Her Outstanding Living People Recalling Events from the Days of Davitt, through James Connolly, Brugha, Collins, Liam Mellows, and Rory O'Connor, to the Present Time* (Dublin: Argenta Publications, 1980).

Mac Giolla Iasachta, Éamonn, *Toil Dé* (Baile Átha Cliath: Oifig Díolta Foillseacháin Rialtais, 1933).

Mac Grianna, Seosamh, *Dá mBíodh Ruball ar an Éan* (Baile Átha Cliath: Oifig an tSoláthair, 1940).

McGuinness, Charles John, *Nomad: Memoirs of an Irish Sailor, Soldier, Pearl-Fisher, Pirate, Gun-Runner, Rum-Rummer, Rebel and Antarctic Explorer* (London: Methuen, 1934).

McKenna, Kathleen, *A Dáil Girl's Revolutionary Recollections* (Dublin: Original Writing, 2014).

McLaverty, Michael, *Call My Brother Back: A Novel* (London: Longmans, Green and Co., 1939).

MacManus, L., *White Light and Flame: Memories of the Irish Literary Revival and the Anglo–Irish War* (Dublin: Talbot Press, 1929).

Manning, Mary, *Mount Venus* (Boston, MA: Houghton Mifflin Company, 1938).

Mullins, Billy, *Memoirs of Billy Mullins: Veteran of the War of Independence* (Tralee: Kenno, 1983).

Mulloy, Patrick, *Jackets Green: A Novel* (London: Grayson & Grayson, 1936).

— *Andy Tinpockets* (London: Thames Publishing Co, 1950).

— *Harvest of the Wind* (unpublished play, 1964).

Murphy, Jeremiah, *When Youth Was Mine – A Memoir of Kerry 1902–1925* (Dublin: Mentor Books, 1998 [2018]).

Ní Ghráda, Máiréad, *An Giolla Deacair agus Scéalta Eile* (Baile Átha Cliath: Comhlacht Oideachais na hÉireann Teo, 1936),

— *An Bheirt Dearbhráthar agus Scéalta Eile* (Baile Átha Cliath: Oifig an tSoláthair, 1939).

— *Stailc Ocrais: Tragóid Stairiúil, Dráma Aonghnímh* (Baile Átha Cliath: Oifig an tSoláthair, 1966).

— *Breithiúnas: Dráma Dhá Ghníomh* (Baile Átha Cliath: An Gúm, 1996).

O'Brennan, Kathleen, *Full Measure: A Play in Three Acts*, NLI, Ms 15,601.

O'Brien, Nora Connolly, *We Shall Rise Again* (London: Mosquito Press, 1981).

Ó Broin, León, *An Mhallacht agus Drámaí Eile* (Baile Átha Cliath: Oifig Díolta Foillseacháin Rialtais, 1931).

Ó Caomhánaigh, Seán Óg, *Fánaí* (Baile Átha Cliath: Oifig an tSoláthair, 1927 [1989]).

— 'Dialann Phríosúin Sheáin a' Chóta', edited by Mícheál Ó Catháin (unpublished PhD thesis, NUI Maynooth, 2012).

O'Casey, Seán, *Two Plays: Juno and the Paycock: The Shadow of a Gunman* (London: Macmillan, 1925).

O'Connor, Anthony, *He's Somewhere in There* (London: Foxgate, 1975).

— *Clubland: The Wrong Side of the Right People* (London: Martin Brian & O'Keefe, 1976).

O'Connor, Frank, *Guests of the Nation* (London: Macmillan, 1931).

— 'A Boy in Prison', *Life and Letters*, August 1934, pp. 525–35.

— *The Big Fellow: A Life of Michael Collins* (London: T. Nelson, 1937).

— *Dutch Interior* (London: Macmillan, 1940).

— *An Only Child* (London: Macmillan, 1961).

— *My Father's Son* (Syracuse, NY: Syracuse University Press, 1968 [1999]).

O'Connor, J. F., *Irish Civil War Exile* (New York: Vantage Press, 1989).

O'Connor, Séamus, *Tomorrow was Another Day: The Irreverent, Humorous Earthy Memories of an Irish Rebel Schoolmaster* (Tralee: Anvil Books, 1970).

O'Donnell, Peadar, *Storm: A Story of the Irish War* (Dublin: Talbot Press, 1925).

— *Adrigoole* (London: J. Cape, 1929).

— *The Knife* (London: Jonathan Cape, 1930).

— *The Gates Flew Open* (London: J. Cape, 1932).

— *On the Edge of the Stream* (London: J. Cape, 1934).

— *Salud! An Irishman in Spain* (London: Methuen, 1937).

— *There Will Be Another Day* (Dublin: Dolemen Press, 1963).

O'Donoghue, Florence, *No Other Law: The Story of Liam Lynch and the Irish Republican Army, 1916–1923* (Dublin: Irish Press, 1954).

O'Driscoll, Garrett, 'A Flippant Young Man: A Story', *Green and Gold: A Magazine of Fiction, etc.*, vol. II, no. 8 (November 1922), pp. 167–76.

— 'The June Babies: A Story', *Green and Gold: A Magazine of Fiction, etc.*, vol. IV, no. 16 (November 1924), pp. 223–34.

— 'Mettle: A Story', *Green and Gold: A Magazine of Fiction, etc.*, vol. V, no. 21 (December 1925), pp. 263–71.

— 'The Blind Man: A Story', *Green and Gold: A Magazine of Fiction, etc.*, vol. V, no. 20 (November 1925), pp. 133–40.

— 'The Lacklander: A Story', *Green and Gold: A Magazine of Fiction, etc.*, vol. V, no. 18 (1925), pp. 1–11.

— *Noreen* (London: George Roberts, 1929).

— 'Lavender in God's Garden', *Catholic World*, March 1932, pp. 676–83.

— 'Soul's Alley', *Catholic World*, June 1934, pp. 274–82.

— 'He That Hath Eyes', *Catholic World*, November 1934, p. 157.

— 'Estuary', *Catholic World*, December 1935, pp. 282–90.

— 'The Bean-a-Tighe Looks Back', *The Meath Chronicle*, 7 September 1935, p. 8.

— 'At That Time', *Catholic World*, March 1937, pp. 661–8.

— 'Fair Day', *Ireland To-day*, vol. II, no. 8, August 1937, pp. 49–57.

— 'The Between-World of Children', *Catholic World*, March 1938, pp. 718–23.

Ó Dubhda, Peadar, *Brian* (Baile Átha Cliath: Oifig Díolta Foillseacháin Rialtais, 1937).

O'Duffy, Eimar, *The Wasted Island* (Dublin: Martin Lester, 1919).

O'Faoláin, Seán, *Midsummer Night Madness: And Other Stories* (London: J. Cape, 1932).

— *Vive Moi! An Autobiography* (Boston, MA: Little Brown, 1964).

— *Vive Moi!* [new edition] (London: Sinclair-Stevenson, 1993).

O'Flaherty, Liam, *The Informer* (London: Jonathan Cape, 1925).

— *The Assassin* (London: Jonathan Cape, 1928).

— *Return of the Brute* (London: Mandrake, 1929).

— *The Martyr* (London: V. Gollancz Limited, 1933).

— *Shame the Devil* (London: Grayson & Grayson, 1934).

— *The Letters of Liam O'Flaherty*, edited by A. A. Kelly (Dublin: Wolfhound Press, 1996).

Ó Gallchobhair, Proinnsias, 'Leaves from a Prison Diary', *Éire & Sinn Féin*, 1924.

Ó Gaora, Colm, 'An Díoghaltas', in *As na Ceithre h-Áirdibh: Cnuasach Gearr-Scéal* (Baile Átha Cliath: Oifig an tSoláthair, 1938).

— *Mise* (Baila Átha Cliath: Oifig an tSoláthair, 1943).

Ó Grianna, Séamus, *Saoghal Corrach* (Baile Átha Cliath: An Press Náisiunta, 1945).

— *The Sea's Revenge and Other Stories*, edited by Nollaig Mac Congáil (Cork: Mercier Press, 2003).

O'Hegarty, P. S., *The Victory of Sinn Féin: How It Won It and How It Used It* (Dublin: Talbot Press, 1924).

O'Horan, Eily, 'Oh, Come All Ye Faithful', *Cork Holly Bough and Weekly Examiner*, Christmas 1936, p. 7.

— 'Christmas Hamper', *Cork Holly Bough and Weekly Examiner*, Christmas 1937, p. 10.

— 'The Old Bog Road', *Chambers's Journal*, vol. VI, 1937, pp. 738–41.

— 'The Young May Moon', *Chambers's Journal*, vol. VI, 1937, pp. 356–60.

— 'Lady of my Delight', *Chambers's Journal*, vol. VII, 1938, pp. 539–44.

— 'The Christmas Candle', *Chambers's Journal*, vol. VII, 1938, pp. 898–903.

— 'Footsteps on the Stairs', *Chambers's Journal*, vol. VIII, 1939, pp. 938–44.

— 'The Tower', *Chambers's Journal*, vol. X, 1941, pp. 657–61.

— 'Tryst at Sheelin', *Chambers's Journal*, vol. XII, 1943, pp. 355–7.

— 'The Quality', *Chambers's Journal*, vol. XIII, 1944, pp. 649–51.

— 'Optimists, a Story', *The Bell*, vol. VII, no. 5, February 1944, pp. 410–17.

— 'The Rustle of Spring, a Story', *The Bell*, vol. XIII, No. 5, February 1947, pp. 28–39.

— 'The Bend of the Road', *Catholic World* 169, no. 1012, July 1949, pp. 263–8.

— 'Ripe Gooseberries', *My Garden*, August 1949, pp. 135–8.

— 'A Touch of Nature', *Catholic World* 169, no. 1014, September 1949, p. 412.

— 'The Proud O'Dempseys', *Catholic World* 170, no. 1018, January 1950, pp. 252–9.

O'Horan, Pádraig, *Roadways of the Heart: Poems* (London: Fortune Press, 1943).

— *The Bright-winged Piper: Poems* (London: Fortune Press, 1945).

— *The Proud and Lovely: Poems* (London: Fortune Press, 1946).

— *Wheat and a Rose: Poems* (London: Fortune Press, 1947).

— *Gabriel Was a Troubadour: Poems of the Nativity* (London: A. R. Mowbray, 1948).

O'Malley, Edward, *Memories of a Mayoman* (Dublin: Foilseacháin Náisiúnta Teoranta, 1981).

O'Malley, Ernie, *On Another Man's Wound* (Dublin: At the Sign of the Three Candles, 1936).

— *The Singing Flame* (Tralee: Anvil Books, 1978).

— *Prisoners: The Civil War Letters of Ernie O'Malley*, edited by Richard English (Dublin: Poolbeg, 1991).

— *Rising Out: Seán Connolly of Longford (1890–1921)* (Dublin: UCD Press, 2007).

— *The Men Will Talk to Me: Galway Interviews by Ernie O'Malley*, edited by Cormac Ó Comhraí and Cormac O'Malley (Cork: Mercier Press, 2013).

Ó Maoileoin, Séamus, *B'fhiú an Braon Fola* (Baile Átha Cliath: Sáirséal agus Dill, 1958).

Ó Siochfhradha, Mícheál, *Deire an Chunntais: Dráma Aon-Mhire* (Baile Átha Cliath: Oifig Díolta Foillseacháin Rialtais, 1932).

Phelan, Jim, *Green Volcano* (London: Peter Davies, 1938).

— *Lifer* (London: Peter Davies, 1938).

— *The Name's Phelan: The First Part of the Autobiography of Jim Phelan* (Belfast: Blackstaff Press, 1943 [1993]).

Pinkman, John A., *In the Legion of the Vanguard* (Cork: Mercier Press, 1998).

Plunkett, Francis, *As the Fool* (London: Wishart, 1935).

Quill, Shirley, *Mike Quill, Himself: A Memoir* (Greenwich, CT: Devin-Adair, 1985).

Rebel Cork's Fighting Story, 1916–1921: Told by the Men Who Made It (Tralee: Kerryman, 1947).

Remarque, Erich Maria, *All Quiet on the Western Front* (English translation of *Im Westen nichts Neues* by A. W. Wheen) (Boston, MA: Little Brown, 1929).

Robinson, Lennox, *The Big House: Four Scenes in Its Life* (London: Macmillan, 1928).

— *Curtain Up: An Autobiography* (London: M. Joseph, 1942).

Ryan, Desmond, *The Man Called Pearse* (Dublin: Maunsel and Company, 1919).

— *James Connolly: His Life, Work & Writings* (Dublin: Talbot Press, 1924).

— *The Invisible Army: A Story of Michael Collins* (London: A. Barker, 1932).

— *Remembering Sion: A Chronicle of Storm and Quiet* (London: A. Barker, 1934).

— *Unique Dictator: A Study of Eamon de Valera* (London: A. Barker, 1936).

— 'Still Remembering Sion', *University Review* 5, no. 2 (1968), pp. 245–52.

Sarr, Kenneth, *Somewhere to the Sea* (London: T. Nelson, 1936).

Scot, Michael, *Three Tales of the Times* (Dublin: Talbot Press, 1921).

Shaw, Desmond, *The Drama of Sinn Féin* (New York: C. Scribner's sons, 1923).

Smithson, Annie M. P., 'Hills O' Home', *Green and Gold: A Magazine of Fiction, etc.*, vol. I, no. 4, September 1921, pp. 255–60.

— 'The Guide: A Story', *Green and Gold: A Magazine of Fiction, etc.*, vol. I, no. 2, March 1921, pp. 81–5.

— The *Walk of a Queen* (Dublin: Talbot Press, 1922 [1989]).

— *The Guide [Short Stories]* (Dublin: Catholic Truth Society, 1923).

— *The Marriage of Nurse Harding* (Dublin: Talbot Press, 1935 [1989]).

— *Myself – and Others: An Autobiography* (Dublin: Talbot Press, 1944).

Stuart, Francis, *Pigeon Irish* (London: Macmillan, 1932).

— *The Coloured Dome* (London: V. Gollancz, 1932).

— *Things to Live for: Notes for an Autobiography* (London: Macmillan, 1935).

— *Black List, Section H* (Carbondale: Southern Illinois University Press, 1971).

Uí Dhiosca, Úna, *Cailín na Gruaige Duinne* (Baile Átha Cliath: Oifig Díolta Foillseacháin Rialtais, 1932).

Walsh, A. T., *Casey of the I.R.A.* (Dublin: Talbot Press, 1923).

Walsh, Louis J., *On My Keeping and in Theirs: A Record of Experiences 'on the Run', in Derry Gaol, and in Ballykinlar Interment Camp* (Dublin: Talbot Press, 1921).

Walsh, Michael, 'Dublin Literary Memories', in Patrick Walsh (ed.), *Along My Father's Hills: A Miscellany by Michael and William Walsh* (Dublin: Colour Books, 1997).

Wynne, Jake, *Ugly Brew* (London: Chatto & Windus, 1936).

3. OTHER PRINTED WORKS

Adamia, Elisa, 'The Truth of Fiction: Some Stories of the Lebanese Civil War', in Karine Deslandes, Fabrice Mourlon and Bruno Tribout (eds), *Civil War and Narrative: Testimony, Historiography, Memory* (New York: Palgrave Macmillan, 2017), pp. 109–28.

Aiken Jnr, Frank, 'Preface', in Bryce Evans and Stephen Kelly (eds), *Frank Aiken: Nationalist and Internationalist* (Dublin: Irish Academic Press, 2014), pp. xv–xx.

Aiken, Síobhra, '"Sinn Féin Permits … in the Heels of Their Shoes": Cumann na mBan Emigrants and Transatlantic Revolutionary Exchange', *Irish Historical Studies* 44, no. 165 (May 2020), pp. 106–30.

— '"The Women Who Had Been Straining Every Nerve": Gender-Specific Medical Management of Trauma in the Irish Revolution (1916–1923)', in Melania Terrazas Gallego (ed.), *Trauma and Identity in Contemporary Irish Culture* (Bern: Peter Lang, 2020), pp. 133–58.

— 'In Aghaidh na Díchuimhne: Dúshlán Mháiréad Ní Ghráda do Mhórscéal Fearúil Réabhlóid na hÉireann', *Léann: Iris Chumann Léann na Litríochta*, 2021, pp. 39–59.

— '"Sick on the Irish Sea, Dancing Across the Atlantic": (Anti-)Nostalgia in Women's Diasporic Remembrance of the Irish Revolution', in Oona Frawley (ed.), *Women and the Decade of Commemorations* (Bloomington, IN: Indiana University Press, 2021), pp. 88–106.

— 'The Silence and the Silence Breakers of the Irish Civil War 1922–2022', *Éire-Ireland*, edited by Sara Dybris McQuaid and Fearghal McGarry, Spring/Summer 2022.

Aiken, Síobhra, Fearghal Mac Bhloscaidh, Liam Ó Duibhir and Diarmuid Ó Tuama (eds), *The Men Will Talk to Me: Ernie O'Malley's Interviews with the Northern Divisions* (Dublin: Merrion Press, 2018).

Alexander, Jeffrey C., 'Toward a Theory of Cultural Trauma', in Jeffrey C. Alexander, Ron Eyerman, Bernard Giesen, Neil J. Smelser and Piotr Sztompka (eds), *Cultural Trauma and Collective Identity* (Oakland, CA: University of California Press, 2004), pp. 1–30.

Allen, Nicholas, 'Frank O'Connor and Critical Memory', in Hilary Lennon (ed.), *Frank O'Connor: Critical Essays* (Dublin: Four Courts Press, 2007), pp. 27–40.

— *Modernism, Ireland and Civil War* (Cambridge: Cambridge University Press, 2009).

— 'Reading Revolutions, 1922–39', in Clare Hutton and Patrick Walsh (eds), *The Oxford History of the Irish Book. Volume V: The Irish Book in English, 1891–2000* (Oxford: Oxford University Press, 2011), pp. 89–107.

Allen-Randolph, Jody, *Eavan Boland* (Washington, D.C.: Rowman & Littlefield, 2013).

— '"If No One Wanted to Remember": Margaret Kelly and the Lost Battalion', in Tina O'Toole, Gillian McIntosh and Muireann O'Cinnéide (eds), *Women Writing War: Ireland 1880–1922* (Dublin: UCD Press, 2016), pp. 133–49.

Aretxaga, Begoña, *Shattering Silence: Women, Nationalism, and Political Subjectivity in Northern Ireland* (Princeton, NJ: Princeton University Press, 1997).

Armitage, David, 'Ideas of Civil War in 17th-Century England', *Annals of the Japanese Association for the Study of Puritanism* 4 (2009), pp. 4–18.

— 'Civil Wars, from Beginning ... to End?', *American Historical Review* 120, no. 5 (2015), pp. 1829–37.

— *Civil Wars: A History in Ideas* (New Haven, CT: Yale University Press, 2017).

— 'Three Narratives of Civil War: Recurrence, Remembrance and Reform from Sulla to Syria', in Karine Deslandes, Fabrice Mourlon and Bruno Tribout (eds), *Civil War and Narrative: Testimony, Historiography, Memory* (New York: Palgrave Macmillan, 2017), pp. 1–18.

Bacopoulos-Viau, Alexandra, 'From the Writing Cure to the Talking Cure: Revisiting the French "Discovery of the Unconscious"', *History of the Human Sciences*, 8 May 2019.

Balaev, Michelle, 'Trends in Literary Trauma Theory', *Mosaic: An Interdisciplinary Critical Journal* 41, no. 2 (2008), pp. 149–66.

Balliett, Conrad, 'The Lives – and Lies – of Maud Gonne', *Éire–Ireland*, vol. 13, no. 3 (Fall 1979), pp. 17–44.

Bashford-Synnott, Marie, 'Annie M. P. Smithson Romantic Novelist, Revolutionary Nurse', *Dublin Historical Record* 64, no. 1 (2011), pp. 47–68.

Bayer, Gerd, 'Trauma and the Literature of War', in J. Roger Kurtz (ed.), *Trauma and Literature* (Cambridge: Cambridge University Press, 2018), pp. 213–25.

Beiner, Guy, 'Between Trauma and Triumphalism: The Easter Rising, the Somme, and the Crux of Deep Memory in Modern Ireland', *Journal of British Studies* 46, no. 2 (2007), pp. 366–89.

— *Remembering the Year of the French: Irish Folk History and Social Memory* (Madison, WI: University of Wisconsin Press, 2007).

— *Forgetful Remembrance: Social Forgetting and Vernacular Historiography of a Rebellion in Ulster* (Oxford: Oxford University Press, 2018).

— 'Memory Too Has a History', *Dublin Review of Books*, 1 March 2015. Available at: https://www.drb.ie/essays/memory-too-has-a-history (accessed 9 February 2020).

Benton, Sarah, 'Women Disarmed: The Militarization of Politics in Ireland 1913–23', *Feminist Review*, no. 50 (1995), pp. 148–72.

Beville, Maria, 'Gothic Memory and the Contested Past: Framing Terror', in Lorna Piatti-Farnell and Maria Beville (eds), *The Gothic and the Everyday: Living Gothic* (London: Palgrave Macmillan, 2014), pp. 52–68.

Bielby, Clare, 'Scripting the Perpetrating Self: Masculinity, Class and Violence in German Post-Terrorist Autobiography', in Clare Bielby and Jeffrey Stevenson Murer (eds), *Perpetrating Selves: Doing Violence, Performing Identity* (London: Palgrave Macmillan, 2018), pp. 85–111.

Bonanno, George A., 'Loss, Trauma, and Human Resilience: Have We Underestimated the Human Capacity to Thrive After Extremely Aversive Events?', *American Psychologist* 59, no. 1 (2004), pp. 20–8.

Borgonovo, John, *Spies, Informers and the 'Anti-Sinn Féin Society': The Intelligence War in Cork City, 1920–1921* (Dublin: Irish Academic Press, 2007).

— '"Exercising a Close Vigilance over Their Daughters": Cork Women, American Sailors, and Catholic Vigilantes, 1917–18', *Irish Historical Studies* 38, no. 149 (2012), pp. 89–107.

Bourke, Joanna, *An Intimate History of Killing: Face-to-Face Killing in Twentieth-Century Warfare* (London: Granta Books, 2000).

— 'Effeminacy, Ethnicity and the End of Trauma: The Sufferings of "Shell-Shocked" Men in Great Britain and Ireland, 1914–39', *Journal of Contemporary History* 35, no. 1 (2000), pp. 57–69.

— 'Sexual Violence, Bodily Pain, and Trauma: A History', *Theory, Culture & Society* 29, no. 3 (May 2012), pp. 25–31.

Boyd, Ernest, 'Joyce and the New Irish Writers', *Current History (1916–1940)* 39, no. 6 (1934), pp. 699–704.

Boylan, Tom, 'Peadar O'Donnell: A Rebellious Relative', in Ciara Boylan, Sarah-Anne Buckley and Pat Dolan (eds), *Family Histories of the Irish Revolution* (Dublin: Four Courts, 2018), pp. 176–89.

Brady, Donal, *Úna Troy 1910–1993: Her Life and Work* (Waterford: Copper Coast Geopark), 2012.

Brennan, Elizabeth, *Out of the Darkness* (Dublin: Metropolitan Publishing Company, 1945).

— *Am I My Brother's Keeper?* (Dublin: Metropolitan Publishing Company, 1946).

Brennan, Fiona, 'Máirín Cregan: Author and Playwright', *Killorglin's River of Memories* (Castleconway: Killorglin Archive Society, 2020), pp. 20–9.

Brown, Laura S., 'Not Outside the Range: One Feminist Perspective on Psychic Trauma', *American Imago* 48, no. 1 (1991), pp. 119–33.

Brown, Terence, *The Literature of Ireland: Culture and Criticism* (Cambridge: Cambridge University Press, 2010).

Bruck, Joanna, '"A Good Irishman Should Blush Every Time He Sees a Penny": Gender, Nationalism and Memory in Irish Internment Camp Craftwork, 1916–1923', *Journal of Material Culture* 20(2) 2015, pp. 149–72.

Burke, John, *Athlone 1900–1923: Politics, Revolution & Civil War* (Dublin: History Press, 2015).

Butler, Ann. M., 'Úna Troy – Author', Copper Coast Geopark, 17 April 2017. Available at: https://coppercoastgeopark.com/una-troy-author/ (accessed 20 August 2020).

Byrne, Susan, '"Keeping Company with the Enemy": Gender and Sexual Violence against Women during the Irish War of Independence and Civil War, 1919–1923', *Women's History Review*, 2 March 2020, pp. 1–18.

Byron, Kristine A., *Women, Revolution, and Autobiographical Writing in the Twentieth Century: Writing History, Writing the Self* (New York: Edwin Mellen, 2007).

Cahalan, James M., *Great Hatred, Little Room: The Irish Historical Novel* (Syracuse, NY: Syracuse University Press, 1983).

Cahill, Susan, '"Far Away From the Busy World": Máirín Cregan's Children's Literature', in John Countryman and Kelly Matthews (eds), *The Country of the Young: Interpretations of Youth and Childhood in Irish Culture* (Dublin: Four Courts Press, 2013), pp. 70–85.

Carty, Ciaran, *Confessions of a Sewer Rat: A Personal History of Censorship & the Irish Cinema* (Dublin: New Island Books, 1995).

— *Intimacy with Strangers: A Life of Brief Encounters* (Dublin: Lilliput Press, 2013).

Carty, Francis Xavier, *Bruises, Baws and Bastards: Glimpses into a Long Life Passing* (Able Press, 2017).

Caruth, Cathy, *Unclaimed Experience: Trauma, Narrative and History* (Baltimore, MD: Johns Hopkins University Press, 2010).

— 'Trauma, Time and Address', in Colin Davis and Hanna Meretoja (eds), *The Routledge Companion to Literature and Trauma* (Milton Keynes: Taylor & Francis Group, 2020), pp. 79–89.

Caulfield, Max, *The Easter Rebellion* (London: Four Square, 1965).

Clark, Gemma, *Everyday Violence in the Irish Civil War* (Cambridge: Cambridge University Press, 2014).

— 'Violence against Women in the Irish Civil War, 1922–3: Gender-Based Harm in Global Perspective', *Irish Historical Studies* 44, no. 165 (May 2020), pp. 75–90.

Clarke, Desmond, and Stephen J. Brown (eds), *Ireland in Fiction. Volume 2: A Guide to Irish Novels, Tales, Romances and Folklore* (Cork: Royal Carbery Books, 1985).

Cobley, Evelyn, 'Narrating the Facts of War: New Journalism in Herr's *Dispatches* and Documentary Realism in First World War Novels', *The Journal of Narrative Technique* 16, no. 2 (1986), pp. 97–116.

Cohen, Dara Kay, *Rape during Civil War* (Ithaca, NY: Cornell University Press, 2016).

Coleman, Marie, *The Irish Revolution, 1916–1923* (Abingdon: Routledge, 2013).

— 'Violence against Women in the Irish War of Independence, 1919–1921', in Diarmaid Ferriter and Susannah Riordan (eds), *Years of Turbulence: The Irish Revolution and Its Aftermath* (Dublin: UCD Press, 2015), pp. 137–56.

Connolly, Linda, 'Towards a Further Understanding of the Violence Experienced by Women in the Irish Revolution', MUSSI Working Paper Series, no. 7 (Maynooth University, January, 2019).

— 'Sexual Violence in the Irish Civil War: A Forgotten War Crime?' *Women's History Review* (6 March 2020), pp. 1–18.

— (ed.), *Women and the Irish Revolution* (Dublin: Irish Academic Press, 2020).

Connolly, Ruth, and Ann Coughlan (eds), *New Voices in Irish Criticism 5* (Dublin: Four Courts, 2005).

Coogan, Tim Pat, *The I.R.A* (London: Palgrave Macmillan, 2002).

Cooper, Matt, *The Maximalist: The Rise and Fall of Tony O'Reilly* (Dublin: Gill & Macmillan, 2015).

Costello, Peter, *The Heart Grown Brutal: The Irish Revolution in Literature from Parnell to the Death of Yeats, 1891–1939* (Dublin: Gill & Macmillan, 1977).

Coughlan, Valerie, 'Writing for Children', in Heather Ingman and Clíona Ó Gallchóir (eds), *A History of Modern Irish Women's Literature* (Cambridge: Cambridge University Press, 2018), pp. 149–66.

Craps, Stef, *Postcolonial Witnessing: Trauma Out of Bounds* (Basingstoke: Palgrave Macmillan, 2012).

Craps, Stef, Bryan Cheyette, Alan Gibbs, Sonya Andermahr and Larissa Allwork, 'Decolonizing Trauma Studies Round Table Discussion', *Humanities* 2015, 4, pp. 905–23.

Cronin, Michael, *Impure Thoughts: Sexuality, Catholicism and Literature in Twentieth-Century Ireland* (Manchester: Manchester University Press, 2012).

Crouthamel, Jason, 'Male Sexuality and Psychological Trauma: Soldiers and Sexual Disorder in World War I and Weimar Germany', *Journal of the History of Sexuality* 17, no. 1 (2008), pp. 60–84.

Crouthamel, Jason, and Peter Leese (eds), *Psychological Trauma and the Legacies of the First World War* (Basingstoke: Palgrave Macmillan, 2016).

Crowley, Ronan, 'Revivalism à Clef, Revivalism sans Clef: Writing the Renaissance in James Stephens, Brinsley MacNamara, and Eimar O'Duffy', *New Hibernia Review* 23, no. 3 (2019), pp. 129–44.

Crowley, Una, and Rob Kitchin, 'Producing "Decent Girls": Governmentality and the Moral Geographies of Sexual Conduct in Ireland (1922–1937)', *Gender, Place and Culture* 15, no. 4 (2008), pp. 355–72.

Crozier-De Rosa, Sharon, *Shame and the Anti-Feminist Backlash: Britain, Ireland and Australia, 1890–1920* (Abingdon: Routledge, 2017).

Davis, Colin, 'Trauma, Poststructuralism and Ethics', in Colin Davis and Hanna Meretoja (eds), *The Routledge Companion to Literature and Trauma* (Milton Keynes: Taylor & Francis, 2020), pp. 36–44.

Davis, Colin, and Hanna Meretoja, 'Introduction to Literary Trauma Studies', in Colin Davis and Hanna Meretoja (eds), *The Routledge Companion to Literature and Trauma* (Milton Keynes: Taylor & Francis, 2020), pp. 1–8.

Dawson, Graham, *Soldier Heroes: British Adventure, Empire and the Imagining of Masculinities* (Abingdon: Routledge, 2013).

— 'The Meaning of "Moving On": From Trauma to the History and Memory of Emotions in "Post-Conflict" Northern Ireland', *Irish University Review* 47, no. 1 (May 2017), pp. 82–102.

D'Cruze, Shani, 'Approaching the History of Rape and Sexual Violence: Notes towards Research', *Women's History Review* 1, no. 3 (September 1992), pp. 377–97.

De Brún, Fionntán, *Seosamh Mac Grianna: An Mhéin Rúin* (Baile Átha Cliath: An Clóchomhar, 2002).

Delaney, Paul, *Seán O'Faoláin: Literature, Inheritance and the 1930s* (Dublin: Irish Academic Press, 2014).

— '"Rising Again": Revision, Trauma, and Frank O'Connor's "Guests of the Nation"', *New Hibernia Review* 23, no. 3 (6 December 2019), pp. 35–54.

DeSalvo, Louise A., *Writing as a Way of Healing: How Telling Our Stories Transforms Our Lives* (Boston, MA: Beacon Press, 2000).

Dietrich, Lisa, 'PTSD: A New Trauma Paradigm', in J. Roger Kurtz (ed.), *Trauma and Literature* (Cambridge: Cambridge University Press, 2018), pp. 83–94.

Diner, Hasia R., *Erin's Daughters in America: Irish Immigrant Women in the Nineteenth Century* (Baltimore, MD: JHU Press, 1983).

Dolan, Anne, 'An Army of Our Fenian Dead: Republicanism, Monuments and Commemoration', in Fearghal McGarry (ed.), *Republicanism in Modern Ireland* (Dublin: UCD Press, 2003), pp. 132–44.

— *Commemorating the Irish Civil War: History and Memory, 1923–2000* (Cambridge: Cambridge University Press, 2003).

— 'Killing and Bloody Sunday, November 1920', *The Historical Journal* 49, no. 3 (2006), pp. 789–810.

— 'Killing in "the Good Old Irish Fashion"? Irish Revolutionary Violence in Context', *Irish Historical Studies* 44, no. 165 (May 2020), pp. 11–24.

— 'Writing the History of the Irish Civil War' [video]. Available at: https://www.youtube.com/watch?v=d6164yPQj3w (accessed 8 July 2020).

Dolan, Pat, and Michael Dolan, 'Our Aunt Eilish's Untold Story of Rebellion, Romance and Religion', in Ciara Boylan, Sarah-Anne Buckley and Pat Dolan (eds), *Family Histories of the Irish Revolution* (Dublin: Four Courts Press, 2018), pp. 37–48.

Dolan Stover, Justin, 'Families, Vulnerability and Sexual Violence During the Irish Revolution', in Jennifer Evans and Ciara Meehan (eds), *Perceptions of Pregnancy from the Seventeenth to the Twentieth Century* (Basingstoke: Palgrave Macmillan, 2017), pp. 57–75.

Dorney, John, *The Civil War in Dublin: The Fight for the Irish Capital, 1922–1924* (Dublin: Merrion Press, 2017).

Dunne, Tom, 'A Polemical Introduction: Literature, Literary Theory and the Historian', in Tom Dunne and Charles Doherty (eds), *The Writer as Witness: Literature as Historical Evidence: Papers Read before the Irish Conference of Historians* (Cork: Cork University Press, 1987), pp. 1–9.

Durnin, David, *The Irish Medical Profession and the First World War* (Basingstoke: Palgrave Macmillan, 2019).

Durnin, David, and Ian Miller (eds), *Medicine, Health and Irish Experiences of Conflict 1914–45* (Manchester: Manchester University Press, 2017).

Earner-Byrne, Lindsey, 'The Rape of Mary M.: A Microhistory of Sexual Violence and Moral Redemption in 1920s Ireland', *Journal of the History of Sexuality* 24, no. 1 (January 2015), pp. 75–98.

Ellis, Timothy Hanson, 'Visual Culture and Visuality in the Politics of the Irish Free State, 1921–1939' (unpublished PhD thesis, Teesside University, 2020).

English, Richard, *Ernie O'Malley* (Oxford: Oxford University Press, 1998).

— 'Green on Red: Two Case Studies in Early Twentieth Century Irish Republican Thought, in D. George Boyce, Robert Eccleshall and Vincent Geoghegan (eds), *Political Thought in Ireland Since the Seventeenth Century* (Abingdon: Routledge, 2008), pp. 161–89.

Enright, Seán, *The Irish Civil War: Law, Execution and Atrocity* (Dublin: Merrion Press, 2019).

Erikson, Kai T., *Everything in Its Path: Destruction of Community in the Buffalo Creek Flood* (New York: Simon and Schuster, 1976).

Fanning, Robert, 'Vivid Faces: The Revolutionary Generation in Ireland 1890–1923', *History Ireland* (blog), 3 March 2015. Available at: https://www.historyireland.com/book-reviews/vivid-faces-the-revolutionary-generation-in-ireland-1890-1923/ (accessed 20 August 2020).

Farquharson, Danine, 'Liam O'Flaherty's *The Martyr* and the Risks of Satire', *The Canadian Journal of Irish Studies* 25, no. 1/2 (1999), pp. 372–87.

Faust, Drew Gilpin, *This Republic of Suffering* (New York: Knopf, 2008).

Felman, Shoshana, and Dori Laub, *Testimony: Crises of Witnessing in Literature, Psychoanalysis and History* (Milton Keynes: Taylor & Francis, 1992), pp. 75–92.

Ferriter, Diarmaid, *Occasions of Sin: Sex and Society in Modern Ireland* (London: Profile Books, 2010).

— *A Nation and Not a Rabble: The Irish Revolution 1913–1923* (London: Profile Books, 2015).

— 'Irish Civil War Has Its Own Contentious Monuments', *The Irish Times*, 27 August 2017. Available at: https://www.irishtimes.com/opinion/diarmaid-ferriter-irish-civil-war-has-its-own-contentious-monuments-1.3198279 (accessed 25 June 2020).

— *Between Two Hells: The Irish Civil War* (London: Profile Books, 2021).

Fitzpatrick, David, *Politics and Irish Life 1913–1921: Provincial Experience of War and Revolution* (Dublin: Gill & Macmillan, 1977).

— 'Commemoration in the Irish Free State: A Chronicle of Embarrassment', in Ian McBride (ed.), *History and Memory in Modern Ireland* (Cambridge: Cambridge University Press, 2001), pp. 184–203.

— *Harry Boland's Irish Revolution* (Cork: Cork University Press, 2004).

Flanagan, Frances, *Remembering the Revolution: Dissent, Culture, and Nationalism in the Irish Free State* (Oxford: Oxford University Press, 2015).

Foster, Gavin, '"No 'Wild Geese' This Time"?: IRA Emigration after the Irish Civil War', *Éire-Ireland* 47, no. 1 (2012), pp. 94–122.

— *The Irish Civil War and Society: Politics, Class, and Conflict* (Basingstoke: Palgrave Macmillan, 2015).

— 'Remembering and Forgetting in Public and Private: Reflections on the Dualities of Irish Civil War Memory in the Decade of Commemoration', *The Old Athlone Society* (2015), pp. 31–50.

— 'Local and Family Memory of the Irish Civil War' [recorded lecture], 12 June 2017. Available at: https://soundcloud.com/history-hub/gavin-foster-local-family-memory-irish-civil-war (accessed 20 August 2020).

Foster, R. F., '"Old Ireland and Himself": William Orpen and the Conflicts of Irish Identity', *Estudios Irlandeses*, 2005, pp. 39–50.

— *Vivid Faces: The Revolutionary Generation in Ireland, 1890–1923* (London: Penguin, 2014).

Foucault, Michel, *Madness and Civilization: A History of Insanity in the Age of Reason* (New York: Vintage Books, 1988).

Frawley, Oona (ed.), *Women and the Decade of Commemorations* (Bloomington, IN: Indiana University Press, 2021).

Freeman, Jody, 'The Disciplinary Function of Rape's Representation: Lessons from the Kennedy Smith and Tyson Trials', *Law & Social Inquiry* 18, no. 3 (1993), pp. 517–46.

Freud, Sigmund, 'Remembering, Repeating and Working-Through (Further Recommendations on the Technique of Psycho-Analysis II)', in James Strachey (ed.), *The Standard Edition of the Complete Psychological Works of Sigmund Freud*, Volume XII (1911–1913) (London: Hogarth Press and the Institute of Psycho-analysis, 1958), pp. 145–56.

Freyer, Grattan, *Peadar O'Donnell* (Lewisburg, PA: Bucknell University Press, 1973).

Fussell, Paul, *The Great War and Modern Memory* (Oxford: Oxford University Press, 2000).

Ganteau, Jean-Michel, and Susana Onega, *Trauma and Romance in Contemporary British Literature* (Abingdon: Routledge, 2013).

Gardiner, Eamonn T., 'An Examination of the Auxiliary Division, Royal Irish Constabulary, Exploring Possible Links between Conduct and Conflict-Related Injury, Traumatic Experiences and Stress' (unpublished PhD thesis, NUI Galway 2017).

Garvin, Tom, *Nationalist Revolutionaries in Ireland 1858–1928: Patriots, Priests and the Roots of the Irish Revolution* (Oxford: Clarendon Press, 2005).

Gibbs, Alan, *Contemporary American Trauma Narratives* (Edinburgh: Edinburgh University Press, 2014).

Gilbert, Sandra M., and Susan Gubar, *The Madwoman in the Attic: The Woman Writer and the Nineteenth-Century Literary Imagination* (New Haven, CT: Yale University Press, 1980).

Gillis, John R., *Commemorations: The Politics of National Identity* (Princeton, NJ: Princeton University Press, 2018).

Gilmore, Leigh, *The Limits of Autobiography: Trauma and Testimony* (Ithaca, NY: Cornell University Press, 2001).

— *Tainted Witness: Why We Doubt What Women Say About Their Lives* (New York: Columbia University Press, 2017).

Glebova, Olga, 'Trauma, Female Identity and the Trope of Splitting in Lessing, Figes, Tennant and Weldon', in Sonya Andermahr and Silvia Pellicer-Ortín (eds), *Trauma Narratives and Herstory* (London: Palgrave Macmillan, 2013), pp. 46–64.

Glennon, Kieran, *From Pogrom to Civil War: Tom Glennon and the Belfast IRA* (Cork: Mercier Press, 2013).

Gonzalez, Alexander, *Peadar O'Donnell: A Reader's Guide* (Chester Springs, PA: Dufour Editions, 1997).

Grant, John, '"I Was Too Chickenhearted to Publish": Seán Ó'Faoláin, Displacement and History Re-Written', *Estudios Irlandeses*, January 2017, pp. 50–9.

Gray, Breda, *Women and the Irish Diaspora* (London: Psychology Press, 2004).

Gronemann, Claudia, 'Autofiction', in Martina Wagner-Egelhaaf (ed.), *Handbook Autobiography/Autofiction* (Berlin: De Gruyter, 2019), p. 241.

Gunne, Sorcha, and Zoe Brigley Thompson (eds), *Feminism, Literature and Rape Narratives: Violence and Violation* (Abingdon: Routledge, 2012).

Halbwachs, Maurice, *On Collective Memory* (Chicago, IL: University of Chicago Press, 1992).

Hanley, Brian, *The IRA, 1926–1936* (Dublin: Four Courts Press, 2002).

— 'Irish Republicans in Interwar New York', *IJAS Online*, no. 1 (2009), pp. 48–61.

Hannifin, Patrick, 'Rewriting Desire: The Construction of Sexual Identity in Legal and Literary Discourse in Postcolonial Ireland', in Didi Herman and Carl Stychin (eds), *Sexuality in the Legal Arena* (London: A&C Black, 2000), pp. 51–66.

Harris, Judith, *Signifying Pain: Constructing and Healing the Self through Writing* (Albany, NY: SUNY Press, 2003).

Hart, Peter, *The I.R.A. and Its Enemies: Violence and Community in Cork, 1916–1923* (Oxford: Oxford University Press, 1998).

Hayes-McCoy, Felicity, *A Woven Silence* (Dublin: Gill & Macmillan, 2015).

Hedgepeth, Sonja Maria, and Rochelle G. Saidel (eds), *Sexual Violence Against Jewish Women During the Holocaust* (Lebanon, NH: University Press of New England, 2010).

Hegarty, Peter, *Peadar O'Donnell* (Cork: Mercier Press, 1999).

Heimo, Anne, and Ulla-Maija Peltonen, 'Memories and Histories, Public and Private: After the Finnish Civil War', in Katharine Hodgkin and Susannah Radstone (eds), *Contested Pasts: The Politics of Memory* (Abingdon: Routledge, 2003), pp. 42–56.

Henke, Suzette A., *Shattered Subjects: Trauma and Testimony in Women's Life-Writing* (New York: St Martin's, 1998).

Henry, Nicola, *War and Rape: Law, Memory, and Justice* (Abingdon: Routledge, 2011).

Herman, Judith Lewis, *Trauma and Recovery* (New York: BasicBooks, 1992).

Herrmann, Gina, '"They Didn't Rape Me": Traces of Gendered Violence and Sexual Injury in the Testimonies of Spanish Republican Women Survivors of the Franco Dictatorship', in Nanci Adler and Selma Leydesdorff (eds), *Tapestry of Memory: Evidence and Testimony in Life-Story Narratives* (New Brunswick, NJ: Transaction, 2013), pp. 77–96.

Higgins, Lynn A., and Brenda R. Silver (eds), *Rape and Representation* (New York: Columbia University Press, 1993).

Higonnet, Margaret R., 'Civil Wars and Sexual Territories', in Helen M. Cooper, Adrienne Munich and Susan Merrill Squier (eds), *Arms and the Woman: War, Gender, and Literary Representation* (Chapel Hill, NC: University of North Carolina Press, 1989), pp. 80–96.

— 'Authenticity and Art in Trauma Narratives of World War I', *Modernism/Modernity* 9, no. 1 (January 2002), pp. 91–107.

Hogan, Patrick Colm, 'Revolution and Despair: Allegories of Nation and Class in Patrick Hogan's *Camps on the Hearthstone*', *The Canadian Journal of Irish Studies* 25, no. 1/2 (1999), pp. 179–201.

Hopkins, Stephen, '"Irish History Unidealised": The Politics of Republican Memoir and Narratives of the Defeated and Defiant', in Karine Deslandes, Fabrice Mourlon and Bruno Tribout (eds), *Civil War and Narrative: Testimony, Historiography, Memory*, (New York: Palgrave Macmillan, 2017), pp. 59–76.

Hopkinson, Michael, *Green Against Green: The Irish Civil War* (Dublin: Gill & Macmillan, 1988 [2004]).

Houghton, Frances, *The Veterans' Tale: British Military Memoirs of the Second World War* (Cambridge: Cambridge University Press, 2019).

Howell, Philip, 'Venereal Disease and the Politics of Prostitution in the Irish Free State', *Irish Historical Studies* 33, no. 131 (2003), pp. 320–41.

Hron, Madelaine, 'The Trauma of Displacement', in J. Roger Kurtz (ed.), *Trauma and Literature* (Cambridge: Cambridge University Press, 2018), pp. 284–98.

Ilie, Paul, *Literature and Inner Exile: Authoritarian Spain, 1939–1975* (Baltimore, MD: Johns Hopkins University Press, 1980).

Inglis, Tom, 'Origins and Legacies of Irish Prudery: Sexuality and Social Control in Modern Ireland', *Éire-Ireland*, vol. 40: 3 and 4, Fall/Winter 2005, pp. 9–37.

Jensen, Meg, *The Art and Science of Trauma and the Autobiographical: Negotiated Truths* (Basingstoke: Palgrave Macmillan, 2019).

— 'Testimony', in Colin Davis and Hanna Meretoja (eds), *The Routledge Companion to Literature and Trauma* (Milton Keynes: Taylor & Francis, 2020), pp. 66–78.

Joly, Maud, 'Las Violencias Sexuadas de la Guerra Civil Española: Paradigma para una Lectura Cultural del Conflicto', *Historia Social*, no. 61 (2008), pp. 89–107.

Joy, James H., 'Victory and Woe: Mossie Harnett and the West Limerick Brigade in the Irish War of Independence, 1915–1923' (unpublished PhD thesis, George Mason University, 2000).

Joyce, Ashlee, *The Gothic in Contemporary British Trauma Fiction* (London: Palgrave Macmillan, 2019).

Kacandes, Irene, 'Narrative Witnessing as Memory Work: Reading Gertrud Kolmar's *A Jewish Mother*', in Mieke Bal, Jonathan V. Crewe and Leo Spitzer (eds), *Acts of Memory: Cultural Recall in the Present* (Lebanon, NH: University Press of New England, 1999), pp. 55–71.

Kansteiner, Wulf, 'Genealogy of a Category Mistake: A Critical Intellectual History of the Cultural Trauma Metaphor', *Rethinking History* 8, no. 2 (1 June 2004), pp. 193–221.

Kaplan, E. Ann, *Trauma Culture: The Politics of Terror and Loss in Media and Literature* (New Brunswick, NJ: Rutgers University Press, 2005).

Karpf, Anne, 'Chain of Testimony: The Holocaust Researcher as Surrogate Witness', in Nicholas Chare and Dominic Williams (eds), *Representing Auschwitz: At the Margins of Testimony* (London: Palgrave Macmillan, 2013), pp. 85–103.

Kavanagh, Úna, 'How Anti-treaty Internees Represent Themselves in an Autograph Book from the Curragh Tintown Camp 1923' (unpublished MA thesis, NUI Galway, 2018).

Kearney, Richard, 'Narrating Pain: The Power of Catharsis', *Paragraph* 30, no. 1 (2007), pp. 51–66.

Keating, Anthony, 'Sexual Crime in the Irish Free State 1922–33: Its Nature, Extent and Reporting', *Irish Studies Review* 20, no. 2 (1 May 2012), pp. 135–55.

Keith, Alison, 'Engendering Civil War in Flavian Epic. After 69 CE – Writing Civil War in Flavian Rome', in Lauren Donovan Ginsberg and Darcy Anne Krasne (eds), *After 69 CE – Writing Civil War in Flavian Rome* (Berlin: de Gruyter, 2018), pp. 295–320.

Kelly, Brendan, *'He Lost Himself Completely': Shell Shock and Its Treatment at Dublin's Richmond War Hospital, 1916–19* (Dublin: Liffey Press, 2014).

— *Hearing Voices: The History of Psychiatry in Ireland* (Dublin: Irish Academic Press, 2016).

Keltner, D., and G. A. Bonanno, 'A Study of Laughter and Dissociation: Distinct Correlates of Laughter and Smiling during Bereavement', *Journal of Personality and Social Psychology* 73, no. 4 (October 1997), pp. 687–702.

Kennedy, Liam, *Unhappy the Land: The Most Oppressed People Ever, the Irish?* (Dublin: Irish Academic Press, 2015).

Keohane, Leo, *Captain Jack White: Imperialism, Anarchism and the Irish Citizen Army* (Dublin: Merrion Press, 2014).

Keown, Bridget, "I Would Rather Have My Own Mind': The Medicalization of Women's Behavior in Ireland, 1914–1920', *Nursing Clio*, 25 October 2017. Available at: https://nursingclio. org/2017/10/25/i-would-rather-have-my-own-mind-the-medicalization-of-womens-behavior-in-ireland-1914-1920/ (accessed 18 May 2018).

— '"She is Lost to Time and Place": Women, War Trauma, and the First World War' (Unpublished PhD thesis, Northeastern University, 2019).

Keown, Damien, *Buddhism: A Very Short Introduction* (Oxford: Oxford University Press, 2013).

Kilfeather, Siobhán, 'The Gothic Novel', in John Wilson Foster (ed.), *The Cambridge Companion to the Irish Novel* (Cambridge: Cambridge University Press, 2006), pp. 78–96.

Kissane, Bill, *The Politics of the Irish Civil War* (Oxford: Oxford University Press, 2007).

— 'On the Shock of Civil War: Cultural Trauma and National Identity in Finland and Ireland', *Nations and Nationalism*, vol. 26, no. 1, 2020, pp. 22–43.

Knirck, Jason K., *Women of the Dáil: Gender, Republicanism and the Anglo-Irish Treaty* (Dublin: Irish Academic Press, 2006).

Knowlson, James, *Damned to Fame: The Life of Samuel Beckett* (New York: Bloomsbury, 2014).

Koopman, Emy, 'Ethical Challenges When Reading Aesthetic Rape Scenes', in Nate Hinerman and Matthew Lewis Sutton (eds), *On Suffering: An Interdisciplinary Dialogue on Narrative and Suffering* (Leiden: Brill, 2020), pp. 73–88.

Kostsonouris, Mary, *Retreat from Revolution: The Dáil Courts, 1920–24* (Dublin: Irish Academic Press, 1994).

Kurtz, J. Roger, 'Introduction', in J. Roger Kurtz (ed.), *Trauma and Literature* (Cambridge: Cambridge University Press, 2018), pp. 1–18.

LaCapra, Dominick, *History and Memory after Auschwitz* (Ithaca, NY: Cornell University Press, 1998).

— *Writing History, Writing Trauma* (Baltimore, MD: Johns Hopkins University Press, 2001).

— *History in Transit: Experience, Identity, Critical Theory* (Ithaca, NY: Cornell University Press, 2018).

Lane, Leeann, *Rosamond Jacob: Third Person Singular* (Dublin: UCD Press, 2010).

— *Dorothy Macardle* (Dublin: UCD Press, 2019).

Lanser, Susan Snaider, *Fictions of Authority: Women Writers and Narrative Voice* (Ithaca, NY: Cornell University Press, 1992).

Laub, Dori, 'An Event without a Witness: Truth, Testimony and Survival', in Shoshana Felman and Dori Laub, *Testimony: Crises of Witnessing in Literature, Psychoanalysis and History* (Milton: Taylor & Francis, 1992), pp. 75–92.

— 'Bearing Witness or the Vicissitudes of Listening', in Shoshana Felman and Dori Laub, *Testimony: Crises of Witnessing in Literature, Psychoanalysis and History* (Milton Keynes: Taylor & Francis, 1992), pp. 57–74.

Leary, Peter, *Unapproved Routes: Histories of the Irish Border, 1922–1972* (Oxford: Oxford University Press, 2016).

Lee, A. J., 'Jim Phelan's Liverpool Home', George Garrett Archive. Available at: https://www.georgegarrettarchive.co.uk/component/content/article/2-uncategorised/73-jim-phelan-s-liverpool-home.html (accessed 18 April 2020).

Lee, Joseph J., *Ireland, 1912–1985: Politics and Society* (Cambridge: Cambridge University Press, 1989).

Lennon, Ivan, *Lennons in Time* (unpublished, c. 2017). Available at: https://www.academia.edu/32727560/LENNONS_IN_TIME (accessed 20 August 2020).

Levi, Primo, *The Drowned and the Saved* (New York: Summit Books, 1988).

Leys, Ruth, *Trauma: A Genealogy* (Chicago, IL: University of Chicago Press, 2010).

Lifton, Robert Jay, 'Interview', in Cathy Caruth (ed.), *Trauma: Explorations in Memory*, (Baltimore, MD: Johns Hopkins University Press, 1995), pp. 128–50.

Litton, Helen, *The Irish Civil War: An Illustrated History* (Dublin: Wolfhound Press, 1995).

Luckhurst, Roger, *The Trauma Question* (Abingdon: Routledge, 2013).

Luddy, Maria, *Prostitution and Irish Society, 1800–1940* (Cambridge: Cambridge University Press, 2007).

Lynch, Claire, *Irish Autobiography: Stories of Self in the Narrative of a Nation* (Bern: Peter Lang, 2009).

Lynch, Robert, *The Partition of Ireland: 1918–1925* (Cambridge: Cambridge University Press, 2019).

Lynch-Brennan, Margaret, *The Irish Bridget: Irish Immigrant Women in Domestic Service in America, 1840–1930* (Syracuse, NY: Syracuse University Press, 2009).

Lyons, F. S. L., *Ireland Since the Famine* (London: Weidenfeld and Nicolson, 1971).

McAreavey, Naomi, 'Reading Conversion Narratives as Literature of Trauma: Radical Religion, the Wars of the Three Kingdoms and the Cromwellian Re-Conquest of Ireland', in David Coleman (ed.), *Region, Religion and English Renaissance Literature* (Abingdon: Routledge, 2016).

McAtackney, Laura, 'Gender, Incarceration and Power Relations during the Irish Civil War (1922–1923)', in Victoria Sanford, Katerina Stefatos and Cecilia M. Salvi (eds), *Gender Violence in Peace and War: States of Complicity* (New Brunswick, NJ: Rutgers University Press, 2016), pp. 47–64.

McAuliffe, Mary, '"An Idea Has Gone Abroad that All the Women Were Against the Treaty"; Cumann na Saoirse and Pro-treaty Women, 1922–3', in Liam Weeks and Mícheál Ó Fathartaigh (eds), *The Treaty: Debating and Establishing the Irish State* (Dublin: Irish Academic Press, 2018), pp. 160–82.

— 'The Homefront as Battlefront: Women, Violence and the Domestic Space during War in Ireland, 1919–1921', in Linda Connolly (ed.), *Women and the Irish Revolution* (Dublin: Irish Academic Press, 2020), pp. 164–82.

Mac Bhloscaidh, Fearghal, 'Objective Historians, Irrational Fenians and the Bewildered Herd: Revisionist Myth and the Irish Revolution', *Irish Studies Review* 28, no. 2 (2 April 2020), pp. 204–34.

McCarthy, Angela, *Personal Narratives of Irish and Scottish Migration, 1921–65: 'For Spirit and Adventure'* (Manchester: Manchester University Press, 2007).

McCarthy, Cal, *Cumann na mBan and the Irish Revolution* (Cork: Collins Press, 2014).

McCarthy, Pat, *The Irish Revolution, 1912–23: Waterford* (Dublin: Four Courts Press, 2015).

Mac Congáil, Nollaig, 'Scéalta Béarla Mháire', *Feasta*, Meitheamh & Iúil 2002.

McCoole, Sinéad, *No Ordinary Women: Irish Female Activists in the Revolutionary Years, 1900–1923* (Dublin: O'Brien, 2003 [2015]).

McDiarmid, Lucy, *At Home in the Revolution: What Women Said and Did in 1916* (Dublin: Royal Irish Academy, 2015).

McDowell, Nicholas, 'Civil Wars of Words: From Classical Rome to the Northern Ireland Troubles', *Global Intellectual History* 4, no. 3 (September 2019), pp. 294–304.

McGarry, Fearghal, 'Revolution, 1916–1923', in Thomas Bartlett (ed.), *The Cambridge History of Ireland. Volume 4: 1880 to the Present* (Cambridge: Cambridge University Press, 2018), pp. 258–95.

Machnik-Kekesi, Gabrielle, 'Gendering Bodies: Violence as Performance in Ireland's War of Independence (1919–1921)' (unpublished MA thesis, Concordia University, 2017).

McInerney, Anne-Marie, 'Internment of the Anti-Treaty I.R.A. in the Irish Free State 1922–4', (unpublished PhD thesis, Trinity College Dublin, 2015).

Mackay, James, *Michael Collins: A Life* (Edinburgh: Mainstream Publishing Company, 1996).

McNally, Richard J., *Remembering Trauma* (Boston, MA: Harvard University Press, 2005).

Macreadie, Rachel Sarah Jo, 'Politicizing the Personal: Reading Gender-Based Violence in Rape Survivor Discourse' (unpublished PhD thesis, University of Melbourne, 2014).

Mac Suibhne, Breandán, *The End of Outrage: Post-Famine Adjustment in Rural Ireland* (Oxford: Oxford University Press, 2017).

Malone, Irina Ruppo, 'Spectral History: The Ghost Stories of Dorothy Macardle', *Partial Answers: Journal of Literature and the History of Ideas* 9, no. 1 (2011), pp. 95–109.

Marchbanks, Paul, 'Elizabeth Brennan', in Alexander G. Gonzalez (ed.), *Irish Women Writers: An A-to-Z Guide* (Santa Barbara, CA: Greenwood Publishing, 2006), pp. 48–50.

Margalit, Avishai, *The Ethics of Memory* (Boston, MA: Harvard University Press, 2002).

Martin, David, *The Road to Ballyshannon* (London: Abacus, 1983).

Mason, Mary, 'The Other Voice: Autobiographies of Women Writers', in Sidonie Smith and Julia Watson (eds), *Women, Autobiography, Theory: A Reader* (Madison, WI: University of Wisconsin Press, 1998), pp. 207–35.

Matthews, Ann, *Renegades: Irish Republican Women 1900–1922* (Cork: Mercier, 2010).

— *Dissidents: Irish Republican Women, 1923–1941* (Cork: Mercier, 2012).

— 'Internment and Women during the Civil War 1922–23', *The Old Athlone Society* (2015), pp. 141–52.

Matthews, James H., *Voices: A Life of Frank O'Connor* (New York: Atheneum, 1983).

Matus, Jill L., *Shock, Memory and the Unconscious in Victorian Fiction* (Cambridge: Cambridge University Press, 2009).

Meaney, Gerardine, 'Identity and Opposition: Women's Writing, 1890–1960', in Angela Bourke, Siobhán Kilfeather, Maria Luddy, Margaret Mac Curtain, Gerardine Meaney, Máirín Ní Dhonnchadha, Mary O'Dowd and Clair Wills (eds), *The Field Day Anthology of Irish Writing V: Irish Women's Writing and Traditions* (New York: NYU Press, 2002), pp. 976–85.

— *Gender, Ireland and Cultural Change: Race, Sex and Nation* (Abingdon: Routledge, 2010).

— 'Fiction, 1922–1960', in Clíona Ó Gallchoir and Heather Ingman (eds), *A History of Modern Irish Women's Literature* (Cambridge: Cambridge University Press, 2018), pp. 187–203.

Micale, Mark S., Paul Lerner and Charles Rosenberg (eds), *Traumatic Pasts: History, Psychiatry, and Trauma in the Modern Age, 1870–1930* (Cambridge: Cambridge University Press, 2001).

Miller, Emma V., 'Trauma and Sexual Violence', in J. Roger Kurtz (ed.), *Trauma and Literature* (Cambridge: Cambridge University Press, 2018), pp. 226–38.

Miller, Kerby A., *Emigrants and Exiles: Ireland and the Irish Exodus to North America* (Oxford: Oxford University Press, 1985).

Mohamed, Saira, 'Of Monsters and Men: Perpetrator Trauma and Mass Atrocity', *Columbia Law Review*, vol. 115, no. 5 (June 2015), pp. 1157–216.

Molidor, Jennifer, 'Dying for Ireland: Violence, Silence, and Sacrifice in Dorothy Macardle's *Earthbound: Nine Stories of Ireland* (1924)', *New Hibernia Review* 12, no. 4 (2008), pp. 43–61.

Morag, Raya, *Waltzing with Bashir: Perpetrator Trauma and Cinema* (New York: Bloomsbury, 2013).

Morgan, Eileen, '"Unbroken Service": Máiréad Ní Ghráda's Career at 2RN, Ireland's First Broadcasting Station, 1927–35', *Éire-Ireland* 37, no. 3–4 (2002), pp. 53–78.

Morley, Vincent, *The Popular Mind in Eighteenth-Century Ireland* (Cork: Cork University Press, 2017).

Morris, Marla, *Curriculum and the Holocaust: Competing Sites of Memory and Representation* (Abingdon: Routledge, 2001).

Morrison, Eve, 'The Bureau of Military History and Female Republican Activism, 1913–23' in Maryann Gialanella Valiulis (ed.), *Gender and Power in Irish History* (Dublin: Irish Academic Press, 2008), pp. 59–83.

— 'Hauntings of the Irish Revolution: Veterans and Memory of the Independence Struggle and Civil War', in Marguerite Corporaal, Christopher Cusack and Ruud van den Beuken (eds), *Irish Studies and the Dynamics of Memory: Transitions and Transformations* (Bern: Peter Lang, 2016), pp. 83–96.

— 'Witnessing the Republic: The Ernie O'Malley Notebook Interviews and the Bureau of Military History Compared', in Cormac O'Malley (ed.), *Modern Ireland and Revolution: Ernie O'Malley in Context* (Dublin: Irish Academic Press, 2016), pp. 124–40.

Murphy, Kim, *I Had Rather Die: Rape in the Civil War* (Batesville, VA: Coachlight Press, 2014).

Murphy, William, *Political Imprisonment and the Irish, 1912–1921* (Oxford: Oxford University Press, 2014).

Neeson, Eoin, *The Civil War in Ireland* (Cork: Mercier Press, 1966).

Ní Bheacháin, Caoilfhionn, 'Seeing Ghosts: Gothic Discourses and State Formation', *Éire-Ireland* 47, no. 3 (14 November 2012), pp. 37–63.

Ní Bhrádaigh, Siobhán, *Máiréad Ní Ghráda: Ceannródaí Drámaíochta* (Indreabhán: Cló Iar-Chonnachta, 1996).

Nic Dháibhéid, Caoimhe, 'Fighting their Fathers' Fight: The Post-revolutionary Generation in Independent Ireland', in Senia Pašeta (ed.), *Uncertain Futures: Essays about the Irish Past for Roy Foster* (Oxford: Oxford University Press, 2016), pp. 148–60.

Ní Dhonnchadha, Aisling, and Máirín Nic Eoin, 'Ar an gCoigríoch: Migration and Identity in Twentieth-Century and Contemporary Irish-Language Literature', *The Irish Review*, 44 (2012), pp. 60–74.

Ní Eaghra, Erin, 'Ní Sciath ar bith Arm ach Tuar Tubaiste Géire – Saighdiúr Stuachach ar son na Síochána: Úna Bean Uí Dhiosca' (unpublished MA thesis, NUI Galway, 2007).

Nic Eoin, Máirín, *Trén bhFearann Breac: An Dílaithriú Cultúir agus Nualitríocht na Gaeilge* (Baile Átha Cliath: Cois Life, 2005).

Nix-Kenefick, Kalene, 'The Woman, the Body and *The Bell*: The Female Voice in the Bell's Short Fiction by Women, 1940–1954', in Ruth Connolly and Ann Coughlan (eds), *New Voices in Irish Criticism 5* (Dublin: Four Courts, 2005), pp. 109–18.

Noakes, Lucy, '"A Disgrace to the Country They Belong to": The Sexualisation of Female Soldiers in First World War Britain', *Revue LISA/LISA e-Journal*, vol. VI – n°4 (September 2008). Available at: https://doi.org/10.4000/lisa.951 (accessed 20 August 2020).

Nolan, Janet A., *Ourselves Alone: Women's Emigration from Ireland, 1885–1920* (Lexington, KY: University Press of Kentucky, 1986).

Norstedt, Johann A., 'Peadar O'Donnell', in Denis Lane (ed.), *Modern Irish Literature* (New York: Ungar, 1988), p. 488.

Novick, Peter, *That Noble Dream: The 'Objectivity Question' and the American Historical Profession* (Cambridge: Cambridge University Press, 1988).

Ó Cadhain, Máirtín, *Barbed Wire* (Baile Átha Cliath: Coiscéim, 2002).

O'Callaghan, Margaret, 'Women and Politics in Independent Ireland, 1921–68', in Angela Bourke et al. (eds), *The Field Day Anthology of Irish Writing V: Irish Women's Writing and Traditions* (New York: New York University Press, 2002), pp. 120–34.

— 'Women's Political Autobiography in Independent Ireland', in Liam Harte (ed.) *A History of Irish Autobiography* (Cambridge: Cambridge University Press, 2018), pp. 133–48.

O'Carroll, Íde, *Models for Movers: Irish Women's Emigration to America* (Cork: Attic Press, 1990).

Ó Céirín, Kit, and Cyril Ó Céirín (eds), *Women of Ireland: A Biographic Dictionary* (Kinvarra: Tír Eolas, 1996).

Ó Ciosáin, Éamon, 'Mairéad Ní Ghráda agus a Saothar Liteartha', in Mairéad Ní Ghráda, *Breithiúnas: Dráma Dhá Ghníomh* (Baile Átha Cliath: Oifig an tSoláthair, 1978), pp. 93–100.

Ó Conaire, Breandán, *Myles na Gaeilge: Lámhleabhar ar Shaothar Gaeilge Bhrian Ó Nualláin* (Baile Átha Cliath: An Clóchomhar, 1986).

Ó Conchubhair, Brian, 'Seosamh Mac Grianna: A Bhealach Féin', in John Walsh and Peadar Ó Muircheartaigh (eds), *Ag Siúl an Bhealaigh Mhóir: Aistí in Ómós don Ollamh Nollaig Mac Congáil* (Baile Átha Cliath: LeabhairCOMHAR, 2016).

O'Doherty, Michael Kevin, *My Parents and Other Rebels: A Personal Memoir* (Donegal: Errigal Press, 1999).

Ó Drisceoil, Donal, *Censorship in Ireland, 1939–1945: Neutrality, Politics, and Society* (Cork: Cork University Press, 1996).

— *Peadar O'Donnell* (Cork: Cork University Press, 2001).

— '"My Pen Is Just a Weapon": Politics, History and the Fiction of Peadar O'Donnell', *The Irish Review*, no. 30 (2003), pp. 62–70.

— 'Appendix A', in Clare Hutton and Patrick Walsh (eds), *The Oxford History of the Irish Book. Volume V: The Irish Book in English, 1891–2000* (Oxford: Oxford University Press, 2011), pp. 644–9.

Ó Drisceoil, Fachtna, *The Missing Postman: What Really Happened to Larry Griffin?* (Cork: Mercier Press, 2011).

Ó Duibhir, Liam, *Prisoners of War: Ballykinlar, An Irish Internment Camp 1920–1921* (Cork: Mercier Press, 2013).

Ó Dúshláine, Tadhg, 'Scéal Úrscéil: *Fánaí*, Seán Óg Ó Caomhánaigh, 1927', *Léachtaí Cholm Cille* 19 (1989), pp. 93–128.

Ó hEithir, Breandán, 'An Lasair a Múchadh Nach Mór', *Comhar* 37, no. 6 (1978), pp. 17–18.

Ó Gadhra, Nollaig, *Civil War in Connacht* (Cork: Mercier Press, 1999).

O'Halpin, Eunan, 'Ulster Says Go: The Forgotten Exodus of Northern Nationalists', *The Irish Times*, 17 June 2015.

O'Leary, Philip, 'The Irish Renaissance, 1890–1940: Literature in Irish', in Margaret Kelleher and Philip O'Leary (eds), *The Cambridge History of Irish Literature*, Volume 2 (Cambridge: Cambridge University Press, 2006), pp. 226–69.

— *Gaelic Prose in the Irish Free State: 1922–1939* (University Park, PA: Penn State Press, 2010).

— 'Presenting a Challenging Past: Piaras Béaslaí's Play *An Danar* (1928)', 39th California Celtic Conference – UC Berkeley, March 2017.

— *An Underground Theatre: Major Playwrights in the Irish Language 1930–80* (Dublin: UCD Press, 2017).

Ó Maonaigh, Aaron, 'The Killurin Ambush and the Outbreak of Civil War in County Wexford', *The Past: The Organ of the Uí Cinsealaigh Historical Society*, no. 33 (2019), pp. 52–67.

Ó Muirí, Pól, *A Flight from Shadow: The Life & Works of Seosamh Mac Grianna* (Belfast: Lagan Press, 1999).

— *Seosamh Mac Grianna: Míreanna Saoil* (Indreabhán: Cló Iar-Chonnachta, 2007).

Onega, Susana, 'Affective Knowledge, Self-Awareness and the Function of Myth in the Representation and Transmission of Trauma: The Case of Eva Figes' *Konek Landing*', *Journal of Literary Theory* 6, no. 1 (20 February 2012), pp. 83–102.

O'Neill, Gerri, '"Looting and Overtures and Acts of Indecency by Black and Tans": The Pursuit of Justice for Acts of Sexual Violence during Ireland's War of Independence (1919–21)', *Studia Hibernica* 47, no. 1 (September 2021), pp. 89–106.

O'Regan, Danae, 'Representations and Attitudes of Republican Women in the Novels of Annie M. P. Smithson (1873–1948) and Rosamond Jacob (1888–1960)', in Louise Ryan and Margaret Ward (eds), *Irish Women and Nationalism: Soldiers, New Women and Wicked Hags* (Dublin: Irish Academic Press, 2004), pp. 80–95.

O'Reilly, Terence, *Rebel Heart: George Lennon: Flying Column Commander* (Cork: Mercier Press, 2009).

O'Toole, Fintan, *The Ex-Isle of Erin* (Dublin: New Island Books, 1997).

Ó Tuama, Seán, *Gunna Cam agus Slabhra Óir* (Baile Átha Cliath: Sáirséal agus Dill, 1964).

Orwell, George, *The Complete Works of George Orwell: A Patriot After All, 1940–1941* (London: Secker & Warburg, 1998).

Palko, Abigail L., 'Queer Seductions of the Maternal in Dorothy Macardle's *Earth-bound*', *Irish University Review* 46, no. 2 (25 October 2016), pp. 287–308.

Pašeta, Senia, *Irish Nationalist Women, 1900–1918* (Cambridge: Cambridge University Press, 2013).

Pawle, Kathleen, *We in Captivity* (New York: Dodd, Mead & Co., 1936).

Pederson, Joshua, *Sin Sick: Moral Injury in War and Literature* (Ithaca, NY: Cornell University Press, 2021).

Pérez, Janet, 'Behind the Lines: The Spanish Civil War and Women Writers', in Janet Pérez and Wendell M. Aycock (eds), *Spanish Civil War in Literature* (Lubbock, TX: Texas Tech University Press, 1990), pp. 161–73.

Phoenix, Eamon, *Northern Nationalism: Nationalist Politics, Partition and the Catholic Minority in Northern Ireland, 1890–1940* (Belfast: Ulster Historical Foundation, 1994).

Pierse, Michael (ed.), *A History of Irish Working-Class Writing* (Cambridge: Cambridge University Press, 2017).

Projansky, Sarah, *Watching Rape: Film and Television in Postfeminist Culture* (New York: NYU Press, 2001).

Quigley, Mark, *Empire's Wake: Postcolonial Irish Writing and the Politics of Modern Literary Form: Postcolonial Irish Writing and the Politics of Modern Literary Form* (New York: Fordham University Press, 2013).

Radstone, Susannah, 'Trauma Theory: Contexts, Politics, Ethics', *Paragraph* 30, no. 1 (2007), pp. 9–29.

Rapp, Dean, 'The Early Discovery of Freud by the British General Educated Public, 1912–1919', *Social History of Medicine* 3, no. 2 (1 August 1990), pp. 217–43.

Rauchbauer, Otto, 'The Big House in the Irish Short Story after 1918: A Critical Survey', in idem (ed.), *Ancestral Voices: The Big House in Anglo-Irish Literature: A Collection of Interpretations* (New York: Georg Olms Verlag, 1992), pp. 159–93.

Redmond, Jennifer, *Moving Histories: Irish Women's Emigration to Britain from Independence to Republic* (Oxford: Oxford University Press, 2019).

Reilly, Catherine W. (ed.), *English Poetry of the Second World War: A Biobibliography* (Boston, MA: G. K. Hall, 1986).

Richardson, Anna, 'Mapping the Lines of Fact and Fiction in Holocaust Testimonial Novels', in Moishe Postone and Eric L. Santne (eds), *Catastrophe and Meaning: The Holocaust and the Twentieth Century* (Chicago, IL: University of Chicago Press, 2009), pp. 53–61.

Robinson, Michael, *Shell-shocked British Army Veterans in Ireland, 1918–39: A Difficult Homecoming* (Manchester: Manchester University Press, 2020).

Roddie, Robert P., 'Pádraig and Eily O'Horan: A Story of Rebellion and Redemption', *Dublin Historical Record* 55, no. 1 (2002), pp. 75–87.

Rogers, Ailbhe, 'Cumann na mBan in Co. Louth, 1914–1921', in Donal Hall and Maguire Martin (eds), *County Louth and the Irish Revolution: 1912–1923* (Dublin: Irish Academic Press, 2017), pp. 35–58.

Rothberg, Michael, *Traumatic Realism: The Demands of Holocaust Representation* (Minneapolis, MN: University of Minnesota Press, 2000).

— *Multidirectional Memory: Remembering the Holocaust in the Age of Decolonization* (Stanford, CA: Stanford University Press, 2009).

— *The Implicated Subject: Beyond Victims and Perpetrators* (Stanford, CA: Stanford University Press, 2019).

Ryan, J. G., 'Máirín Cregan', *Kerry Magazine*, iss. 23, 2013, pp. 50–1.

Ryan, Louise, '"Drunken Tans": Representations of Sex and Violence in the Anglo-Irish War (1919–21)', *Feminist Review*, no. 66 (2000), pp. 73–94.

— 'Splendidly Silent: Representing Irish Republican Women, 1919–1923', in Ann-Marie Gallagher, Cathy Lubelska and Louise Ryan (eds), *Re-Presenting the Past: Women and History* (London: Longman, 2001), pp. 23–42.

— '"In the Line of Fire": Representations of Women and War (1919–1923) through the Writings of Republican Men', in Louise Ryan and Margaret Ward (eds), *Irish Women and Nationalism: Soldiers, New Women and Wicked Hags* (Dublin: Irish Academic Press, 2004), pp. 45–61.

Said, Edward, *Reflections on Exile and Other Essays* (Cambridge, MA: Harvard University Press, 2000).

Sampson, Denis, 'The Big House in Seán O'Faoláin's Fiction', in Jacqueline Genet (ed.), *The Big House in Ireland: Reality and Representation* (New York: Barnes & Noble 1991), pp. 179–90.

Samuelson, Meg, 'The Disfigured Body of the Female Guerrilla: (De)Militarization, Sexual Violence, and Redomestication in Zoë Wicomb's *David's Story*', *Signs* 32, no. 4 (2007), pp. 833–56.

Saunders, Max, *Self Impression: Life-Writing, Autobiografiction, and the Forms of Modern Literature* (Oxford: Oxford University Press, 2010).

Scully, Diana, and Joseph Marolla, 'Convicted Rapists' Vocabulary of Motive: Excuses and Justifications', *Social Problems* 31, no. 5 (1984), pp. 530–44.

Seery, Aidan, and Karin Bacon, 'Auto/Biographical Research and the Family', in Julie M. Parsons and Anne Chappell (eds), *The Palgrave Handbook of Auto/Biography* (Basingstoke: Palgrave Macmillan, 2020), pp. 143–56.

Showalter, Elaine, 'Feminist Criticism in the Wilderness', *Critical Inquiry* 8, no. 2 (1981), pp. 179–205.

— *The Female Malady: Women, Madness, and English Culture, 1830–1980* (New York: Pantheon Books, 1985).

Sielke, Sabine, *Reading Rape: The Rhetoric of Sexual Violence in American Literature and Culture, 1790–1990* (Princeton, NJ: Princeton University Press, 2009).

Smith, Leonard V., *The Embattled Self: French Soldiers' Testimony of the Great War* (Ithaca, NY: Cornell University Press, 2014).

Smith, Nadia Clare, *Dorothy Macardle: A Life* (Dublin: Woodfield Press, 2007).

— 'From Dundalk to Dublin: Dorothy Macardle's Narrative Journey on Radio Éireann', *The Irish Review*, no. 42 (2010), pp. 27–42.

Smith, Sidonie, and Julia Watson, *Reading Autobiography: A Guide for Interpreting Life Narratives* (Minneapolis, MN: University of Minnesota Press, 2001).

Steele, Karen, 'When Female Activists Say "I": The Veiled Rebel and Counterhistories of Irish Independence', in Gillian McIntosh and Diane Urquhart (eds), *Irish Women at War: The Twentieth Century* (Dublin: Irish Academic Press, 2010), pp. 51–68.

— 'Revolutionary Lives in the Rearview Mirror: Memoir and Autobiography', in Marjorie Howes (ed.), *Irish Literature in Transition, 1880–1940*, Volume 4 (Cambridge: Cambridge University Press, 2020).

Steiner, Rudolf, *Psychoanalysis in the Light of Anthroposophy: Five Lectures*, translated by May Laird-Brown. Literary Licensing, LLC, 2013. Available at: https://wn.rsarchive.org/Medicine/Psych/English/AP1946/PsyAnt_index.html (accessed 20 August 2020).

Storey, Michael L., *Representing the Troubles in Irish Short Fiction* (Washington, D.C.: Catholic University of America Press, 2004).

Surridge, Lisa Anne, *Bleak Houses: Marital Violence in Victorian Fiction* (Athens, OH: Ohio University Press, 2005).

Tal, Kalí, *Worlds of Hurt: Reading the Literatures of Trauma* (Cambridge: Cambridge University Press, 1996). Revised edition available at: http://worldsofhurt.com (accessed 20 August 2020).

Thomas, Richard, '"My Brother Got Killed in the War": Internecine Intertextuality', in Brian Breed, Cynthia Damon and Andreola Rossi (eds), *Citizens of Discord: Rome and Its Civil Wars* (Oxford: Oxford University Press, 2010), pp. 293–308.

Tiernan, Sonja, *Eva Gore-Booth: An Image of Such Politics* (Manchester: Manchester University Press, 2012).

Titley, Alan, *An tÚrscéal Gaeilge* (Baile Átha Cliath: Clóchomhar, 1991).

Tomkins, Phil, *Twice a Hero: From the Trenches of the Great War to the Ditches of the Irish Midlands 1915–1922* (Cirencester: Memoirs Publishing, 2013).

Townshend, Charles, *The Republic: The Fight for Irish Independence, 1918–1923* (London: Penguin, 2013).

Troupe, Shelley, 'TSI: Teresa Deevy, or What Do We Know about The Reapers?', Teresa Deevy Archive, NUI, Maynooth, 2014. Available at: https://www.academia.edu/7135600/_TSI_Teresa_Deevy_or_What_do_we_know_about_The_Reapers_ (accessed 20 August 2020).

Uí Laighléis, Gearóidín, *Gallán an Ghúim* (Baile Átha Cliath: Coiscéim, 2017).

Valente, Joseph, 'Ethnostalgia: Irish Hunger and Traumatic Memory', in Oona Frawley (ed.), *Memory Ireland. Volume 3: The Famine and the Troubles* (Syracuse, NY: Syracuse University Press, 2014), pp. 174–92.

van der Kolk, Bessel, *The Body Keeps the Score: Mind, Brain and Body in the Transformation of Trauma* (London: Penguin, 2014).

Voynich, Ethel Lillian, *The Gadfly* (New York: Henry Holt and Co., 1897).

Wallace, Nathan, 'The Importance of Being Ernie O'Malley in Ken Loach's *The Wind That Shakes The Barley*', in *Modern Ireland and Revolution: Ernie O'Malley in Context*, edited by Cormac O'Malley (Dublin: Irish Academic Press, 2016), pp. 55–75.

Walsh, Oonagh, '"Her Irish Heritage": Annie M. P. Smithson and Autobiography', *Études Irlandaises* 23, no. 1 (1998), pp. 27–42.

Ward, Margaret, *Unmanageable Revolutionaries: Women and Irish Nationalism* (London: Pluto Press, 1983).

— 'Gendered Memories and Belfast Cumann na mBan, 1917–1922', in Linda Connolly (ed.), *Women and the Irish Revolution* (Dublin: Irish Academic Press, 2020) pp. 47–67.

— 'Review of Adrian Frazier, *The Adulterous Muse*', 7 March 2017. Available at: https://womenshistoryassociation.com/book-reviews/review-of-adrian-frazier-the-adulterous-muse-by-dr-margaret-ward/ (accessed 20 August 2020).

Whelan, Bernadette, 'Women on the Move: A Review of the Historiography of Irish Emigration to the USA, 1750–1900', *Women's History Review* 24, no. 6 (2 November 2015), pp. 900–16.

White, Hayden V., 'The Historical Text as Literary Artifact', in idem, *Tropics of Discourse: Essays in Cultural Criticism* (Baltimore, MD: Johns Hopkins University Press, 1978), pp. 81–100.

Whitehead, Anne, *Trauma Fiction* (Edinburgh: Edinburgh University Press, 2004).

Whittier, Anthony, 'Frank O'Connor', in Cowley, Malcolm (ed.), *Writers at Work: The Paris Review Interviews* (New York: The Viking Press, 1958), pp. 161–82.

Wilk, Gavin, *Transatlantic Defiance: The Militant Irish Republican Movement in America, 1923–45* (Manchester: Manchester University Press, 2014).

— '"No Hope for Him Unless He Can Be Got Out of the Country": Disabled Irish Republicans in America, 1922–1935', *New Hibernia Review / Iris Éireannach Nua* 18, no. 1 (2014), pp. 106–19.

Wills, Clair, *Dublin 1916: The Siege of the GPO* (Boston, MA: Harvard University Press, 2009).

Wilson, T. K., *Frontiers of Violence: Conflict and Identity in Ulster and Upper Silesia 1918–1922* (Oxford: Oxford University Press, 2010).

Winter, Jay, *Remembering War: The Great War Between Memory and History in the Twentieth Century* (New Haven, CT: Yale University Press, 2006).

Wydenbach, Joanna, 'Emily Ussher and *The Trail of the Black & Tans*', *Revue LISA/LISA e-Journal. Littératures, Histoire Des Idées, Images, Sociétés Du Monde Anglophone – Literature, History of Ideas, Images and Societies of the English-Speaking World*, vol. III–n°1 (1 January 2005), pp. 22–38.

Yeates, Pádraig, *A City in Civil War: Dublin 1921–1924: The Irish Civil War* (Dublin: Gill & Macmillan, 2015).

Young, James E., 'Regarding the Pain of Women: Questions of Gender and the Arts of Holocaust Memory', *PMLA* 124, no. 5 (2009), pp. 1778–86.

Younger, Calton, *Ireland's Civil War* (London: Frederick Muller, 1968).

Zneimer, John, *The Literary Vision of Liam O'Flaherty* (Syracuse, NY: Syracuse University Press, 1970).

ACKNOWLEDGEMENTS/
NÓTA BUÍOCHAIS

This is a pandemic book, written in lockdown between Salthill, Co. Galway and Ardee, Co. Louth. I could have never contemplated undertaking this project without the support of family, friends and colleagues who shared expertise, read drafts, provided materials and even checked page numbers.

I owe a sincere debt of gratitude, first of all, to Louis de Paor at the Centre for Irish Studies, National University of Ireland, Galway, who supervised the dissertation on which this book is based. I am forever grateful to Louis for his guidance, patience and keen editorial eye. I was also very privileged to have been supported in this research as an NUI Hardiman PhD Scholar, as a recipient of Sparánacht Bhreandáin Uí Eithir, and, later, as an Irish Research Council Government of Ireland Postgraduate Scholar. I am incredibly thankful to my PhD examiners Guy Beiner and Ríóna Ní Fhrighil, who gave advice on turning the dissertation into a monograph. Alan Titley has been a key support as my mentor through the Foras na Gaeilge writers' mentorship scheme and I am also very grateful to Brian Hanley for his astute suggestions on an earlier draft of this manuscript.

The research on the many remarkable figures discussed in this book was greatly enhanced by insights and materials provided by family members. I am indebted to Cormac O'Malley, Caitríona Nic Mhuiris, Francis Xavier Carty, Gareth Mulloy, Ivan Lennon, Pat Dolan and Michael Dolan for their assistance. Many thanks also to Kilmainham Gaol Museum and to Iseult White for permission to use Catalina Bulfin McBride's beautiful portrait on the cover.

My colleagues at both NUI Galway and Queen's University Belfast were a huge support throughout this process: my heartfelt thanks to Méabh Ní Fhuarthain, Verena Cummins, Samantha Williams, Nessa Ní Chróinín and Leo Keohane in Galway, and Greg Toner, Marcas Mac Coinnigh and Mícheál Ó Mainnín in Belfast. I am also grateful to the many scholars who generously gave up their time as reviewers and editors to read my work and offer feedback during my doctoral studies. My sincere thanks, therefore, to Ailbhe McDaid, Enda Delaney, Fearghal McGarry, Liam Chambers, Liam Mac Amhlaigh, Máirín Nic Eoin, Marie Coleman, Melania Terrazas Gallego, Nicholas Wolfe, Oona Frawley, Vera Kreilkamp and others. I am also incredibly grateful to the many people who encouraged me with this project, answered research questions, gave feedback on drafts and saved me from many errors. A huge thanks to Aisling Ní Churraighín, Ashley Cahillane, Breandán Mac Suibhne, Ciaran McDonough, Conor McNamara, Deirdre Ní Chonghaile, Eoin Magennis, Eoin Ó Broin, Fearghal Mac Bhloscaidh, Fionntán de Brún, John Borgonovo, John Cunningham, José Brownrigg-Gleeson, Kieran Fitzpatrick, Laoighseach Ní Choistealbha, Leeann Lane, Liam Mac Mathúna, Lorraine Grimes, Michael Lydon, Mícheál Mac Craith, Niall Murray, Pádraig Yeates, Stephen O'Neill and Úna Kavanagh.

I am incredibly grateful to all of the archivists and librarians who helped me track down sources, order books and scan material throughout the pandemic. My thanks to the staff at the James Hardiman Library in NUI Galway, especially to Ríona Moggan, Aisling Keane, Barry Houlihan, Geraldine Curtain, Margo Donohue and Kieran Hoare. Many thanks also to all at the National Library of Ireland, and especially to Joanna Finegan. My research on Pádraig O'Horan was greatly enhanced by the expertise of Robin Roddie at the Methodist Historical Society of Ireland Archive in Belfast. I am also indebted to the staff at the UCD archives for generously providing digital copies of resources and allowing me to include material that otherwise would not have been possible to access at height of the pandemic. Equally, I am indebted to the staff at Wilson Special Collections Library at University of North Carolina at Chapel Hill, the Special Collections in the University of Reading, and Cnuasach Bhéaloideas Éireann in UCD. Aoife Torpey at Kilmainham Gaol Archive has been a constant support and a fountain of knowledge. I was very fortunate also that Grace McCarthy was able to track down sources on my behalf at the National Library of Scotland, Edinburgh. I am grateful, too, to Ailbhe Rogers, Ciarán Ó Brolcháin, Mick O'Farrell, Caitlín Nic Íomhair and others for helping me fill missing references. Sincere thanks also to Michelle Griffin for her editorial assistance.

Despite the often isolating circumstances over the last year and half, I was fortunate to have the support of a strong network of friends and colleagues. Mo bhuíochas mór ó chroí le Club Snámha na mBan i mBóthar na Trá: Ailbhe Nic Giolla Chomhaill, Cassie Smith-Christmas, Katie McGreal,

Katie Ní Loingsigh agus Ríóna Ní Fhrighil. I also benefited immensely from the support of Alison Garden's Belfast-based remote writing group. My sincere thanks to all the writers for encouraging me through the final push of this project and for giving advice on drafts, especially to Alison Garden, Ann-Marie Foster, Anna Liesching, Eliza McKee, Sophie Cooper and Susie Deedigan. Mo shíorbhuíochas freisin le mo chairde dílse Seán Peril, Maedhbh Ní Dhuinn, Maitiú Ó Cribín, Tadhg Ó Murchú, Sinéad Hodgins agus Deirdre Ní Cheallacháin.

It has been a pleasure to work with Irish Academic Press. My thanks to Conor Graham, who took an interest in this project from the start, to Wendy Logue for her stellar editorial work, to copyeditor Heidi Houlihan, to Patrick O'Donoghue and to Maeve Convery for her work on the cover design. This book was further supported by a National University of Ireland Grant towards Scholarly Publications, a bursary from the Irish Association of Professional Historians and an Anna Parnell Grant from the Women's History Association of Ireland. I am incredibly grateful that these supports were available to me, and, indeed, to other scholars.

The long days of 'lockdown three' were spent in the company of Eolann Aiken and Bryony Archer, and I am so grateful for their support and comradery. My heartfelt thanks to my parents, Iseult Aiken agus Paddy Griffin, for their selflessness, dedication and love – and for their willingness to read drafts and discuss this work with me. This book is of course inspired by my many conversations (over occasional glasses of wine and jazz music) with my granddad, Frank Aiken, whose honest and nuanced engagement with the past has informed this project. I am indebted, indeed, to all my grandparents – Eileen Aiken (née O'Loughlin), Anne Stuart and Gerry Griffin – for fostering in me a deep appreciation of not only the various strands of my family history, but also the importance of education, resilience and hard work. Sincere thanks also to my in-laws Rick and Ann Mahoney for their hospitality on visits to the US and for letting us know that we always have a second home in Connecticut.

Agus do m'fhear céile agus mo leathbhádóir, Pádraig: mo bhuíochas ó chroí leat as do chomhluadar, do chúnamh agus do chomhairle stuama. Ní fhéadfainn tabhairt faoin tionscnamh seo murach do thacaíocht shíoraí.

Síobhra Aiken
An Sruthán Milis, Béal Feirste, Earrach 2022

INDEX